The Writing Revolution

THE LANGUAGE LIBRARY

Series editor: David Crystal

The Language Library was created in 1952 by Eric Partridge, the great etymologist and lexicographer, who from 1966 to 1976 was assisted by his co-editor Simeon Potter. Together they commissioned volumes on the traditional themes of language study, with particular emphasis on the history of the English language and on the individual linguistic styles of major English authors. In 1977 David Crystal took over as editor, and *The Language Library* now includes titles in many areas of linguistic enquiry.

The most recently published titles in the series include:

Ronald Carter and Walter Nash	*Seeing Through Language*
Florian Coulmas	*The Writing Systems of the World*
David Crystal	*A Dictionary of Linguistics and Phonetics, Fifth Edition*
J. A. Cuddon	*A Dictionary of Literary Terms and Literary Theory, Fourth Edition*
Viv Edwards	*Multilingualism in the English-speaking World*
Amalia E. Gnanadesikan	*The Writing Revolution: Cuneiform to the Internet*
Geoffrey Hughes	*A History of English Words*
Walter Nash	*Jargon*
Roger Shuy	*Language Crimes*
Gunnel Tottie	*An Introduction to American English*
Ronald Wardhaugh	*Investigating Language*
Ronald Wardhaugh	*Proper English: Myths and Misunderstandings about Language*

The Writing Revolution

Cuneiform to the Internet

Amalia E. Gnanadesikan

A John Wiley & Sons, Ltd., Publication

This edition first published 2009
© 2009 Amalia E. Gnanadesikan

Blackwell Publishing was acquired by John Wiley & Sons in February 2007.
Blackwell's publishing program has been merged with Wiley's global Scientific,
Technical, and Medical business to form Wiley-Blackwell.

Registered Office
John Wiley & Sons Ltd, The Atrium, Southern Gate, Chichester, West Sussex, PO19
8SQ, United Kingdom

Editorial Offices
350 Main Street, Malden, MA 02148-5020, USA
9600 Garsington Road, Oxford, OX4 2DQ, UK
The Atrium, Southern Gate, Chichester, West Sussex, PO19 8SQ, UK

For details of our global editorial offices, for customer services, and for information
about how to apply for permission to reuse the copyright material in this book please
see our website at www.wiley.com/wiley-blackwell.

The right of Amalia E. Gnanadesikan to be identified as the author of this work has
been asserted in accordance with the Copyright, Designs and Patents Act 1988.

Library of Congress Cataloging-in-Publication Data

Gnanadesikan, Amalia E.
    The writing revolution : cuneiform to the internet / by Amalia E. Gnanadesikan.
        p. cm. – (The language library)
    Includes bibliographical references and index.
    ISBN 978-1-4051-5406-2 (hardcover : alk. paper) – ISBN 978-1-4051-5407-9
(pbk. : alk. paper) 1. Writing–History. 2. Alphabet–History. I. Title.

    P211.G58 2009
    411.09–dc22

                                                                    2008014284

A catalogue record for this book is available from the British Library.

Set in 10/13pt Palatino by Graphicraft Limited, Hong Kong
Printed in Singapore by Utopia Press Pte Ltd

1   2009

Contents

Illustrations

Plates

Figures

Preface

One day during my sophomore year of college I returned to my dorm excited by a piece of information I had encountered.

"Is it true," I asked my neighbor, Joan Kim, "that Korean uses an alphabet you can learn in a single day?" Naïve Westerner that I was, I thought all East Asian languages, including hers, had very complicated scripts.

"Faster than that," she replied. "Here, I'll show you." And she did.

So began a love affair with writing systems which has culminated many years later in this book. It is written for people who, like my college-age self, are curious to know what the apparently meaningless squiggles of written symbols actually stand for, where they came from, and how they have adapted to and shaped the cultures that have used them through the centuries.

All of the world's major scripts are here, though the inclusion of important extinct ones means that not every modern script is discussed in the detail its present cultural prominence would merit. Also given pride of place are some minor scripts whose stories I could not resist telling, while many other of the world's smaller written traditions are at least mentioned. Enthusiasts may be disappointed, however, at the absence of Easter Island's rongo-rongo, the virtual absence of Anatolian hieroglyphs, the scanty treatment of runes, or other slights and omissions. Scholars may equally find that their field of specialty is touched on too quickly, with a lack of the nuance they rightly see as its due. To them I offer my apologies, pleading the constraints of length. To other readers I offer this book as an invitation to a fascinating topic of global importance.

I would like to acknowledge here a number of people who have helped my work along the way. Of foundational importance was

John McCarthy, whose inspired teaching and mentorship helped me become a phonologist, giving me the tools to understand many of the linguistic aspects of writing systems. I was also fortunate to receive his introduction to the editors at Wiley-Blackwell. My thanks also go to people who have taught me or helped me practice their scripts over the years: Joan Kim, Sandeepa Malik, Sheela Jeyaraj, and Lydia Peters. Thanks to Bill Poser for writing-system discussion, to the folks in the tablet room of the UPenn museum for showing me their work, and to Gillett Griffin for sharing with me Princeton's Mayan collection (and his own). Thanks to Yukiyo Yoshihara and Keith Rodgers for the Japanese proverb quoted in chapter 7. Some of the ancient scripts included in the figures and occasionally in the text are in the Alphabetum Unicode font, designed by Juan-José Marcos and used here with my thanks.

At Wiley-Blackwell I would like to thank Ada Brunstein for enthusiastically supporting the book in its early days, and Danielle Descoteaux and Kelly Basner for seeing it through to the end. My gratitude also goes to the members of the production team, especially to Fiona Sewell for her expert copyediting. Thanks also to David Crystal and three anonymous reviewers who made a number of useful suggestions and corrections. Remaining errors – and stances taken on controversial topics – are entirely mine. Thanks to Susan Hines, Patricia Athay, John Kilgore, and especially Lisa Fishman Kim for their comments on chapter drafts.

The paradox of the writing life is that it is both essentially communicative and essentially solitary. My heartfelt thanks, therefore, to John Hawthorn for being there in those moments when I emerged from my cave. Finally, my love and everlasting gratitude go to my dear ones, Anand and Gitanjali, who gracefully combined constant support and love with the role of literary critics and (in Gita's case) Chinese tutor.

1

The First IT Revolution

This sentence is a time machine. I wrote it a long time before you opened this book and read it. Yet here are my words after all this time, pristinely preserved, as good as new. The marvelous technology that allows the past to speak directly to the future in this way is by now so pervasive that we take it for granted: it is writing.

Imagine a world without writing. Obviously there would be no books: no novels, no encyclopedias, no cookbooks, no textbooks, no telephone books, no scriptures, no diaries, no travel guides. There would be no ball-points, no typewriters, no word processors, no Internet, no magazines, no movie credits, no shopping lists, no newspapers, no tax returns. But such lists of objects almost miss the point. The world we live in has been indelibly marked by the written word, shaped by the technology of writing over thousands of years. Ancient kings proclaimed their authority and promulgated their laws in writing. Scribes administered great empires by writing, their knowledge of recording and retrieving information essential to governing complex societies. Religious traditions were passed on through the generations, and spread to others, in writing. Scientific and technological progress was achieved and disseminated through writing. Accounts in trade and commerce could be kept because of writing. Nearly every step of civilization has been mediated through writing. A world without writing would bear scant resemblance to the one we now live in.

Writing is a virtual necessity to the societies anthropologists call *civilizations*. A civilization is distinguished from other societies by the complexity of its social organization, by its construction of cities and large public buildings, and by the economic specialization of its members, many of whom are not directly involved in food procurement or production. A civilization, with its taxation and tribute systems, its trade, and its public works, requires a sophisticated system of record keeping. And so the early civilizations of Mesopotamia, Egypt, China, Mesoamerica, and (probably) India all developed a system of writing. Only the Peruvian civilization of the Incas and their predecessors did not use writing but instead invented a system of keeping records on knotted color-coded strings known as *quipu*.

Early writing had three essential functions. It was used in state administration and bureaucracy, in trade and commerce, and in religion. The ancient Sumerians invented writing for administration and trade. The ancient Chinese used it to record what questions they had asked of Heaven. The ancient Maya used it to establish the divine authority of kings, and the ancient Egyptians used it to gain eternal life. In the case of trade and adminstration, the advantage of keeping written records is clear. The natural affinity of writing with religion is less transparent, but may well stem from the relative permanence – immortality, almost – of the written word. From ancient Egypt to the modern world, writing has been used to mark burials (bestowing a form of immortality on the deceased), as well as to dedicate offerings and record the words of God. Literature, which we now tend to consider the essence of written language, was a much later development – and in the case of some writing systems, never developed at all.

Writing was invented from scratch at least three times: in Mesopotamia, in China, and in Mesoamerica. In Egypt and in the Indus Valley, writing may have been invented independently, or the basic idea may have been borrowed from Mesopotamia. When the first words were written down in what is now southern Iraq in the late fourth millennium BC, history was made in more senses than one, for it is writing that separates history from prehistory, the time that can be studied through written records from the time that can be studied only through archaeology. Thanks to the time-machine technology of writing, a selection of the thoughts and words of earlier peoples have come down to us.

Writing is one of the most important human inventions of all time. It is rivaled by agriculture, the wheel, and the controlled use of fire, but by little else. The goal of this book is to shed light on how this remarkable technology actually works, where it came from, what it has done for us, and why it looks so different in different parts of the world.

Writing was invented to solve a particular problem: information only existed if someone could remember it. Once it was gone from memory, it was gone for good. As human societies became more complex, those attempting to control them found that their memories were overtaxed. What they needed was an external storage device. What they came up with is writing.

Let's say I owe you five dollars. If I say "I will repay you next April," the words are gone the instant I utter them. They exist only in my memory and in the memory of anyone who has heard me. And who is to say I will continue to remember them? You may well want more lasting evidence of my promise. Nowadays I could record my words electronically, but the inventors of writing lived more than five millennia before the invention of the phonograph, the tape recorder, or the digital voice recorder. Nor was capturing human speech their intention; they needed a way to record *information*. The memories of non-literate people are good, but they are far from infallible, and the human memory was not made for book-keeping.

So is there any way to keep my promise alive? How can we be sure exactly what has been said, or thought, or done? I could tell someone else, who would tell someone else, who would tell someone else . . . and, as in the party game "telephone," where each person whispers a message to the next person in a circle, the message would be very different by the end. But let's say I write down the words on a piece of paper and pass the paper around the circle. The words are just the same at the end as at the beginning. There is no amusing party game left, but in recording the words we have achieved reliable transmission of information.

This is the essence of writing. Writing represents language, but it outlasts the spoken word. The oldest examples of writing have lasted over five thousand years. Others will last only until I press my computer's delete key. But all have the potential to outlast the words I speak, or the words I put together in my head. A spoken (or mentally composed) message unfolds in *time,* one word replacing the previous one as it is uttered. Writing arranges the message in *space,* each word following the previous one in a line. Writing is therefore a process of translating time into space.

Being spatial, writing is visible. But being visible is not crucial to its definition. Braille, for example, is a writing system for the blind designed to be felt with the fingers. It represents letters as a series of raised bumps that can be read by touch. In both reading by touch and reading by sight, time has been translated into space. There are also forms of language which are inherently visible and spatial, such as American Sign Language (ASL). But such languages are akin to spoken languages in their essential properties: they too unfold in time. Like spoken words, signed words are gone the moment they are produced. By contrast, writing is a transformation of language, a technology applied to language, not language itself.

Writing takes words and turns them into objects, visible or tangible. Written down, words remain on the page like butterflies stuck onto boards with pins. They can be examined, analyzed, and dissected. They can be pointed to and discussed. Spoken words, by contrast, are inherently ephemeral. So written language seems more real to us than spoken language. Nevertheless, writing is only a means of expressing language; it is not language itself. In a highly literate culture it is easy to confuse the two, since much communication is mediated by writing, and the standards of written language influence our sense of "proper" language. But writing is not language, nor is it necessary to language.

Humans everywhere use language. It is a natural and normal human behavior. Although babies are not born speaking a language, all children who are raised around other people, who can perceive the language spoken around them (they are not, say, deaf in an environment where no sign language is used), and who are within normal range in certain mental and physical facilities will inevitably learn at least one language. They pick up their mother tongue naturally over the first few years of life. Indeed they cannot really be taught it, and will resist instruction if parents try too hard to correct their baby talk. Reading and writing do not come so naturally and must be taught. By the time children learn to read and write the vast majority of their language learning (other than further vocabulary growth) has already taken place.

As far as we can tell, language has been with us since the human race began. By contrast, writing is not a fundamental aspect of human life despite the profound impact it has had on human history. All human societies have had language, but many have had no writing. The organization SIL (originally the Summer Institute of Linguistics) has counted 6,912 languages spoken in the world today. Thousands more were once spoken but are now dead. The exact tally of languages is open to dispute, as it is often difficult to determine what forms of speech are dialects of a single language and which are different languages; also, languages change constantly, and two dialects may grow into distinct languages (especially in the absence of a common written form); languages may also die out, and are now doing so at increasing rates. Thousands of the world's languages use no writing system; no more than a hundred languages have produced a significant literary tradition.

Although writing is secondary to language, it often enjoys higher prestige. Writing is generally done more deliberately than speaking, so finished written pieces are much more carefully crafted than a typical spoken sentence. Written texts can thus convey their message more precisely, adding to the sense that writing is worth more than speech. Until the development of modern recording and broadcasting techniques, writing could reach a larger audience than the spoken word, and continue to communicate to people over a long period of time. Writing is associated with education, and education with wealth and power. The small percentage of languages that have a well-established written tradition include all the languages of national and international influence. Most of the unwritten languages are spoken by small minority groups, and many of these languages are not expected to survive the twenty-first century. Language conservation efforts must therefore include the development of writing systems and literacy programs.

Nowadays individuals faced with the task of designing a writing system for a language can draw on a wealth of literacy experience and linguistic theory. The original inventors had no such luxury. Later pioneers had the benefit of knowing that writing was possible, but still had to make most of it up as they went along.

Take King Njoya, for instance. King Ibrahim Njoya ruled the Bamum people of Cameroon from 1880 to 1931, the seventeenth king to rule from the ancient capital of Foumban. Njoya lived in a changing world, as strange people with strange new technologies encroached on traditional lands. To the north were invading Arabs, and they gave credit for their victories to a small book. Impressed, Njoya became a Muslim. Then Europeans came along with superior fire power. When asked where their strength came from, they also pointed to a book. Their book was larger, and their power the greater. Njoya therefore considered adopting Christianity, but could not accept its requirement of monogamy.

One thing was clear, however: writing was a powerful technology, and his people needed it. So in 1896 Njoya set out to invent a writing system for his language, Shü-mom, gathering together his best thinkers and best artists to help him.

The job he faced was not an easy one. His advisors were bright, but none of them had any prior experience with writing, and so none knew how the technology worked. What should Njoya write? What aspects of the Shü-mom language should be recorded?

Could he perhaps bypass the words of language and just record the thoughts he wanted to convey? When European scholars first encountered Egyptian hieroglyphs they thought the elaborate drawings represented pure thought. They believed that the hieroglyphic signs were *ideograms* – symbols that stood for *ideas*, not specific words. This misunderstanding set the decipherment of Egyptian hieroglyphs back considerably. The ideogram hypothesis was more than just a bad guess for Egyptian, however. As it turns out, a full writing system that bypasses the encryption process of language is not possible. In other words, *information* separate from *language* is not the place to begin writing.

Rudimentary systems of such a type do exist. A road sign that shows a car skidding will convey its meaning whether you say to yourself, "Slippery when wet," or, "Watch out, you might skid," as you "read" it. Similarly, mathematical symbols and equations convey a meaning that can be expressed in any one of many languages, or even several ways within a language. What is essential in an expression such as $\int dx/(a + bx^2)^2$ is not what it sounds like in English words, but what mathematical operation it refers to.

The graphical systems of road signs and mathematics work because they apply to a very limited part of human communication. By contrast, one of the essential properties of human language is the infinite range of what can be communicated using only a finite number of basic words. If we could distill human thoughts into a finite number of concepts that could be written down, could we resist giving them names – *words*? No. We would "read" the symbols by pronouncing them as words. Written symbols cannot systematically bypass language.

So King Njoya's writing system had to encode language. But this did not make the problem much easier. The system of encoding and communicating information that we call *language* has many layers. Which layer or layers should Njoya make symbols for?

The most obvious layer of language is its words. However, to make a truly different symbol for each word of a language would result in far too many symbols. To take an example from English, the 160,000 entries of the second edition of *Webster's New World College Dictionary* would require 160,000 different symbols. But the number of entries in a dictionary actually underestimates the number of words in a language. For example, the entry for *girlish* also mentions *girlishly* and *girlishness* – both words of English, but not given their own entries. It would be silly, though, to try to create a writing system that had one symbol for *girl*, an entirely different one for *girlish*, and another completely different one for *girlishness*. The words *girl*, *girlish*, and *girlishness* have pieces in common. They all contain the piece *girl*, while *girlish* and *girlishness* share -*ish* as well. The -*ness* of *girlishness* is also a piece that recurs over and over in English. These pieces of words are called *morphemes*. There are far fewer morphemes in a language than words, and the morphemes can be combined and recombined in so many ways that it is hard to say how many words a language actually has. It is not surprising, therefore, that no one has ever managed to create a usable writing system that uses full words rather than morphemes as its level of encoding.

A morpheme has two aspects, its *meaning* and its *pronunciation*. Writing systems that concentrate on representing morphemes – as complete meaning–pronunciation complexes – are called *logographic* (the name, meaning "word-writing," is traditional, though it ignores the difference between morphemes and words), and the individual symbols are called *logograms*, as shown in figure 1.1 Although those of us who have been trained to use an alphabet find it natural to divide words up into individual vowels and consonants (in other words, separating meaning from its pronunciation and representing only pronunciation), the first inventors of scripts did not. For them it was more natural to consider the morphemes as a whole. Core morphemes at least (those like *girl*, rather than -*ish* or -*ness*) can be uttered on their own in many languages and thus are natural units in which to think of language.

The first version of King Njoya's writing system was therefore logographic. He compiled a list of little schematized pictures that could stand for individual morphemes. After a while he had 465 of them. A symbol for every morpheme in the language was clearly going to take a lot more than that. And so he was forced to a decision that all complete writing systems have had to make in some form or another: he was obliged to begin using symbols to represent *pronunciation*.

The pronunciation (or *phonology*) of language also has several layers. Words are made of one or more morphemes, but they are also made of one or more *syllables* in the way they are pronounced. A word

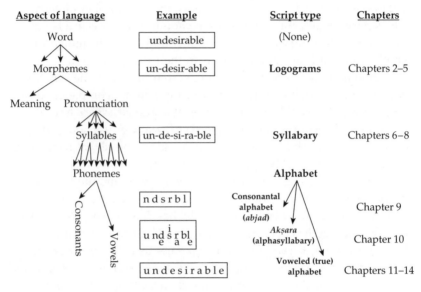

Figure 1.1 How different writing systems represent language. Logograms represent morphemes, both their meaning and pronunciation, while syllabaries and alphabets represent only pronunciation. In the column of examples, the word *undesirable* is used to illustrate how the various writing systems would divide up such a word. A morphemic (logographic) system would use three symbols, a syllabary five, and so forth. In an akṣara system, the vowels are written as appendages to the consonants.

like *cat* has a single morpheme and a single syllable, but a word like *undesirable* contains three morphemes and five syllables. Thus a logographic writing system would give *cat* one symbol and *undesirable* three, while a *syllabary* would give *cat* one and *undesirable* five. That lengthens the spelling of *undesirable*, but lessens the number of symbols needed in all, as there are fewer distinct syllables in a language than there are distinct morphemes.

So King Njoya converted a number of his symbols into *syllabograms*, standing for syllables – just a pronunciation, unconnected to any meaning. The meaning would come only when the syllabograms were put together to make up words. He worked on his script over a period of many years, ending with a syllabary of 73 signs, plus 10 numerals. He put the writing system to good use, compiling a law code, designing a calendar, and founding schools.

Other ways of writing were theoretically open to him. Syllabaries come in different kinds. Most represent only *core* syllables (a single consonant + short vowel sequence) and find a variety of workarounds to represent other kinds of syllables. A few include symbols for *closed* syllables (those that contain a final consonant), and a few writing systems of the world split the syllable in two, representing the consonant(s) at the beginning (the *onset*) with one symbol and the rest (the *rhyme*) with another.

More familiar to Westerners is the kind of writing system that ignores syllables entirely and looks at the individual sounds out of which syllables are made. This requires knowing what counts as an "individual sound." Consider for a moment the words *feel* and *leaf*. They appear to contain the same sounds, in reverse order. However, if you say the two words slowly, and pay close attention to your tongue as you say the *l*s, you may notice that the *l* in *feel* has the back of the tongue pulled back and upward compared to the *l* in *leaf*. Chances are, however, that you have never noticed it before. Similarly, the *p* in *spoof* is pronounced quite differently from the *p* in *poof* – you can blow out a candle by pronouncing the latter but not the former.

There are many such variations in sound that native speakers of a language disregard and typically have lost the ability to hear unless they have had training in phonetics. Native speakers of a given language will consider an entire range of sounds to be the "same." That "same sound" that native speakers perceive is called by linguists a *phoneme* of that language. The actual sounds of language are infinitely varied, as they are uttered by different people in different circumstances. It would be pointless to try to capture this variation in writing. But most languages have between 20 and 37 phonemes, and phonemes can be written down. An alphabet that is strictly phonemic would have the same number of letters as phonemes (though English does not).

Technicalities aside, an important point here about these abstract phonemes and syllables is that although writing represents information about how words are pronounced, it does not record the identifying details of any individual utterance of those words. It records *language*, but not actual *speech*. Even in cases of dictation or courtroom stenography, much information about the actual speech is lost, such as intonation and emotional content. As a result, reading is not at all the same as listening to a recording (and can therefore, fortunately, proceed much faster).

Writing systems that represent individual phonemes are called *alphabets*. It is therefore inaccurate to refer to the "Chinese alphabet" or the "Japanese alphabet," as these writing systems do not work at the phonemic level. A further level of distinction separates alphabets into those that represent only or primarily consonants (consonantal alphabets, also known as *abjads*), those that represent vowels as somehow dependent on the preceding consonant (*akṣara* systems or *alphasyllabaries*), and those that give vowels and consonants equal status ("true" or voweled *alphabets*).

All writing systems find themselves somewhere in the range from morphemic to phonemic (see figure 1.1). The more morphemic writing systems may also do a little to directly represent the semantic aspect of a morpheme in the form of clues to meaning known as *determinatives* (thus the symbol for "cat" might include a symbol showing that it is an animal). But no writing system is so completely morphemic that it pays no attention to the phonology (syllables and/or phonemes) of the language. Some scripts are fully phonological, representing either the phonemes or the syllables of the language. On the other hand, no written language is simply a record of uttered sounds: that is left up to a less significant invention, the phonograph, and its modern descendants.

The earliest writing systems were, like King Njoya's first efforts, all highly logographic. Later writing systems are typically more phonologically based and use far fewer logograms. This is not to say that logographically based scripts are primitive. Logograms have the advantage of using space very efficiently, needing only one sign per morpheme, where alphabets need several. They are also more convenient in contexts where pronunciation varies significantly, making phonologically based writing hard to standardize. Yet an alphabet, with its limited number of signs, is the more easily memorized and can therefore spread faster in a context of limited schooling. What kind of writing system a language uses is largely determined by the accidents of history and by the properties of the language itself.

King Njoya's labors had a sad ending. The French colonial forces burned his books and exiled him from Foumban in 1931. Today, despite Cameroon independence, his writing system is nearly forgotten. His grandson, the present king, sponsors classes in it at the royal palace in Foumban, but it sees very little actual use. Other scripts have been luckier. Born into more propitious time they have enjoyed a more extensive history. The following chapters tell their stories.

First, in chapters 2 through 5 are the stories of ancient logographic systems – Mesopotamian cuneiform, Egyptian hieroglyphs, Chinese characters, and Maya glyphs – along with their syllabic or consonantal compromises. Next, chapters 6 through 8 tell of syllabaries, from the Bronze-Age Linear B used for Greek, through the two Japanese syllabaries, to the modern invention of the Cherokee script. Phonemic scripts follow, with consonantal alphabets, akṣara systems, and voweled alphabets in turn. In the final chapter the effects of secondary writing technologies – printing, typing, word processing, and the Internet – are considered, along with the globalization of the Roman alphabet.

A book about writing systems faces one significant obstacle: transliteration. The phonemes, syllables, and morphemes recorded by the world's writing systems cannot all be recast into the Roman alphabet in a single, unambiguous way. The languages of the world contain some 600 distinct consonants and 200 different vowels. Not all of these have yet been converted into writing, but clearly there needs to be a way to translate the scripts we do not know into one we recognize, so that we know what they say. Many languages already have established ways of being transliterated into the Roman alphabet or use the Roman alphabet themselves. For many transliterated languages the general operative principle is "consonants as in English, vowels as in Italian." Such a system glosses over a lot, as there are only so many consonants in English and so many vowels in Italian. Furthermore, languages that already use the Roman alphabet do so in many different, mutually incompatible ways.

Therefore I will use standard spellings and transliteration systems where their meaning is clear, but will supplement them where necessary with the International Phonetic Alphabet (IPA). The IPA is designed to represent all the phonemes of human languages. By transcribing an alphabet into the IPA we can tell what phonemes that alphabet encodes: it is a sort of decoder ring for alphabets.

The IPA is reprinted in the appendix (figure A.1). Examples of English phonemes transcribed into the IPA are given in figure A.2. When using IPA symbols to describe a pronunciation, I will write them between square brackets. This is to emphasize that what is being referred to is a *sound*, not a letter of the Roman alphabet. Thus **b** is a letter, but [b] is a sound. In many cases the IPA symbol represents the same sound that the Roman letter does in English, but this is not always so, especially in the case of vowels, where the symbols taken from the Roman alphabet generally have the sound values that they do in most continental European languages (such as Italian).

Sounds that do not occur in English will be explained where relevant in later chapters. However, much can be learned about them from studying the IPA charts. The purpose of laying out the IPA vowel and consonant symbols in charts is that even if your language does not contain a particular sound, you can get a fairly good idea of what it sounds like from the description and its place on the chart. For instance, English does not have the [x] sound. However, the consonant chart describes it as a fricative, in the same row as [f], [v], [θ], [ð], [s], and [z], which do occur in English (as in *fine*, *vine*, **thin**, **thine**, *sin*, and *zen*). A fricative is, like any of these sounds, a sound that you can keep on making (unlike a plosive, such as [b]), but that makes a turbulent sound of rushing air (unlike, say, [l]). The column [x] is in shows that it is a "velar" sound. This tells us that it is made in the same part of the mouth as [k] and [g], at the soft palate toward the back. It is therefore the "ch" sound of Scottish *loch* or German *ach*. Most English speakers find this sound impossible to pronounce correctly. However, with the IPA they can at least talk about it, even if they can't produce it.

The vowel chart also has many sounds that English does not possess, such as [y]. It is described by the chart as "close" and "front." Even if those terms do not mean anything to you, you can tell from the chart that it is similar to [i], the vowel in English *see*. But unlike [i], it is "rounded." This means that it is made with pursed lips, like [u], the vowel in *food*. If you say [i] and then try to say it with your lips pursed, you may manage the vowel [y]. Most English speakers have a great deal of trouble with it. It is the vowel sound in French *tu*.

A full understanding of the IPA is not necessary to this book. However, if you find yourself wondering what sounds the symbols in a script actually refer, you can get a rough idea by using the IPA chart.

2

Cuneiform: Forgotten Legacy
of a Forgotten People

Our story begins in the Middle East, in what is today southern Iraq. Nestled between the southern reaches of the Tigris and Euphrates rivers was a land whose earliest recorded name is Sumer (see map in the appendix, figure A.3). The land was rich and fertile, but dry. With irrigation, however, the land yielded enough and to spare; the extra food encouraged the growth of trade and the development of specialized professions and stratified social classes. Over time these developments led to the birth of a true civilization in the centuries between 3500 and 3000 BC.

It was a momentous period. Facing a drying climate, people living in northern Mesopotamia moved south to avail themselves of the benefits of irrigation. The necessity of feeding a larger population was the mother of a number of inventions: the plow, the grain sled, the potter's wheel, wheeled vehicles, and the sail. These technologies allowed people to plant more food and to store, transport, and trade it more easily. To keep pace, irrigation technology had to be improved, and larger-scale irrigation systems built. Such public works required concerted community effort, encouraging the rise of strong community leaders. With fertile land at a premium, scattered villages began to be replaced with more compact, centralized cities. As the cities grew in size and complexity of organization, so their leaders accumulated power and wealth.

The growth of civilization required yet another advance in technology. The complex society of a city-state requires administration, and administration requires record keeping. Early attempts to meet this need included the working out of a numerical tally system and perhaps the use of tokens, which stood for farm animals, quantities of grain, trade goods, or other objects that needed to be recorded. But these advances

Bureaucracy

were not enough to meet the culture's growing bureaucratic needs. The technology that emerged to meet those needs – writing – filled a prosaic but essential purpose: accounting. The impetus behind its invention was not a desire to faithfully record language, but to record trade transactions, crop yields, and taxes – to record and preserve *information*, not *language*. It was the first – and most important – information technology revolution. It succeeded in preserving information, however, by representing language – crudely at first, but with increasing precision. As the technology matured and spread, it came to be used for languages of five separate linguistic families and inspired the development of several other scripts; it shaped forever the world that came afterwards.

Commodities such as wood, stone, and metal had to be imported into Sumer, but thanks to the Euphrates and Tigris rivers the land was rich in mud. The right kind of mud produced clay. Almost everything in Sumer was made of clay: bricks for houses and temples, tools, and even writing surfaces. Clay left to dry of its own accord is fairly durable; baked clay is virtually indestructible. It is because of this property of clay that ancient Mesopotamian writing is preserved for us: early unbaked tablets have come down to the present rather crumbly but often still legible after five millennia, while tablets that experienced the sacking and burning of cities were merely strengthened by the process. Later tablets were sometimes intentionally baked to preserve them.

The earliest writing known to archaeologists is found on small clay tablets unearthed from the ancient city of Uruk. Uruk (biblical Erech, modern Arabic Warka) was once a thriving city on the banks of the Euphrates. It is now a large and desolate heap 12 miles from the Euphrates, the river bed having shifted over the course of the millennia. Arguably, the name has changed less with time than the geography.

Modern excavations began at Uruk in 1912. As is usual in archaeology, the periods of occupation have been named from the top (latest, but first to be unearthed) downward. Thus Uruk I is more recent than Uruk II, and so forth. It is during the period Uruk IV that writing is first attested, around 3400 or 3300 BC. In the Uruk III period (c.3200–3000 BC), a few other Sumerian cities also show evidence of writing. Either independently or by the inspiration of the Sumerians, writing also appears around this time east of Mesopotamia at Susa – recording the as yet undeciphered proto-Elamite language – and to the west in Egypt.

Though the earliest known writing comes from Uruk, we cannot be entirely certain that this is where writing was actually invented. However, later Sumerian legend also places the first writing there. The invention is ascribed to Enmerkar, said to have been king of Uruk after the Great Flood of Sumerian legend. Enmerkar was engaged in a contest of wills with the lord of far-off Aratta. He had sent three messages demanding tribute and had been denied three times. His final move was to send a written clay tablet. The written message reduced the lord of Aratta to submission, perhaps in recognition of the significance of the invention.

The first written tablets are in a script we call proto-cuneiform. About 85 percent of them are of an administrative or accounting nature, while the remaining 15 percent are lists of words. The latter were spelling lists, used by scribes practicing the signs for the various professions, agricultural produce, and commodities. The same word lists, written in the same order, were used for hundreds of years; conveniently, this fact allows modern Sumerologists to use the later lists to identify early proto-cuneiform signs.

Proto-cuneiform was scratched, or drawn, into damp clay tablets (see figure 2.1). Numerals figure prominently in the early business records: of the roughly 800 different signs that have been identified, 60 or so are numerals. This is a lot, compared to the 10 digits we use today. But the early Sumerians did not use numerals abstractly, without reference to what was being counted. Instead, different systems of numerals were used for counting different things: for discrete entities, for areas of land, for periods of time, for quantities of grain, and so forth. This was probably a holdover from the tally systems of the preliterate period, when numerals that told you something about what was being counted were an advantage rather than a cumbersome inconvenience.

Of the remaining signs, some were straightforwardly pictographic – stylized pictures of identifiable objects – like the sign for "head," *sag*, or the sign for "fish," *ku*, shown in the left-hand column of figure 2.2. In such cases the shape of the sign indicated fairly clearly what the meaning of the word was. In other cases the relationship between the appearance of the sign and its meaning was looser, and would only be apparent after one already knew what the meaning was. Still other signs were from the beginning entirely arbitrary or highly abstract, like the sign for "sheep," *udu*.

15

Figure 2.1 A proto-cuneiform tablet. Administrative tablet with cylinder seal impression of a male figure, hunting dogs, and boars. 3100–2900 BC. Jamdat Nasr, Uruk III style, southern region, Mesopotamia. Clay, H. 2 in. (5.3 cm). Purchase, Raymond and Beverly Sackler Gift, 1988 (1988.433.1). The Metropolitan Museum of Art, New York, NY, U.S.A. Image copyright © The Metropolitan Museum of Art/Art Resource, NY.

Yet to have a separate sign for each word (even just those consisting of a single morpheme, like *sheep*) requires a great many signs, and if one is relying on pictography there is the problem that not all words are easily drawn. Modern players of Pictionary can attest to this fact. The early Sumerians came up with a number of workarounds for this obstacle. Less easily pictured words often used the same sign as one that was more easily pictured but had a similar meaning. Thus the sign for "mouth," *ka*, which indicated the position of the mouth on a picture

Proto-cuneiform c.3000 BC	Early cuneiform c.2400 BC	Late (Neo-Assyrian) cuneiform c.700 BC	Transcription and meaning
			sag "head"
			ka "mouth"
			du/gin/gub "go/walk/stand"
			gud "ox"
			udu "sheep"
			ku "fish"
			dug "pot"
			gi "reed, to render"

Figure 2.2 The development from proto-cuneiform, through early Sumerian cuneiform, to later Akkadian cuneiform. Proto-cuneiform signs were often pictographic, though not always, as the sign for "sheep" shows. By late cuneiform the pictographic origins are hard to spot. At some point between the second and third columns the orientation of signs (and tablets) was rotated by 90 degrees.

of the head, could also mean "tooth" (*zu*), "word" (*inim*), "voice" (*gu*), or "speak" (*du*), depending on context. Another way to represent words was to combine or modify other, simpler signs. Thus a sign that showed a jar (*dug*) became, with the addition of stippling or cross-hatching, *kaʃ*, the beer that was kept inside such a jar.

Some signs were not meant to be read aloud, but functioned as determinatives – unpronounced signs that told the reader what class of thing was being referred to. Early determinatives marked divine names, wooden objects, and male and female names. The use of determinatives is common in logographic writing systems, but they are not unknown elsewhere. In English, for example, we vary letters between upper and lower case. The words *frank* and *Frank* are pronounced the same and spelled with the same letters, but the capitalization of *Frank* informs us that it is a name, while *frank* is an adjective. The use of upper case thus serves as a determinative in English.

In contrast with determinatives, some signs were used precisely because of their pronunciation. For example, *gi* meant "reed." But the word that meant "to render" in Sumerian was pronounced precisely the same, so the reed symbol was also used to mean "render." Similarly, *ti* meant "arrow," but it could also mean "life," so a sign depicting an arrow could mean either one. This use of an easily pictured object to stand for its more abstract homonym is known as *rebus writing*. Proto-cuneiform used it sparingly, but enough to allow us to identify proto-cuneiform as the writing of language rather than merely concepts, and to convince some scholars that the language represented was indeed Sumerian. Without these homonym pairs we would know very little about the pronunciation of proto-cuneiform.

The written messages of proto-cuneiform tablets are all rather telegraphic. All grammatical information, such as verb tense or noun case, was omitted, and only the core morphemes of words were shown, without any prefixes or suffixes. The signs were arranged in boxes outlined on the tablets, one statement per box. The order of the signs within a box did not follow the order of spoken language, and some have even described it as random. Yet there do seem to be patterns: they tended to first record numerals, then the objects counted, and then other relevant information about them, such as "3 sheep temple," meaning, presumably, that three sheep had been given to the temple. Different types of transactions appear to have been organized differently. But there is much about the arrangement of proto-cuneiform signs that is not obvious to the modern reader; the ancient scribes would have been able to use a significant amount of contextual understanding that is lost to us.

The proto-cuneiform system was limited and full of ambiguities. However, for the purposes to which it was put it was quite adequate, and context provided the necessary disambiguation. As a technological and intellectual development, it was like nothing the world had seen before.

The dawn of the third millennium BC saw the emergence of true cuneiform. The name *cuneiform* refers specifically to the wedge-shaped impressed lines that make up the individual signs of the script. Drawing curved lines on clay is relatively hard; stamping marks into clay is much easier. And so over time the curvilinear signs of proto-cuneiform gave way to the angular signs of true cuneiform, pressed into the clay with a stylus made from the end of a reed. In the process the pictographic origins of the signs (where there were any) became obscured (as in the second column of figure 2.2).

The writing now ran consistently from left to right within the boxes. Over time the boxes widened, so that the writing eventually ran in lines across the full face of the tablet. The number of signs grew substantially to about 1,200, then shrank again as the writing system became systematized and the phonological aspect of the script grew. By the middle of the third millennium BC the number of different signs in use was about 800, and by the end of the millennium it had stabilized at about 600.

It is early in the third millennium BC that we begin to truly recognize the Sumerian language in its writing. The proto-cuneiform tablets contain relatively little phonological information, and no grammatical information, so they tell us relatively little about their language. From later tablets we learn that Sumerian was an *agglutinative* language, which means that it expressed grammatical information and the relationships between words by adding prefixes and suffixes to its words. As in English, grammatical features such as verb tense, possession, and plurality would be expressed with *affixes* (the collective term for prefixes and suffixes). Thus there were Sumerian analogs for the English past tense *-ed*, the possessive *-'s*, and the plural *-(e)s*. But unlike in English, other grammatical features were also expressed with affixes. We use prepositions like *from*, *to*, and *with* and modal verbs like *will*, *would*, and *could* as free-standing words, while in Sumerian these concepts would have been expressed with affixes. Nouns and verbs carried up to three suffixes, while verbs could have up to six prefixes and nouns one or none.

None of these many affixes was written in early Sumerian texts. The recording of affixes began about 2900 BC with a greater use of rebus writing, and increased gradually over the next millennium, spurred by increasing numbers of readers for whom Sumerian was a foreign language. These readers could not so easily fill in missing affixes

19

from context and a personal knowledge of the language. By the time the affixes were being fully represented, Sumerian had probably ceased to be a living, spoken language. It had become a classical language of literature and science, much as Latin did in the centuries following its development into the separate Romance languages. With the death of Sumerian as a spoken, everyday language, the written language was called upon to preserve knowledge of the grammatical details. The death of spoken Sumerian is impossible to date exactly, but probably occurred early in the second millennium BC.

The recording of the first affixes, and of personal names, forced an expansion of the writing system. The early signs inherited from proto-cuneiform were logograms representing the core morphemes of words – the core nouns and verbs apart from their affixes. Having a sign for simple, unaffixed words like "ox" and "barley" and even abstract words like "life" and "give" is one thing. Being able to represent the arbitrary sounds of a foreigner's name, or to indicate grammatical details such as verb conjugations and a system of 10 noun cases, was a significant step forward.

The way the Sumerians went about expanding their writing system was to listen to the sounds of their words. Already in the proto-cuneiform period they had occasionally used rebus writing, using one logogram to represent another word that sounded the same. Now they began to use signs to represent only a part of a word, to represent *just a syllable*, regardless of whether that syllable meant anything in itself. This syllable could be used in spelling out an affix, a personal name, or a foreign word.

This use of syllabograms was a significant advance, not just in writing, but in linguistics. The logical individual unit of language is the core morpheme, like *sheep*, *house*, or *go*. Pronouncing incomplete pieces of words by themselves is not natural. Given a word like *feeling*, we might find ourselves with reasons to mention the core morpheme, *feel*, but we rarely find ourselves called upon to pronounce the suffix *-ing* by itself, and we are even less likely to think about the fact that when we speak, the final syllable of *feeling* is in fact *-ling*, including part of the core as well as the suffix. Yet the Sumerians realized that their words were made up of smaller, pronounced units – syllables. And so a sign like *gi* came to mean not only "reed," and not only "render," but also merely the syllable [gi], independent of what word it appeared in.

Thus cuneiform became what we call a *logosyllabary*, a mixed system
in which some signs were logograms and some were syllabograms. Many
of the signs could be either one depending on context. The syllabograms
were also pressed into service as *phonetic complements*: a word spelled
with a logogram could take an additional syllabic sign to indicate which
of various possible pronunciations of the logogram should be used.
Thus *ka*, "mouth," plus the phonetic complement *me* was the word
that had to do with the mouth but ended in the syllable [me], in other
words *eme*, "tongue."

The complexities of the Sumerian logosyllabary can be summed up
as follows:

1   The signs could either be logograms or syllabograms (or both).
2   Because of the logographic origins of the writing system, words
    that were pronounced the same were often written with different
    signs. In other words, there were many homonyms. Thus, for ex-
    ample, the spoken word *gu* could mean "shout," "thread," or 12 other
    things, each of which was written with its own logogram. The
    English use of *two*, *too*, and *to* is a pale reflection of the same idea.
3   On the other hand, many signs were polyvalent. In other words,
    the same sign could stand for two or more morphemes that
    meant different things and were pronounced in different ways.
    For example, the sign known to Sumerologists as APIN could be
    read either *apin* ("plow") or *engar* ("farmer"). But the different
    morphemes were generally related in meaning, and would have
    shared a pictogram in proto-cuneiform. The correct word would
    be deduced from context, as in English, where context can usu-
    ally tell us whether *house* should be pronounced [hauz] and mean
    "to provide shelter for," or be pronounced [haus] and mean "a
    place where people live."
4   To reduce the chance of confusion brought on by the polyvalence
    of the signs, the Sumerians used determinatives and phonetic
    complements. Determinatives provided clues as to what kind of
    meaning a word would have, while phonetic complements
    spelled out part of a word syllabically so as to indicate which
    reading of a polyvalent logogram was being used.

The system may appear baroque to the modern mind, and especially
to those used to an alphabet. Attaining literacy in cuneiform required

21

hard work, as attested by the long word lists that student scribes studied and copied. Throughout its history Sumerian cuneiform retained aspects of having been a first invention. There was no earlier writing system to learn from, no pre-existing concept of literacy to compare with, no idea that a writing system could be more or less efficient or learnable. Yet it more than filled the need for which it had been invented. When Sumerian administrators first put reed to tablet it is doubtful that anyone dreamed that their invention would be used to write history, literature, and science texts. It took some 500 years, yet eventually that is precisely what happened.

Sumer occupied only the southernmost part of Mesopotamia, a land of growing city-states in the first half of the third millennium. The language of the Sumerians was unrelated to any other language that we know of. It was a *language isolate*, like Basque, with no known relatives. East of Sumer was the land of Elam, where the Elamite language was also a language isolate. North of Sumer, in what is now central Iraq, was the land of Akkad. The Akkadians spoke a Semitic language related to Hebrew, Aramaic, and Arabic, but entirely unrelated to Sumerian. The linguistic diversity of the region may be reflected in the biblical story of the tower of Babel, which describes the building of a ziggurat (temple) at Babylon, near the Sumer–Akkad border.

Despite differences of language and culture, the elites of Akkad adopted many Sumerian customs, including the building of ziggurats. Even before Sargon I (2334–2279 BC) conquered Sumer and instituted Akkadian as the language of administration, Akkadian scribes had worked out ways to adapt Sumerian cuneiform to their own language. Quite simply, they took the *meanings* of some of the logograms and supplemented them with the *sounds* of the syllabograms. Thus the sign for "reed," Sumerian *gi*, was now pronounced *qanuum*, or, when it meant "to render," *taarum*. But it could also still stand for the syllable [gi] in a word spelled out syllabically! The original unifying pronunciation that made sense of the use of this one sign for three purposes was lost. In other words, while the three uses of the sign had all been pronounced [gi] in Sumerian, Akkadian word lists tell us they were pronounced [qanuːm], [taːrum], and [gi] in Akkadian.

This apparently nonsensical arrangement would have made sense to Akkadian scribes, however, since they would have been bilingual in Akkadian and Sumerian. In order to learn to read and write, the earliest Akkadian scribes had had to learn Sumerian. From then on it became a tradition: an educated person learned Sumerian. This pattern has been repeated many times throughout history. A language that is written becomes dominant over other languages in its region, inspiring a great deal of second-language study by speakers of other languages.

An important contribution of the Akkadians to the cuneiform writing system was the expansion of the syllabary, with the result that Akkadian, unlike Sumerian, was written mostly in syllabograms with the occasional logogram thrown in, rather than vice versa. This expansion and adaptation brought about the full maturation of the script.

The Sumerians had tended to be imprecise about the match between syllabograms and spoken syllables. Like English, Sumerian allowed closed syllables – syllables formed of a consonant plus a vowel plus another consonant, schematically notated CVC. But the number of possible CVC syllables is quite large, and it was impractical to have a separate symbol for each one. The Sumerians tended to write CVC sequences as simply CV, leaving it up to the reader to recognize from context what consonant had been left out. This may be one reason for the apparently large number of homonyms.

Syllabaries are naturally more apt for some languages than for others, as the number of possible syllables varies from language to language. Most syllabaries in the history of writing have consisted of only – or almost only – CV syllabograms, with a few additional V syllabograms for vowel-initial words. Languages whose spoken syllables are also entirely or almost entirely of CV form are well served by a syllabary, while those with more complex syllables are not (such as English, whose longest single syllables are *strengths*, phonologically CCCVCCC, and *twelfths*, CCVCCCC). If written syllabically, these languages must resort to representing either more vowels or fewer consonants than the spoken word actually contains.

Akkadian possessed closed syllables with a vengeance. Furthermore, as a Semitic language, it entrusted the core meaning of its words to its consonants. In Semitic languages most word cores consist of three consonants, with the addition of vowels and/or the doubling of consonants providing inflectional information. So, for example, you conjugate a verb by changing the vowels. This is like English *sang* being the past tense of *sing*, but much more systematic. Thus the sequence of three consonants *p-r-s* was the core of the verb meaning "to render a decision," but the present tense form of the verb was *iparras* (doubling of the second consonant being part of the inflection) and the past tense was *iprus*. The infinitive was *paraasu*. A spelling system that did not allow Akkadian scribes to indicate all the consonants in a word like *iprus* – with its VC.CVC structure – would have forced them to leave out the essential meaning of the word. So they began to use some syllabic signs for VC sequences. They could then break up closed CVC syllables into two signs, one CV and the other VC. Thus *iprus* could be spelled *ip-ru-us*. There was some ambiguity in this, as the sequence *ru-us* could be used to spell a syllable pronounced [ruːs] (with a long vowel) or [rus] (with a short vowel). The trouble of inventing and remembering a symbol for every CVC syllable was averted, however.

The Akkadians also systematized the appearance of the signs. In Akkadian cuneiform the individual wedge-shaped lines that made up the signs all had their heads at the left (for horizontal or diagonal signs) or at the top (for vertical signs). The effect can be seen in the contrast between the second-column and third-column versions of the signs given in figure 2.2. The Akkadian versions (on the right) draw from a smaller and more organized repertoire of shapes.

After the fall of Sargon's dynasty around 2100 BC, Sumerian once more became the administrative language of the unified land called "Sumer and Akkad." Later dialects of Akkadian known as Babylonian and Assyrian eventually replaced Sumerian, but Sumerian continued to be studied by scribes and scholars, and a considerable portion of the extant literature in Sumerian was collected by the late Assyrian king Assurbanipal (668–627 BC) and housed in his library at Nineveh. Akkadian also went on to produce a large corpus of legal, scientific, and literary texts, such as the law code of Hammurabi, observations of the planet Venus (plate 1), and the Epic of Gilgamesh (originally a tale about a Sumerian hero, but put into its final form by Akkadians). In fact, due to the durability of clay tablets – which were preserved rather than destroyed whenever a city was put to the torch – the period of Akkadian cuneiform has left us more primary documents than any other time up to the invention of the printing press.

From the seventh century onwards cuneiform was rivaled by the Aramaic alphabet, and with the conquest of Mesopotamia by Alexander the Great (336–323 BC) it lost its official support. The last known cuneiform text is an astronomical tablet dating to AD 75.

In its heyday, however, cuneiform covered a wide area. The invention of writing constituted a revolution in bureaucratic technique, and like any other successful revolution, its effects could not be contained. Soon after the development of proto-cuneiform, in the Uruk III period at the end of the fourth millennium BC, early writing inscribed on clay tablets also appeared in the land of Elam, east of Sumer, now part of Iran. It is not entirely clear how much the appearance of writing in Elam owes to the development of writing in Sumer. Most likely, the idea of using writing for accounting purposes had reached the people of Elam, but they may or may not have seen proto-cuneiform before they set out to develop their own script. The script, known as proto-Elamite, is thus far undeciphered. Like proto-cuneiform, it was used for concise administrative accounts and not for lengthy prose. Unlike proto-cuneiform, it did not develop further, and so we don't have more elaborated versions of the script to use for decipherment, nor do we know what language the proto-Elamite scribes spoke.

Instead of continuing to adapt and develop their own script, the people of Elam later borrowed the cuneiform script of their Mesopotamian neighbors and used it for over 2,000 years. At first they wrote in Akkadian, then adapted the script to their own language, which we can now identify as Elamite, a language with no known relatives. Unlike the Akkadians, the Elamites had no particular loyalty to the ancient Sumerian way of doing things. They considered logograms unnecessary complications: why learn a separate sign for a word if you can just spell it out with a syllabary? They ruthlessly cut down the number of signs, arriving at about 130, compared to the roughly 600 signs required to write Akkadian. Most of the signs were syllabic – either CV (or just V), VC, or sometimes CVC. As in Akkadian, most CVC syllables did not have their own sign and were written CV-VC.

Interestingly, the number of logograms gradually increased over time, a trend that is noticeable in other phonologically written languages too. At first the most important consideration is to develop a system that can be easily learned, and so additional signs that can only be used for a single morpheme are an unnecessary complication. After a while, though, literacy is taken for granted, and it becomes more important to write efficiently. A single sign for a common word can be written more quickly than the individual syllables or phonemes (consider how annoying it would be to write out "dollar" every time, rather than "$"), and so the Elamites came to use about 20 common logograms.

Cuneiform also spread north. In an area covering northern Syria, northern Iraq, and part of Turkey, the Hurrian civilization flourished for about a thousand years, starting toward the end of the third millennium BC. Like the Elamites, the Hurrians borrowed syllabic cuneiform from the Akkadians, cutting the number of signs to achieve an efficient syllabary. A related language, Urartian, readapted the script, preserving more of the logograms, in the period 830 to 650 BC.

Cuneiform was also adapted to the Hittite language of Asia Minor in the middle of the second millennium BC. Hittite was an Indo-European language, a member of the same linguistic family as English. Like the Urartians, the Hittites chose to borrow a good number of the ancient Sumerian logograms along with the Akkadian syllabary.

Thus the original Sumero-Akkadian cuneiform was used for or adapted to languages of five different families: Sumerian and Elamite (both isolates), Akkadian (Semitic), Hurrian and Urartian (related to each other but not to other languages), and Hittite (Indo-European).

The *idea* of cuneiform – a script consisting of impressed wedge-shaped signs – spread yet further. Old Persian, the Indo-European language that came to share and then dominate the Elamite language area, is the language of a number of cuneiform-type royal inscriptions from the Achaemenid dynasty, which ruled Persia from 559 to 331 BC and included the famous kings Cyrus, Darius, and Xerxes. Luckily for later decipherers of cuneiform, Darius had a fondness for commemorative inscriptions; but the Old Persian script was not otherwise much used. It was midway between an alphabet and a simple syllabary. Some signs were simple consonants (C), some simple vowels (V), and some a syllabic CV combination, for a total of 36 phonologically based characters, plus a word divider, 5 logograms, and numerals. The wedge-shaped lines that make up the signs were selected from those of Akkadian cuneiform, but the actual signs were completely different.

There is one final use to which the cuneiform style of writing was put. The last version of cuneiform to become known to the modern world was discovered in 1929 at what is now Ras Shamra on the coast of Syria. The site was once the Canaanite city of Ugarit, which flourished between the fifteenth and twelfth centuries BC.

The Ugaritic script consisted of only 27 to 30 signs, depending on the context in which it was used. A script with so few signs is almost bound to be an alphabet – with each sign representing a single consonant or vowel – rather than a syllabary. And indeed it was an alphabet. Within a year of its discovery it had been deciphered; not only was it an alphabet, but it turned out to be a transliteration into cuneiform-type characters of the ancient Semitic alphabet which spawned the Phoenician, Hebrew, and Arabic scripts, and which ultimately lies behind our own alphabet as well. The letters were shaped entirely differently from those of the other Semitic alphabets, but the names of the letters and the alphabetical order were the same. Ironically, the oldest evidence for the ancient alphabetical order that we still follow when we recite "A, B, C" is from a Ugaritic cuneiform tablet of about 1400 BC, and not from letters related in shape to ours or to any of the other Semitic-derived alphabets.

And so the method of writing impressed cuneiform signs on clay tablets was used for logograms, for syllabaries, and even for an alphabet. This remarkably adaptable and long-lived tradition finally died in the early years of our own era, and the very fact that such writing had once existed was forgotten.

Meanwhile the Mesopotamian tablets lay buried in the shifting sediments of time. Whole cities were abandoned and forgotten, along with the public inscriptions their kings and conquerors had erected in them. Not a word of any form of cuneiform could still be read, and when in the seventeenth century AD reports reached the West of a wedge-shaped form of writing on the ancient stones of the Middle East, some scholars refused to believe that it could actually be a kind of writing. Today we can read the inscriptions of Darius the Great, the astronomy of the Babylonians, the laws of the Akkadian kings, and the myths of the Sumerians. How did this happen?

The ego of the Persian king Darius (521–486 BC) played a not insignificant role in the decipherment of cuneiform. Darius had his exploits and decrees inscribed in various public places in and around his new capital city, Persepolis. His son Xerxes (486–465 BC) followed his example. To ensure that no one missed the point, the inscriptions were written out in three languages: Old Persian, Elamite, and Babylonian Akkadian.

But even the glory of kings passes. In the seventeenth century AD no one could read a word of Darius' and Xerxes' boasts. No one knew who had written them, what three languages they were in, or even that they were in three different languages.

The first accurate copies of Persepolis inscriptions reached the hands of Western scholars between 1772 and 1778, published by Carsten Niebuhr, a Dane who had spent time in Persepolis meticulously copying the cuneiform inscriptions. He was the first to realize that there were three different wedge-like scripts represented. He was also able to confirm that the writing ran from left to right, and he assembled a list of the individual characters in the Old Persian script. But there was still no way to know what the inscriptions actually said. How could anyone go about deciphering a text in an unknown language with no readable translation?

The first part of the answer took the form of an inspired guess: if you don't know what the text says, what do you think it *should* say? Taken too far this method can be disastrous, and many false decipherments of forgotten scripts have been based on such an error (a sixteenth-century Dutch doctor, for example, tried hard to prove that the language recorded by ancient Egyptian hieroglyphs was in fact Dutch). But it is common knowledge that monumental public inscriptions were generally made at the behest of kings and made frequent mention of those kings in their texts. It is also true that the names of kings are sometimes preserved in the records of other peoples. Thus we owe to the Greeks the memory of the names of the Achaemenid Persian kings as well as many of the Egyptian pharaohs. Both the decipherment of cuneiform and that of Egyptian hieroglyphs began with the names of these monarchs.

The German school teacher Georg Grotefend (1775–1853) was the one to make the inspired guess. On the basis of later Persian inscriptions written in the recently deciphered Sassanian script, he guessed that there would be a repeating formula of the style "so-and-so, the king, king of kings, son of so-and-so, the king, king of kings." And sure enough, the texts did contain repeated phrases (hypothesized to be "the king, king of kings") interspersed with sections of text short enough to be names. If his hypothesis was correct, then one text mentioned "x, the king, king of kings, son of y, the king, king of kings," while another text mentioned "y, the king, king of kings, son of z." Clearly, then, z was not a king. So who were x, y, and z?

The genealogies of the Persian kings were preserved by the Greeks. Given the general time period, the names must have been Xerxes, his father Darius, and Darius' father Hystaspes, who was not a king. With an informed guess as to what these names would have sounded like in Persian (rather than Greek), Grotefend was able to assign phonetic values to some of the signs. The name of the last king, Xerxes, began with the same letters as the hypothesized word for "king," and indeed in Persian they both began with the sounds [xʃ]. So the language was

Persian, a language that (in other versions and written in another script) was fortunately becoming known to Western scholars at the time. Decipherers who followed up on Grotefend's initial work could thus check their guesses and deductions against what was known about the language: if the text could be made to make sense in Old Persian, the decipherment was likely to be correct. Here the budding field of historical linguistics played a key role, enabling scholars to make systematic use of different varieties of Persian and of related languages such as Sanskrit to reconstruct the properties of Old Persian.

The most famous and longest of the trilingual inscriptions covers a large part of a cliff face at Behistun (also known as Bīsitun or Bisotun). The British army officer Henry Rawlinson (1810–95) copied the inscription at some personal risk and made it available to Western scholars.

With the publication of the Behistun inscriptions, further progress could be made. The Irishman Edward Hincks was able to make significant headway, demonstrating that the Old Persian script was at least partly syllabic. He also studied the other versions of the trilingual text, recognizing the second script (now known to be Elamite) as a simpler version of the third (now known to be Babylonian Akkadian), and the third as being the same (generally speaking) as that of tablets being found in great number at Assyrian and Babylonian sites in neighboring Mesopotamia (see figure 2.3).

Hincks applied Grotefend's name formula to the Elamite and Babylonian inscriptions, beginning the decipherment of these scripts. He deduced that the third language was Semitic, and used his knowledge of common Semitic properties to work on Akkadian. Akkadian presented a significant challenge, owing to the complicated nature of the writing system, with its polyvalence of signs and combination of logograms and syllabograms. Elamite, by contrast, had a much simpler script, but the language itself was more difficult to understand because it had no recorded relatives.

At the time, much of the credit for the decipherment of cuneiform after Grotefend's initial progress went to Rawlinson, with Hincks understood as having achieved similar results working independently but a little more slowly. It is not unlikely, however, that it was Rawlinson who trailed Hincks, making use of Hincks's results as they became available.

Hincks was a clergyman and a prolific scholar who also did much in the decipherment of Urartian. His was also the honor of bringing

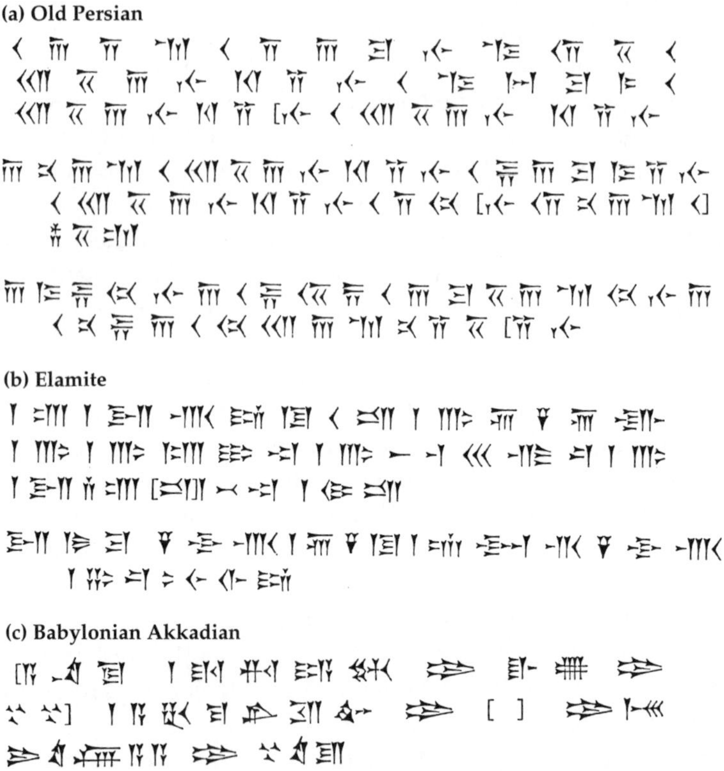

(a) Old Persian

(b) Elamite

(c) Babylonian Akkadian

Figure 2.3 The first sentence of Darius the Great's trilingual cuneiform inscription at Behistun in (a) Old Persian, (b) Elamite, and (c) Babylonian Akkadian. Note that the Old Persian, being partly alphabetic, is the longest, while the Babylonian version, being logosyllabic, contains more complex signs. The sentence reads, "I am Darius, the great king, the king of kings, the king of Persia, the king of the provinces, the son of Hystaspes, the grandson of Arsams, the Achaemenian." The Babylonian version is more succinct than the other two (and, where in brackets, partly restored through comparison with other inscriptions). For those interested in trying their hand at decipherment, the first words of the Old Persian can be transliterated as *a-da-m da-a-ra-ja-va-u-ʃ x-ʃa-a-ja-θ-i-ja va-z-ra-ka* (I, Darius, great king), with signs belonging to the same word separated by hyphens. The lone angular sign with which the sentence begins is a word divider.

the decipherment of Akkadian cuneiform to a close in 1852 by correctly identifying an Akkadian tablet that listed a number of logographic signs and gave their pronunciation spelled out in syllables. He had found the Akkadians' own ABC. Such a sign list would have been used in the training of ancient Akkadian scribes; it and the many other sign lists that have since been found have also proved invaluable to the study of Akkadian by modern scholars.

But where in all this were the Sumerians? The decipherment of cuneiform proceeded largely backward, from the relatively late (and streamlined) Old Persian to the ancient and elaborate (one might even say baroque) Akkadian. The Persians were known to history, and so were the Akkadian-speaking Assyrians and Babylonians. The Sumerians had been lost entirely. The Sumerian language first re-emerged at the site of the royal library at Nineveh. As Akkadian became fully readable, it was obvious that some of the texts at Nineveh were written bilingually in Akkadian and something else. For a while some scholars believed that the "something else" might not even represent a real language – it could be some sort of code version of Akkadian, or a scribe's game.

But other evidence was accumulating that pointed to the existence of a form of cuneiform older than that of Akkadian. For one thing, the syllabic and logographic versions of Akkadian signs did not sound the same. Why, for example, was one sign pronounced [gal] when it denoted just a phonological syllable sound, but [rabuːm] when it was functioning as a logogram meaning "great"? Wouldn't it make more sense if the syllabic use of the sign were based on the logographic use and pronounced like it? Where had the syllabic values of the signs come from, if not from Akkadian words? Assyriologists began to suspect that a different language underlay the Akkadians' use of cuneiform. But what was it? The answer came from early Akkadian records in which the ancient kings called themselves "king of Sumer and Akkad." The unknown language must have been that of this hitherto unknown land, Sumer. And sure enough, tablets from the Early Dynastic period in southern Mesopotamia began to come to light. These were written in the same language as the mysterious texts assembled much later at Nineveh.

And thus the words of the Sumerians were restored to us. Once people were willing to believe that the bilingual tablets contained a real language – Sumerian – much about that ancient language could be deduced. The disparity between the syllabic and logographic readings of the signs disappeared: in Sumerian, the word for "great" was *gal*. The use of the same sign for "reed" and "render" and the syllable [gi] became obvious: in Sumerian, they were *all* pronounced [gi]. Sumerian, it turned out, explained a lot about how Akkadian was written.

Nevertheless, to this day Sumerologists are plagued by the fact that we can only read Sumerian because we can read Akkadian, an unrelated language. Thus we do not know precisely how the Sumerians pronounced their language. We know that the *Akkadians* thought that the Sumerian word for "great" sounded like [gal], and that the Sumerian words for "reed" and "render" sounded like [gi], but whether the Sumerians would have agreed is a somewhat different matter. Conversely, the writing of Akkadian was somewhat hampered by the traditions of writing Sumerian. The number of different sounds represented in Sumerian influenced which sounds were distinguished in writing Akkadian. Thus Akkadian was always written with what might be considered a Sumerian accent. But when we look for evidence as to what Sumerian sounded like, we have to take the Akkadians' word for it, and so we now read Sumerian with an Akkadian accent!

The spoken words of the Sumerians and Akkadians disappeared long ago. Yet through the efforts of decipherers we can read words 5,000 years old, even if we do so in an accent the ancient writers would never recognize. Most other languages of the time – the vast majority of languages around the ancient world – were not so lucky. They perished without a trace or mutated into new forms. Language is inherently ephemeral; writing lasts, particularly if it is written on baked clay tablets.

3

Egyptian Hieroglyphs and the Quest for Eternity

A Sumerian or Akkadian scribe keeping records in cuneiform would have been astounded to learn that his text would survive for millennia. An Egyptian scribe incising hieroglyphs for a commemorative or funerary text would merely have considered such permanence a job well done. The Egyptians were probably the second people to develop a writing system, but they trailed the Mesopotamians only slightly if at all, and they soon caught up to apply their unique script to the full range of bureaucratic, religious, and literary uses. They also made writing into an art form that still inspires fascination and admiration today. The lasting popularity of hieroglyphs is quite apt: writing both encouraged and expressed the Egyptians' devotion to permanence and the pursuit of eternal life.

The Egyptians' preoccupation with eternity was fostered by their physical surroundings, where life flourished in the narrow valley of the Nile River, surrounded by changeless deserts and a changeless sky. The Nile defined the Egyptian country and culture. The river creates a slim band of cultivable land extending the length of the country, widening out into the fan-shaped delta in the north as it flows through its own deposits of sediment to reach the Mediterranean Sea. On either side of the narrow line of green are inhospitable deserts. These deserts were formed in prehistoric times, driving their inhabitants to settle in the Nile Valley where water continued to be available. There the migrants found plenty of game in the marshlands fed by the river. The yearly flooding of the Nile brought fertile sediments and moisture to the riverbanks, allowing edible plants to flourish. The prehistoric Egyptians discovered that they could control the growth of plants by sowing, irrigating, and harvesting crops. With the development of agriculture, the population grew, and as the population grew, swamps were drained and put into cultivation. As the cultivated land expanded, so did the need for irrigation. As in Mesopotamia, the collective labor required for irrigation appears to have played a part in the increasing complexity of society and the birth of civilization in Egypt.

Since the habitable land was very narrow, the population did not tend to cluster into towns and cities as it had in Mesopotamia, but remained spread out along the river in villages. As civilization began and the political power of chieftains grew, their domains therefore were not city-states but stretches of the Nile. By the end of the prehistoric period, Upper Egypt was a cohesive cultural and political region in contrast to Lower Egypt, which contained the delta. (Upper Egypt was southern Egypt, as the Nile runs downhill from south to north. The Egyptians always thought of south as "up" and north as "down." Similarly, "left" could mean "east" and "right" "west.")

Toward the end of Egypt's prehistoric period, the Egyptians must have come into contact with the Mesopotamians. They borrowed the cylinder seal (which originated in the Uruk period of Sumer), and certain artistic and architectural styles. They soon rejected these borrowings for their own developing native styles. More importantly, the Egyptians may have learned at this time of the recent breakthrough in Sumerian record keeping – the ability to record words by stylized markings on a durable surface.

It is likely that the Egyptians at least heard about Sumerian writing, but it is unclear exactly how much the Egyptians learned about proto-cuneiform, and it is even possible that somehow they did not hear of it at all, for they certainly went about creating their writing system in their own way. Egyptian hieroglyphs make their first appearance in the archaeological record around 3150 BC, as Egypt was making the transition from its pre-dynastic to dynastic period.

According to later Egyptian tradition, the nation's history began around 3100 BC with the unification of Upper and Lower Egypt into a single kingdom under the first pharaoh of the first dynasty, Menes. Menes has never been identified historically, but he was said to have been a king of Upper Egypt who conquered the delta land of Lower Egypt. Despite uncertainty as to the precise date (it may have been a little earlier than 3100 BC) or the actual name of the pharaoh, by 3100 BC Egypt had become the first nation-state in the world, unified under the command of divine kings, with all the administrative requirements that this entailed. The success of this new political arrangement depended on their new invention, writing.

For all we know, the Egyptian writing system may have been the invention of a single person, or it may have required the collaboration of many over a considerable period of time. If the latter, then the early stages of development have been lost to archaeology. Although the oldest surviving inscriptions – labels on ceramic vessels and stelae (commemorative stones) – are terse and hard to read, they appear to contain the same essential characteristics as later Egyptian writing: logograms supplemented with three different kinds of phonograms. In Mesopotamia, by contrast, the maturation of the script was much slower. While changes and elaborations in the Egyptian system did occur along the way, these characteristic elements were present from its earliest surviving uses.

The first and longest-lived form of Egyptian writing was what we now call *hieroglyphic* after the Greek term for "sacred carving." While hieroglyphs were often carved into stone, they could also be written with a brush and ink on pottery or on papyrus, a heavy, paper-like material made from the papyrus reed. Unlike cuneiform, whose original pictograms eventually lost all visual connection to the real world, Egyptian hieroglyphs always remained pictorial (see plate 2). Individual hieroglyphs were pictures of actual beings or objects. They could be elegantly carved and painted, as they often were in commemorative and sacred inscriptions, or they could be drawn in outline, a style known as cursive hieroglyphs and usually used for writing with brush and ink. The two styles are attested from the earliest stages of hieroglyphic writing. The fancier style may be an elaboration of the simpler, or the simpler style may be a reduced form of the fancier. In either case, the two styles were adapted to their different uses and the different surfaces on which they were written.

An individual hieroglyphic sign could have one or more of three possible functions: logogram, phonogram (phonological sign), or determinative. Probably the first signs to be developed were logograms, as in Mesopotamia. Such a sign would stand for the word that named the object pictured. Oft-cited examples include ⊓ (*pr*), a schematic of a house plan meaning "house," and ⊙ (*rꜥ*), a depiction of the sun's disk meaning "sun" and also, by extension, *hrw*, "day." A number of other easily depicted things, such as animals, body parts, and everyday objects, could be written with logograms.

The inventors of Egyptian writing would soon have realized, however, that designing a logogram for every word in the language would be a tall order. Thus in practice, words written with merely a logogram were relatively rare; when they did occur, they were usually followed by a stroke below or beside them to indicate their logographic use: ⸢ʔ or ⊙ı.

For a fully developed writing system, something else was needed. The Egyptians may have heard of the rebus principle from the Sumerians, or they may have discovered it independently. At the heart of rebus writing is the idea that the sound of a word is separable from its meaning, so that a pictorial logogram for one word can be transferred to another word of the same sound but a different meaning. The rebus principle eventually led the Sumerians and Akkadians to dissociate sound and meaning enough to create syllabograms – phonologically based signs with no inherent semantic meaning. In Egypt the rebus principle was applied differently because of some crucial differences between the Egyptian and Sumerian languages.

The Sumerians had begun by developing symbols for simple monomorphemic words – a practice known as "nuclear writing" as it represents just the uninflected core of the words. From there they used rebus writing to represent homonyms, to add phonetic complements, and eventually to spell out words and names syllabically.

A crucial aspect of the Sumerian nuclear writing, however, was that the cores of words were themselves words. The same is true in English. The word *breath* can function alone, or it can form the core of the plural *breaths*, the verb *breathe*, the adjective *breathless*, or the derived noun *breathalyzer*. The logograms of early Sumerian nuclear writing sometimes represented full words (like *breath*) and sometimes just the core of longer words.

The logograms of the Egyptians represented full words. So ⊏⊐ı was "house" and ⊙ı "sun," etc. Unlike in Sumerian or English, however, the cores of the words *were not themselves words*. This takes a little linguistic theory to explain.

The Egyptian language belonged to the Afro-Asiatic language family, to which also belong the Semitic languages of western Asia (such as Hebrew, Arabic, and Akkadian) and a number of languages of North Africa such as Berber. Egyptian and Akkadian are the earliest attested Afro-Asiatic languages.

Like Akkadian and other Semitic languages, Egyptian generally built its words around a core of three consonants. The derivation of one word from a related word was usually done by changing the vowels that were intermingled with those consonants, as well as by the repetition of consonants or the addition of affixes. Thus related words shared consonants, just as English *drink*, *drank*, and *drunk* do, with vowels carrying the difference in meaning.

The core three consonants of an Egyptian word constituted the root morpheme of the word, while the vowels that were interspersed with these consonants carried the inflection, varying with the grammatical form of the word and functioning like prefixes and suffixes do in other languages. For example, the consonant sequence *n-f-r* meant "good" or "complete." The masculine form of this word was probably **nafir*, where the asterisk shows that the word is a reconstruction made by historical linguists, not a form of the word that has ever been firmly attested. The feminine form of the word had a -*t* suffix, but it would also have had different vowels: it was probably **nafrat*. In these two words not only are the vowels different (*a* and *i* versus *a* and *a*), but they are placed differently among the consonants. Both the particular vowels used and their placement affected the meaning of words.

In Egyptian, unlike in Sumerian, there was a difference between a simple unaffixed word (like **nafir*) and the core of the word (*n-f-r*). The core of a word was not composed of a consecutive string of sounds pronounceable as a syllable or two. The feminine **nafrat*, for example, could not be formed by the addition of -*t* to **nafir*. Instead, the word core was an unpronounceable sequence of discontinuous consonants. A symbol that represented the core of a word therefore *represented its consonants*. In other words, the Egyptians realized that the common element of **nafir* and **nafrat* was the triconsonantal root *n-f-r*.

The written consequence of this property of Egyptian was that both **nafir* and **nafrat* and many another word built on the same core (such as the name of Queen Nefertiti) were spelled with the symbol ⸙, representing the consonant sequence *n-f-r*. Thus Egyptian developed a repertoire of about 70 signs (some of which are shown in figure 3.1) which represented many of the commonly used triconsonantal word cores.

Some word roots in Egyptian had only two consonants, and they were accordingly given signs that represented only two consonants. It was at this point that the Egyptians applied the rebus principle. They applied it to these biconsonantal cores and developed a purely phonological use for the biconsonantal signs. A biconsonantal sign like ⊓, *pr*, could be used logographically to mean "house" (if written with a

Some biconsonantal signs			
ḥr	wn	wr	pr
mn	mw	mt	ms
zꜣ	nb	sw	ḏd
wꜣ (also used for **o** in foreign names)	rw (also used for **l** in foreign names)	kꜣ	bꜣ
Some triconsonantal signs			
nfr	ꜥnḫ	ḏꜥm	wꜣs
ꜣbw	nṯr	ḫpr	bit
tyw	ḥtm	ḥtp	iwn
nḏm	rwd/rwḏ	ꜥḥꜥ	ḥrw
Some determinatives			
woman	man	enemy, foreigner	mummy, likeness
king, god	queen, goddess	eye, seeing	walk, run
fish	horse	tree	house, building
pyramid	desert, foreign country	sun, light, time	book, writing, abstract concept

Figure 3.1 Some of the biconsonantal signs, triconsonantal signs, and determinatives used in Egyptian hieroglyphs. For the phonetic values of the transcriptions, see figure 3.2. The signs could face either rightward or leftward, depending on the direction in which they were intended to be read. Rightward-facing was the ordinary direction, but leftward-facing texts were made in the interests of artistic harmony. Hieroglyphs embedded within the text of this book therefore face leftward, while those in this chart face rightward.

stroke after it) or simply to mean the two consonants *p* and *r*. Thus the spelling of ⌐ꜣ *prt*, "winter", began with ⌐. There were about 80 common biconsonantal signs.

Once the signs were used for their consonantal value alone, the principle could be extended yet further, and the Egyptians also developed a series of 25 signs which stood for individual consonants, the so-called "hieroglyphic alphabet" (shown in figure 3.2). The values of some of these signs may have been derived from the first consonant in the word for the object depicted: the horned viper, ⌣, *fy*, stood for the consonant *f*.

Except in foreign names, the Egyptians did not generally use the uniconsonantal signs as a true alphabet with which to spell out whole words phoneme by phoneme, although the insight that phonemes could be represented with individual signs later served as the inspiration for the ancestor of our own alphabet (see chapter 9). Rather, the Egyptian uniconsonantal signs had two specific purposes. The first was to serve as phonetic complements. Putting a uniconsonantal sign after a biconsonantal sign, such as ⌐, *r*, after ⌐, emphasized that the word was being spelled phonologically rather than logographically – as the consonants *pr*, rather than the word meaning "house." Phonetic complements emphasized phonological readings; they did not add new sounds to the word. Thus adding the ⌐ to ⌐ did not add another *r* sound.

Uniconsonantal signs could also be added as phonetic complements to triconsonantal signs. When they followed triconsonantal signs, however, they did not mean the sign was being used purely phonologically. Unlike biconsonantal signs, triconsonantal signs generally remained associated with a particular core morpheme, resisting rebus applications. Thus similar-sounding words that did not share the same core meaning would tend not to use the same triconsonantal sign.

Supporting bi- and triconsonantal signs with uniconsonantal phonetic complements makes reading hieroglyphs much easier, as there are continual reminders of what the last one or two consonants in a sign are. Thus *n-f-r* could be written ⌐ (nfr), ⌐ (nfr-f-r), or ⌐ (nfr-r), the latter two cases containing built-in reminders of how ⌐ was to be read. Using uniconsonantal signs to complement biconsonantal or triconsonantal signs was the norm rather than the exception; but whether they were used, and how many of them were used, could vary according to the space that was available.

Symbol	Transliteration	IPA	Object depicted
𓅐	ꜣ	[ʔ]	vulture
𓏭	y or i	[j] or [i]	reed leaf
𓏮 or //	y	[j] (usually word–final)	double reed leaf or archaic dual sign
⌐	ꜥ	[ʕ]	forearm
𓅱 or 𓍢	w	[w] or [u]	quail chick or curl of rope
𓃀	b	[b]	foot
▢	p	[p]	stool
⌐	f	[f]	horned viper
𓅓	m	[m]	owl
﹏	n	[n]	water
⌒	r	[r], later also [l]	mouth
𓉐	h	[h]	enclosure
𓎛	ḥ	[ħ]	rope
⊜	ḫ	[x]	placenta (?)
⌐●	ẖ	[ç]	belly and udder
—∞—	s	[s], originally [z]	door bolt
𓏏	s	[s]	bolt of cloth
▭	š	[ʃ]	pool
◺	q	[q]	hill
⌒	k	[k]	basket with handle
𓎼 or 𓎽	g	[g]	jar stand or bag
⌒	t	[t]	loaf of bread
⌐	ṯ	[tʃ]	tether
⌐	d	[d]	hand
𓆓	ḏ	[dʒ]	snake

Figure 3.2 Egyptian uniconsonantal signs, the so-called hieroglyphic alphabet, in rightward-facing orientation. The order is modern convention; the ancient order is not fully known.

The other important use of uniconsonantal signs was to spell out affixes. Thus the feminine *nafrat* was spelled ⌡⌣ (nfr-(r)-t), showing the feminine suffix -*t*, ⌣.

The structure of the Egyptian language thus led the inventors of hieroglyphs down a different path than the Sumerians. Unlike the Akkadians, the Egyptians were laboring under no allegiance to the Sumerian system. When they applied the rebus principle, separating sound from meaning, the signs took on the values of consonants, rather than syllables. And thus the Egyptian writing system became the first to represent individual phonemes (often unpronounceable by themselves) as opposed to syllables, which are the natural pronounceable unit of speech. The mixed system of logograms and consonant symbols that resulted is described as *logoconsonantal*, as opposed to cuneiform's logosyllabic nature.

Besides the logograms, the tri- and biconsonantal morphological cores, and the purely phonological uses of bi- and uniconsonantal signs, there remains an extensive series of determinatives – unpronounced signs that served to give some information about a word's meaning. The determinative(s) came last in the spelling of a word, after the phonetic complements, so they were handy for indicating the ends of words in a time before the invention of word spacing. They would also have suggested to the reader which one of a family of words was to be read from the consonantal core, and they would have disambiguated homonyms.

Some determinatives were quite broad in their application, giving the general class of object or idea that was being referred to. For example, a scroll, ⌐⌐, was used with words that dealt with writing, books, or abstract concepts. A sparrow was used with things that were considered small, weak, or evil; it is thus known to modern Egyptologists as the "little bird of evil." Other determinatives were very specific. The sign △ was used with the names of pyramids and towns located near pyramids. The introduction of the horse during Egypt's New Kingdom brought the introduction of a horse determinative: 🐎. Occasionally the use of a determinative would add non-linguistic information. For example, the word for "mother" would normally be written with a "woman" determinative, but if a divine mother was being referred to, the determinative would be that for a goddess, showing a distinction in writing that was not reflected in the pronunciation of the word (as we might write "the Mother" if referring to a goddess).

Thus far there has been no mention of vowels. The vowels of an Egyptian word varied according to what form of the word was being used and were therefore predictable on the basis of the conjugation of the word. So a word's vowels could generally be inferred from context or from the determinative that followed the word. A person who spoke Egyptian could easily supply the correct vowels. The problem for modern Egyptologists, however, is that there is no longer any very clear evidence for what those vowels were. Some evidence can be garnered from the spelling of Egyptian names in other ancient languages, such as Greek and Akkadian. But foreigners' ideas of how names are pronounced tend to be unreliable, so even this minimal evidence must be taken with a grain of salt.

Other evidence comes from Coptic, the liturgical language of Egyptian Christians and a direct descendant of ancient Egyptian. Although Coptic died out as a native spoken language around the end of the seventeenth century AD, it is still used in church liturgy and, most importantly, it is written with vowels. This evidence is valuable to historical linguists but is still somewhat unreliable, as vowels are notoriously changeable aspects of language. (In English, for example, the pronunciations of all the long vowels have changed since AD 1400, and the pronunciation of vowels varies considerably from one region to another.)

Therefore, while the ancient Egyptian language can nowadays be read quite easily by Egyptologists, pronouncing it is another matter. By convention an [ɛ] vowel (as in the English word *met*) is usually pronounced between consonants. Thus the feminine form *n-f-r-t* is nowadays usually pronounced [nɛfrɛt] or [nɛfɛrt] (as in Nefertiti), rather than the more historically probable **nafrat*. Exceptions to the default [ɛ] are made for the so-called "weak consonants" *ꜣ* ([ʔ]), *y* ([j]), and *w*, which are pronounced [ɑ], [i], and [u] respectively. So *kꜣ*, "spirit," is today pronounced [kɑ], rhyming with English *ma*; *yb*, "heart," is pronounced [ib], rhyming with *grebe*, and *nwt*, the sky goddess, is pronounced [nut], rhyming with *loot*. The *ꜣ*, *y*, and *w* consonants belong to a class known as glides or semivowels, and are notorious for flip-flopping between more vowel-like and more consonantal pronunciations in various languages. Reading them as vowels is thus not unreasonable. The Egyptians themselves would often omit glides in writing, probably considering them part of the previous or following vowel. (Try pronouncing "three ears" and "three years," and you will see how easily a [j], spelled "y," can be lost among the vowels.)

In all, hieroglyphic writing used about 500 common signs at any given time. Some signs were lost or added with time; some occurred relatively rarely. The classic hieroglyphic texts draw from a repertoire of about 700 signs. In Roman times, however, when the use of hieroglyphs had become the exclusive knowledge of the priesthood, there was a final flowering of hieroglyph invention, which put the total number of attested Egyptian hieroglyphs up over 6,000.

In writing hieroglyphic texts Egyptian scribes were ever conscious of the aesthetic effect of their labors. The individual signs were not simply arranged one after the other in rows or columns. While texts did in general progress along a row or down a column, the individual signs were grouped so as to make a series of square or rectangular boxlike clusters. Large signs would form a box of their own, while small signs were grouped together as their shape permitted. Signs within a box were read from top to bottom and then either right to left or left to right depending on the orientation of the text in general. Variant spellings (with more or less phonetic complementation, for example) could be used to fit texts to the space assigned to them.

The direction of writing could vary. The default direction for hieroglyphic writing was either from top to bottom in columns, with the columns progressing from right to left, or from right to left in rows written from top to bottom. In some cases, however, columns or rows of hieroglyphs could be written from left to right. This option was called upon in the interests of symmetry, for example for two columns of writing flanking an illustration. Both columns would thus face the picture. The particular direction a text is to be read in can almost always be determined by the direction which the humans and animals in the text are facing. Hieroglyphs are read so that you encounter the faces or fronts of things first. When interspersed with modern texts, hieroglyphs are usually presented in the less typical direction, left to right; this is after all consistent with the traditional Egyptian principle of harmonious arrangement in context.

The Egyptians never lost sight of the pictorial value of their written signs. Unlike in Mesopotamia, where writing was reduced to practical wedges that ran willy-nilly across any attending artwork, writing in Egypt was never fully separated from art. When illustrations and writing occurred together, they were knit into a harmonious whole, and it is not always evident where the art leaves off and the writing begins. For example, illustrations of the judgment of souls show the heart of the deceased being weighed against a feather. But the feather is a hieroglyph for the goddess Maat, who personified justice and right living. Is the heart then being weighed against a literal feather, or against the ideal of justice and right living?

The illustrations accompanying a text also affected the order of writing. Whichever way the images of people were facing, that would be the direction in which the hieroglyphs labeling the image (i.e. the caption) would be facing. Thus the large illustrating picture and the little pictures that made up the text of the caption would all be facing the same direction. Similarly, inscriptions on the left and right sides of a statue would be written in two different directions, so that the beings composing each inscription faced the same way the statue itself was facing.

In fact, illustrations and statues influenced writing even more deeply. Normally the name of a person (or god) would be followed by a determinative, showing whether the name was that of a man, woman, child, god, or goddess. But when the name occurred in the label of an illustration or statue of that person, the determinative was generally left off. Why include a sign which is essentially the picture of a goddess, if the object being labeled is a bigger picture of a goddess? Thus a portrait of a person could play the written role of a determinative.

A well-executed text in hieroglyphs was indeed a work of art, and to the Egyptian mind art and hieroglyphs served much the same function. Specifically, they both preserved the essence of a person for eternity. Many of the most extensive surviving hieroglyphic texts are related to the Egyptian cult of the dead. Egyptian culture displayed a constant preoccupation with eternity and the afterlife, particularly on behalf of the pharaohs. The Old Kingdom (2650 to 2150 BC) saw the building of the pyramids, which were intended to be eternal earthly dwelling places of the pharaoh's spirit – a particularly effective spirit embodying divine kingship. It was clear to the Egyptians that being deprived of food and drink would cause a person's spirit to depart from their body; thus clearly the spirit (*k3*, usually spelled *ka* in English) needed to be sustained with food and drink. Cults were established to continue serving the deceased pharaohs in perpetuity, and great pyramids were built to house and commemorate them. The pyramids of Khufu, Khafra, and Menkaura at Giza were built during the fourth dynasty, from 2575 to 2465 BC. But after a couple of centuries – and a change in dynasty – the pharaohs must have noticed (and perhaps even encouraged) the fact that the temple cults of these long-dead kings were petering out. People and institutions, they realized, were ephemeral, while the need for sustenance in the afterlife was eternal.

To solve this problem, the pharaohs turned to the written word, inscribing their burial chambers with hieroglyphs that described the offering of food and drink to the king. They also wrote incantations to ensure the overcoming of all obstacles in the afterlife, and to point the king's soul (*b3*, now usually spelled *ba*) to the heavens. Words were considered to have magical efficacy, and writing, they realized, could effect this magic permanently on their behalf. And they were right: the cults of the pharaohs are long gone, but many of these Old Kingdom funerary inscriptions, known as Pyramid Texts, still survive.

In the Middle Kingdom (c.2040–1780 BC), the use of funerary texts spread downward to the nobility, and the texts were often painted on the coffins of the deceased. These Coffin Texts were considered to be extremely powerful: the words were intended to be eternally alive. In fact, the words were composed of pictures, often of living things. But if those words were alive, might it not be dangerous to put them so close to the body of the deceased, home of a living spirit? Indeed. The most dangerous animal, the horned viper (, representing *f*), began to appear cut in two, and by the end of the Middle Kingdom potentially dangerous animals were often shown dismembered or mutilated in Coffin Texts.

The New Kingdom (1550–1070 BC) saw a further evolution of funerary texts into a genre collectively known as the Book of the Dead. These texts were written on papyrus in cursive hieroglyphs and buried with the dead (plate 2).

Hieroglyphic texts were strongly conservative in their language, perpetuating not only the spirits of the dead but also their language. The earliest connected texts in hieroglyphs are written in a form of the language known as Old Egyptian, spoken from about 2600 to 2100 BC. This was the language of the Pyramid Texts. The classical phase of the language followed, known as Middle Egyptian. As far as we can tell, Middle Egyptian was spoken from about 2100 to 1600 BC. Yet the permanence of the written word (especially in carefully executed hieroglyphs) had by then so impressed the Egyptians that Middle Egyptian remained the language of hieroglyphic texts from then on. Just as Akkadian-speaking scribes continued to learn Sumerian after it was otherwise dead, Egyptian scribes continued to read and write in a form of their language that was no longer spoken.

This is one of the stranger consequences of the invention of writing. Originally meant to preserve information, it ended up preserving language, with the result that people could (and still do today) read and write in languages that have been dead for centuries. In a preliterate society the idea of using an extinct language would have been bizarre. Who would you speak it with? How would you learn it? A literate society, however, preserves messages from the dead.

The preserving nature of writing was put to good use by the Egyptians in their quest for the eternal, and it both expressed and fueled their quest. On the one hand it allowed them a look into their own past, giving them the opportunity of perpetuating traditions and language that were already ancient; on the other hand they used it to preserve for the everlasting future their culture and even their own spirits.

Although many literary and scholarly Egyptian texts do survive, the majority of surviving ancient Egyptian texts are funerary in nature. This is partly due to the priorities of the Egyptians, who placed great emphasis on ensuring a blessed afterlife for their kings and, by extension, themselves. Much effort was expended in this endeavor, as attested by the Great Pyramid of Khufu, whose base covers 13 acres. The production of a great quantity of written material for the same eternal purpose is not surprising.

Another significant reason for the preponderance of funerary texts is that everyday texts were used in everyday locations, while funerary texts were placed in holy preserves at the edge of the bone-dry desert, well away from the damp of the irrigated land. The sere environment has allowed the funerary texts to stand the test of time, just as they were intended to. By contrast, papyri dealing with national administration, for example, have generally not survived. Yet those that do tell a rather different story.

The requirements of administrative record keeping and those of eternal commemoration are quite different; not all uses of writing are inherently artistic or spiritual. As Egyptian civilization emerged it also needed writing for more prosaic purposes – for running its bureaucracy and storing everyday information. Writing put to these purposes had to be quick and easy, and so cursive hieroglyphs began to be written with less pictorial accuracy and more ligatures between signs. This process soon led to the development of *hieratic*, a script that was used in the everyday affairs of the nation. Hieratic worked on the same principles as hieroglyphic, being simply a more efficient way of writing the same signs, but the pictorial nature of most of the signs was obscured, while certain frequently occurring sequences of two hieroglyphs were merged into one connected sign. The relationship between hieratic and hieroglyphic was thus not unlike that between modern cursive handwriting and type, though somewhat less obvious. Hieratic was written from right to left in rows or in columns.

Despite the preponderance of hieroglyphs in the archaeological record – and their perennial mystique – hieratic was the common script of ancient Egypt and was used for both bureaucratic records and literary works. Most writing was done in hieratic; thorough knowledge of hieroglyphs, by contrast, would have been rare even among scribes. Since it was well adapted to being written in ink on papyrus, hieratic eventually came to be used for religious works as well, so that during the Third Intermediate Period (1070–650 BC) the papyri of the Book of the Dead were written in hieratic.

Since hieratic was generally used for less formal purposes, the language used and the spellings employed tended to be less archaic than in hieroglyphic texts; so it is the hieratic texts that tell us of changes in the Egyptian language. From these texts we know that Middle Egyptian was succeeded in the spoken arena by Late Egyptian, the language of about 1600 to 650 BC. The form of the hieratic script itself was also more open to evolution, the needs of efficient record keeping favoring any change that allowed written signs to flow more easily from the scribe's hand. Thus hieratic evolved over the centuries and eventually diverged into two styles, a "book hand" for literary and formal texts and a "chancery hand" for business and other mundane matters. With an absence of strong central government, the Third Intermediate Period saw the chancery hands of the now-separated Northern Egypt and Southern Egypt diverge into two increasingly cursive forms, eventually mutually unintelligible.

With the reunification of the country under the twenty-sixth dynasty (672–525 BC) the northern style of writing was given official sanction in a form we now call *demotic*. Hieratic book hand continued to be used for religious texts; thus Clement of Alexandria described it accurately in about AD 200 when he gave it its modern name, meaning "priestly" or "sacred" in Greek. The demotic script (meaning "of the people") was used for more mundane purposes and remained in use until the fifth century AD. The purposes to which demotic was put meant that there was no strong pull toward preserving antique forms of the language, and so it represents more closely the form of Egyptian spoken at the time, also known as Demotic.

Though the ultimate root of demotic was the hieroglyphic script, demotic and hieroglyphic look completely different. Demotic did not look pictorial at all. The numerous abbreviations and ligatures it used make it now impossible to accurately transcribe texts in demotic into hieroglyphs or vice versa, while hieratic, on the other hand, always remained interchangeable with hieroglyphs. Demotic and hieroglyphic illustrate the opposing pressures in the evolution of a script: on the one hand a script should be easy to write, so as to enable rapid copying and recording of information. On the other hand, using a script preserves information for future ages, and if the script changes much, later generations will not be able to read it. (Modern software designers face the same problem.) The Egyptians resolved the tension by using different scripts for different purposes: the relatively unchanging hieroglyphs for eternal purposes, and the evolving hieratic and demotic for more temporal records.

The twenty-sixth dynasty was followed by conquest at the hands of the Persians in 525 BC, and thereafter self-rule was never achieved for very long. By the Ptolemaic period (332–30 BC), when Egypt was ruled by Greek foreigners, hieroglyphs and even hieratic were increasingly the domain of the very few within the temples. The ruling elite used Greek, but demotic continued to be used for documents written in Egyptian and even occasionally for monumental inscriptions.

In an attempt to consolidate his power, Ptolemy V co-opted the traditional cult of the pharaoh, having himself declared a god in all the temples of the land. The commemorative texts surrounding the event were written by Egyptian priests (none of the Ptolemaic officials spoke Egyptian) in 196 BC and set up on stelae with Greek, demotic, and hieroglyphic texts. And thus it is to Ptolemy V's divine aspirations that we owe the Rosetta Stone, which was to provide the key to reading the Egyptian scripts.

With the defeat of Cleopatra VII by Octavian (later Caesar Augustus) in 30 BC, control of Egypt passed to the Romans. As the religious scribes continued to use hieroglyphs for their own private purposes during the Ptolemaic and Roman periods, we see an explosion in the number of hieroglyphic signs and the use of word-play in texts – a sort of ivory-tower effect, in which scholars delighted in multiplying complexities, freed from the need to communicate their meaning to the uninitiated. The number of attested hieroglyphs rose to over 6,000. This complexifying trend culminated in the third century AD, in which one surviving but persistently obscure text was written almost entirely in crocodile signs, and another largely with rams.

Yet despite this apparent flowering, indigenous culture – and thus writing – languished, at times from neglect and at times from outright repression by the Romans. The last dated hieroglyphic text is inscribed on a wall of the temple at Philae, in the extreme south of Egypt, farthest from Rome. It dates from AD 394, three years after the Christian emperor Theodosius banned worship in pagan temples. Demotic outlived both hieroglyphic and hieratic, yet it too eventually succumbed: the last known demotic texts are graffiti, also at Philae, from AD 452.

With the death of demotic, knowledge of the ancient Egyptian writing systems was lost for nearly fourteen hundred years. Yet the death of Egyptian writing did not imply the death of the Egyptian language, which continued to be spoken by the common people of Egypt, though not by the governing class. This stage of the language is Coptic, which means merely "Egyptian," the term being used to describe both the phase of the Egyptian language that succeeded Demotic and the script it was written in. The Coptic script was adapted from the Greek alphabet. The twenty-four Greek letters were supplemented with eight letters (later reduced to six) borrowed from demotic and used to represent sounds in Egyptian that did not occur in Greek.

The first use of the Coptic script seems to have been in the first century AD for writing magical incantations. Since the Greek alphabet shows a word's vowels, the first writers of Coptic may have borrowed Greek characters in order to convey more precisely the magical words, leaving no possibility for mispronunciations that would cause the backfiring of the spell. The use of the Coptic alphabet only became well established in the third century, however, and later with the death of demotic it became the only way the Egyptian language was recorded.

The rise of the Coptic script is associated with the spread of Christianity in Egypt. In its first two centuries, Egyptian Christianity remained an urban Greek phenomenon, but in the third century AD it became established among the native population and took on a distinctively Egyptian flavor. The new Egyptian Christians were mostly commoners; they knew neither Greek nor the demotic script, but they wanted to read the Christian scriptures for themselves. The script that came to hand for the purposes was Coptic.

It has been surmised that the choice of Coptic over the indigenous Egyptian scripts was part of the Christians' rejection of their pagan past. The feeling must have been mutual – the priests presiding over the dying temples would never have wanted to share their treasured knowledge of hieroglyphs or of hieratic with the Christian upstarts. However, the connection between *demotic* and paganism would have been relatively tenuous; by then any connection between hieroglyphs and demotic was completely imperspicuous and may well have been forgotten. Yet very few ordinary folk could have read demotic at the best of times, as the scribes' profession was a highly exclusive one. As previously illiterate Egyptians began to read the new scriptures, a simple 32-character alphabet based on Greek would have been easier to learn, both for the native Egyptians and for their Greek-speaking missionaries.

Coptic is indeed much easier to learn than hieroglyphs or their descendants. A script of 500 signs simply is harder to memorize than one of 32. Yet the hieroglyphic script, once learned, is not hard to read. The reinforcing effect of phonetic complements and of word-final determinatives makes a line of hieroglyphs easy to scan. Modern Egyptologists find, by contrast, that the few attempts made in Greco-Roman times to write Egyptian alphabetically using only uniconsonantal hieroglyphic signs are quite difficult to make out. Similarly, the earliest uses of the Greek alphabet for Egyptian are also hard to read, in part because Greek did not yet use spaces between words.

The Coptic script continued to be used by native speakers of Coptic Egyptian until the eleventh century. Thus Coptic literature extended the written attestation of the Egyptian language for several more centuries: from its first hieroglyphic beginnings in the late pre-dynastic or early dynastic period, the Egyptian language was written down for over four millennia. This is a world record that has yet to be surpassed, and it provides a valuable case study of the changes that occur in a language over time. The Coptic stage of the language is, however, the only one for which the vowels are attested.

After the Islamic conquest of the seventh century, the Coptic language was officially replaced by Arabic and was eventually retained only by the minority that remained Christian. After the last texts written by native speakers in the eleventh century, it continued to be spoken by a dwindling number of people until at least the late seventeenth century. It is still used as a liturgical language, though not a conversational, everyday language. In that liturgy, however, a few letters with very ancient roots are still being used.

After the death of demotic, all knowledge of how to read the papyri and inscriptions of the ancient Egyptians was lost. The only surviving knowledge of ancient Egyptian times was that passed on to the West by Greek and Roman writers and by the Egyptian historian Manetho, who wrote in Greek. In the process, the principles of how the hieroglyphic script had worked became confused. It was thought that hieroglyphs represented ideas expressed allegorically through pictures. Thus a goose was reported to mean "son" because geese were devoted to their offspring. (Actually, the bird is a duck, 𓅬 , and it is a biconsonantal sign for *z3*, which meant "son," the phonological value of the sign being based on the word for "duck," *zt* or *z3t*.) There was a germ of truth here in that some logograms were used to denote ideas related to the object represented, as ⊙ could mean *hrw*, "day," as well as *rˁ*, "sun," and could also serve as a determinative with other words relating to time. But the allegory explanation proved to be more misleading than helpful.

As scholars of the Renaissance rediscovered classical authors, they also learned about Egypt, a strange land of crocodiles and hippopotamuses, gods and goddesses, divine kings, and mysterious carved writings. Clearly much ancient wisdom lay locked in those meticulously carved pictures. Early attempts at decipherment accepted the idea of mysterious symbolism in the hieroglyphs, often reading meanings into the signs by a process much resembling free association.

By the end of the eighteenth century, little true progress had been made. It had been surmised – correctly – that the rings, or "cartouches," in hieroglyphic texts encircled royal names, and that the direction of writing could be determined from the way the figures faced. The Coptic language had become known to Western scholars, although its potential usefulness in deciphering hieroglyphs had not.

Then in 1799 the stimulus to further progress was found. Napoleon Bonaparte had arrived in Egypt the previous year with an expedition of military troops, engineers, and scholars, bent on wresting the country from the Ottoman Empire and on unlocking the secrets of its splendid past. On August 20, 1799, a group of soldiers working on the foundations of a military fort near the town of Rosetta (now Rashid) uncovered a large black stone covered with three kinds of writing, one of which was Greek.

The 762-kg Rosetta Stone (figure 3.3) was passed along to Napoleon's scholars, who saw immediately that the stone might have great significance in the attempt to decipher hieroglyphs. The inscription was written in Greek, in hieroglyphs, and in an unfamiliar script now known to be demotic. The assumption was that the three scripts said the same thing, and that the Greek version could be used to decipher the hieroglyphic and demotic texts.

While stationed in Egypt, the French fleet suffered a severe defeat at the hands of the British navy, with the result that the Rosetta Stone was carried off to England as a war trophy and ended up in the British Museum, where it can still be seen today. Luckily, the French scholars had already made ink rubbings of the stone and sent them to various distinguished European scholars. Later the English made additional copies in the form of plaster casts and engravings. Although they had lost the Rosetta Stone, Napoleon's scholars brought back from Egypt a wealth of information, drawings, and artifacts, inspiring a wave of "Egyptomania" which engulfed France and much of Europe. Deciphering the mysterious hieroglyphs became a scholarly obsession.

As it turned out, the Rosetta Stone was something of a disappointment. The hieroglyphic version of the text was badly damaged. The other undeciphered text, demotic, appeared more promising. A sensible place to start was with the names, which could be assumed to read roughly the same in Greek as in Egyptian. Lining up the names would thus be more an exercise in transliteration than translation. In 1802 the French scholar Sylvestre de Sacy was able to identify where in the demotic texts the names Ptolemy and Alexander occurred. His pupil, the Swedish Johan Åkerblad, went on to identify the rest of the proper names, finding that the names were spelled out phonemically and that the same phonemic signs were used elsewhere in the text. From a knowledge of Coptic and the values of the letters occurring in the proper names, he was able to identify a number of recognizably Egyptian words in the demotic text. Unfortunately, this convinced him that demotic was entirely alphabetic in nature, a conclusion that hindered further progress on his part.

In 1814 the Englishman Thomas Young was the first to observe a similarity between some demotic signs and certain hieroglyphic signs, leading him to suppose that demotic used logograms as well as alphabetic signs. Later, in examining newly published funerary documents,

Figure 3.3   The Rosetta Stone, with inscriptions in hieroglyphs, demotic, and Greek. Found in 1799 by Napoleon's soldiers at Rashid (Rosetta) in Egypt, the stone sparked hopes for a decipherment of Egyptian hieroglyphs. The inscriptions date from 196 BC and record a decree affirming the divinity of Ptolemy V. Image copyright © British Museum/Art Resource, NY.

he concluded that the hieroglyphic script had evolved into hieratic and further into demotic. Thus the two Egyptian scripts on the Rosetta Stone were related to each other, and to a third form of Egyptian writing.

If the personal names were spelled out phonologically in the demotic text, then perhaps they were done similarly in the hieroglyphic text, since even a primarily logographic script needs some way to spell out the names of foreigners. The only surviving name in the hieroglyphic text is that of Ptolemy V: (▢ ⌒ ≈ 𝄄𝄀). Young ascribed phonological values to the signs (some correctly, some incorrectly) and to those of a cartouche from a different inscription naming the Ptolemaic queen Berenice. Beyond this he failed to go, as he was sure that most hieroglyphic inscriptions were logographic or ideographic. Phonological use of hieroglyphs was, he thought, restricted to the spelling of foreign names, and he believed that the cartouche signaled that this unusual type of spelling was being used.

The Frenchman Jean-François Champollion (1790–1832) was the one to make the decisive breakthrough. Champollion was inspired from a young age by the challenge of Egyptian decipherment. He studied Coptic, Arabic, Hebrew, Persian, and Aramaic in his determined attempt to break the code, trying meanwhile to avoid being drafted into the army long enough to do so. Like Young, Champollion was able to identify the name of Ptolemy on the Rosetta Stone. In 1822 he received a copy of another bilingual inscription, that of an obelisk from Philae, containing both the name Ptolemy and the name Cleopatra, that of several Ptolemaic queens. The great usefulness of this pair of names was that they had signs (and sounds) in common. Thus Champollion was able to assign phonological values to the signs more accurately than Young had.

He then went on to other cartouches, filling in values that he had so far deduced, and then guessing the rest of the signs once the name looked recognizable. In this way he identified the spellings of Alexander, Berenice, Caesar, and Autocrator, the Greek version of Caesar. So far all of these were names of the Greco-Roman period and did not undermine Young's assumption that phonological spelling was confined to foreign names.

Yet Champollion himself was beginning to doubt this assumption. He had counted the hieroglyphic signs on the Rosetta Stone and gotten 1,419. If hieroglyphs each represented a word, why was the number so much larger than the 486 words in the Greek text? The words must be written with more than one hieroglyph apiece.

The breakthrough came as Champollion was studying the cartouche ⟨ ☉𝖒𝖕𝖕 ⟩. The last two signs he knew to stand for [s]. The first sign looked like a sun, and Champollion knew that the Coptic word for sun was pronounced [re], not unlike English *ray*. This led him to suspect that the name was that of Rameses, reported by Manetho as the name of many pharaohs of the nineteenth and twentieth dynasties. That would mean that the 𝖒 sign stood for [m]. (Actually, it is a biconsonantal *m-s*, but since the *s* was repeated as a phonetic complement Champollion's further inferences were not thrown off by this mistake.)

Another text had the cartouche ⟨ 𝕴 𝖒𝖕 ⟩, beginning with an ibis, which Champollion knew from Greek sources to be the symbol of the god Thoth. This gave thoth-mes, or Tuthmose, a pharaoh of the eighteenth dynasty.

Thus Champollion was able to show that the hieroglyphic script mixed logograms and consonantal phonograms, and that foreign names were not unique in using phonological spellings. He applied the sign values he had deduced so far to words that were not royal names, corroborating his results with the Coptic forms of words. And so, one sign at a time, the words of the ancient Egyptians were revived and the modern study of Egyptology could begin.

Champollion died at only 41 in 1832, while his work was still opposed by many scholars. Others built on his work: Richard Lepsius found that phonograms could contain not just one but also two or three consonants, while the prolific Edward Hincks (who was simultaneously contributing to the decipherment of cuneiform) demonstrated that the script contained no vowels.

Today Egyptian can be read as easily as the classical languages, despite the fact that its vowel-less character means that no one knows how to pronounce it. The ancient scribes, enjoined to preserve forever the words offered to their pharaohs, succeeded admirably. Fossilized in writing, their language long outlasted the civilization that used it.

4

Chinese: A Love of Paperwork

The fields of the Chinese village of Xiao Tun in the district of Anyang yielded the occasional bonus crop. After a rainfall, or after being plowed, the earth would occasionally heave up an ancient bone. These "dragon bones" were sold to the local apothecary, who dispensed them in small pieces to be ground up into traditional Chinese medicines. Occasionally a bone would turn up inscribed with symbols that looked like writing. The apothecary carefully scraped off these scratchings before selling the pieces; dragon bones, no matter how magical, would look inauthentic with writing all over them.

So runs the modern legend surrounding the oldest form of Chinese writing yet found. In 1899 fragments of inscribed bone came to the attention of the antiquarian Wang Yi-Jung, who realized to his astonishment that he was looking at the long-lost ancestor of the Chinese writing system. The writing dated from the latter part of the Shang dynasty (China's second dynasty) in the period between 1200 and 1040 BC, when the Shang had their capital at Anyang (see map in the appendix, figure A.4).

Though the art of writing was well established in Egypt and Mesopotamia long before the Shang period, Chinese writing seems to have been an entirely indigenous development. Just how and when the Chinese developed the technology is not clear, however. The climate of China is significantly different from that of Mesopotamia or Egypt. In China's wetter climate, perishable materials duly perish, leaving much less for the archaeologist's spade. The Shang bones thus remain the oldest surviving form of Chinese writing. Some scholars have interpreted marks incised on pottery during the Neolithic period, some as much as six thousand years old, as the forerunners of Chinese writing. But while the marks do appear to have been meaningful symbols, and while the use of symbols is an important prerequisite for writing, there is no firm evidence that the pottery symbols evolved into a true script, either the Shang script or any other.

The "dragon" bones – actually the shoulder blades of cattle and the breast-plates of turtle shells – are the remains of the Shang system of divination. To inquire of the spirits (ancestors and deities), the diviner would hollow out a small oval in the back of a polished turtle shell or ox scapula, leaving the bone very thin inside the oval. The diviner would then apply heat to a point at the edge of the oval, and the bone would crack. The resulting T-shaped crack would convey a positive or negative answer to the diviner by some system of interpretation now forgotten. In some cases the diviner would write down what the question had been, scratching it into the bone after the divination had taken place. The questions were mostly about sacrifices and warfare, but also on such topics as rain and crops. Unfortunately, it is rare to find the answer recorded along with the question. A few bones are not divinatory but record calendars of sacrifices or reports on warfare or hunting expeditions. Despite their narrow topical focus, these oracle bone inscriptions, as they are now called, are a significant source of information about Shang society; it is always easier to understand an ancient society when we have access to their own words, in writing, than when we have only mute artifacts to work with (see plate 3).

Despite the passage of three thousand years since the last oracle bone was used for divination, the shape of the divinatory crack is preserved in the modern character for "to divine," 卜 (*bǔ*; see figure 4.3 for a pronunciation guide). This crack shape is not the only enduring legacy of Shang Chinese. The characters on the Shang oracle bones embody the same principles that are used to write Chinese today.

Early Chinese scribes, like other pioneers of writing, seem to have started with stylized pictograms of easily depicted things or ideas, which they used as logograms to encode complete morphemes. They sided with the Mesopotamians rather than with the Egyptians in that they chose an abstract, schematic way to make their pictograms.

The most basic Chinese characters are thus stylized pictures of objects, such as "sun," 日 (*rì*), "moon," 月 (*yuè*), "tree," 木 (*mù*), and "horse," 馬 (*mǎ*), whose original Shang characters are shown in figure 4.1. Generally speaking, any residual pictorial element in the modern character is only visible in retrospect, after one knows the meaning of

Shang origins of modern characters			
Shang	"Standard" traditional	Simplified	Pronunciation and meaning
 �	女	女	nǚ "woman"
	王	王	wáng "king"
	日	日	rì "sun"
	月	月	yuè "moon"
	雨	雨	yǔ "rain"
	木	木	mù "wood (tree)"
	龜	龟	guī "turtle"
	買	买	mǎi "buy"

Historical forms of three characters			
			Oracle bone
			Large seal
			Small seal
		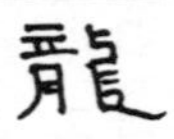	Clerical script
	龍	虎	Standard (traditional)
龙	虎		Modern simplified
			Cursive
"horse"	lóng	hǔ	Modern pronunciation
	"dragon"	"tiger"	Meaning

Figure 4.1 At left, a few of the Shang characters that have identifiable modern descendants. At right, the stages of evolution of two characters from oracle bones to modern standard and cursive scripts. About 2,200 characters received simplified forms in the People's Republic of China in the mid-twentieth century. Some of these characters, such as that for "turtle," seem to have been begging for simplification.

the character. Other simple characters depict a more abstract idea, such as "center," 中 (*zhōng*), "above," 上 (*shàng*), "below," 下 (*xià*), and the numbers "one," 一 (*yī*), "two," 二 (*èr*), and "three" 三 (*sān*). Although these characters illustrate the idea behind a word, it is the *word* that they represent. Thus, for example, in contexts where the word *liǎng* is used instead of *èr* to mean "two" (as we use the word *pair* sometimes, rather than *two*), the character is 兩 (or 两), not 二.

Any aspiring developer of a writing system soon realizes the limitations of pictography, not to mention the limitations of human memory that come into play if one abandons pictography and attempts to devise arbitrary symbols for each of the language's thousands of morphemes. These limitations would have led the Chinese to discover the rebus principle, by which the sign for one word was used to indicate a different word of the same or similar sound. A few simple rebus characters still exist, such as 萬 (*wàn*) for "ten thousand," derived from a Shang character that meant "scorpion". To resolve ambiguities caused by rebus writing, the Chinese, like their predecessors in the Middle East, added clues to meaning in the form of semantic determinatives.

But here is where the Chinese took a crucial step differently than other peoples. They put the determinatives and the rebus signs together into a single compound character. As a result, most Chinese characters are compound – sometimes multiply compounded. One part of the character is the rebus, or phonological element, which contains another character (possibly itself compound) whose pronunciation is similar to the one being written. The other part of the character is the semantic determinative, which identifies the semantic category of the morpheme being written. For example, 馬 is the traditional (i.e. not simplified in mid-twentieth-century reforms in the People's Republic of China) character for "horse," *mǎ*. The character for "woman" is 女, *nǚ*. The word for "mother," *mā*, belongs to the same semantic class as "woman," but it sounds like "horse," though pronounced with a different pitch of the voice. The character for "mother" is thus 媽, incorporating the meaning "woman" on the left with the sound [ma] on the right. As can be seen from the way the parts are squeezed together, it is a single, compound character, not a sequence of two characters. The compound character is the same size as either of the original two characters. No matter how many times a character is compounded (the practical limit seems to be about six), all the parts must be squeezed into the same-sized box.

The position of the parts within a character is not fixed; so, for example, the character originally meaning "tree" and now "wood," 木, *mù*, serves as the semantic determinative in various types of trees or wooden objects. When added to 容, *róng*, "face," it yields 榕, "banyan tree," also pronounced *róng*, but with the "tree" determinative added on the left. *Róng* can also mean "hibiscus," but in that case it has the "grass" determinative, adapted from the character 艸, *căo*, added to the top, indicating that a hibiscus is, like grass, a smaller plant than a tree: 蓉. The "tree" determinative itself can occur in other positions within a character, sometimes on the bottom, as in 栗 (*lì*, "chestnut tree"), and occasionally on the top, as in 杏 (*xìng*, "apricot"). So it is not always obvious which part of a character is the semantic determinative and which is the phonological component.

Over 80 percent of modern Chinese characters are semantic–phonological composites of this type. Since the size, location, and precise shape of the components of a compound character will vary, each character must be treated as a unified entity by writers, typesetters, and word processors.

This practice of squeezing phonological and semantic elements into the same character is part of why the Chinese script has remained logographic and not become logosyllabic like cuneiform or logo-consonantal like Egyptian hieroglyphs. As in all scripts, phonological components are extensively used, but in Chinese they are not used as separate characters. The use of rebus signs without semantic determinatives did not become well established, so the Chinese writing system did not develop purely phonological signs. Chinese characters refer directly to morphemes.

Another reason why the Chinese script resisted a move toward a logosyllabic system lies in the nature of Chinese morphology. Unlike Sumerian, which expressed grammatical relations by adding affixes to root morphemes, the Chinese language does not inflect its words, and uses very few affixes. The need for phonological signs to spell out affixes was therefore absent in Chinese.

Chinese morphemes are usually a single syllable long. Therefore, one logogram stands for a single morpheme, but simultaneously for a single syllable. The most common source of two-syllable words is compounds, which are made up of two smaller words, just as English *doghouse* and *Scotland* are. Chinese compound words are written with two characters (or occasionally three, if three morphemes are compounded), but the characters within a word will be spaced no more closely together than characters that belong to separate words. Each written unit on the page is thus one character long, which is rather misleading to Westerners used to defining a "word" as something that is written with a space after it.

When words of two or more syllables are borrowed into Chinese from other languages, they will be written with as many characters as syllables, in keeping with Chinese speakers' general sense that each syllable is a separate morpheme and each morpheme has its own character. What keeps the Chinese system from being a syllabary, however, is that each character is vested with a meaning. Exceptions do occur in the writing of foreign words (such as the Sanskrit terms of Buddhism), and foreign names, but even in such cases the individual syllables tend to acquire meaning; marketers of foreign brands must be careful what characters they use for their products' names, so as to avoid any unsavory connotations. The symbols are not used as pure sounds dissociated from meaning as they would be in a true syllabary.

The Chinese script thus remains true to the logographic principles of its Shang ancestor. Yet despite the clear relationship between Shang writing and the modern Chinese script, reading Shang Chinese is no easy task. Of the roughly 4,500 identified characters, about a third have recognizable modern descendants or have been deciphered, while the rest of the characters are still not well understood.

Besides the oracle bones and short texts in an elaborated version of the script on commemorative bronze vessels, no other examples of Shang writing have survived. Bones have a durability convenient to archaeologists, but the practice of divination with oracle bones was discontinued soon after the Shang were conquered by the Zhou, leaving a silent period in the archaeological record of Chinese writing.

The Zhou (whose dynasty lasted in some form or other from about 1122 to 221 BC) seem to have learned to write from the Shang shortly before they conquered the Shang region and established themselves as rulers of the Chinese heartland. The Zhou took to writing with the zeal of the converted. Aristocrats and courtiers were expected to be literate, and bureaucratic paperwork blossomed. Orders were written down, apparently just for the sake of the impressive flourish with which they could be read out to underlings. The first Chinese histories were written.

Yet very little original Zhou material remains. Early Chinese books were written on bamboo strips which were strung together to make a book. Bamboo, unlike clay tablets or stone inscriptions, is highly perishable. Some examples of bamboo strips do survive from the very end of the Zhou dynasty (dating from the Warring States period of 403–221 BC), but these are about six hundred years younger than the latest Shang inscriptions. The surviving literature from the Zhou period has been copied and recopied, so that the early forms of the characters are no longer preserved. As a result, the history of many Shang characters cannot be traced into Zhou times, with the result that reading Shang Chinese today is to a large extent a matter of deciphering an unknown script.

During the Warring States period, China was divided into seven separate pieces. It is perhaps not surprising that when China was unified under the First Emperor, Qin Shi Huangdi (221–210 BC) of the short-lived but dynamic Qin dynasty (221–207 BC) that gave China its Western name, he found that his realm had no standard way of writing. The original Shang characters had spread and developed regional and idiosyncratic forms in the intervening Zhou period. Unchecked, the writing system might have gone on to produce mutually illegible descendant scripts used for more and more widely diverging local languages. But the First Emperor was both shrewd and literate, and he recognized the power of the written word. He had his minister of justice, Lǐ Sī, create an official list of characters in an official style. The resulting 3,300-character list was the first Chinese dictionary, and the style of writing was known as the "small seal" script, based on the "large seal" script, one of the styles in use during the Zhou period. (In a less kindly recognition of the power of writing, Shi Huangdi and Lǐ Sī burned a great many of the books extant at the time. The target was free-thinking philosophers. Spared were books owned by members of the Academy of Learned Scholars, books of official history, and books on practical subjects such as agriculture.)

The small seal script did not entirely win the day. New writing materials (the camel's-hair brush, and silk cloth as a writing surface) allowed characters to be written with a new ease and fluidity of motion – a development that both spurred the art of calligraphy and affected the forms of characters written for more everyday purposes. Writing that is put to practical use is subject to evolutionary pressure: the clerks and bureaucrats who actually lived by the written word were more interested in getting things written down quickly and accurately than in what style was official. A style known as "clerical" script became popular, and it is this clerical style that eventually became the new standard and underlies the forms of characters usually used in modern times (see figure 4.1, right-hand side).

There seems to have been some attempt to move away from strict logography in the centuries following Lǐ Sī. Characters were sometimes used just for their phonological value, without a semantic component. This flirtation with phonological writing was quashed by Xǔ Shèn, who in AD 121 published an impressive 15-volume dictionary of about 10,000 characters complete with definitions, analysis, and classification. Xǔ Shèn introduced a system of sorting characters by semantic determinatives and described the various legitimate ways of composing a character. Characters were to remain logographic, with phonological information restricted to only part of a character.

The original function of semantic determinatives was to provide a clue to the general meaning of a word. With Xǔ Shèn's standardization, however, the determinatives were pressed into service as a classification scheme for characters. The entire corpus of characters was divided into 540 groups, according to the 540 determinatives that Xǔ Shèn identified. Later the determinatives were reclassified (and sometimes oversimplified) into a total of 214, then raised to 227 in modern times. These determinatives or semantic classifiers are often called "radicals" in English – a term that can be misleading. The classifiers are not the "roots" or cores of characters, though as determinatives they do suggest something about the meaning of characters.

What does it mean to classify characters? In our alphabetic system of writing, words can be easily sorted into ordered lists based on the alphabetical position of the letters they contain. As a result, all kinds of information can be stored for easy retrieval. One type of information that is typically stored in alphabetical order is that found in dictionaries. If you know the spelling – near enough – of a word, you can look it up in a dictionary and find its meaning. In a language like English, where the phoneme-to-letter correspondence is relatively poor, you may also need to look up the pronunciation. Dictionaries, or their antecedents, word lists, have served as technical manuals to literacy since the times of the Sumerians and Akkadians.

But how do you find a word in a Chinese dictionary? From the days of Xǔ Shèn until modern times the answer has been that first you identify the character's radical – which may not be easy, as it may be at the top, bottom, left, or right of the character. The characters are listed in the dictionary under their respective radicals, which are themselves ordered according to their complexity of shape – measured in terms of how many strokes of the brush or pen are required to write them. Then you count the number of strokes that the character contains in addition to the radical. The character will be found after characters requiring fewer strokes and before characters requiring more strokes.

This is one reason why the principle of strokes is so important to the tradition of written Chinese. In learning to write Chinese characters, children are taught not just the shapes of characters, but a set order in which to make their component lines. These lines are known as strokes – traditionally what is drawn with a single motion of the brush. Properly drawn strokes are important, as every literate person is to some extent expected to be a calligrapher. In fact, the Chinese invented calligraphy – the art of beautiful but abstract writing. While the Egyptians made their writing beautiful, it was left to the Chinese to invent an art form in which the abstract lines of the written word were rendered beautiful in themselves. In the more calligraphic and cursive styles of handwriting, the order in which strokes are made influences the way the lines of a character get run together. If you can't identify the way the strokes have been connected, the cursive styles are illegible.

In addition to the calligraphic value of stroke order, the standardization of strokes has served the standardization of the written language. And by counting strokes and identifying radicals, one can look up a word in a Chinese dictionary and find its meaning.

But what about the pronunciation? While it is true that a large majority of Chinese characters have a phonological component to them, the system is far from precise enough to make the pronunciation of an unfamiliar character obvious. For example, the character for "mother," 媽, contains the rebus component for "horse," 馬, but the two are not pronounced identically. The word for "mother," *mā*, is pronounced with a high tone (the voice at a high, level pitch), while the word for "horse," *mǎ*, is pronounced with a tone that starts fairly low, dips lower, then rises. Tone is a feature that some languages use to distinguish one word from another; the same syllables pronounced with different pitches mean different things. The accents which are used to indicate the tones in Romanized transcriptions of Chinese represent fairly well the movement of the voice pitch for each tone. So *mā* has the high, level tone and *mǎ* has the dipping tone. The other two tones used in standard Mandarin Chinese are the rising tone (sounding like a question to an English speaker) of the word *má*, meaning "hemp," and the sharply falling tone of the word *mà*, meaning "to call someone names" or "to scold."

A difference in tone is only one source of imprecision in the phonological component of a character. Another major factor is the changes in the Chinese language since the script was codified. All spoken language changes with time. Written language, which by its very nature transcends the temporal limitations of speech, tends to become fossilized. The language on which the phonological components were based was that of Old Chinese, spoken during the Shang and Zhou periods. A great many changes in the language have occurred since then. The result is that while the rebus components of characters can tell us something about which words were pronounced similarly, they cannot tell us precisely how those words were actually pronounced in Old Chinese, nor can they tell us whether the words are pronounced the same today. They cannot even tell us whether the two words were pronounced identically in Old Chinese, as it is not clear how close a pronunciation originally had to be in order to be considered close enough for use in the rebus component.

The historical changes in the pronunciation of Chinese serve to reduce the phonological component of the modern Chinese script and to strengthen its logographic nature, as the phonological component has become increasingly imprecise. For example, characters that have the phonological component 工, pronounced *gōng* in modern Mandarin, can be pronounced *gōng, gòng, gǒng, gāng, gàng, hòng, hóng, xiàng, jiāng, qióng, kōng,* or *kǒng*. This is a great deal of variety, yet the range of possibilities is not limitless. It is quite clear than a character with the 工 component is not to be pronounced *mǎ*, for example. Meanwhile the semantic classifiers are also subject to becoming dated – pillows are no longer made of wood, but the character, 枕, *zhěn*, still uses the "tree/wood" radical. It is therefore impossible to predict with certainty either the pronunciation or the meaning of an unfamiliar character.

In the first Chinese dictionaries the only way of unambiguously indicating the pronunciation of a character was to supply a homonym – another character with the same pronunciation. But not all morphemes had homonyms. The earliest surviving solution to this problem dates from AD 601, when Lù Fǎyán published his pronouncing and rhyming dictionary. In Lù Fǎyán's dictionary, the pronunciation of each character was given in terms of two others, one of which had the same initial sound and one of which rhymed with it. This is as though we showed the pronunciation of *show* by listing the words *sheep* (same initial sound) and *though* (a rhyme). The system works, but only if one already knows the pronunciation of the two reference characters.

Lǐ Sī and Xǔ Shèn's concern with standardizing the script set the stage for a use of writing of which the Chinese were to become the masters. China, the Middle Kingdom, has always had a strongly centripetal organization. Its cohesion has allowed China to recover after periods of conquest and fragmentation, and to remain in this day of crumbling empires one of the largest nations of the world geographically, and the largest in population. A standardized writing system has been part of that cohesion since the days of Lǐ Sī and the First Emperor.

Writing standardizes language and serves to mark the identity of national groups. Written Chinese became the touchstone for all Chinese people, regardless of how widely their spoken language diverged. To some extent, this happens whenever there is a written tradition. A shared written standard serves to indicate which varieties of speech belong to the same language. For example, American English and British English sound quite different, but the Americans and the British write very much the same – in fact, the minor differences in spelling do not reflect the rather significant differences in pronunciation between the two varieties.

In Europe, the traditional dialects of the Netherlands shade off into the dialects of lowland Germany almost imperceptibly, as the dialects of France once did with the dialects of Italy. Yet the Dutch speak Dutch, the Germans speak German, and the Italians speak Italian for two interconnected reasons. One is the presence of a national boundary, and the other is the presence of national written standards. The difference between Dutch and German is more about where the national border is and what standard written language is learned in school than it is about any clear, sharp line between people's everyday speech.

In China, the Chinese people (known to themselves as the Han, as distinct from other ethnic groups who live within China's borders) distinguish themselves from other peoples by their written language. The Han have probably always spoken a wide array of dialects. Today the spoken versions of Chinese fall into seven broad categories that linguists rarely hesitate to classify as distinct languages. But the Han themselves insist that they all speak the same language, and they adhere to the same written standard; so the seven Chinese languages are generally referred to as dialects. The Mandarin Chinese of the north is mutually unintelligible with the Yue or Cantonese Chinese of the south, for example. Words that are distinctively Cantonese can in some cases be written in nonstandard, Cantonese characters, but in other cases – and in all other "dialects" – they must be left out of written texts entirely. Yet words that are etymologically related in Mandarin and Cantonese, no matter how differently they are pronounced, can be written with the same character. Characters may be read out in any dialect, though in standard written Chinese the formation of compound words and of sentences will be distinctively Mandarin, as they used to be distinctively Classical. However, the order in which words are arranged into sentences is pretty similar across the Chinese "dialects," making written Mandarin fairly accessible to speakers of other dialects.

This dialectal flexibility is extremely useful. The Chinese languages or dialects share a common ancestor, just as the Romance languages all descend from vernacular Latin; but the seven main types of Chinese differ from each other more than the Romance languages do. For example, the number of tones ranges from four in Mandarin to eight or nine (depending on how you count) in Cantonese. Cantonese dialects allow words to begin with [ŋ], the *ng* sound that ends the English word *thing*, and allows them to end in such exotic sounds (to a speaker of Mandarin) as [t], [p], or [k]. Mandarin, on the other hand, allows its words to contain the sound [ɹ], similar to the *r* of American English, while Cantonese contains no *r*-like sound at all. The sharing of a written language between such widely differing spoken forms is only possible because of the logographic nature of the script.

The logographic script, therefore, has been a unifying force in a nation committed to the ideal of unity. Centralization was a constant theme in the Chinese Empire, with the emperor continually working to hold in check the power of regional noble families who might have weakened his authority. One way of achieving this centralization was through a large state bureaucracy, fed by the civil service examination, a notable Chinese invention. The roots of the civil service exam are in the former Han dynasty (206 BC to AD 9) under the emperor Wudi (141–87 BC), who expanded the bureaucracy and established an Imperial

Academy whose students were taught the Confucian classics and, upon passing an examination, were eligible for a government appointment.

Another unifying emperor, Wendi, reassembled China in AD 589 after a period of disunion and disorder, founding the Sui dynasty (AD 589–618). Like Qin Shi Huangdi, Sui Wendi then faced the task of solidifying China's unification. He created a new bureaucracy, staffed at least in part with officials who had passed a written examination testing their general learning. The system grew during the following Tang dynasty (618–907) and became fully developed under the Northern Song dynasty (960–1127).

Schools to prepare candidates for the civil service exams were established, and a system of blind grading was introduced to counteract bias against low-born candidates. Education became a highly prized attainment, a powerful means of upward mobility. The successful candidate joined the bureaucratic class, while the emperor received into his service an official without pre-existing powerful connections. Nevertheless, there was also a "protection" system, which allowed officials to nominate family members for government positions. Government service was thus partly hereditary and partly meritocratic. In this way hereditary power was held in check, but not so much as to provoke aristocrats to revolution. In the period from 998 to 1126, during the Northern Song period, nearly 50 percent of prominent officials came from poor (non-aristocratic) families.

The examination system was abolished by the Mongol emperor Kublai Khan (AD 1260–94), partially restored (with quotas and discrimination against Han candidates) by his Mongol successors, and fully revived under the Ming dynasty (1364–1644), when power returned to the hands of Han rulers. It was finally abolished in 1905 in the final years of the last dynasty, that of the Manchu Qing (1644–1912). Meanwhile the civil service exam was adopted by the Koreans and Vietnamese; the idea of the exam (though not the specific content) also inspired the Prussian and British civil service exams.

The curriculum on which the civil service exams were based was in most periods the Confucian classics. From Ming times on, candidates were required to write an essay on a Confucian quotation and to compose a poem in beautiful calligraphy. While this was arguably not the best preparation for an administrative career, it did mean that officials had imbibed deeply of Confucian philosophy, which taught the principles of ethical rule and emphasized one's duty in a hierarchical social structure headed by the emperor. The exam also stressed that most ancient of bureaucratic skills, literacy – a skill not easily attained in a logographic script, and therefore subject to much variation in mastery.

The difficulty of learning and remembering several thousand characters was commensurate with its rewards. Literacy was the path to worldly advancement, to wisdom (through the Confucian and Daoist classics), and to artistic expression (through calligraphy). The skill was therefore highly prized and not shared lightly. Such valuable knowledge could not be entirely contained, however. With the establishment of a merchant class during the Southern Song dynasty, writing came to be used in trade and business. Drama and fiction written in the vernacular became popular in succeeding centuries, though attempts at mass literacy were unheard of until the twentieth century.

Mass literacy is of course useless if access to writing materials and written texts is limited. Such was the situation in the ancient and classical worlds, when all texts had to be produced by hand, generally written on materials whose quantities were limited (with the exception of clay) or which, like stone, made writing a truly labor-intensive activity. Early Chinese books were written on strips of bamboo, as we have seen, each strip carrying one or more columns of characters. With a thong passed through the strips they became a book, with bamboo pages. The character cè, 冊, meaning a book, register, or table of statistics, depicts the ancient book. The range of meanings associated with the character suggests the early bureaucratic uses to which books would have been put. This character is found in much the same shape in oracle bone inscriptions, though unfortunately no Shang books have survived. The utility of a book that holds only one or two lines of text per page remains limited, however.

The innovation of using woven cloth, usually silk, as a writing surface and the invention of the camel's-hair brush spurred the further development of book making as well as the art of calligraphy. Cloth made for a porous, smooth surface that could be made in large enough strips to make a scroll.

Yet the truly great Chinese innovation – the second great information technology revolution – was the invention of the world's first true paper, traditionally dated to AD 105. Papermaking turned scraps into a culturally and financially valuable commodity. Paper made possible cheap and dense information storage, and was to earlier bamboo strips or clay tablets what a modern rewritable CD is to an old five-and-a-quarter-inch floppy disk. Imagine any modern volume as a collection of half-inch-thick clay tablets and the impact of the paper revolution will begin to come clear. The Chinese invented paper books, paper money, packing paper, and even toilet paper, four things we would hate to do without.

The word *paper* comes from *papyrus,* the everyday writing surface of the ancient Egyptians. Papyrus resembles paper and has many of the same useful properties, but it was made differently, was thicker, and could not be folded. It was also limited in its availability. The papyrus reed once grew abundantly in marshy ground along the Nile River but is now virtually extinct in Egypt, though still found here and there around the Mediterranean. Writing papyrus was made from the pith of the reed. Strips of pith were laid down side by side, wetted and perhaps pasted, and covered with strips laid down the other way, perpendicular to the first layer. The two layers were pressed together, and stuck. The process was not unlike the making of very thin plywood.

True paper is made from fibers which have been broken apart and disintegrated and are then matted together into a thin sheet. Paper can thus be considered a very thin form of felt, which is also made by matting together fibers. Early Chinese paper was made from scraps of fabric, with flax, hemp, the inner bark of trees, and even old fishnets soon joining the list of raw materials. Anything that would provide the necessary fibers could be used, and many such things were either scraps or highly renewable resources. The second IT revolution was thus built on the recycling of trash. Ink made from lampblack (later known as "India ink" in English) made a liquid pigment that could easily be brushed onto paper.

It is easy to underestimate paper. It is ubiquitous, it is cheap, and it takes up very little space. But that is exactly the point. As long as writing materials remained expensive, bulky, and rare, the uses of literacy were restricted. There would have been very little point in inventing movable type, for instance, if not for paper. Even today, the "paperless office" has yet to materialize; the computer revolution has triggered the use of more paper than ever, just as the printing revolution did in its time.

The Chinese people had a great respect for paper and papermakers. Paper was put to lofty use, carrying the words of Confucius and other sages. Paper also made a very effective burnt offering. Almost anything, from money to goods to pet dogs, could be copied in paper effigy and offered to one's deceased ancestors. Prayers were written on paper and ritually burned; the prayer would thus ascend to heaven.

It was in fact prayer that inspired the earliest known printing of text on paper, ushering in the third great IT revolution. Paper spread from China to Korea and onward, reaching Japan around AD 610. By this time the technology for printing was available in China. The Chinese used inked seals to transfer a design onto paper, cloth, or leather, and took rubbings from stone inscriptions. They may also have been printing texts on paper. But the first true printing of text onto sheets of paper that history has remembered occurred in Japan in the eighth century.

The reigning monarch of the time, Empress Shōtoku (reigned 749–58 and 765–9), was a Buddhist who ordered the printing (in Chinese) of one million Buddhist prayers. These were to be inserted into miniature pagodas and set in various temples throughout Japan. It is not known whether she herself devised the means for producing the million prayers, whether she left that to her advisors, or whether the technique was imported wholesale from China. Whether "a million" actually meant a million or just "a very great number" is also unclear, but many prayers and pagodas were produced in the years from 767 to 770, and some have survived to the present day. Thus printing made possible piety on a new scale entirely.

Woodblock printing on paper (xylography) came to be used for other purposes as well in China, Japan, and Korea. The first printed book, the *Diamond Sutra*, was printed in China in AD 868 (figure 4.2), and many books of the Chinese classics and Buddhist canon followed, first in scroll form and later in books with pages. Engravings and text could be combined on the same printing block and be transferred together onto the same page, a feat impossible to later movable-type printing presses.

Movable type, using a ceramic font, was also invented in China, by Bi Sheng between 1041 and 1048. Yet the Chinese did not consider movable type particularly useful, partly because the early ceramic type was easily broken, partly because the art of handwriting was so highly valued, and partly because any relatively complete font for Chinese requires thousands of characters.

The Chinese traded paper westward along the silk route, but the technique of papermaking was a jealously guarded secret until 751, when a number of Chinese papermakers in Samarkand were taken as prisoners of war by the Arabs. Samarkand soon became an important Islamic papermaking center. From there, knowledge of the process spread

Figure 4.2   The printed *Diamond Sutra*, the oldest surviving woodblock-printed book in the world, dating to AD 868, during the Tang dynasty. The frontispiece illustration shows the Buddha surrounded by his disciples. Found in Buddhist temple caves at Dunhuang, China. British Library, London. Image copyright © Werner Forman/Art Resource, NY.

slowly westward, finally arriving in Europe in the twelfth century, a thousand years after its invention in China.

Until the early twentieth century, the language of most Chinese books was Classical Chinese, based on the written language described by Lù Fǎyán's dictionary of AD 601. The spoken language of that period is now known as Middle Chinese. A great number of changes had already occurred from the language recorded in the first Old Chinese texts. It is also probable that the literary language had already diverged considerably from the spoken language and was written in an artificially terse and abbreviated style. Thanks to this artificial style, and the further changes that occurred in the development of Middle into Modern Chinese, Classical Chinese texts are now unintelligible when read aloud in modern pronunciation.

As Middle Chinese gave way to Modern Chinese, many distinctions of sound were lost, with the result that many of the syllables (and thus morphemes) began to be pronounced the same. The process did not occur uniformly in the different areas of China, leading to significant differences in pronunciation in the different Chinese "dialects" of modern China. Modern Chinese, and especially the Mandarin group of northern dialects, has lost a great number of sound distinctions that older versions of Chinese possessed, especially at the ends of syllables.

In Mandarin, the reduction left only about 1,300 separate syllables, less than a third of what Middle Chinese had had. Spoken language adapts, however. As the number of homophones – and thus the potential for misunderstanding – grew, so did the number of compound words. Rather than calling something by a single, ambiguous syllable, words grew to contain (usually) two syllables, with two morphemes reinforcing each other's meaning. For example, 報告, *bàogào*, "to report," is made of two morphemes, literally meaning "to announce–inform." The addition of the reinforcing morpheme is important, because *bào* alone (in spoken, not written, form) can also mean "to embrace," "a leopard," "cruel," "an abalone," "a sudden rain," or "to explode." Together, *bàogào* is unambiguous. The script continues to be written on the syllable/morpheme level, so that many a word that is still ambiguous halfway through its spoken form is already disambiguated in written form by the character for the first morpheme/syllable.

Added to the changes in pronunciation since Middle Chinese are the inevitable grammatical differences between the older and newer forms of language, shifts in word meanings that have occurred, and classical allusions that the modern reader may fail to grasp. Furthermore, the artificially telegraphic classical style meant that only the first syllable would be written in words that may already have been bisyllabic in the spoken language. All in all, Classical Chinese is very difficult to master. Due to its rampant ambiguities, it is meaningless when read aloud or transliterated into Roman letters. Yet written in characters it makes some sense to a literate reader of Modern Chinese – it is the pronunciations that have changed, not the written characters.

Until the fall of the last imperial dynasty, the Qing (1644–1912), Classical Chinese was the standard for written Chinese. It was then replaced by a modern written form, which uses the grammatical patterns and compound words of modern spoken Mandarin, the dialect of Beijing. The same characters remained in use, but the ways of using them in sentences changed. The changes have made written Chinese much more accessible to ordinary people and have encouraged the spread of literacy.

Learning to read and write Chinese is both easier and harder than English. Each written symbol in Chinese is pronounceable, and children easily learn to read words, without the painful struggle to "sound out" letters that English-speaking children experience. The learning process continues longer, however. To read the first 90 percent of a typical text requires a knowledge of 1,000 characters. To read 99 percent requires 2,400 characters. To reach 99.9 percent takes 3,800; 99.99 percent requires 5,200. An educated reader who is not an expert in Chinese literature or history will know 3,500 to 4,000 characters; a scholar may know 6,000. Popular dictionaries list about 8,000. Unabridged dictionaries, however, tell an even more daunting story: every time a new morpheme enters the language and is written down, a new character is born. Thus dictionaries grow through the ages; recent ones list around 60,000 characters. For some of the more obscure characters, no one today knows either the meaning or the pronunciation. For others, the meaning is known but not the pronunciation.

For all that, there are many Chinese words that cannot be written at all. Colloquial expressions often have no written form, especially in the non-Mandarin dialects. So, for example, a writer from Shanghai will not be able to write using local colloquial vocabulary, but must use the vocabulary for which cognates exist in written Mandarin.

Users of alphabets are quick to see the disadvantages of Chinese characters. The system does not easily absorb new or colloquial expressions. It is hard to use characters to convey information about pronunciation, and they are difficult to organize into a dictionary, or indeed into any searchable database. This last point is becoming more important. These days, a system that does not easily allow the sorting of information is disadvantaged. Telephone books, dictionaries, encyclopedias, library catalogues, book indexes, mailing lists . . . such compilations of information are becoming more and more common, and more and more essential. As databases become larger, it becomes vital to have a sorting scheme, such as alphabetical order, that even a stupid computer can follow. The alphabet is a small, ordered set; you simply sort by the first letter of a word, then by the second, and so forth.

The latest IT revolution has not made Chinese logograms look good. Besides the difficulty of storing information for easy retrieval, there is the fact that nowadays communication is expected to occur instantaneously, via keystrokes typed into a computer in combinations of around 45 keys. Keyboarding is not easily done in Chinese characters.

An earlier invention, telegraphy, was also poorly adapted to characters: telegraphs were sent as sequences of four-digit numbers. Each number represented a character, which had to be looked up in a list.

To overcome these obstacles, the People's Republic of China has instituted an official Romanization: pīnyīn (see figure 4.3). School-children are taught pīnyīn, and then taught the standard Mandarin pro-nunciation of characters via pīnyīn. A person doing word processing can type in pīnyīn and have the computer convert it into characters (as I have done for the characters in this chapter; the Romanized spellings of Chinese words are also in pīnyīn). Language learners can use pīnyīn to learn the sounds of Chinese words, and nowadays dictionaries present characters in alphabetical order according to their pīnyīn spelling.

In Taiwan another script, known as bōpōmōfō or guóyīn zìmŭ, is used to indicate pronunciation. It is a system of 37 symbols derived from very simplified characters. The symbols are used purely phonolo-gically and indicate a syllable's initial consonant, its medial semivowel (if any), its ending (which may consist of a vowel, a diphthong, or a vowel followed by [r], [n], or [ŋ]), and its tone, for a total of three to four symbols per syllable. Yet pīnyīn and bōpōmōfō are used as auxiliary scripts only, and characters continue to be used by increas-ing numbers of people as the literacy rate grows.

In an effort to encourage literacy, in 1964 the government of the People's Republic of China published a list of 2,238 characters which were given new, simplified forms. The result has been that Chinese living in Taiwan, in Hong Kong, and abroad now have trouble reading mainland publications, and vice versa. But the basic system of using characters remains strong.

Why, if they are so cumbersome, are Chinese characters still used? Why not just use pīnyīn (or bōpōmōfō)? One reason which looms large in the consciousness of Chinese people is the large number of homophonous syllables. Because written Chinese represents each syllable/morpheme separately, the Chinese are more oriented to syl-lables than to complete words as the units of their language. They are therefore very aware of the information that appears to be lost when characters are translated into pīnyīn. Distinct characters that clearly have different meanings get spelled the same in pīnyīn. The problem is not intractable, however. After all, the Chinese manage to communicate in speech perfectly well. They rely on context: the context of a morpheme

75

Initial	IPA	Final	IPA	Final	IPA
b	[b̥]	a	[a]	ing	[iŋ]
c	[tsʰ]	ai	[ai̯]	iong	[i̯oŋ]
ch	[tʂʰ]	an	[an]	iu	[i̯ou̯]
d	[d̥]	ang	[ɑŋ]	u	[u]
f	[f]	ao	[au̯]	ua	[u̯a]
g	[g̊]	e	[ɤ]	uai	[u̯ai̯]
h	[χ]	ei	[ei̯]	uan	[u̯an]
j	[d̥ʑ]	en	[ən]	uang	[u̯ɑŋ]
k	[kʰ]	eng	[əŋ]	uo	[u̯ɔ]
l	[l]	er	[əɹ]	un	[u̯ən]
m	[m]	o	[ɔ]	ui	[u̯ei̯]
n	[n]	ong	[oŋ]	ü	[y]
p	[pʰ]	ou	[ou̯]	üan	[yɛn]
q	[tɕʰ]	i	[ɻ] after **ch,** **r, sh, zh**	ue	[yɛ]
r	[ɻ]/[ʐ̩]		[i] after **c,** **s, z**	ün	[yn]
s	[s]		[i] elsewhere		
t	[tʰ]	ia	[i̯a]		
w (initial form of **u**)	[u̯]	ian	[i̯ɛn]		
x	[ɕ]	iang	[i̯ɑŋ]		
y (initial form of **i**)	[i̯] (silent in **yi**)	iao	[i̯au̯]		
z	[d̥z]	ie	[i̯ɛ]		
zh	[d̥ʐ̥]	in	[in]		

Tone markings: ā high tone   á rising tone   ǎ dipping then rising tone   à falling tone

Figure 4.3 Chinese pīnyīn Romanization, with IPA equivalents. By tradition, Chinese syllables are divided into initial consonants and finals (everything after the first consonant), and the system of pronouncing pīnyīn follows this division. Tone markings are shown at the bottom, illustrated on the letter *a*.

within a word, and of a word within a sentence. Similarly, when a pīnyīn text is considered on a word-by-word basis, rather than a syllable-by-syllable basis, the ambiguities largely evaporate.

The concern over homophony applies more aptly to the Chinese classics, which, thanks to their telegraphic style and the subsequent neutralization of sound distinctions, are now unintelligible when read aloud. They would be equally unintelligible in pīnyīn.

One of the consequences of the technology of writing is the very existence of classical texts. Once created, classical texts give a people a strong incentive to maintain backwards compatibility – to keep writing in an antique style, the better to emulate and to continue appreciating the classics. English is no exception: many of our odd spellings, such as *could* and *might*, derive from earlier versions of English, and much of the argument against spelling reform is that it would make older works inaccessible to modern readers.

Yet their writing system has a much stronger hold over the Chinese than their love of the classics. Chinese characters made China China. They fostered a unified Chinese civilization, which, far from being backward in the area of information technology, in fact produced the second great IT revolution (paper) and a significant part of the third (printing). A phonological system such as pīnyīn favors one form of Chinese (in this case, Mandarin) over the others much more strongly than the current standard of Mandarin-based logographic writing does. A phonological system could lead to the development of regional written languages – perhaps the end of the Han as a unified people.

Chinese writing developed hand in hand with Chinese civilization, and the Han enjoyed a cultural and literary monopoly in Asia for many centuries. When writing began to spread to other Asian peoples, they first wrote in Chinese, just as the Akkadians first wrote in Sumerian. The Koreans, Japanese, and Vietnamese all adopted Chinese characters, to write first in Chinese and later in their own respective languages. The Vietnamese switched to a version of the Roman alphabet in the 1940s, and the North Koreans have likewise abandoned Chinese characters; but the Japanese and South Koreans still use them in combination with their own native forms of writing, presented in later chapters.

Yet Chinese logograms are not particularly adaptable. A Chinese logogram stands for a particular morpheme *in Chinese*. Another language can in principle use logograms for morphemes of corresponding meaning, but that relies on the language having morphemes that match the meaning of Chinese morphemes (and vice versa). Relatively few languages fit the bill. Chinese has very little inflectional morphology, so that 馬, *mǎ*, for example, can mean "horse," or "horses," depending on context. Languages that add morphemes (like the English -*(e)s*) to distinguish the two words cannot be properly represented using only Chinese characters.

Rather than try to adapt Chinese characters to their language, some neighbors of the Chinese chose to create their own scripts. Just as Mesopotamian cuneiform inspired the creation of similar-looking scripts such as Old Persian and Ugaritic, so Chinese logograms inspired the creation of Chinese-looking ("siniform") scripts in Asia. Scripts were invented by various peoples living to the north or northwest of the Han – by the Khitan in AD 920, the Tangut in 1,036, and the Jurchin in 1,120. However, none of these scripts enjoyed a long lifespan. More recently scripts have been invented for some of the minority languages of southwest China, such as Lisu and Yi, but these are not widely used. A syllabic "women's script" has traditionally been used in part of Hunan province, but has largely gone out of use with the expansion of women's education in China. Chinese characters still dominate East Asia.

The Chinese script, the most stubbornly logographic of the ancient invented forms of writing, is the only one of those early writing systems still in use today. Used for Chinese as well as (to varying extents) for Japanese and Korean, it encodes the languages of a quarter of the world's population and continues to hold together the Middle Kingdom.

5

Maya Glyphs: Calendars of Kings

The Earth's geography played a strong supporting role in giving the world a script so distinctive and visually complex that its nature as a true writing system was widely misunderstood until the late twentieth century. The Bering land bridge connecting Siberia and Alaska had allowed human migration to the New World in Paleolithic times. But with the end of the last ice age the land bridge was submerged, leaving today's Bering Strait, and the New World was cut off from the Old World until the voyages of Leif Erikson and Christopher Columbus. In the absence of any outside stimulus, the New World fostered its own civilizations and its own scripts. While the civilizations of Peru used nongraphical record-keeping systems, such as the Inca's *quipu* system of knotted cords, those of Mesoamerica (a cultural area stretching from southern Mexico to northwest Costa Rica) developed a number of graphical recording systems. Some of these systems were developed to the point of true writing while others remained conventionalized pictographic systems that were used to record certain types of information but not the full language of the speakers.

Of these Mesoamerican scripts and proto-scripts, the most advanced – and the most amply preserved for modern epigraphers – was the hieroglyphic system of the Maya. Carved on monuments in the cities of the Classic Maya and painted on their fine polychrome vases, the script was also used to make books through Post-Classic times until the Spanish conquest. It was then neglected, actively repressed, and ultimately forgotten. But the carved monuments remained, increasingly hidden by the encroaching jungle, to enthrall later generations of explorers, art historians, and decipherers.

The ultimate origin of the Maya script lies with the cultural predecessors of the Maya, the Olmec. The Olmec were the first civilization to arise in Mesoamerica, flourishing between 1200 and 400 BC (see map in the appendix, figure A.5). A number of distinctive aspects of common Mesoamerican culture had their roots in Olmec traditions: all the successors of the Olmec used a distinctive 52-year calendar (with local variations), and many of them developed writing or advanced pictographic systems that verged on true writing. The various Mesoamerican scripts are quite diverse, but they share a bar-and-dot system of numerals and the signs for the names of the calendar days. As the very earliest surviving inscriptions record almost exclusively dates, it seems likely that all the Mesoamerican scripts evolved from a calendrical system of the Olmec period.

In fact, the use of a complex calendar seems to have been the intellectual stimulus for developing writing in Mesoamerica. The 52-year Calendar Round consisted of two pieces, the Sacred Round and the Vague Year. The Sacred Round was in use before 600 BC and is still used among the Maya today. Its 260-day ritual cycle pairs 13 numbers with 20 named days. Each day that dawns has a number and a name associated with it; the following day will have the next day number in the sequence, coupled with the next name. Thus 1 Imix is followed by 2 Ik, which is followed by 3 Akbal – not unlike the way Monday the 1st (of some month) is followed by Tuesday the 2nd and Wednesday the 3rd. The fourteenth day of the sequence has the number 1 again, but not the name Imix, as the list of 20 day names will not yet be exhausted. Rather, it will be 1 Ix, followed by 2 Men, and not reaching Imix until the eighth day. It takes 260 days to run the cycle all the way around from 1 Imix through to the last day, 13 Ajaw, arriving back at 1 Imix on the two-hundred-and-sixty-first day.

Running concurrently with the Sacred Round was the calendar of the Vague Year, so called because it contained 365 days, nearly a true solar year. The Vague Year contained 18 named months of 20 numbered days each (progressing in a way more familiar to us – Pop 1 decorously followed by Pop 2, Pop 3, etc.), with an extra inauspicious five days at the end. Just as it took several individual cycles of the names and numbers of the Sacred Round to complete a full cycle from one 1 Imix around to the next 1 Imix, so the combination of the Sacred Round and the Vague Year – the time it took for a date in the Vague Year to correspond to the same number and day in the Sacred Round again – took many turns to complete, a total of 52 years. A Calendar Round date will thus repeat after 52 years, and inscribed dates using only the Calendar Round must be interpreted with the help of other archaeological evidence to determine which 52-year cycle they occur in.

The urge to record important dates seems to have spurred the forebears of the Maya to take the intellectual and technological leap into writing. Just as Sumerian writing developed in the context of conjoining numbers with words, in the need to record *how many* of *what* were to be entered in the accounting system, so the conjunction of numbers and words (here day names) may have first stimulated writing in Mesoamerica. Primitive tallies record numbers, but do not record *what* is being counted. Pictures, on the other hand, may record objects, but show a given number of objects by drawing that number of objects. Neither tallies nor pictures of objects are writing. But when the two are put together, they connect numbers and objects in the same way that language does, allotting one sign to the number and one to the object, just as language gives one word to each. This allows the signs to be read back in phrases, such as "four oxen" (as in Mesopotamia) or "1 Imix" (as in Mesoamerica), and the germ of writing is born. Thus while the uses of the first writing in Mesoamerica appear to be for historical rather than economic records, the intellectual roots of the system may be the same here as in Mesopotamia – in the conjunction of numbers with other words in the context of record keeping.

The Olmec had taken their first steps toward writing, based on their calendrical system, by about 650 BC. To what extent they elaborated the system into full-fledged writing is still unknown. When Olmec influence began to decline, other cultural groups asserted themselves, and by the Late Pre-Classic Period (400 BC to AD 200), three related scripts had arisen out of the Olmec prototype: the Isthmian, the Oaxacan, and the Maya. These cultures used writing as a way of legitimizing the newly developed concept of divine kingship in the emerging states. Writing served as a powerful form of propaganda, literally fixing in stone the lineage of the kings, their great deeds, and the ritually significant dates on which these deeds were supposed to have occurred. Of these writing systems, only that of the Maya is known to have reached full maturity, able to faithfully record anything they might have wanted to say.

Maya writing never forgot its debt to the calendar. Crucial to the recording of official history, in the minds of the Mesoamericans, was the recording of dates. The Maya and other Mesoamerican peoples were preoccupied with time, and dates take up a great deal of space in the ancient inscriptions.

Perhaps because of the ambiguity of the Calendar Round, the Maya of the Classic Period (AD 200 to 900) added to their dating system an additional calendar called the Long Count. The Long Count was a tally of the passage of days, retroactively begun on August 13, 3114 BC. Twenty days, or *k'ins*, made 1 *winal*. Eighteen *winals* made a *tun* of 360 days, 20 *tuns* made a *k'atun*, and 20 *k'atuns* a *baktun* (for pronunciation guidance, see figure 5.1).

Modern Mayanists have also adopted the Long Count, in the sense that it now defines the Classic Period of Maya civilization, the time during which the Maya were erecting monuments inscribed with Long Count dates. In the previous, Late Pre-Classic Period, however, much of Maya civilization was set in place. Cities were built, centered on temples and pyramids which, as in Egypt, housed dead kings. Writing appeared, and the first stelae (commemorative stone pillars) were erected in temple plazas. The earliest dated, readable Maya inscription is from AD 199.

It is during the Classic Period, however, that Mayan writing truly flourished. Although no writing on perishable materials survives from that time, there is writing painted on murals, ceramics, and cave walls, as well as carved on stelae, tombs, lintels of durable sapodilla wood, and smaller objects of pottery, jadeite, bone, and shell (see plate 4).

Maya civilization was concentrated around relatively small city-states, the chief of which seem to have been Calakmul and Tikal. Society was divided into commoners and nobility, with a hereditary king at the top. Scribes – both those who painted glyphic dedications on pottery and those who carved official history on stelae – were members of the nobility. As in other parts of the ancient world, writing was an exclusive skill, not intended for the common people, and never meant to be easy.

The Maya city-states seem to have waged nearly constant small-scale warfare with each other. A large number of the surviving records revolve around battle and the taking and subsequent torture and sacrifice of high-ranking captives. Another important theme is the ritual shedding of blood by the king and other important nobles, apparently intended to nourish the earth and to bring on visions of gods and ancestors.

In the end, the kings failed in their efforts to sustain their people and their land. The ninth century was one of increasing environmental degradation, overpopulation, and warfare. The city-states fell, and no more monuments were erected. Yet the Post-Classic Maya went on writing. They wrote in books, made of a paper-like substance produced from the inner bark of fig trees by a method reminiscent of papyrus making. Pieces of this paper were joined together into a long strip which was then folded, fan-like, into a book with pages. The surface was coated with a thin layer of a plaster-like substance, and the texts and illustrations were painted on the surface in much the same way that the stucco murals of Classic times were painted. Books are depicted in vase paintings from the Classic period, but the only Maya books now extant are four codices from Post-Classic times, one of which even post-dates the Spanish Conquest. A fifth codex exists as a decomposing fused lump of paper and plaster, unreadable and even unopenable, at least with today's technology.

The Spanish Conquest of the Maya area began in 1527. In the eyes of the Christian Spaniards, the Maya books were filled with the most horrific idolatry, celebrating bizarre-looking gods with a gruesome taste for blood. The sooner the native people were converted to Christianity, they felt, the better. Mission schools were established to teach the Christian faith and the Roman alphabet, though academic instruction was not the only means of persuasion the early Spanish missionaries used to convert the Maya.

One man stands out, paradoxically, as both the great destroyer and the great preserver of Maya culture and writing. Diego de Landa, a Franciscan priest and later bishop of Yucatán, had a genuine interest in Maya culture and a love for the Maya people. He even went so far as to learn at least a portion of the Maya script. Yet when he saw that the Maya books were sustaining traditional beliefs and encouraging backsliding among new Christian believers, he held a now infamous grand bookburning in 1562. Other Franciscans had already burned books on smaller scales, but Landa also inflicted torture on unrepentant backsliders in his zeal to redeem their souls. Recalled to Spain to explain his actions, he wrote his *Account of the Affairs of the Yucatán*, giving a detailed description of all aspects of Maya life.

Among other things, Landa provided in his *Account* the names and glyph signs for the 20 named days of the Sacred Round and the 18 months of the Vague Year. He also recorded what he called an "ABC," giving Maya signs as equivalents of Spanish letters, admitting that this was only a small sample of the system. Although many would-be decipherers were thrown, either by taking Landa's ABC to mean that the Maya script was alphabetic or by dismissing Landa altogether on the grounds that the script was clearly *not* alphabetic, Landa's text was in fact the only Rosetta Stone the Maya script was ever to have. What Landa had written down were signs which stood for the *syllables* that the Spanish pronounced as A, B, C ([a], [be], [se]), etc.

Exonerated by the authorities in Spain, Landa returned to Yucatán as bishop and died there seven years later. His *Account* presumably stayed in Spain, but all that now remains is an abridged copy made a century later. Thanks in part to his repression, knowledge of the Maya script was probably gone from the northern part of the Yucatán Peninsula by 1600. Yet the Spanish Conquest of Mesoamerica was a piecemeal operation, and the last Maya kingdom, that of the Petén Itza of Guatemala, remained independent until 1697. Sometime after that, in the first decades of the eighteenth century, the last Maya scribe must have died.

The literacy rate had never been high among the Maya, writing having been the sacred preserve of the nobility. Knowledge of the script was therefore relatively easy to stamp out, leaving only an unusually tough puzzle for decipherers.

Meanwhile, the copy of Landa's *Account* languished uncatalogued in the Royal Academy of History in Madrid. Three of the four surviving Maya codices, having been brought to Europe at some point in early colonial times, led similarly obscure lives in Dresden, Paris, and Madrid. The fourth led an even more obscure existence, possibly in a cave in Chiapas, Mexico. The jungle continued to hide the great Classic cities.

The first decipherment of an ancient script was published in 1754, when the Abbé Barthelémy read his paper on the Palmyrene script to the Académie des Inscriptions in Paris. Decipherments of Phoenician and Sassanian Persian followed; these scripts were all consonantal alphabets of a general type already familiar to scholars of Hebrew. In the nineteenth century came decipherments of the great logographic scripts, Egyptian hieroglyphs and Mesopotamian cuneiform. Thus the combination of curiosity and academic rigor that made ancient scripts both intriguing and decipherable was an Enlightenment phenomenon which the living Maya script missed by mere decades.

In the last decades of the eighteenth century and first half of the nineteenth, explorers began to visit the ruins of Palenque and Copán and eventually the other great cities of the Classic Maya, publishing reports of the great ruined buildings, the imposing pyramids, and the stelae with their intricately carved pictures and accompanying hieroglyphs.

Even when it was realized that the Maya codices were in the same script as the monumental inscriptions of the ruined cities, progress on decipherment was slow. First there was a scarcity of accurate reproductions from which to work. Then there was the trouble of identifying the language. Despite the continued presence of the Maya people (today numbering 5 or 6 million speakers, divided among the 31 related languages of the Mayan language family), it was some time before scholars accepted that the language the script recorded actually was Mayan, and that the cities had been built by the Maya people. Surely, they thought, such a great civilization must have belonged to a more advanced people than the North Americans – perhaps even to the citizens of lost Atlantis. The rediscovery of Landa's *Account* in 1862 put paid to that idea, but making a careful study of the modern Mayan languages, such as Champollion made of Coptic, did not occur to most of the early Mayanist scholars. Similarly, very few of those working on Maya glyphs had a background in other ancient scripts, a background which would have suggested a number of useful parallels.

Misapplication of Landa's ABC as an alphabet rather than a syllabary delayed the decipherment as well. The other information Landa recorded, regarding the day and month names, proved much more useful, but paradoxically the progress made on deciphering Maya dates slowed the linguistic decipherment of the script and its acceptance as a full writing system rather than merely an intricate calendar. The extant codices dwell heavily on astronomical cycles and calendrical almanacs, while the monumental inscriptions give pride of place to dates; so the misperception of the Maya script as being almost entirely calendrical in nature was an easy one to acquire.

A typical Maya inscription begins with the so-called Initial Series. First there is the Initial Series Introductory Glyph (shown in figure 5.2), usually given double sized, not unlike the capital letters that begin chapters in many modern books. Then follows a Long Count date, usually given in full, with the number of *baktuns*, *k'atuns*, *tuns*, *winals*, and *k'ins* that had passed since August 13, 3114 BC. Then follows a Calendar Round date, with the day name and number of the Sacred Round, and the numbered day and named month in the Vague Year. Between the two parts of the Calendar Round date there is usually inserted a Supplementary Series indicating which of the nine Lords of the Underworld ruled that particular day, the phase of the moon, the name of the current lunar month, and the length (29 or 30 days) of that month. All this before any content regarding what happened on that date and who did it!

It is no surprise, then, that the astronomical and calendrical aspects of the Maya script were the first to be understood. Much of the credit goes to Ernst Förstemann, who in 1867 became the librarian at Dresden and thus curator of the Dresden Codex. The basic system of numerals was very simple and already understood: the Maya used a dot to represent one, and a bar to represent five. Förstemann realized that the Maya number system was vigesimal (base 20), rather than decimal (base 10) like ours, and that it used a sign for the completion of a unit of 20 that could function as a place-holder in larger numbers – effectively the equivalent of the place-holding zero that makes our decimal system of Arabic numerals so efficient. He worked out how the Long Count and the Sacred Round worked, and identified tables in the Dresden Codex that referred to cycles of the planet Venus and of the Moon.

Were the Maya inscriptions, then, just records of sacred dates carved by a race of calendar priests? Given that the dates could be read, while any other content remained undeciphered, this was a reasonable hypothesis. But that view was to change, starting in 1958 when Heinrich Berlin, a German settled in Mexico, published his discovery of what he called Emblem Glyphs. These were glyphs of a particular structure: the upper and left-hand parts were invariant, while the main signs varied according to the location where they were found – Tikal, Naranjo, Yaxchilán, Palenque, Copán, etc. Whether they recorded the names of these cities or their dynasties, tutelary deities, or rulers, the Emblem Glyphs seemed rooted in the geo-political world of the Maya rather than in abstract dates.

Then in 1960 the Russian-American Mayanist Tatiana Proskouriakoff made a remarkable discovery. Studying the rows of stelae standing in front of the Maya pyramids, she noted that each row of stelae recorded dates within a relatively narrow range – arguably a single lifespan. Perhaps the dates recorded the reigns of individual rulers, she reasoned. Two dates in each series received special prominence and occurred with particular glyphs; these particular dates were not repeated on rows of stelae found elsewhere, but the accompanying glyphs were. So the specific dates, which were separated by a period ranging from 12 to 31 years, were significant to only one ruler, but the events that occurred then (recorded in the accompanying glyphs) were shared by other rulers.

Proskouriakoff concluded that the dates recorded the birth and accession of the Maya kings.

With Berlin's and Proskouriakoff's discoveries, it became clear that the stelae of the Maya cities recorded actual historical events (at least the "official" history) rather than being dedicated to the abstract concept of time. The stelae were actually *saying something*, and it became the more incumbent upon Mayanists to find out what.

With careful analysis it became possible to identify which glyphs were the names of rulers and which identified the events they commemorated. But as there was yet no way to actually read out the glyphs in Mayan, the glyphs took on colorful nicknames. The "upended frog" glyph indicated birth, while the "toothache" glyph represented accession to the kingship (figure 5.2). Royal personages were given nicknames like Shield Jaguar, 18 Rabbit, and Lady Beastie.

In retrospect we know that by the time Proskouriakoff published her discoveries, an important breakthrough in unlocking the linguistic content of Maya glyphs had already been made. But it had been made in Russia, by Yuri Valentinovich Knorosov in the 1950s. Cold War politics did little to make Knorosov's ideas attractive to Western scholars, and certain inconsistencies in his approach left him open to much criticism. In fact, few of the specific decipherments that he put forward have stood the test of time, though his general approach marked a significant turning point.

Unlike many other Mayanists, Knorosov was well acquainted with other ancient scripts. Given the number of signs in the Maya script (around 700), he reasoned that it was likely to be a logosyllabary, like Akkadian cuneiform. Landa's alphabet, he correctly guessed, was actually a disguised syllabary, the signs standing for the syllables with which the Spanish pronounced the letters of the alphabet. This would explain why Landa had listed, along with the letters of the alphabet, some clearly syllabic signs, including ones labeled "ca" and "cu." The syllabic signs, Knorosov assumed, would often be used as phonetic complements, so that if he knew how a syllabogram was pronounced, he could find (at least part of) the phonetic value of the accompanying logogram, and vice versa. Confirmation of correct readings came from the pictographic nature of the logograms, from illustrations accompanying the text in the Dresden Codex, and from Mayan dictionaries of the colonial period. Thus the syllable *tzu* plus the syllable *lu* made *tzul*, which was recorded to mean "dog" in an early post-Conquest Maya dictionary. Furthermore, the word *tzul* appeared over a picture of a dog god in the Dresden Codex. This confirmed the decipherment of the syllables *tzu* and *lu*.

As is usually true in a syllabary, the signs stood for a consonant–vowel (CV) sequence. But since Mayan words generally end in a consonant if they do not have suffixes appended to them, spelling a word out syllabically often left a silent vowel at the end of the word. By a principle Knorosov called "synharmony," the silent vowel would match the previous vowel, a spelling strategy reminiscent of the recently deciphered Linear B script of Crete (see chapter 6). So *tzu* plus *lu* was to be read *tzul*, not *tzulu*. There turned out to be many exceptions to the principle of synharmony, and these apparent inconsistencies helped to justify the disbelief with which Knorosov's work was almost universally greeted in the West. The exceptions have only recently been given a satisfactory explanation: when synharmony fails, and a final silent vowel is different from the previous, pronounced vowel, it indicates something about the quality of the previous vowel – that it is long, or followed by [h] or a glottal stop ([?], the unspelled sound that begins both syllables of *uh-oh*). At first this seems to be a bizarre interpretation, but it is in fact not unreasonable: after all, the length of vowels in English is frequently indicated by a final silent vowel, in words such as *make*, *line*, and *home*.

Despite Knorosov's progress, some Western scholars continued to deny that there was any phonological component to Maya writing at all, and to claim that the glyphs were not true writing but merely ideograms, representing *concepts* but not actually recording *language*. Things began to change in the 1970s, however, as more American Mayanists became convinced that Knorosov had been on the right track. Mayanists began to get together to collaborate on decipherment and exchange ideas in brainstorming sessions, often at the instigation of art historian Linda Schele.

The linguist Floyd Lounsbury gave the decipherment efforts some much-needed rigor with his study of substitutable glyphs. Glyphs that could be substituted for each other in the same context must either (a) represent the same sound, (b) represent the same meaning, or (c) be contrasting members of the same category (in the sense that, for example, the English suffixes -*ed* and -*ing* are both in the category of verbal inflections – they can both be used as suffixes to a verb like *walk*, but they cannot be used simultaneously).

The decipherment crept forward, slowly gaining momentum, until the 1980s, which saw the opening of the floodgates. This was in part thanks to the young David Stuart, who was raised on Maya archaeology and presented his first paper on Maya decipherment in 1978 at the age of 12. Since then Stuart has remained at the forefront of Maya decipherment, rigorously applying the principle of phonetic complements and substitution patterns, and carefully testing his proposed decipherments both in the context of associated illustrations and in the context of other texts. Does a proposed reading of a glyph, he asks, produce a meaning that squares with what the associated illustrations suggest is being discussed in the text? And does the reading combine with glyphs in other texts to produce a meaningful reading?

Other Mayanists, many of them art historians, have contributed to the effort. Just as Champollion's recognition of the ibis as a symbol for the god Thoth was important to his breakthrough in Egyptian hieroglyphs, so a growing understanding of Maya iconography has been important to the Maya decipherment.

The decipherment is now significantly advanced. Many logograms can be read, and reconstruction of the syllabary is nearly complete (figure 5.1). In recent years the phonological decipherment has advanced to the point where texts can be read well enough to give linguistic detail on the language, rather than just bare outlines. This means that a particular question can now be considered with some hope of an answer: which Mayan language, exactly, do the inscriptions record? Earlier work suggested either a language of the Ch'olan subfamily or the Yucatecan subfamily, or a mixture of both; but recently David Stuart and collaborators Stephen Houston and John Robertson have made a strong case that the language of the glyphs was a prestige language they have dubbed Classic Ch'olti'an, which belonged to the Ch'olan subfamily. In other words, the Maya followed the same pattern as other literate cultures: a particular version of the language, once written down, became fossilized and spread beyond its original sphere to others who wished to acquire writing. The written language ignored many of the differences of language and dialect that occurred over time and space in the spoken language.

Even without an individual Champollion, the Maya glyphs have finally been persuaded to divulge the majority of their secrets. While early Mayanists may be faulted for their lack of cross-cultural training (of the sort that allowed Knorosov to make his breakthrough) or for

	a	e	i	o	u
b					
ch (= [tʃ])					
ch' (= [tʃ'])					
j (= [h])					
k					
k'					
l					
m					
n					
p					
s					
t					
tz (= [ts])					
tz' (= [ts'])					
w					
x (= [ʃ])					
y (= [jl])					

Figure 5.1 The Maya syllabary (incomplete). Additional variant signs exist, and continued decipherment is identifying further signs.

their lack of interest in actually learning Mayan languages, it is nevertheless true that the Maya decipherment has been an objectively difficult task. For one thing, there simply has not been available the extensive corpus that exists for Egyptian hieroglyphs or for Mesopotamian cuneiform (most of whose hundreds of thousands of excavated tablets have yet to be read, due to their overwhelming quantity). The longest Maya inscription ascends along the hieroglyphic stairway of Copán. It describes Copán's dynastic history in the space of about 2,500 glyphs. Most surviving Maya texts are much shorter. Many of the longer texts are painted or carved on ceramics; these may number up to 84 glyphs. This is very short indeed compared to the Egyptian funerary papyri of the Book of the Dead, or the Akkadian Epic of Gilgamesh. The range of topics dealt with is also limited: dates take up much of the inscriptions, and virtually all texts are in the third person singular. First- and second-person forms are so rare that they have only recently been identified.

A final and not insubstantial reason for the slow decipherment of Maya glyphs is the system's complexity. It was difficult to decipher because the system just plain *is* very difficult. Unlike Egyptian hieroglyphs, where each sign stands alone as a discrete picture of something that is often recognizable even to modern eyes, Maya glyphs are hard to take in visually. Complex patterns and grotesque faces are jammed together into ornate, dice-shaped blocks. While the principles of Maya writing may be familiar to those acquainted with cuneiform or Egyptian hieroglyphs, visually Maya glyphs are like nothing found outside Mesoamerica.

Here, roughly, is how the system works. A Maya text is composed of visually discrete *glyph blocks*. These are nearly square, but with rounded corners, like dice. The glyph blocks are laid out in one of several possible arrangements: a line, column, L- or T-shape, or grid. The reading order is face-on, which is almost always left-to-right, and top-to-bottom. A grid of glyph blocks is read in double columns, so that the leftmost two glyphs of the top row are read first, followed by the leftmost two of the second row, until the bottom is reached and the reading picks up at the third and fourth glyphs of the top row, etc.

A glyph block is usually composed of two or more pieces – the individual *signs* of the Mayan logosyllabary. (This is like the Egyptian practice of putting hieroglyphs into square or rectangular arrangements, or the Chinese practice of squeezing together compound characters, but there is no open space left between individual parts of a glyph block.) Within a glyph block, one sign – the *main sign* – will be shown larger than the others, and squarer (though still with rounded edges). The main sign will often be a logogram and represent the root of a word, but syllabograms may also occur as main signs. Surrounding the main sign will be one or more *affixes* (meaning here *graphical* signs added to the main sign, not *linguistic* affixes added to the root of a word). The affixes are longer and narrower than the main sign. They may be appended on the left, top, right, or bottom of the main sign and are hence known as prefixes, superfixes, postfixes, and subfixes respectively. Affixes tend to be numbers, phonetic complements, pronouns, or verbal suffixes. Yet there is no formal distinction between what may be a main sign and what may be an affix: the affix of one glyph block may appear, plumped out, as a main sign in another. The orientation of an affix will change according to whether it is being used horizontally (as a superfix or subfix) or vertically (as a prefix or postfix). Thus an affix that stands tall and narrow as a prefix to the left of one main sign will appear rotated 90 degrees as a short and wide superfix on another main sign. A glyph block is generally, but not always, read in the order prefix, superfix, main sign, subfix, postfix (in other words, left, top, center, bottom, right). Figure 5.2 shows examples of glyph blocks.

A glyph block can be further complicated by including two slightly overlapping main signs, or by conflating signs – that is, adding distinctive aspects of one sign to the general shape of another.

One bewildering aspect of the Maya script is its rich variety. As in other early scripts, spellings could alternate between phonological and logographic forms, and vary in the number of phonetic complements used. Sometimes the variations were due to the requirements of space, but the Maya scribes appear to have taken special delight in using as many different spellings as possible. Even logograms could occur in more than one form. Humans, animals, gods, and other supernatural creatures (which included units of time in this calendrically obsessed culture) often had both a *symbolic* (abstract) form and a *head variant*, showing the individual in profile with its identifying features. Even numbers, normally the easiest part of the Maya system, had head variants, the numbers 1 through 12 represented by their patron deities, and 13 through 19 represented by a conflation of the deity for 10 and those for the numbers 3 through 9. As if two versions of the logograms were not enough, sometimes a being rated a *full-figure* glyph, a miniature-scale portrait, complete with associated objects and attributes, embedded in the text.

To further complicate matters, the Maya system, like cuneiform, contains a fair amount of polyvalence, by which a single sign may be read in more than one way. This on top of the various ways to spell a single word, or to spell two words that are homonyms! This apparently

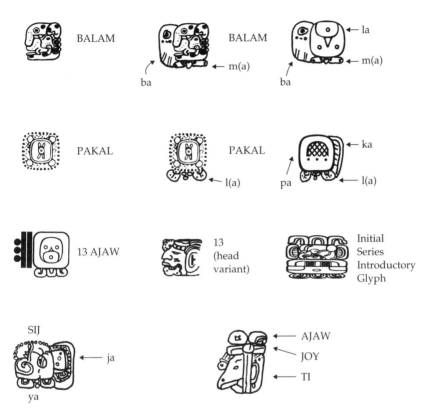

Figure 5.2 Examples of Maya glyphs. Top two rows: variant spellings of *balam* ("jaguar") and *pakal* ("shield"), using logograms, phonetic complements, and syllabic spellings. Third row, a date in the Sacred Round, 13 Ajaw, showing the bar-and-dot system of numerals and the tripod cartouche for day signs. Also shown are the head variant form of 13 and a version of the Initial Series Introductory Glyph. Bottom row: the "upended frog" and "toothache" glyphs identified by Proskouriakoff, signifying birth and accession to kingship.

inefficient variety is typical of early writing systems, and Knorosov's education prepared him for this aspect of Maya. Other Mayanists, however, found the complication unintuitive and were the less inspired to believe that Knorosov's approach to decipherment was going in the right direction.

In one way, however, Maya does not behave like other early scripts. Given a logosyllabic system with heavy use of phonetic complements, where are the semantic determinatives? If the Maya did use determinatives, it was on nowhere near the scale of the Akkadians, the Egyptians, or even the Chinese with their system of radicals. The cartouche on three legs that surrounds the day signs of the Sacred Round may be a determinative; as far as anyone knows there was no pronunciation associated with it. But it is still not settled which signs or parts of signs, if any, may have functioned as determinatives. The less conspicuous presence – or even absence – of determinatives in the Maya system serves as a reminder that each of the ancient traditions of writing was an intellectual accomplishment in its own right, created with its own quirks and idiosyncrasies.

Despite the restricted content of surviving Maya material, it is clear – from the extent of the syllabary, if nothing else – that the Maya could have written down anything in their language that they cared to. In this respect they outstripped their neighbors, and even their cultural successors. The Aztecs, whose empire rose in the fourteenth and fifteenth centuries only to be destroyed by the Spanish in 1521, used their proto-writing as a labeling or captioning system in their illustrated books, but not to write out texts.

Though knowledge of the Maya script was lost in the eighteenth century, the Maya themselves are still there, still living and speaking Mayan languages in their traditional homeland. Since the days of Bishop Landa, those languages have been written in the Roman alphabet. But with the advances in modern decipherment and a new spirit of cooperation between Mayanist scholars and the modern Maya, the script is now being returned to its original people. Maya glyphs can finally be removed from the long and tragic casualty list of the Old World's collision with the New.

6

Linear B: The Clerks of Agamemnon

Although we revere the Greeks of the classical period (480 to 323 BC) as the founders of Western civilization and its literary tradition, their forebears were another matter. The Greeks of the late Bronze Age (roughly 1600 to 1100 BC) were not democrats, playwrights, and philosophers. They were more like Greek-speaking, Bronze-Age Vikings, living in small fortified city-states and engaging in trade, piracy, and sacking and pillaging in the waters of the Aegean; and though they experimented with literacy, it didn't stick.

Nevertheless, the Greeks of this era – known as the Mycenaean period, the age memorialized in the epics of Homer – developed a complex enough society that for a while keeping written records seemed like an awfully good idea. Accounts were kept in Greek for about two and a half centuries, between 1450 and 1200 BC, before the Mycenaean cities suffered destruction and collapse. The population declined dramatically, and the technology of writing was lost as Greece sank into its Dark Age. Even the memory of Greek writing was lost, so that when the alphabet was introduced in the ninth century BC, it was hailed as a new technology, and when modern archaeologists rediscovered Bronze-Age Greek documents, it was hardly conceivable that the writing could be Greek.

The story of the rediscovery of the first Greek script, Linear B, starts with Heinrich Schliemann, a nineteenth-century German businessman turned archaeologist. Schliemann was possessed by an idea that most experts in the field of Greek history at the time considered to be ludicrous: that Homer's *Iliad* and *Odyssey*, telling of the Bronze-Age Trojan War and its aftermath, were based on actual historical events. Armed with Homer's descriptions, he went looking for the city of Troy. In 1871 he found its remains on the coast of Asia Minor (see appendix, figure A.6), and although later generations of excavators have shown that he misidentified which archaeological layer would have coincided with the Trojan War, he proved that there was at least a germ of truth to the old legends that described an advanced Aegean civilization during the Bronze Age.

Schliemann then turned to mainland Greece, home of the attackers of Troy, called Achaeans by Homer. According to Homer, the foremost Greek city at the time of the Trojan War was Mycenae, ruled by the great king Agamemnon. The wife of Agamemnon's brother, Menelaus, was Helen, whose abduction by Paris of Troy started the war. Schliemann located Mycenae in 1876, complete with gold-filled burials, one of which he was sure was that of Agamemnon. Once again, he had gotten the date wrong (the burials would have been centuries before Agamemnon), but he succeeded in attracting world attention to Greek archaeology as he conjured history out of legend with his rediscovery of Mycenae and its riches.

Schliemann's discoveries were of particular interest to the Englishman Arthur (later Sir Arthur) Evans. The son of an amateur archaeologist and paleontologist, Evans was more aware than most that Europe must have had historical roots much earlier than the classical Greeks and Romans, with whom nineteenth-century history classes began. People had lived in Europe during the Stone Age and Bronze Age – why weren't more people interested in finding out about them?

Evans visited Schliemann in Athens, where his imagination was captured by the Mycenaean civilization. Where had it arisen? How had it developed? And on what did it keep its records? A civilization that advanced, he reasoned, must have had writing – why had it not been found? Evans had a keen appreciation of the cultural importance of writing: his father was a paper-mill owner at a time of rising literacy rates in Victorian England. Evans had also inherited from his father an interest in ancient coins and their inscriptions. He was particularly struck by some small gemstones and rings that Schliemann showed him. Engraved with tiny designs, they had obviously been used as seals, to create a distinctive impression on soft clay or wax.

One of the designs was an octopus, a symbol typically associated with the Aegean islands, not mainland Greece. Could the source of Mycenaean civilization lie out in the Aegean? On a later trip to Greece Evans found more engraved sealstones in an antique shop. The small symbols engraved on them had a vaguely hieroglyphic look. Could they be writing? The stones came from Crete, he was told. So Evans headed to Crete.

According to Greek legend, Crete had once been ruled from the city of Knossos by a powerful king, Minos. Minos had employed the brilliant inventor and architect Daedalus, who had built for him the famous maze-like Labyrinth beneath his palace. The Labyrinth imprisoned the Minotaur, the half-man, half-bull son of Minos' wife, Pasiphaë, and a bull.

Not far outside the city of Candia (today's Heraklion) was a hill still known by tradition as Knossos, though its official name was Kephála. Evans was not the first to eye the site with an excavator's interest, but the island was under Turkish control at the time, and excavation permits were difficult to obtain. Evans managed to buy a quarter-share of the site in 1894, ensuring that no one else could beat him to the digging, and went on to explore the rest of the island. He found many more sealstones; their ancient purpose long forgotten, they were worn by nursing peasant women as charms to aid their milk production. Crete was clearly the home of the sealstones; surely it was here that he would find the Bronze-Age source of Aegean writing and civilization.

Excavation was delayed by revolution and civil war on Crete, and Evans's first concern on returning to the island in 1898 was relief work on behalf of its citizens. With the spring of 1900, however, he began digging at Knossos. A week later he had found his first written clay tablet. The finds piled up: soon he had hundreds of tablets, and by the end of the first year's digging he had over a thousand.

Meanwhile more glamorous discoveries were also being made at Knossos. The ruins of the Palace of Minos, as Evans called it, began to be unearthed. A truly impressive structure larger than Buckingham Palace, the Palace of Minos served as an administrative and religious center, as a storage facility, and quite possibly as the domicile of a royal family, whether or not any of the kings were actually called Minos. Long, complicated passageways adorned with brightly painted murals led to a large central court. The size and intricacy of the floor plan would quite naturally have suggested a confusing Labyrinth to those who viewed its ruins in the centuries after its fall. Excavating the grand Palace of Minos was to occupy most of the rest of Evans's life.

Crete had been home to other palaces as well, though the one at Knossos was the largest. Good-sized palaces at Phaistos and Mallia came to light under the spades of other archaeologists in the early twentieth century, and a few smaller palaces have been found since. The flowering of the Cretan civilization that produced these complexes preceded that of Mycenaean Greece, and Evans was able to show that much of Mycenaean art could trace its inspiration to Crete, to the civilization he dubbed *Minoan*. The sensitivity and elegance of Minoan ceramics and wrought gold pieces remain exceptional today, three and a half millennia later.

Evans came to believe firmly in the cultural superiority of the Minoans over all of their Aegean contemporaries: the Mycenaeans were warlike barbarians by contrast. And so Evans did not long entertain the possibility that the tablets he had excavated could be Greek. The more he uncovered of the Minoan age, the less possible it looked. The tablets must record the forgotten language of the Minoans.

Looking over his tablets, Evans was able to identify three distinct forms of writing. The oldest he dubbed *Cretan hieroglyphic* because, like the Egyptian hieroglyphic script, it consisted of fully drawn pictograms. This was the script of the sealstones and of a small number of clay tablets. The second two scripts consisted not of full pictures but of stylized lines, and he called these *Linear A* and *Linear B*. Linear A was found on clay tablets and occasionally on objects worked in stone or metal, while Linear B only appeared on clay objects: tablets, labels and sealings, and the occasional ceramic jar.

Cretan hieroglyphic was the earliest to develop, as the palatial centers arose at Knossos, Phaistos, and Mallia. Its birth may have been as early as 1900 BC, and it remained in use until around 1600 BC. Cretan writing did not develop in a cultural vacuum, however. The cultures of Egypt and Mesopotamia were already literate; Minoan traders would have encountered writing and brought home tales of a strange but useful technology, inspiring the development of a native script. (The Anatolians similarly invented their own hieroglyphic script and the Canaanites developed the earliest consonantal alphabet during the Bronze-Age expansion of civilization in the region.)

Linear A appears to have derived from Cretan hieroglyphic, but was drawn with simpler lines. It seems to have been used from the eighteenth century BC to the mid-fifteenth century BC. Its birth is hard to pinpoint, however, as most of the surviving examples come from the very end of the period, when the palaces were destroyed by fire and the clay tablets on which Linear A was written were accidentally baked (none of the Cretan tablets was baked deliberately).

Linear A was used in palaces all over Crete, but the surviving examples are few; the majority of them come from an archive of about one hundred and fifty small and poorly preserved tablets found in the royal villa of Haghia Triadha near Phaistos, baked in a fire of the fifteenth century.

Linear B succeeded Linear A, but for many years it looked like Linear B had been used only at Knossos and on the occasional vase exported to the mainland. When the other palaces were destroyed, Knossos suffered only partial damage and was rebuilt, enjoying a renaissance between 1450 and 1350 or 1300 BC, when it was finally destroyed.

Linear B is related to Linear A, but the precise nature of the relationship is not entirely clear. Telling them apart is not too difficult, however, as Linear B tablets tend to be neater than Linear A tablets, with the text written on ruled lines. Otherwise they are quite similar: the two scripts have about the same number of signs, many of which are the same or nearly so. But some signs of Linear A do not survive in Linear B, and some signs of Linear B have no precedent in Linear A. There are even a few Linear B signs that more closely resemble Cretan hieroglyphs than the corresponding signs in Linear A. So Linear B, though younger, may be more a sibling than a direct descendant of Linear A.

The material in Cretan hieroglyphic and in Linear A was – and remains – relatively scanty. The number of Linear B tablets available was much bigger, however, so Linear B was the obvious place to start a decipherment. To Evans the Linear B script was clearly the product of the advanced Minoan culture in its golden age. It was a special, royal script, developed at the palace at Knossos and used during the period when Knossos was the undisputed leader of civilization not only in Crete but in the entire Aegean world. It would surely record the lost language of the Minoans.

It was apparent, however, that neither the Linear B nor the Linear A tablets had all that much to say: judging from the length of the texts, the numerals, and the accompanying pictograms, they were clearly accounting tablets, more parallel to proto-cuneiform accounting records than to the Epic of Gilgamesh or other literary cuneiform texts.

But what was the language of the Minoans? Eager would-be decipherers suggested connections to Basque or to Etruscan. One thing seemed obvious: it was not Greek. For one thing, the Minoans were culturally distinct from and far more advanced than the Greeks of the time; they would surely not have used the Greeks' language. A second and more convincing reason came from a related script from Cyprus.

The Cypriot syllabary is clearly related to Linear A and B but was used in Cyprus to write Greek from sometime after the Greek colonization of the island around the twelfth century BC until the third or second century BC, when standardization of writing spread through the Greek world in the wake of Alexander the Great (336–323 BC). It was deciphered in the 1870s using bilingual Phoenician–Cypriot inscriptions, with later confirmation from biscriptal Greek inscriptions, written both in the Greek alphabet and in the Cypriot syllabary.

The Cypriot syllabary is a CV syllabary of the typical kind, each sign standing for a consonant–vowel sequence, except for a few signs which stand for plain vowels. Like most syllabaries (Akkadian being a notable exception), it lacks VC or CVC signs. This makes it a poor fit for Greek. Greek syllables may begin with a sequence of consonants, and may also end with a consonant, as in the Homeric name *Ktesippus*. As a result, Cypriot spelling was only approximate, sometimes leaving out consonants, and sometimes adding additional, unpronounced vowels. For example, words of Greek may end in the consonants *r*, *n*, or *s*. To write these final syllables, Cypriot used signs for *re*, *ne*, and *se*. Thus *Ktesippus* would have been spelled *ke-te-si-pu-se*. The sign for *se* in Cypriot, ⱶ, looked just the same as one of the signs in Linear B. If that sign had the same pronunciation in both scripts, any Greek text written in Linear B should have many words ending in ⱶ. None did. So apparently the texts were not Greek.

The decipherment of Linear B was delayed by Evans's slow approach to publishing the tablets. In 1909 he published the hieroglyphic texts he had found, and he planned to go on to publish the Linear A and B texts, but the more exciting work of publishing his other finds at the palace intervened, and continued to do so for much of the rest of his life. The inclusion of some tablets in the fourth volume of his *Palace of Minos* in 1935 brought the total number of published Linear B tablets up to only 120, a tiny amount of material considering that each tablet holds only a very brief text.

Sir Arthur Evans died in 1941 at the age of 90, without having published the remaining Knossos tablets. They were eventually edited by a colleague and published in 1952. Even before his death, however, Evans had lost his monopoly on Linear B. In 1939 the American archaeologist Carl Blegen began digging at a site in mainland Greece that he believed to be the ancient city of Pylos, mentioned in Homer as the capital of wise King Nestor. The very first day's digging brought to light clay tablets written in Linear B. By season's end, it was clear that a Mycenaean king's palace had indeed stood here, and that written records had been used in its administration. Then World War II forced a pause in the excavations. The Pylos tablets were not published until 1951, and further excavation was delayed until 1952. In 1952 a few tablets were also found at Mycenae. Since then tablets have been found at Tiryns, at Thebes, and a few at Chania, thus far the only site in Crete outside of Knossos to yield samples of Linear B.

The mainland Linear B tablets dated from later than the Knossos tablets, to the preserving fires of a period of widespread destruction around 1200 BC, near the close of the Bronze Age. But the style of writing was the same, and its presence on mainland Greece was perplexing. Had the Mycenaeans imported their scribal class from Crete? This was not impossible, as they clearly looked to Crete for many cultural imports. Had the Mycenaean upper class learned Minoan in order to learn to write, as earlier Akkadian scribes had learned Sumerian? Only the decipherment of the tablets would yield the answer.

The decipherment of an unknown script requires a great deal of preliminary analysis, some of which could be done even without full publication of the texts. The basic subject matter of Linear B texts was pretty obvious: they were accounting tablets. A typical tablet has words written out in Linear B, followed by an ideogram, followed by a numeral (see plate 5). The use of the term *ideogram* is for once accurate here. In many cases these ideograms are pictographic, showing the type of entity being counted: horses (𓃗), chariots (𓃟), people (𓀀,𓀁), jars (𓎺). In some cases the ideogram is stylized so as not to be recognizable by the uninitiated (e.g. 𓇋, "grain"). In others it is completely abstract, being derived from the signs with which the relevant words are written (e.g. 𓏤, from 𓏥𓏦𓏧, *a-re-pa*, "ointment"). But unlike logograms in a logosyllabary, the ideograms do not appear mixed in among the syllabic signs. They only appear next to numerals, indicating what kind of thing is being counted. There is no evidence that they were even pronounced. With decipherment it became clear that they repeated information spelled out in the syllabic text of the tablets, so in all likelihood they were *not* pronounced. If they were, readers of the tablets would have said things like "Horses, horses 12," repeating themselves a great deal. The ideograms served as a visual organization for the numbers recorded on the tablets, much as a dollar sign today may head up a list of numbers and identify what kind of thing is being counted.

For twentieth-century scholars, the ideograms were of great help in guiding and evaluating decipherment attempts. Even before the decipherment, the tablets could be sorted by topic. They were clearly about food, livestock, trade commodities, weapons, and other concerns of a centralized Bronze-Age bureaucracy. Any decipherment that claimed to find in these mundane tablets an ode to the goddess Athena, say, was bound to be wrong.

Aside from the ideograms and numerals, the core of the script consisted of about 87 signs, some uncertainty being due to the rarity of certain signs and the variation between different handwriting styles. The number of signs was a clue to the nature of the script. While the occasional language with 87 or more phonemes does exist, most languages have far fewer; so Linear B was probably not an alphabet. A logographic system with only 87 signs is even less likely. Even a complex syllabary of the Akkadian type, encompassing CV, VC, and even a few CVC syllables, would have required more than 87 symbols. In all probability, then, Linear B was a syllabary of the open-syllable CV type that Cypriot was already known to be.

There were no bilingual texts for Linear B. Nor did history record any royal names that one could expect to find, the way Grotefend identified Darius' and Xerxes' names in Old Persian cuneiform. The names of mythological characters like Minos and Daedalus were unlikely to show up, and indeed have never been found on a Linear B tablet. The language, and even the language family, was completely unknown. Where, then, to start?

One possibility was with the Cypriot syllabary, transferring the syllabic values of the Cypriot signs to similar ones in Linear B. Only seven of the signs are the same or nearly the same, though some additional ones are similar. Nevertheless, Evans himself used Cypriot to successfully read the first Linear B word, though he rejected it as a coincidence. On one particular tablet the ideograms showed horses' heads. One was smaller and had no mane, while the other was larger and complete with mane. The smaller was accompanied by a word, ⹊⼂, which, if supplied with Cypriot values, read *po-lo*. Evans was struck by the similarity to the Greek *pōlos*, meaning "foal," but was so sure that the language could not be Greek that he did not pursue this approach. If he had, he might have noticed that the missing final *s*, rather than an added *se,* suggested that the spelling conventions of Cypriot did not apply to Linear B, undermining the argument that it could not be Greek.

The similarities with Cypriot were not strong enough to allow a decipherment, and those who worked on the decipherment wisely did not assume that signs that looked similar in Cypriot must have the same reading in Linear B. Comparisons between the Greek and Roman alphabets, where P stands for [r] in Greek but [p] in Latin, for example, show the dangers of such an approach.

The American Alice Kober's particularly clear-thinking approach was to look for evidence as to what *kind* of language the tablets recorded. Working between 1943 and her death in 1950, she was to make the most progress before the actual breakthrough. Scrutinizing the published texts, analyzing the syllabically written words in the context of the ideograms and numerals, she looked for evidence of how the language assembled its words. Luckily (and unlike the early alphabetic inscriptions of later Greek), it was clear where one word ended and another began, the break between one word and the next usually being shown by a short vertical line.

Some tablets recorded several numerals, with a total at the bottom of the tablet. Kober found that the word preceding the totals had two forms, one used for men and a certain class of animals, and another, with the same first syllable but a different final syllable, used for women and another class of animals. The language of Linear B therefore had gender, dividing the world up into masculine and feminine things, like Spanish, French, or ancient Greek. In fact, the particular way the masculine and feminine forms were related (by a difference in the final syllable, rather than by the presence or absence of a suffix) made it very likely that Linear B recorded a language of the Indo-European family, to which Greek, Latin, and even English belong.

Perhaps most significantly, Kober found sets of words whose endings varied in regular ways. These came to be called "Kober's triplets" (see figure 6.1). Kober rightly concluded that these words shared a core morpheme but had different endings depending on their grammatical form. In English, for example, *Canada* is the name of a country. But the adjectival version of the word is *Canadian,* whose meaning is obvious from the combination of *Canad-* and *-ian,* but is not formed simply by adding a suffix *-n* to the end of *Canada. Bermuda* and *Bermudian,* and *Argentina* and *Argentinian,* form pairs according to the same pattern. The language of Linear B words formed triplets rather than pairs.

𐀓𐀸𐀴𐀷   𐀀𐀖𐀛𐀰   𐀓𐀜𐀰
𐀓𐀸𐀴𐀍   𐀀𐀖𐀛𐀍   𐀓𐀜𐀍
𐀓𐀸𐀴𐀴   𐀀𐀖𐀛𐀴   𐀓𐀜𐀴

𐀠𐀴𐀵   𐀴𐀱𐀵
𐀠𐀴𐀍   𐀴𐀱𐀍
𐀠𐀴𐀴   𐀴𐀱𐀴

Figure 6.1 Some of Kober's triplets, which she took as evidence for inflection in Linear B. The triplets were foundational to Ventris's logical grid of consonants and vowels and also provided the key to the phonological decipherment of Linear B when Ventris guessed that they recorded the names of places in Crete. The ones at the top refer (from left to right) to Amnisos, Knossos, and Tylissos. At bottom left is Phaistos, at right Lyktos.

Kober's triplets revealed something even more important. If *Canada* and *Canadian* are divided syllabically, you get *ca-na-da* and *ca-na-di-an*. There are two different third syllables in these words, *da* and *di*, but they begin with the same consonant. By analogy, it was possible to predict that certain syllables shared a consonant. In the triplet 𐀠𐀴𐀰, 𐀠𐀴𐀍, and 𐀠𐀴𐀴, 𐀰 and 𐀍 were likely to have the same first consonant, as were 𐀴 and 𐀴. By comparing one triplet set to another, it was possible to predict that certain other syllables shared a vowel. *Ber-mu-di-an* and *Ar-gen-ti-ni-an* have the same vowel in the second-to-last syllable, as they both have the *-ian* suffix. Similarly, in the suffixed forms 𐀠𐀴𐀍 and 𐀓𐀸𐀴𐀍, 𐀍 and 𐀍 both came before 𐀴 and were therefore likely to share a vowel. For every pair of signs for which Kober hypothesized a shared vowel or consonant, she was correct. She also pointed out, wisely, that Linear A probably recorded a different language than Linear B. For all the similarity of the two scripts, the Linear A tablets record not a single word that is also found in Linear B.

At this point leadership in the decipherment passed to a young British architect by the name of Michael Ventris. Ventris had been fascinated by the mystery of Linear B since 1936, when at the age of 14 he had met Sir Arthur Evans. His own pet theory was that the language was Etruscan, and he held to this idea until the final steps of his solution showed him that it could not be. Ventris followed up on Kober's work, organizing the signs of Linear B into a grid, with 15 rows of signs that he believed shared a consonant and 5 columns of signs that he believed shared a vowel. Yet it was his ability to entertain hunches, as well as his painstaking work producing ever more complete versions of his syllabic grid, that led him to a solution.

The Pylos tablets were published in 1951, finally making available enough data to allow a true decipherment. Ventris quit his job to focus on Linear B. He filled in his grid with instances where signs probably shared a consonant or a vowel, gathering evidence from variant spellings of what were probably the same word; from still-visible erased signs (indicating a corrected spelling mistake, and thus perhaps a similarity between the incorrect and the correct spelling); from inflections, including the kind in Kober's triplets (of which many more examples were now available); from masculine and feminine endings; and from singular and plural forms of words (identifiable by the accompanying numerals). He noted that three signs favored the first position in a word. These were probably vowels – plain V rather than CV signs – which are especially needed at the beginnings of words. Ventris was able to build his grid with a high (but not perfect) degree of accuracy, based on the *relative* values of the signs, with as yet no good idea of what the actual phonological values of any of the signs were. In other words, he could have told you that Ŧ and ∕Λ shared a consonant, but he could not have told you what that consonant was.

With this careful groundwork laid, what was still needed was an inspired guess. Ventris had noticed that the triplets Kober had found in the Knossos tablets did not occur in the Pylos tablets. Might they then be the names of places on Crete, with suffixes on adjectival forms (like *Canada, Canadian*)? What places were they likely to be? Some Cretan place names known from classical times were clearly of ancient, pre-Greek origin, as they share a suffix that is meaningless in Greek: Amnisos (the harbor nearest Knossos), Knossos, Tylissos, Phaistos, Lyktos. One of Kober's triplets began with one of the signs Ventris had identified as a vowel. The uninflected form had four syllables: ⼁𐃑𐃯. Might this be Amnisos, spelled syllabically as *a-mi-ni-so*? At this point Ventris called upon some similarities with the Cypriot syllabary. The Linear B sign Ŧ was very similar to the Cypriot sign for *na*, Ŧ. If the similarity could be trusted, and if Ħ really was *a*, then Ŧ should be in the column headed by Ħ. It was. This identified the *-a* column, and by implication the *n*-row (for a grid layout of the signs of Linear B, see figure 6.2). Another sign similar in Linear B and Cypriot was *ti*, ∕Λ. If the signs really

	a	e	i	o	u
Basic syllabary	a	e	i	o	u
	da	de	di	do	du
	ja	je		jo	ju
k = [k], [kʰ], or [g]	ka	ke	ki	ko	ku
	ma	me	mi	mo	mu
	na	ne	ni	no	nu
p = [p], [pʰ], or [b]	pa	pe	pi	po	pu
q = [kʷ], [kʰʷ], [gʷ]	qa	qe	qi	qo	
r = [r] or [l]	ra	re	ri	ro	ru
	sa	se	si	so	su
t = [t] or [tʰ]	ta	te	ti	to	tu
	wa	we	wi	wo	
z = [dz] or [ts]	za	ze		zo	
Optional symbols	a₂ (= ha)	a₃ (= ai)	au		
	dwe	dwo	nwa		
	pa₃?	pu	pte		
	ra₂	ra₃	ro₂		
	swa?	swi?			
	ta₂	two			
Unidentified symbols					

Figure 6.2 The Linear B syllabary. At the top are the signs of the basic syllabary. Also listed are optional symbols that seem to have been used occasionally to avoid certain ambiguities in spelling. At the bottom are symbols which occur so rarely that their value has not yet been established.

were the same, this identified the *t*- row and the -*i* column. The third syllable of the proposed *a-mi-ni-so*, should be in the -*i* column and the *n*- row. It was. The second syllable, should also be in the -*i* column, and indeed it was. This suggested an identification of the *m-* row. Guessing that the fourth syllable, ⴲ, was *so* allowed more of the grid to be filled in.

Another of Kober's triplets, ⵯⵘⴲ, now read *?-no-so*, a close match for Knossos. That made the unknown syllable, ⵯ, *ko*. Working in this way with known place names and the string of inferences that could be made whenever a value was added to the grid, Ventris was able to identify the spellings of many places in Crete. This gave him the values of many signs, but the language of the inscriptions was still unknown, as place names are often quite independent of regional language. Deciphering only place names such as *Connecticut* and *Quebec*, for example, would not tell you if a coded text was in English, French, or even a Native American language.

But then Ventris turned to the longer members of Kober's triplets, to the words for "total," and to those for "girl" and "boy". The longer forms of the *Amnisos* triplet were *a-mi-ni-si-jo* and *a-mi-ni-si-ja*, which could be construed as "men from Amnisos" ("male Amnisians") and "women from Amnisos" ("female Amnisians") in Greek. "Boy" and "girl" were *ko-wo* and *ko-wa*, plausible syllabic spellings of what these words were in early Greek, probably *korwos* and *korwā*. "Total" was *to-so* in the masculine, and *to-sa* in the feminine; again, it looked Greek.

Could Linear B actually be Greek? Was Evans wrong? Why would the Minoans write in Greek? Claiming that Linear B was Greek was a bold step to take, and Ventris did not take it all at once. At first he only claimed to have found some Greek words in the inscriptions.

Ventris had good reasons to hesitate. For one thing, the Greek that emerged was very poorly spelled. Greek is not a good language for a CV syllabary. Many phonemes were omitted from spellings, and many distinctions between phonemes were not made. For another thing, the Greek – if it was Greek – of the tablets was four hundred to six hundred years older than the earliest known alphabetic Greek. No language stays the same for that amount of time, so the texts were bound to look odd to a student of Classical Greek. Some archaic words were known from Homer, who lived early in the period of renewed Greek literacy and deliberately used archaic language to describe ancient events, but Homer used only words that fit the meter of his poetry. Other archaic words were lost. It is also true that the tablets probably contain some words that are not Greek: Mycenaeans living in Crete might well have incorporated some native Minoan words into their vocabulary.

One of the first to believe Ventris's suggestion of a Greek solution was John Chadwick, who assisted in the final stages of the decipherment. Chadwick's ready acceptance of the fractured syllabic spelling of Greek may have stemmed from his knowledge of Japanese, which made him familiar with the way a language (or writing system) with a simple syllable structure adapts words that do not fit the allowed patterns (in Japanese, for example, "Christmas" is *kurisumasu*). Thanks to his academic training, he was also able to guide Ventris in matters of ancient Greek dialectology. Ventris had been concerned because he had found no trace of a definite article in the tablets – no "the," in other words. Chadwick was able to reassure him on that score: while Classical Greek had a definite article, historical linguists had already worked out that Greek of earlier periods did not.

Acceptance of the Greek hypothesis was slow in coming, the spelling system of Linear B being one significant reason for it. Trying to spell Greek in an open CV syllabary is very much a business of fitting a square peg into a round hole. Furthermore, not all the CV syllables of Greek are distinguished. The difference between syllables starting with *p-* and those starting with *b-* (a sound which is like *p*, but is pronounced with the vocal cords vibrating) or *ph-* ([pʰ], pronounced like *p*, but aspirated, and only pronounced *f* in much later Greek) was not indicated, nor was the difference between the related sounds *k-* and *g-* and *kh-* ([kʰ]), or between *t-* and *th-* ([tʰ]). The difference between long and short vowels was not indicated, nor was the difference between *r* and *l*.

As a result of these mismatches between the syllabary and the spoken language, words in Linear B look strange to scholars of Greek, even accounting for the antiquity of the language. But there is systematicity, even to the mismatch. Syllable-final consonants (*l, m, n, r, s*) are regularly omitted in spelling. Thus *khalkos* "bronze" is spelled *ka-ko* and *patēr* "father" is spelled *pa-te*. If more than one consonant begins a syllable, a copy of the upcoming vowel is used to turn the single spoken syllable into two written ones: *ti-ri-po* spelled *tripos*, a tripod cauldron. (This spelling convention inspired Knorosov's principle of "synharmony," with which he began the phonological decipherment of Maya glyphs.) An initial *s-* is omitted, however, so that *pa-ka-na* was the spelling of *sphagana*, "swords." The system is regular, but it leaves some significant ambiguities, especially to the modern reader, who is not a native speaker of the language and does not have the clear understanding of a tablet's context that a Mycenaean clerk would have had.

Startling confirmation of Venris's decipherment came in 1953 when Carl Blegen, the excavator of Pylos, began studying some tablets he had found the previous year but had not yet published. Using Ventris's values, one of the tablets matched spelled words and pictograms too well to be coincidence: the word *ti-ri-po* (*tripos*) occurred with an ideogram of a tripod cauldron, ⛋. *Ti-ri-po-de* (*tripode*, "two tripods") occurred next to the same tripod ideogram and the numeral 2. There followed a list of vessels, described in syllabic Greek as having three, four, or no handles – with perfectly matching accompanying illustrations. Not only were these Greek words, but the use of the correct archaic dual form (in "two tripods") showed that the words were being used with Greek grammar, not just sprinkled into another language as loanwords. Linear B was Greek.

The mystery of Linear B was solved, but the solution created a number of further puzzles. What was Mycenaean Greek doing on Crete? Why did the Mycenaeans take up writing only to abandon it? Where in all this were Evans's culturally superior Minoans? Presumably theirs was the language recorded with Linear A. At some point their island was conquered by the Mycenaeans, who may have considered it expedient to rule the land from which so many of their imports came. Around 1450 BC, the palaces of Crete were destroyed, leaving only Knossos standing. This destruction marks the Mycenaean invasion. The Mycenaeans were accustomed to borrowing from the Minoans culturally, however, and they left little mark of their residence at Knossos for later archaeologists to uncover. They brought with them their language and their weaponry, but apparently very little else. They adopted many Minoan ideas, including the technology of syllabic writing.

The mainland Linear B tablets date from somewhat later, around 1200 BC. The new technology may have taken a while to spread back to the mainland. But it is also true that only destruction by fire preserved the tablets, and so we have the last, but not the first, tablets that were written. At the end of the Mycenaean period, the cities of the Mycenaean world were destroyed, preserving their tablets. Knossos fell first, and later Pylos, Mycenae, and the other Greek city-states of the time. Civilization declined, and around 1100 BC Greece entered its Dark Age.

With the loss of central administration came the loss of writing. The Greeks had used writing for the same purpose as the early Sumerians had: as a means of bureaucratic record keeping. Over time the Meso-potamians went on to discover other uses of writing – as literature, correspondence, and instructional texts – but the Mycenaean Greeks never took this leap. The second stage of the writing revolution – the expansion of writing from its original record-keeping function – seems never to have happened in the Mycenaean world. Literacy was probably restricted to employees of the palace administration, and may quite literally have died with the sack of the cities that preserved the last of the Linear B tablets for rediscovery in the twentieth century. The idea of writing as a medium of culture apparently never occurred to the early Greeks.

Perhaps the ambiguities involved in writing Greek in Linear B helped to persuade them that the potential applications of the technology were limited. They did not, after all, have the VC and CVC syllabograms that the Akkadians developed. The texts on the tablets would have been fairly clear in their administrative context (just as proto-cuneiform was), but the chances for misunderstandings would have been much greater in other contexts. Had they really wanted a better writing system, however, they probably could have created one. Already the script contained some signs that were not simple CV syllables, such as *pte*, and the diphthongs *ai* and *au*. These signs were considered optional, and were used sporadically, apparently to reduce ambiguity (see figure 6.2). More systematic use of such signs would have been a first step toward a more flexible script.

Whatever the reason, the Bronze-Age Greeks, unlike their classical descendants, were not very interested in the written word and left us only the uninspiring texts of the Linear B tablets. It is possible that a certain amount of writing on perishable materials has been lost. References to "this year" and "last year" in the tablets suggest that a clay tablet was normally kept for only a year, and the clay then softened in water and recycled. Whether the year's records were first collated in some other form – on some more valuable but perishable material such as papyrus – is unknown. It is telling, however, that the range of preserved uses is so small. The older and more scantily preserved Linear A shows up occasionally on stone or metal objects, recording what may have been religious dedications; but not so Linear B. Not only is there no surviving trace of writing used for anything but bureaucratic purposes – no religious, monumental, or private texts – but there is no writing imported from elsewhere. Cuneiform was used all over the Near

East at the time, but not a trace of cuneiform – not a letter, not a treaty, not a receipt – has been found in Crete or Greece, despite obvious trade contacts. The only Egyptian hieroglyphs are inscriptions on scarabs which were apparently brought back as decorative souvenirs – the writing on them is incidental.

The people who kept their records in Linear B – the last of the Mycenaean Greeks before troubled times in the Mediterranean region destroyed their cities – were the people that Homer describes in the *Iliad* and the *Odyssey*. It is natural to hope for some reference to Homeric individuals or events in the tablets, but there is none. Names of people occur, but the name Nestor, king of Pylos, does not occur on the tablets of Pylos, nor is Minos recorded at Knossos, or Agamemnon at Mycenae. Homer calls Nestor a charioteer, and indeed the Pylian tablets include an inventory of chariot wheels (though the inventory of the chariots themselves is still missing). This is as close to Homer's Nestor as we can get.

Instead of literature, the Mycenaean Greeks, like the Vikings after them, possessed a rich tradition of oral epic poetry – stories, myths, and legends that told them who they were, where they had come from, and what their place in the world was. These were not private stories to be enjoyed alone, curled up with a good book. They were shared stories that affirmed and nurtured a community.

This is speculation, to some extent, because an oral tradition leaves no archaeological imprint. Yet when the curtain of history lifted again, and the Greeks again took up writing around 800 BC, the last of the oral poets were still practicing their craft. One of the greatest of these must have been Homer. His work is in the traditional oral style, yet with a polish and magnitude that suggests the influence of writing. Although later tradition describes him as blind, there is no real evidence for this; he may well have recorded the *Iliad* and the *Odyssey* himself, as a compilation and refinement of his best work. Like other oral poets, he took traditional material and shaped it to his own purposes. Each telling would have been unique, at least until it was written down.

Writing set the stories in stone, fixed in the new medium. Was the fixing intentional or unintentional? Possibly it was unintentional, and Homer recorded his stories fully expecting later poets to rewrite them. I like to think, however, that it was intentional, that Homer was widely recognized in his day as a poet of unrivalled ability, and that as he grew older the impending loss of this great poet began to weigh heavily on his community. Was there any way to evade this loss? The newly introduced alphabet served just the right purpose.

Since Schliemann revealed a historical core to Homer's epics, it is tempting to look to them to put a face on the inhabitants of the ancient cities, the people who wrote in Linear B. But the oral tradition does not have the same kind of strict accuracy that writing does, and that writing was invented for. Some details may survive the centuries with startling accuracy, but others will be seriously distorted and still others forgotten and replaced by anachronisms. We will probably never fully know which details in Homer fall into which category; the decipherment of Linear B has been only marginally useful in this respect. Neither the epics of Homer nor the Linear B texts give us a clear picture of Mycenaean times.

Yet it is best not to dismiss individual details too hastily. Had Evans taken Homer more seriously, he might have been more willing to accept the presence of Greeks on Crete, and he might have believed his own reading of *pōlos*, garnering for himself the achievement of deciphering Linear B. On Crete, Homer says in the *Odyssey*, "First come the Achaeans [Greeks], then the native Cretans . . . Central to all their cities is magnificent Cnossos." Greeks at Knossos should have been no surprise.

We owe the works of Homer to renewed Greek literacy, as it was only with the reintroduction of writing into Greece that Homer's genius was preserved for posterity. On the other hand, Homer's epics were born of the great Greek oral tradition, whose roots stretch back to the Mycenaean age. We owe them, therefore, to Greek *illiteracy*, to the value the early Greeks placed on the spoken word to the neglect of the written. We owe them, in other words, to the death of Linear B.

7

Japanese: Three Scripts are Better than One

In Japan, as elsewhere, the history of writing is marked by both invention and staunch conservatism. Yet the Japanese have managed a unique balance between the two, on the one hand creating for themselves not just one but two syllabaries, while on the other hand continuing throughout their literary history to favor the Chinese logograms with which they first learned to write. The resulting syncretism of three scripts used simultaneously qualifies as the most complex writing system in modern use.

According to Japanese tradition, Chinese characters came to Japan with the arrival of Wani, a Korean scholar, at the court of Emperor Ōjin. Wani brought with him the *Analects* of Confucius and became tutor to one of Ōjin's sons. It is not clear how accurate the legend is, or when exactly Ōjin reigned, but somewhere between the late third century and the early fifth century AD, the Chinese written language came to Japan.

The Japanese court's first reaction to the new technology was not to adapt the system to Japanese, but rather to learn Chinese, just as the Koreans had before them and as the Akkadians had once learned Sumerian. Such foreign language study is in fact a common response to the introduction of writing – a response justified not only by the difficulty of adapting an existing writing system to a very different language, but also by the fact that one of the important uses of written language is not actually writing, but *reading*. There was as yet nothing to read in Japanese. The Chinese, by contrast, had been literate for well over a thousand years and had produced great works such as the Confucian classics and the translations of and commentaries on the Buddhist scriptures.

By the seventh century the Japanese had begun to write for themselves. At first the only way they could do so was to write in Chinese, using Chinese characters arranged in Chinese syntax – in other words, with the words arranged in the order found in Classical Chinese. In a Chinese sentence, the verb is placed between the subject and the object, as it is in English. In Japanese, however, the verb always comes at the end, after the subject and the object. In this respect and in many others, Japanese is very different from Chinese. In fact, despite numerous worthy efforts, Japanese has not convincingly been shown to be genetically related to any other language, though Korean is generally considered the best candidate. Unlike Chinese, Japanese is rife with inflections and follows each noun with a particle that indicates its function in the sentence. The Chinese writing system contains no equivalents for these morphemes, and so Chinese characters could not straightforwardly be adapted to Japanese. Despite the fact that few Japanese could speak Chinese, writing in Classical Chinese became the official, educated style of writing prose and remained so for centuries.

It soon became clear, however, that not everything that Japanese writers wanted to say could be written in Chinese. For one thing, how should they write their names? Names are more than their meanings: they are inextricably bound to their pronunciations, which in this case were in Japanese. The written form of a name therefore had to reflect its pronunciation. There was a precedent for a solution to this problem, in the way the Chinese wrote foreign names or the untranslatable Sanskrit terms of Buddhism. They used characters for their phonological value, divorced from their meaning. This rebus-style use of characters always remained marginal in Chinese, but it was to become widespread in Japan and lead eventually to the development of its two native syllabaries.

A second stumbling block was honorifics. Speakers of Japanese showed respect to people they considered their social superiors by using a special set of pronouns and inflectional suffixes when addressing them. These distinctions could not be written in Chinese, but they were important to the Japanese. To solve this problem, certain characters were given peculiarly Japanese interpretations as honorifics. A style of "modified Chinese" developed, with Japanese honorifics and a more Japanese word order. The Chinese verb placement was confusing to Japanese readers and writers, and in informal works such as diaries and personal letters they tended to slip into a more natural verb-final style. However, it was not until the time of the Kamakura shogunate (1192–1333), during the feudal period, that official documents were allowed to stray from correct, Classical Chinese and began to be written in modified Chinese.

Works written in Chinese could be read back either in Chinese or, with some mental gymnastics, in Japanese. The individual characters could be pronounced either in Chinese or as Japanese words of equivalent meaning. For example, 山, "mountain," which is *shān* in modern Mandarin, could be pronounced in Japan either in Chinese or as the native Japanese word *yama*. A full sentence of characters, if read back in Japanese, had to be reorganized to get the correct word order, and the reader had to infer the appropriate Japanese inflections and particles. Because of this flexibility of reading, it can be difficult to determine precisely what language early Japanese documents were intended to be read in. The modified Chinese style, with its Japanese honorifics and un-Chinese word order, seems to have been intended to be read in Japanese, or perhaps a Japanese–Chinese hybrid. Poetry that rhymed was clearly meant to be Chinese, as Japanese poetry did not rhyme. Other documents could have been read either way. However, many words relating to philosophy, education, and high culture were borrowed into Japanese from Chinese, so there was only one way to say the word, no matter which language one was supposedly reading in.

By the ninth century it is clear that many Chinese texts were being read in Japanese, as priests studying Buddhist texts began to annotate the characters with dots to show which words received which particles, helping readers to construct Japanese sentences out of Chinese text. This was no doubt cumbersome, but easier to do with logographic characters than with a phonological script. Many Japanese learned to read Chinese texts without actually learning Chinese.

From these texts, words flooded into educated Japanese from Chinese in much the same way that Latin and Greek words entered English and many other European languages. Yet Chinese and Japanese are even more different from each other than English and Greek, and the newly borrowed words had to be altered to fit Japanese. Chinese morphemes were generally each a single syllable, but the Japanese language allowed only very simple syllables. So some Chinese syllables were simplified and others were spread out into two syllables. Chinese words were stripped of their distinctive tones, while the phonemes they contained were converted into the nearest Japanese equivalents. These adaptations caused rampant homophony in Japanese. A particularly egregious case is *ka*, which is the Chinese-based (Sino-Japanese) pronunciation of 31 different characters on the modern list of 1,945 commonly used *kanji*, as Chinese characters are known in Japan. Modern Mandarin pronunciations of the same characters are (in pīnyīn) *xià, xiá, jiā, jià, jiǎ, huā, huà, huá, guǎ, guò, guǒ, huǒ, kē, kě, hé, gē,* and *gè.*

The borrowing of Chinese words occurred in three major waves. The first began with the introduction of Buddhism, traditionally dated to AD 552 and credited to a missionary from Korea. The Japanese pronunciation of the new religious vocabulary was probably adapted from that of southern Wu Chinese dialects of the time (see appendix, figure A.4). The second wave took place during the Nara period (AD 710–93), a time of stable imperial government built around Confucian ideals and state-sponsored Buddhism. Students were sent to China to study, and government officials were sent on diplomatic missions. They brought home many new words associated with Confucian philosophy, government affairs, and secular education. The Japanese pronunciation of this large set of Chinese loanwords was adapted from the standard dialect of the ruling dynasty of the time, the Tang.

The third and smallest wave of borrowings occurred in the fourteenth century with the arrival of a new sect of Buddhism, Zen. These words are mostly concerned with Zen, and their pronunciation in Japanese was probably adapted from their fourteenth-century pronunciation in Hangzhou, in southern China.

The effect of these multiple borrowings at different times and from different kinds of Chinese was to permanently complicate written Japanese. When kanji are read in Japanese each character may have up to three Sino-Japanese pronunciations, known as *on* readings, as the morpheme may be part of loanwords from up to three phases of borrowing, taken from three different Chinese languages. Additionally there is the *kun* reading – the native Japanese pronunciation of a word of the same meaning. Luckily, the majority of kanji have only one Sino-Japanese *on* pronunciation. In China characters also have many different pronunciations, but the variation there is from one dialect to another – within a dialect, a character usually has a single pronunciation. In Japan, the particular pronunciation to be used depends on context.

Sino-Japanese words, including new compound words made in Japan out of Sino-Japanese parts (many of which have since been borrowed back into China), now comprise about half the words in Japanese. Most simple, commonly used words remain Japanese, however. Compared to native words, Sino-Japanese words are considered more formal, technical, and precise, just as words of Latin and Greek origin are in English. In English, a word like *water* is an everyday, native English word. When the concept of "water" is used to make up scientific compound words, however, we use the Greek *hydro-* (in words like *hydrology* and *hydroponics*), or Latin *aqua-* (in words like *aquatic* and *aquarium*). If we were writing English like Japanese, the free-standing word *water* as well as *hydro-* and *aqua-* would be all written with the same character. We would then know that a word of a single character was to be read back as a native word (*water*), while the ones in compound words of technical vocabulary would receive a foreign pronunciation (*hydro-* or *aqua-*) depending on the topic of the word and the morphemes it was compounded with (*-ology* versus *-ium*).

The Chinese language left a permanent mark on Japanese, not only in its writing system and its vocabulary, but also in its phonology. Chinese words were adapted to fit Japanese syllables, but they also exerted their own pressure on Japanese syllables, creating what are known as heavy syllables, which contain either a long vowel or a final consonant: CVV (also noted CV:) or CVC. The types of closed (CVC) syllables in Japanese are still extremely restricted, but it is due to Chinese influence that they exist at all.

Meanwhile, as the Japanese intellectual class blossomed during the Nara period, writing in Chinese or even modified Chinese was found to be inadequate for certain purposes, even if texts could be translated into Japanese on the fly by an adequately nimble reader. Writers could express most of their ideas in Chinese, especially as they owed so much of their intellectual culture to the Chinese, but what about their poetry? Poetry, like names, is deeply rooted in sound, not just meaning. The form of poetry is untranslatable between languages as different as Chinese and Japanese. To write Japanese poetry, therefore, required a way of writing *Japanese*. The initial solution to this problem was to expand the rebus technique used to write Japanese names: Chinese characters were used for their syllabic values, not their meanings. A syllabic system of writing known as *man'yōgana* emerged in the eighth century, named after the *Man'yōshū* collection of poetry compiled around 759. Early written poetry, such as that found in the *Man'yōshū*, used a combination of characters used for their *kun* (native Japanese) readings and a syllabic use of characters for their sounds alone, the man'yōgana syllabary. Texts in this logosyllabic style faithfully represented the Japanese language, including all its particles and inflections.

The man'yōgana syllabary was large and inefficient. The syllabic value of a character could be derived from either its *on* reading or its *kun* reading. A number of different characters could be used for the same syllabic sound. Twelve different characters could spell *ka*, for example. This is a lot, but fewer than it could have been, considering the 31 kanji with that pronunciation. In the *Man'yōshū*, 480 characters were used for their syllabic *on* values, and a smaller number for their syllabic *kun* values, all for the roughly 90 different Japanese syllables of the time.

The man'yōgana of early Japanese poetry is remarkably like Akkadian cuneiform, despite the lack of any visual similarity or historical connection. Both used a bulky logosyllabary, with phonological values being supplied by two different, unrelated languages (Sumerian and Akkadian being as different as Chinese and Japanese). Like Akkadian cuneiform, the Japanese system was cumbersome but worked: Japanese had become a written language. Nevertheless, writing in Japanese did not enjoy high prestige. Man'yōgana was reserved for poetry and proper names; other eighth-century texts were in either proper Chinese or modified Chinese. Within the restricted field of poetry, however, the *Man'yōshū* had a tremendous literary influence, and its style, containing virtually no Chinese loanwords, became the model for native-style poetry. In the aesthetic context of poetry, native vocabulary was valued, in sharp contrast with the importance of Chinese in formal documents. Where people's hearts were involved, they wrote in Japanese.

The need to record the Japanese language accurately also arose in the cases of imperial rescripts and Shinto prayers, which were written in a style known as *senmyōgaki* (imperial rescripts are *senmyō* in Japanese). The Shinto prayers were of native Japanese origin and were supposed to be repeated accurately, word for word. Similarly, the emperor's words were taken down so as to be read back exactly, and of course the emperor spoke Japanese. In senmyōgaki, kanji were used with their *kun* readings, with the particles and inflection written in smaller man'yōgana characters. The result was the first truly Japanese prose.

The Nara period was succeeded by the Heian period, which lasted from 794 until 1192. During the first hundred years, Japanese literature languished, but the tools with which to create it were refined, and the two Japanese syllabaries still in modern use were born.

Japan's first native syllabary, hiragana, developed out of a cursive version of man'yōgana characters. (The shared element -*gana* of *hiragana* and *man'yōgana* is derived from *kana* and means "syllabary." In the formation of certain compound words the *k* becomes a *g* – a "hard" [g] sound – while in others it remains *k*.) The cursive man'yōgana characters were reduced to simple, rounded shapes of only a few strokes apiece. The result was hiragana, "smooth kana." Even an inexperienced eye can pick out the hiragana in a page of modern Japanese, as the signs are noticeably more curved – and usually simpler – than the accompanying kanji. The word *kanji*, for example, is written (in kanji) 漢字, while *kana* (in hiragana) is the much simpler かな. The circular element at the bottom of the *na* sign would never occur in (noncursive) kanji, where only slight curves are permitted.

According to tradition, hiragana was invented by the sainted Kōbō Daishi, founder of the Shingon sect of Buddhism. Probably the tradition is not entirely accurate, as hiragana seems not to have fully taken shape within Kōbō Daishi's lifetime, from 774 to 835. Little documentation of the development of hiragana remains, but it seems to have been an evolutionary process rather than the invention of an individual or of a moment. Different ways of simplifying man'yōgana characters were tried, and at first some of the man'yōgana syllabary's redundancy was inherited, with more than one sign for the same syllable. Eventually, a lean syllabary of 50 signs was achieved.

At nearly the same time, another form of kana was being created out of man'yōgana characters. Buddhist monks and their students, poring over Chinese texts, would annotate the texts, showing the pronunciation of unfamiliar kanji, or recording the particles and inflections needed to turn the sentences into Japanese. The spaces between characters were not large, however, and students were often under time pressure as they took notes during lectures. In response to these pressures, they began writing only *part* of the man'yōgana characters as a kind of abbreviation, giving birth to "partial kana" writing, or *katakana*. Abbreviated writing had been practiced before, both in Japan and in China, but the usefulness of this new kana, not just as shorthand but as a way of writing Japanese rather than Chinese, could not be overlooked. Like hiragana, katakana took a while to become standardized, with rival forms – varying in which part of the character got simplified, or which character got simplified – existing for some time.

Because katakana was abbreviated from standard (noncursive) characters, it retains the angular shape of noncursive kanji, but is much simplified. ひらがな is "hiragana" in hiragana, while the same word appears more angular in katakana as ヒラガナ. In some cases the hiragana and katakana signs were based on the same man'yōgana character. Sometimes this is obvious: hiragana か and katakana カ (both *ka*) are derived from the 加 character, meaning "to add," which was also pronounced *ka* in its *on* reading and was used as one of the many man'yōgana characters for that syllable. At other times the derivation from the same character is not obvious: hiragana め and katakana メ (*me*) are both derived from 女, pronounced *me* in its *kun* reading, meaning "female." In other cases, due to the redundancies available in the man'yōgana syllabary, equivalent characters in hiragana and katakana were taken from different characters: hiragana は *ha* (also used for the particle *wa*) is from 波 *ha*, meaning "wave," while the corresponding katakana sign, ハ, is taken from 八, meaning "eight" and pronounced *hachi*. Figure 7.1 shows the hiragana and katakana syllabaries.

Unlike Akkadian or Mycenaean Greek, Japanese is well suited to be written with a syllabary. At the time the kana were being developed, Japanese consisted of only light syllables: CV (or just V). In their stabilized and standardized forms, hiragana and katakana each comprised 50 signs. Of these, 45 are still used. A forty-sixth has since been added, and new uses of some signs have been developed, to account for changes in the Japanese language since the ninth century. Due to the influence of Chinese, modern Japanese syllables may contain a long vowel or could be closed in one of two ways. First, a syllable may be closed by a nasal sound. If the nasal is followed by a consonant, it will be pronounced in the same part of the mouth as that following consonant, as in familiar Japanese words like *tempura* (itself a loanword from Portuguese) and *Honda*. If the nasal is not followed by a consonant it is pronounced as a rather indeterminate nasal sound far back in the mouth. The other way of closing a syllable in Japanese is by doubling the consonant that begins the next syllable. In a word like *Hokkaido*, for example, the first *k* closes the first syllable. The mouth remains closed, prolonging the *k*, until it is time to pronounce the vowel of the second syllable.

The forty-sixth sign – hiragana ん and katakana ン – represents the adopted syllable-final nasal. A small version of the *tsu* syllable is used for the other kind of closed syllable: っ in hiragana, or ッ in katakana, indicates that the upcoming consonant is doubled. Another special application of kana symbols occurs for what the Japanese call "twisted" sounds and linguists call *palatalized*. Palatalized consonants sound

あ ア a	い イ i	う ウ u	え エ e	お オ o
か カ ka	き キ ki	く ク ku	け ケ ke	こ コ ko
さ サ sa	し シ shi (= [ʃi])	す ス su	せ セ se	そ ソ so
た タ ta	ち チ chi (= [tʃi])	っ ツ tsu	て テ te	と ト to
な ナ na	に ニ ni	ぬ ヌ nu	ね ネ ne	の ノ no
は ハ ha (wa)	ひ ヒ hi	ふ フ fu (= [ɸu])	へ ヘ he (e)	ほ ホ ho
ま マ ma	み ミ mi	む ム mu	め メ me	も モ mo
や ヤ ya (= [ja])		ゆ ユ yu (= [ju])		よ ヨ yo (= [jo])
ら ラ ra	り リ ri	る ル ru	れ レ re	ろ ロ ro
わ ワ wa				を ヲ (w)o
ん ン n (syllable-final nasal)				
が ガ ga	ぎ ギ gi	ぐ グ gu	げ ゲ ge	ご ゴ go
ざ ザ za	じ ジ ji (= [dʒi])	ず ズ zu	ぜ ゼ ze	ぞ ゾ zo
だ ダ da	ぢ ヂ ji (= [dʒi])	づ ヅ zu	で デ de	ど ド do
ば バ ba	び バ bi	ぶ ブ bu	べ ベ be	ぼ ボ bo
ぱ パ pa	ぴ ピ pi	ぷ プ pu	ぺ ペ pe	ぽ ポ po

Figure 7.1 The Japanese syllabaries, with hiragana on the left and katakana on the right. The Romanization follows the Hepburn style, with IPA interpretation where needed. The basic syllabaries are above the double line, secondary symbols with diacritics below. A smaller version of the *tsu* character is used for the first part of a double consonant.

almost as if they are followed by a *y* ([j] in the International Phonetic Alphabet), and so are transliterated *kya*, *kyu*, *kyo*, etc. In kana they are written with two symbols, the second one written smaller to emphasize that there is actually only one syllable. So the syllable *kya* is written as though it were *ki-ya*: き や. The representation of palatalized sounds did not begin until the middle of the Heian period, but it is not clear whether these syllables developed under the influence of Chinese, or were native but left out of the original kana in the interests of achieving a smaller, more easily memorized set of signs.

The 46 basic signs do not distinguish between syllables that begin with *g* versus *k*, *s* versus *z*, or *t* versus *d*. These pairs of sounds are distinguished by the phonological property of *voicing*: in [g] the vocal cords are vibrating, creating a person's voice, while in [k] the vocal cords do not vibrate, and the sound is effectively whispered. So, for example, *ka* and *ga* were originally both か in hiragana. Evidence from man'yōgana shows that Japanese of the Heian period did distinguish between voiced and voiceless sounds, but it is not unusual for a syllabary to ignore this difference in return for a smaller syllabary. Linear B did the same, and even English fails to mark one voicing distinction, spelling as *th* both the voiced [ð] of *either*, and the voiceless [θ] of *ether*.

In order to distinguish syllables with the voiced sounds *g*, *z*, *d*, and *b* from their voiceless counterparts, diacritical marks were added during the feudal period. So か is *ka* in hiragana and が is *ga*. Also added was a diacritical mark to distinguish syllables beginning with *p* from those beginning with *h*. At some point in the history of Japanese, [p] came to be pronounced as [h] (except before [u], where it is pronounced [ɸ], a sound similar to [f]). The result was that [b] came to be considered the voiced equivalent of [h]: は is hiragana *ha*, and ば is *ba*. A special diacritic is nowadays used to make *pa*: ぱ. The [p] sound is now limited to doubled consonants (it is the doubled version of *h*), consonants occurring after the nasal, onomatopoeic words, and foreign loanwords.

Hiragana and katakana both evolved in the ninth century from the same source, man'yōgana. However, they were developed, and continued to be used, in different environments. Katakana arose in the austere, masculine environment of Buddhist scholarship; its use in the Heian period was restricted to men. By the end of the Heian period, katakana had replaced the small man'yōgana characters for Japanese particles and inflections in the senmyōgaki style of writing, yielding a form of written Japanese that mixed kanji and katakana.

Meanwhile, hiragana came to be used at court by aristocratic women and their correspondents. Although they had not created it, women of the nobility adopted hiragana as their own. Studying kanji was not considered proper for women, but hiragana – perhaps because of its home-grown, informal associations – was fair game. In their hands, hiragana matured in the high cultural and aesthetic environment of the tenth-century Heian court. Aristocratic women studied calligraphy, composed and memorized poems, and wrote diaries. Women used their diaries to write colorful narrative memoirs in hiragana, while men recorded in theirs the day's events in a more formal modified Chinese style. Women's diaries became an established literary genre, to the extent that one man, Ki no Tsurayuki, had to circulate his hiragana diary in 935 under a female pseudonym. Part of Sei Shōnagon's *Pillow Book* of around 1001, one of the two most famous works of the period, is in diary style, though it also contains poems, opinion essays, and lists.

Noblewomen were highly protected creatures, hidden from view behind screens and curtains. From there they had the leisure to observe and reflect on the characters and behavior of the people around them, and to incorporate their insights into their writing, giving Japanese fiction a new level of depth and maturity. Murasaki Shikibu's *Tale of Genji*, written in the first decade or two of the eleventh century, is considered by many to be the world's first true novel, as contrasted with earlier epics and tales with more two-dimensional characters.

Genji is not only a remarkable literary accomplishment; it is also a valuable first-hand account of the role of writing among the Heian nobility. Women could not be looked upon, but they could be corresponded with; and their beauty of soul and character was supposedly expressed in their handwriting. Great importance was laid on the kind of paper used, the elegance of the (hiragana) handwriting, and the allusive and literary beauty of the poems that were exchanged between correspondents. Despite the protective measures surrounding women, romantic affairs were frequent (though probably, then as now, more frequent in fiction than in real life) and were relatively well tolerated, provided the woman was single and the man's rank did not disgrace her. Writing was crucial to the romance: by custom the successful consummation of an affair required a "morning after" letter from the man.

The literary style of *Genji* and other works of the late tenth and early eleventh centuries, mostly by women, marked a high point in

Japanese literature. The style was almost pure Japanese, with very few Chinese loanwords. The deliberate cultivation of a high aesthetic in court circles was expressed in literature by the development of an elegant, evocative native style. The fact that the vocabulary was native – in the mother tongue, rather than the stilted, intellectual borrowed Chinese vocabulary – meant that both the hiragana prose and poetry of the period had an emotional resonance that other styles did not.

Paradoxically, this success at writing the mother tongue spelled the end of writing in a spoken style. Written down – fossilized – the graceful eleventh-century style was imitated in the writing of pure Japanese for centuries thereafter, with the result that the written and spoken languages soon diverged.

Although Japanese writing had come of age, having attained its own formalized, classical style, it was still not considered fit for official purposes. Official documents were still written in Chinese, and many male poets composed poetry in Chinese. Unofficially, however, the two separate written traditions – native Japanese in kana and formal Chinese in kanji – gradually began to merge. The beginnings of the modern compromise began to be reached as, starting in the twelfth century, literary styles appeared that were in Japanese but made free use of Chinese loanwords and were written in a mixture of kanji and kana, most often katakana.

In the succeeding feudal period (1192 to 1602), the first inklings of compromise touched officialdom. The influence of the imperial court and the old aristocracy was greatly diminished, and real power was in the hand of the shogun and of feudal lords. They were served by the samurai, men of the warrior class, who became the new bureaucrats. Without the education of their predecessors at the imperial court, the samurai gave up on proper Chinese and used modified Chinese in official documents.

The shogunate of Tokugawa Ieyasu ushered in a period of peace and prosperity known as the Edo period (1603 to 1867). Literacy spread from the highest-placed samurai throughout the warrior class. Schools were also established for children of commoners, and literacy in kana, with some kanji, began to spread. Printing techniques improved, and the publishing business prospered.

During the Edo period Japan was closed to outside influence, with small and carefully monitored exceptions made for Chinese, Korean, and Dutch traders. With the dawn of the succeeding Meiji era (1868 to

1911), Japan took stock of its position as compared to the West and decided it was time to modernize. Education was reformed and made compulsory. Written language, it was decreed, should more closely resemble the spoken language. Official documents were now to be written in Japanese syntax, with katakana mixed in with the kanji to provide particles and inflections. After more than a millennium's dominance, writing in Chinese or modified Chinese finally lost its special status. The syntax of written Japanese, however, was still heavily influenced by the Classical Japanese of the Heian period until the twentieth century.

Japanese written style was far from homogeneous, however. Words could be written in kanji, in hiragana, or in katakana, or in some mixture of the three, the proportions in the mixture being open to variation. A small minority of zealous reformers even advocated replacing both kanji and kana with the Roman alphabet.

The present orthographic conventions in Japan are based on policies implemented after World War II. Modern Japanese writing finds a place for kanji, hiragana, and katakana, with the result that Japanese texts are written in three different scripts. Most nouns, verbs, and adjectives, plus some adverbs, are written in kanji. There are 1,945 characters on the government's list of "common kanji," with 284 more to be used in personal names and place names. The most frequently used 2,000 kanji account for 99 percent of the kanji in most texts. However, since specialized fields have their own specialized vocabulary, a total of 4,000 or 5,000 kanji are in active use in Japan today.

The 1,945 common kanji have, between them, 4,087 readings, a little over two readings per character, on average. Most have at least one Sino-Japanese (*on*) reading and at least one native (*kun*) reading. There may be more than one *on* reading, and there may also be more than one *kun* reading, as synonyms or near synonyms in the native vocabulary may be written with the same kanji. A fair number have only *on* readings. A few kanji have been created in Japan and therefore lack *on* readings (though one of them has actually acquired a pseudo-*on* reading). A few also lack *on* readings in the officially recommended list of kanji, due to the government's efforts to rein in the explosion of kanji readings, but they have had *on* readings in the past.

Given the multiplicity of readings, it can be difficult to know how to read kanji, especially where proper names are involved (the same can be said of English, actually, where a family named *Cholmondeley* may live at *Greenwich*, on the *Thames*). Words consisting of a single kanji are usually read in their *kun* readings. Compounds are usually, but not always, given *on* readings, and the particular *on* reading will depend on the meaning of the compound. Some compounds are to be read as *kun*, though, and a few are mixed between *on* and *kun*.

Native Japanese words that are not assigned to a kanji are normally written in hiragana. This includes auxiliary verbs, many adverbs, and any other words whose kanji have become obsolete. Hiragana is also used for the particles that follow nouns, and for inflectional suffixes of nouns, verbs, and adjectives. Questions as to which *kun* reading of a character is intended are often resolved by the inflectional material in hiragana that follows, which may repeat part of the word stem as a kind of phonetic complement. For example, if the kanji 捕, meaning "to catch, grasp," is followed by hiragana らえる, *raeru*, then it is read *toraeru*. If it is followed by まえる, *maeru*, then it is read *tsukamaeru*, another *kun* reading with the same basic meaning. Hiragana is also used to spell out the *kun* readings of kanji when needed.

Katakana, on the other hand, serves a function in modern written Japanese much like that of italics in English. Like italics, it conveys emphasis. It also expresses that a particular word is not an everyday word of Japanese. An increasing number of words from European languages, and especially English, are flooding into Japanese. These modern loanwords appear in texts in katakana, as do foreign words and names transliterated into Japanese. Certain specialized names of plants, animals, and chemicals are written in katakana, especially in scientific writing. Some female given names lack a kanji version and are written in katakana. Another class of words written in katakana includes onomatopoeia and similar, often reduplicated words with evocative sounds (analogous to words like "eensy-weensy" or "pitter-pat" in English). Katakana is also used for specialized children's vocabulary, exclamations, colloquialisms, and slang. Telegrams are written and sent in katakana. *On* readings of kanji are transliterated into katakana to distinguish them from *kun* readings, transliterated into hiragana.

The Japanese mixture of three scripts is a complicated writing system that takes years to master and discourages many a foreigner from even attempting to learn the language. Japanese readers are nowadays also exposed to increasing amounts of Romanized text, especially in advertising, raising the number of scripts used in some contexts to four. Yet anything written in Japanese could theoretically be written in either of the two kana scripts: why not just keep hiragana, say, and dispense with the rest? Hiragana is easily learned, and the Japanese language, with its simple syllable structure, is well suited to a syllabary. As compared to an alphabet, a syllabary is easy to learn to read. The process of sounding out words actually produces words: the pronunciation of the sequence of signs is the pronunciation of the word itself. Compare ひらがな "hiragana," which can be read off as *hi-ra-ga-na*, with a very simple alphabetic word like English *bet*. The word *bet* is not pronounced as the sequence of its letters, *bee-ee-tee* (phonetically [biː iː tiː]), nor of the sounds we tell children they stand for: [bə ɛ tə]. The consonant sounds that *b* and *t* represent are not pronounceable except when combined with vowel sounds. Sounding out words, therefore, involves far more than just learning the alphabet. By contrast, in a syllabary consonants and vowels come in precombined pronounceable packages. There are more symbols to memorize, but once they are learned, reading is easy. Indeed, most Japanese children learn hiragana before starting formal schooling. The educational system assumes children entering the first grade know hiragana, and concentrates on teaching katakana (first three grades) and kanji (the object of at least nine years of study).

Though kana is easy, kanji are objectively difficult to learn – the more so because the phonetic complements embedded in kanji characters, vague enough in Chinese, have no bearing at all on their Japanese *kun* readings. Kanji that are seldom used are easily forgotten (though, to be fair, so are spellings in English). Despite its complexities, the kanji–kana mixed writing system is retained. And it works. Japan manages an impressive literacy rate: virtually all students emerge from the nine years of compulsory education with at least functional literacy of a level that enables them to hold productive jobs in their modern industrial society. Most people do better: a well-educated reader knows about 3,000 kanji, 1,000 more than the official list. A large number of classroom hours are devoted to studying written Japanese, yet Japan also does well at educating its students in math and science.

An important reason for the retention of such a complex writing system is the fact that the needs of the *user* and the needs of the *learner* of a technology are often quite different. A hiragana-only writing system would be simple to learn, and it would do its job adequately (especially if word spacing were added), but kanji would be sorely missed by experienced readers, and not only for sentimental reasons.

127

1) 夫婦ゲンカは、犬も食わぬ。　　　　(mixed kanji–hiragana–katakana)
2) ふうふげんかは、いぬもくわぬ。　　(hiragana only)
3) フウフゲンカハ、イヌモクワヌ。　　(katakana only)
4) Fūfu genka wa, inu mo kuwanu.　　(Romanization – rōmaji)
5) couple quarrel (topic) dog even eat not.　(word-for-word translation)
6) Even a dog doesn't eat a couple's *quarrels*.　(English translation)
7) A dog, who will eat just about anything,　(interpretation)
   will not eat a couple's quarrels – so you
   shouldn't get involved either.

Figure 7.2 A Japanese proverb written in (1) a mixture of kanji, katakana, and hiragana, (2) hiragana only, (3) katakana only. Also given are the Romanization (known as rōmaji in Japanese), a word-for-word translation, English translation, and interpretation. To a Japanese reader, the kanji words for "couple," "dog," and "eat" stand out as content words. The use of katakana for the word for "quarrel" indicates emphasis; in kanji it would be 喧嘩. The grammatical words and particles (topic marker, "even," and negative particle) are in hiragana. Thus the first version provides more linguistic clues than the second or third (kana-only) versions.

A text in mixed kanji–kana conveys a considerable amount of information that would be lost in a purely phonological script like hiragana. At a glance, the content words – which convey what the text is actually about – are distinguished from the grammatical words and suffixes, the former written in kanji and the latter in hiragana (see figure 7.2). The contrast between content words and grammatical words like *the*, *in*, *at*, *with*, and *it* is one that is nowhere marked in English orthography, but it is nevertheless a linguistically real distinction. By visually marking it, Japanese orthography gives clues to the syntactic function of its individual words. Skimming a text is made much easier, as the important words stand out from the grammatical window dressing.

Users of kanji also value the ability of the logograms to distinguish between homophones, of which Japanese has a large number, especially in its formal, Sino-Japanese vocabulary. If written in hiragana, the words 四 "four," 市 "city," 紙 "paper," 矢 "arrow," plus 43 other Sino-Japanese words would all be rendered simply as し, *shi*. Understandably, writers resist such "simplification," realizing that written language, divorced as it is from the interactive context of speech, must work harder to avoid ambiguity. In kanji, even if it isn't obvious whether the *on* or *kun* reading is intended, the basic meaning will be clear. The Japanese writing system puts more emphasis on conveying the *meaning* of a word than on conveying its *pronunciation*.

The use of katakana rather than hiragana also conveys useful linguistic information. In most uses, katakana signals that there is something unusual about the word recorded – it draws attention to it as a collection of sounds, outside the usual category of Japanese words. This is especially helpful in the case of loanwords. The restricted number of syllables in Japanese means that foreign words must be adjusted to fit a native shape. Because the writing is syllabic, this adjustment happens both in speech and in writing. The resulting words, if written in hiragana, would not signal their foreignness in the way that foreign words often do in alphabetic spellings. To take an example from English, *Przewalski's horses* were clearly not named after an Englishman. English words do not contain *prz*-sequences, though the letters *p*, *r*, and *z* are all part of the writing system. In a syllabary, however, the syllabic adjustments to a foreign word make it look normal (although very strange to the foreigner: *strawberry*, for example, comes out *sutoroberi*). So it is the use of katakana that signals that the word is foreign.

The linguistic richness of the Japanese writing system exacted a price, however: Japan missed out on the typewriter age. The first successfully marketed American typewriter appeared in the 1870s. By contrast, the first Japanese kanji–kana typewriters came out only in 1915. These were monstrous things – expensive, slow, with huge trays full of symbols, and requiring specially trained operators. Few businesses could afford one; most subcontracted out their typing. The vast majority of office documents were handwritten.

The first katakana typewriter appeared in 1923, prior to the postwar script reforms that favored hiragana over katakana. It never became popular: by 1958 only about 10,000 katakana typewriters were in use in the entire country. They were fast, portable, and efficient, but people complained that they could not easily read the text. For one thing, the writing was horizontal, as compared to the traditional top-to-bottom orientation. For another, people found the spelling of homophones confusing, as also the inefficient, oddly spaced-out nature of the text, as it unrolled its message slowly, syllable by syllable. Typists had to remember to include spaces between words to avoid serious ambiguities (word spacing is not normally used in Japanese, as the switch from kanji to kana signals that one is reaching the end of a word).

Nevertheless, some companies adopted katakana typewriters for their billing departments. In this restricted context they were adequate and efficient.

A hiragana typewriter was brought out in 1962, but it also failed to become popular. By this time, however, it was clear that Japan was falling behind the West in the area of office automation, in contrast with its impressive levels of industrial productivity. Fax machines and photocopiers were adopted enthusiastically, but could help only so much, as the originals of most office documents still had to be handwritten. Typing was reserved for a final, clean copy of documents when it was worth the expense. Proponents of Romanization and of kana-only writing had a strong argument: Japan should abandon kanji in order to keep its place as a modern, industrial nation. This would mean turning its back on its own history and entirely revamping its educational infrastructure, but wasn't it worth it, for the sake of progress?

As it turned out, Japan's history was saved by its technology. The prospects for kanji began to brighten in 1978, when Toshiba unveiled a word processor that could handle both kanji and kana. The user would type in kana and at the press of a button the word processor would convert appropriate stretches into kanji, giving the user choices in cases of homophones. (I have used the same basic system to type the Japanese in this chapter: I type on the Roman keyboard, which appears on screen in hiragana, which will convert to kanji if I press "enter.")

The first word processor or *waa puro* as it became known in Japan (short for *waado purosessaa*), weighed 220 kilograms and cost 6.3 million yen (at the time, roughly $37,000 in American dollars). Not surprisingly, it was marketed to businesses and not to private individuals. Other companies soon brought out their own word processors, however, and prices began to drop in the 1980s. The year 1987 saw the application of artificial intelligence to Japanese word processing, greatly increasing the accuracy and efficiency of the kana-to-kanji conversion function.

Some of the most enthusiastic adopters of word processing were office workers who felt they had bad handwriting. Since the time of *Genji* at least, Japanese conventional wisdom has held that one's handwriting is a window on one's character. This belief led to a self-consciousness from which many a messy writer was pleased to escape. On the other hand, private individuals who enthusiastically embraced word processing were sometimes criticized for giving their personal correspondence an impersonal look, hiding their souls. Tradition has a valid point: handwritten material, its symbols shaped by the writer's own body, carries along with its linguistic message a certain amount of personal information that is absent from a typed text, just as a spoken message in turn carries more information about the speaker (in its intonation, volume, and timbre of voice) than a written one does.

Not only has word processing allowed Japan to become competitive in the area of office automation, it has given Japan access to the Internet. Because of the late arrival of word-processing programs, Internet use was slow to catch on. But the nation has made up for lost time: Japanese is now the third most commonly used language on the Internet.

Besides the economic advantages of word processing, the technology has bolstered the private use of kanji. It is now easier for writers to use kanji that they may have partly forgotten (an effect similar to that of spell-checkers in English). Whereas a writer would once have resorted to hiragana in the face of a word whose kanji was forgotten or never mastered, with the *waa puro* a writer need only *recognize* characters, not create them perfectly from memory. The internal dictionary of the average word processor contains all 6,355 characters of Levels 1 and 2 of the Japan Industrial Standards, making available thousands more than the 1,945 of the government's list of common kanji. A trend since the nineteenth century of using fewer and fewer kanji (and more kana) has been halted and may even be reversing. The chances of kana replacing kanji anytime in the near future are therefore slim and getting slimmer.

The Japanese word processor was created independently of Western models. The technology behind it spread to China, Taiwan, and South Korea, strengthening the hold of characters over each country in turn. The tradition of Chinese characters thus continues to bind the region together culturally. Where the characters are the same (and they are not always, as Japan and South Korea do not use the full range of characters, the People's Republic of China has simplified some 2,000 of its characters, and Japan has independently simplified a few hundred), a reader of one of these languages can make some sense out of a text written in another, although certain meaning differences do exist between one country's use of a character and another's. Written phonologically, however (either alphabetically or syllabically), a text in one language is entirely meaningless to speakers of the other languages.

Japan is not about to abandon kanji, the logograms its most revered author, Murasaki Shikibu, was not supposed to know – though she did. Yet the elegant hiragana syllabary in which Lady Murasaki wrote *Genji* is also alive and well, though relegated to a supporting role. The competing syllabary, katakana, has its place too. A complex but effective compromise has been reached in the Land of the Rising Sun.

8

Cherokee: Sequoyah Reverse-Engineers

No doubt about it, Sequoyah was a genius. This visionary Cherokee, whose English name was George Gist (sometimes spelled *Guess*), was an able silversmith, an artist, and a veteran of the Creek War of 1813–14. More importantly, he was the first person known to history to have achieved literacy by single-handedly inventing a writing system. Unable to read or write, he nevertheless brought literacy to his people.

All writing is an invention, but the inventors of the world's ancient writing systems are lost to history. Cuneiform, whose early history is best preserved, took centuries – and the input of numerous individuals – to develop from a book-keeping system to a complete orthography for the Sumerian and Akkadian languages. Over the succeeding millennia other individuals created new scripts or altered old ones to fit new languages; but these innovators were already literate and understood how writing worked. Sequoyah, on the other hand, was a monolingual Cherokee speaker who never learned to read the Roman alphabet. A few individuals have since replicated his achievement, as King Njoya did in Cameroon and Shong Lue Yang did for the Hmong language of Southeast Asia. Compared to the original inventors of writing, these modern script creators have had the advantage of knowing that writing exists and that language – at least *some* languages – can be represented by written signs. Nevertheless, the intellectual achievement of these men is staggering, the more so when we manage to stop taking our own literacy for granted and imagine ourselves in their shoes – setting aside all knowledge of what the marks on a page mean and in what way they are related to speech.

Few details of Sequoyah's life are known with certainty. He was born sometime around 1770 in the former Cherokee village of Tuskegee on the Little Tennessee River, just upstream from the Tennessee River in

Tennessee (see appendix, figure A.5). The village site is now under the waters of the Tellico Reservoir, though a museum has been erected nearby in his honor. Sequoyah was born into the Cherokee tribe, which numbered about 12,000 at the time, far fewer than a few generations earlier, when smallpox arrived. The tribe held lands in southern Appalachia and surrounding areas, lands that now constitute parts of Virginia, Kentucky, North Carolina, South Carolina, Tennessee, Georgia, and Alabama. These holdings were rapidly shrinking with the relentless encroachment of white settlers onto traditionally Cherokee territory. Sequoyah's own father was white, but left when Sequoyah was an infant, leaving the child to be raised by his mother. Cherokees reckoned their clan affiliations though the mother's line, and so Sequoyah was never considered anything but Cherokee. He grew up speaking only his tribal language.

Sequoyah lived during a critical time for the Cherokee people. Land-hungry whites were pressing in upon them, unwilling to recognize the territorial claims of a people who marked no borders, held no deeds to their land, and sowed crops in only a small fraction of their soil. The Cherokees resisted, in some cases by taking on those aspects of white culture that whites scorned them for not having. They organized into a formal nation with a representative constitutional government. The Nation's lands extended from the Tennessee River southward in Alabama and Georgia, and from the river eastward in Tennessee and into North Carolina. Some took up plantation agriculture and had their children educated in English at mission schools.

Increasingly, the federal and state governments pressured the Cherokees to move west, to sell their homeland in exchange for lands in Arkansas and in Oklahoma, designated Indian Territory. The state of Georgia, in particular, wanted its share of Cherokee lands, which the federal government had promised in 1802 to buy for it as soon as it peaceably could. Georgia became especially insistent after the discovery of gold on tribal lands in 1829. The Nation spent much of the 1830s staving off deportation, which finally came in the form of the Trail of Tears, during which many Cherokees died on the way to Indian Territory over the winter of 1838 to 1839.

Sequoyah was not subjected to the Trail of Tears, having already moved to Arkansas in 1818 with other Cherokees who emigrated westward at the urging of the federal government. Although Sequoyah apparently liked his new home in Arkansas, he was deeply opposed to the white government's treatment of his people. While pondering the power of the ever-advancing whites he made an astute observation: there was a close relationship between the power of whites and the marks they made on paper, which let them communicate, like magic, across long distances. He was right, of course. Writing is indeed a powerful tool – or weapon.

At the time, literacy had reached unprecedented rates among Europeans, becoming part of their cultural self-image. Europeans, in their own eyes, were literate and civilized, unlike the illiterate red savages of the New World (Maya literacy was conveniently forgotten by now). This intellectual accomplishment helped justify the Europeans' belief that they were superior to the Native Americans. Sequoyah acknowledged the power of the technology but set out to disprove the doctrine of superiority.

According to later accounts, Sequoyah began thinking seriously about writing in about 1809, claiming to his friends that the white man's skill in making and reading marks could not be so very hard to duplicate. He was roundly ridiculed for his presumptuous claims. How could an Indian language be written down? No one had ever seen it done. How indeed? This question was to occupy him on and off for years. He never knew it, but these same years saw Champollion laboring on the decipherment of Egyptian hieroglyphs across the Atlantic in France. Both men were engaged in a quest to reverse-engineer the technology of writing. Both puzzles were long and difficult ones, but Sequoyah was to solve his a year before Champollion, in 1821.

Details of how Sequoyah went about it vary in later accounts – there was certainly no one there to make written records of it at the time. He himself never wrote the story down, perhaps out of modesty, or perhaps because it never occurred to him. He was interested in a technology that would help him keep business accounts and communicate with people in distant places. In his culture, events and exploits were recounted in the oral tradition, and so the use of writing to create history seems not to have occurred to him, just as it failed to occur to the Mycenaean Greeks before him.

When Sequoyah first began experimenting with symbols to represent language, he scratched them with a nail on a whetstone or on wooden shingles. Later he bought a pen and paper. Making marks was not hard. What was very hard was deciding what the marks should symbolize. Some say he started with symbols for entire sentences – units of information that a person might want to convey. "I arrived safely" would be a single symbol, for example. The symbols multiplied rapidly, and Sequoyah abandoned this approach as impossibly cumbersome. How about a symbol for each word? Most accounts relate that he worked for some time at inventing symbols for words. His inventory of logograms mounted up. And up. After a while he had a few thousand, and could no longer remember what the earlier ones stood for. It was time to try a new approach.

I suspect that the reason Sequoyah – with most other modern script inventors – abandoned logographic writing so quickly was that it was obvious to him from the outset that his system would have to apply to his entire language. The ancient Sumerian book-keepers and the ancient Maya calendar-keepers probably did not realize when they first assigned symbols to commodities and to days and months that in time every word of their language would have to be writable. In order to get to that point, all logographic systems – even the Chinese – had to call on some sort of phonological representation. Sequoyah also realized that phonological representation was necessary, but unlike the ancients, he had no existing logographic tradition to honor.

Sequoyah had built himself a cabin for his literary labors and would sequester himself there, to the neglect of his family and all other work. His preoccupations, typical of genius, must have made him infuriating to live with. His wife is said to have burned his cabin – or at least his work – in frustration, hoping to get him back to more productive labors. Sequoyah was discouraged but soon returned to his quest, and this time the solution began to take shape (plate 6).

Words, he realized, were made of smaller pieces. They were made up of sounds, which could recur in many different words. The number of *sounds* was much smaller than the number of *words*. It was the *sounds* he should represent.

Sequoyah set about trying to determine how many sounds there were in his language. For an illiterate person with no background in linguistics, this is a difficult task. What, after all, is a distinct sound? Does the word *Sequoyah* have three sounds – *se-quo-yah* – or six – [s ɪ kʷ o y ɑ]? There was no one to explain to him about phonemes and syllables. He had to work it out for himself, pronouncing words slowly and carefully, over and over, trying to isolate the recurring pieces. He must have sounded like a madman. Small wonder his friends and family looked askance at his project.

He came up with about 200 phonological pieces. Still too many, he considered. What he wanted was a system that people could easily memorize. He set about trying to streamline the system. Were there sounds that were so much alike that they could share a symbol? What kinds of symbols were easy to write? He whittled away at the system and eventually arrived at a set of 86 – later reduced to 85 – signs, some of whose final shapes (but not sounds) he took from a sample of English text which he inspected closely but could not read. His young daughter, Ahyokeh, was the first convert to his cause, helping him in the final streamlining and testing of his new system.

The system Sequoyah ended up with was a CV syllabary. A syllabary does not match the Cherokee language as well as it does Japanese, but it is a much better fit than it would be for English – and far better than Linear B was for Greek. Most Cherokee words end in vowels, but there are some word-internal sequences of consonants, and the language has more distinct consonant sounds than the syllabary indicates. Cherokee makes considerable use of aspiration, but the syllabary distinguishes between aspirated and unaspirated consonants in only a few cases (this may be, in part, because the pronunciation of aspiration differs between slow, careful speech and more rapid speech, and Sequoyah may not have considered it a consistent enough effect to pin down in writing). The syllabary also ignores long vowels, the glottal stop ([ʔ], as in the unspelled first sound of *uh-oh*), and the distinctive pitch that may distinguish one word from another. Sequoyah knew that his syllabary did not spell Cherokee words exactly as they sounded, but for a speaker of Cherokee who knew how the words should sound there was no serious problem, just as writing without vowels was no obstacle to native speakers of ancient Egyptian. More important, Sequoyah felt, was a system that could be easily memorized.

A CV syllabary (including word-initial V symbols) encodes the smallest consistently pronounceable units of a language, since many consonants (the ones known as *plosives*) cannot be pronounced without an accompanying vowel. As Sequoyah spoke the words of his language aloud to himself, CV chunks would have been the smallest pieces he would consistently have observed, and so his system encoded those CV chunks. Nevertheless, Sequoyah employed one brilliant exception to the syllabic structure of his script, one that would have stood the ancient Mycenaeans in good stead. He included one phonemic (non-syllabic) symbol, for the hissing sound [s]. The [s] sound is one that is used by many languages, including English, Greek, and Cherokee, at the edges of syllables to make other, longer syllables. In English, for example, we can add [s] to either side of *park* to get *parks*, *spark*, or *sparks*. Thus the [s] can be either a prologue or epilogue to a normal syllable. It is not a plosive, so you can say [s] and go on saying it, with no need for a vowel. In sounding out his words Sequoyah must have noticed the special qualities of [s] and tarried thoughtfully over its hissing sound. He assigned this sound a symbol of its own, Ꮝ making it the only consonant phoneme in Cherokee to have its own symbol. He must have lingered over its sound in his own name, as he always wrote ᏍᏏᏉᏯ, *s-si-quo-ya*, with an extra initial *s*.

The use of the Ꮝ symbol goes a long way toward making the Cherokee syllabary fit Cherokee syllables. When syllables are closed by consonants other than [s], a dummy vowel is used, as in Maya. The selection of the vowel varies: if a related word includes a vowel in that position, that vowel will be used, but otherwise the selection is up for grabs. Unlike English, Cherokee has never been subjected to authoritative spelling rules.

Satisfied that his system worked, Sequoyah taught some relatives and neighbors in Arkansas the new system. He then traveled back to the Cherokee Nation, bearing letters from Arkansas Cherokees to their friends and family back east. He gave a public demonstration of his syllabary before the tribal council in 1821, assisted by little Ahyokeh. His initial reception was deeply skeptical. How were his listeners to know he wasn't merely remembering his own words? As a test, Sequoyah and Ahyokeh were placed out of earshot of each other and instructed to take dictation. Much to the surprise of everyone present except Sequoyah and Ahyokeh, when the messages were exchanged father and daughter could read each other's writing back word for word. Was there some sort of witchcraft at work? Or was the accomplishment natural and replicable? For answer, Sequoyah taught the syllabary to a number of young lads, and they could soon replicate Ahyokeh's feat with no signs of occult disturbances.

After that, interest in the new technology took off. Previously illiterate Cherokees found that they could learn to read and write in a matter of days. In fact, the Cherokees with the least schooling in English often proved the most adept at the new system. The syllabic nature of the system and the consistency of its spelling meant that it was much easier to learn to read Cherokee than English. Sequoyah stayed east to teach his script, then returned to Arkansas, again carrying letters.

The letters were crucial to the acceptance of Sequoyah's syllabary. He had done his work at the most strategic historical moment: Cherokee families and clans were for the first time divided, with substantial numbers of tribe members now living out west. Miraculously, they were now able to stay in touch and communicate directly with their distant friends. In this context, the new literacy spread like wildfire. Formal surveys were not conducted, but some estimated that by the late 1820s a majority of Cherokees could read and write the syllabary.

When the white missionary Samuel A. Worcester arrived in the Cherokee Nation in 1825, charged with the task of learning Cherokee and translating the Bible, he found Sequoyah's syllabary waiting for him. He also found an able tutor and collaborator in Elias Boudinot, a Cherokee Christian convert well educated in English and in Christian theology. Together they struggled to translate Christian concepts into a language that had never before expressed them. Worcester learned the syllabary and sent off to Boston to have type cast for it. They set up a printing press, and in 1828 Boudinot became the first editor of the *Cherokee Phoenix*, the first Native American newspaper ever, with columns in both English and Cherokee. The press was later used for Worcester and Boudinot's Cherokee New Testament and Cherokee hymnal, two works that remain critical to Cherokee literacy today.

Samuel Worcester was unusual among white Americans of his day in his respect for the Cherokee people to whom he had been sent. Rather than assume he could improve on a natively developed script, he adopted it enthusiastically, adding only the alphabetical order that it uses today (figure 8.1). He firmly opposed deportation of the Cherokees, winning for himself over a year's jail time for his civil disobedience on their behalf. His adoption of Sequoyah's syllabary made the Christian message more attractive to the Cherokees. Many of them converted, though never Sequoyah.

After the Trail of Tears, only a remnant of the Cherokee people remained in the east. A few hundred lived on lands in North Carolina outside the Cherokee Nation's boundaries and had been exempt from the removal orders. There were also Cherokees who had managed to hide out in the mountains and avoid deportation. These two groups were the ancestors of today's Eastern Band of Cherokees, based in the Great Smoky Mountain region of southwestern North Carolina.

Ꭰ a	Ꭱ e	Ꭲ i	Ꭳ o	Ꭴ u	Ꭵ v (v = [ə̃])
Ꭶ Ꭷ ga ka (g = [k], k = $[k^h]$)	Ꭸ ge	Ꭹ gi	Ꭺ go	Ꭻ gu	Ꭼ gv
Ꭽ ha	Ꭾ he	Ꭿ hi	Ꮀ ho	Ꮁ hu	Ꮂ hv
Ꮃ la	Ꮄ le	Ꮅ li	Ꮆ lo	Ꮇ lu	Ꮈ lv
Ꮉ ma	Ꮊ me	Ꮋ mi	Ꮌ mo	Ꮍ mu	
Ꮎ Ꮏ Ꮐ na hna nah	Ꮑ ne	Ꮒ ni	Ꮓ no	Ꮔ nu	Ꮕ nv
Ꮖ qua (qu = $[k^w]$, $[k^{hw}]$)	Ꮗ que	Ꮘ qui	Ꮙ quo	Ꮚ quu	Ꮛ quv
Ꮝ Ꮜ s sa	Ꮞ se	Ꮟ si	Ꮠ so	Ꮡ su	Ꮢ sv
Ꮣ Ꮤ da ta (d = [t], t = $[t^h]$)	Ꮥ Ꮦ de te	Ꮧ Ꮨ di ti	Ꮩ do	Ꮪ du	Ꮫ dv
Ꮬ Ꮭ dla tla (dl = $[t^l]$)	Ꮮ tle (tl = $[t^{hl}]$)	Ꮯ tli	Ꮰ tlo	Ꮱ tlu	Ꮲ tlv
Ꮳ tsa	Ꮴ tse	Ꮵ tsi	Ꮶ tso	Ꮷ tsu	Ꮸ tsv
Ꮹ wa	Ꮺ we	Ꮻ wi	Ꮼ wo	Ꮽ wu	Ꮾ wv
Ꮿ ya	Ᏸ ye	Ᏹ yi	Ᏺ yo	Ᏻ yu	Ᏼ yv
ᏣᎳᎩ tsa-la-gi "Cherokee"	ᏍᏏᏉᏯ s-si-quo-ya "Sequoyah"				

Figure 8.1 The Cherokee syllabary, as invented by Sequoyah and arranged by Samuel Worcester. Only in a few cases does the syllabary make a distinction between aspirated and unaspirated initial consonants (transliterated as voiceless and voiced consonants respectively). Where no distinction is made (i.e. there is only one symbol in the box) the symbol can be used for either an aspirated or unaspirated consonant. At the bottom of the chart are the Cherokee spellings for "Cherokee" and "Sequoyah." The name Sequoyah is often spelled as *s-si-qua-ya*, but he himself spelled it *s-si-quo-ya*, as witnessed by surviving examples of his signature.

Meanwhile, the Cherokee Nation reconstituted itself in the west, many of its administrative functions served by Sequoyah's syllabary. To its great misfortune, the Nation sided with the Confederacy during the Civil War, as the wealthier and more assimilated Cherokees had taken up slaveholding when they adopted plantation agriculture. The war left the Nation battered and impoverished, with few resources and little energy to support its distinctive literacy. Oklahoma statehood in 1907 entailed the end of autonomous government for the Cherokees.

During the late nineteenth and the twentieth centuries Cherokee literacy declined, with some renewal of interest beginning in the 1960s. The spoken language also lost ground in the face of English, especially in North Carolina, so that among the Eastern Band of Cherokee today, only about 10 percent speak Cherokee and a much smaller proportion are literate in the syllabary. Since the rise of the telephone, the script's wondrous effect of allowing communication at a distance has been less important. In the early twentieth century, government educational policies enforced monolingual education in English, and children were often punished for speaking Cherokee on school grounds. Only since the 1970s have Cherokee-speaking children in Oklahoma been allowed bilingual programs. In North Carolina, Cherokee children are now permitted to study Cherokee as a subject in school. The syllabary is taught, but (in the east, at least) transcriptions into Roman letters are used much more than the syllabary and students usually do not become comfortable using it.

Oddly enough, the Cherokee syllabary is now considered difficult to learn by Cherokee speakers, though in its early years it was famous for being easy. One reason for the difference is probably that most Cherokees nowadays first learn to read in English, which means that their expectations for how writing works become adjusted to an alphabet rather than a syllabary. English literacy probably also makes it difficult for them to reassign meaning to symbols that also occur in the Roman alphabet and to read **D** as *a*, **S** as *du*, and **A** as *go*, etc. The syllabary also uses distinctions that a user of the Roman alphabet would be trained not to notice: **R** is *e* but **Ꝛ** is *sv* (phonetically [sə̃], the tilde indicating a nasal vowel); **W** is *la* but **Ꮃ** is *ta*. Another factor is that learners who are not already fluent in Cherokee would be far more troubled than fluent speakers by the information omitted in Cherokee spelling, not being sure if a consonant is meant to be aspirated, and if a vowel is to be pronounced short or long, or even omitted. The syllabary therefore functions more readily as a writing system for first-language speakers than for second-language learners.

The mainstays of Cherokee literacy have been the Bible and traditional medicine. Reading the Bible in their own language has special meaning for the many Christian Cherokees, while formulas of traditional medicine are recorded by traditional practitioners in their own language and script. Sequoyah's syllabary remains closely linked with Cherokee identity; the single most widely recognized word is probably ᏣᎳᎩ, *tsa-la-gi* ("Cherokee"), which actually has its own keyboard key in the Cherokee font used in this chapter.

Sequoyah died in 1843 on a trip to Mexico, searching for a group of Cherokees who had supposedly settled there and whom he hoped to reunite with the Cherokee Nation. His grave is unmarked and unknown. Sequoyah himself remains a cultural icon among the Cherokees, and even white Americans idolized him during the nineteenth century. His name has been given to a county in Oklahoma, and also (spelled *Sequoia*) to a particularly large and long-lived subfamily of trees, a presidential yacht, and, more recently, a Toyota SUV.

9

The Semitic Alphabet: Egypt to Manchuria in 3,400 Years

The alphabet has been touted as one of humankind's greatest inventions – and not without cause. Equally, though, the alphabet is a monument to human stupidity and hidebound conservatism. Originally conceived as a dumbed-down version of writing for the illiterate, it was simple enough to spread easily from one language to the next; however, it was rarely adapted thoughtfully to the new language. Throughout its history, innovation has been astonishingly rare.

An alphabet is a writing system in which the individual symbols stand for phonemes (individual, distinct sounds) rather than whole syllables or morphemes. *The* alphabet refers to the first script whose letters stood for phonemes and whose letters began with something that sounded like *aleph* and *bet* (which became *alpha* and *beta* in Greek), and by extension to its vast family of descendants. The early alphabet wrote only consonant phonemes, however, and therefore some scholars reserve the term *alphabet* for scripts in which *all* phonemes are written (though they may not each have a unique symbol); for them *the* alphabet is the Greek script and its descendants, which record all their vowel phonemes. The distinction between a consonantal alphabet (also known as an *abjad*) and a fully voweled alphabet of the Greek type is perhaps overrated; even among the Greek family of scripts very few languages manage a perfect one-to-one correspondence between letters and phonemes.

David Sacks has compared the alphabet to the wheel: a simple, elegant invention that, once arrived at, cannot really be improved upon. Arguably, the *idea* of the alphabet fits this description, but the actual alphabet rarely has. In theory, each symbol in an alphabet stands for a single phoneme of the language, but this theoretical ideal is seldom achieved and if once achieved is often lost again. A language changes over time, and an alphabet that fits a language perfectly at one stage

143

in its history will not be such a perfect fit at another. And an alphabet that fits one particular language perfectly is unlikely to be perfect for another. This slippage has rarely prompted substantial adaptations to the alphabet, and the result is often far from elegant.

The conservatism is not without reason. For one thing, reading is a matter of habit. Fluent readers do not sound out words letter by letter; they employ a great deal of top-down processing, identifying whole words and phrases at a glance, and using context to tell them what words to expect next. It is a brilliant performance, really. With top-down processing readers can become quite fluent even in scripts that indicate the sounds of a word only vaguely. However, this expertise is only gained with practice; change the system and years of practice go down the drain.

It is not only reading fluency that is lost. Once a written tradition exists, there is strong motivation to continue writing the same way one's ancestors did. As long as the writing system remains, the information stored by previous generations is still readable. Change your writing system and you lose your history. No wonder innovation is rare.

Crucially, the early users of the alphabet had no particular interest in history, at least not the history that had so far been written, which wasn't theirs. They spoke a Semitic language, probably Canaanite, and though they lived in Egypt they were not particularly interested in Egyptian literature. It is this kind of lack of interest that allows for true innovation in the technology of writing: Sequoyah managed it, having no interest in English literature, but the Nara Japanese, who wanted to read the Chinese classics, did not.

The earliest samples of alphabetic writing yet found were discovered in the 1990s in a dry valley in Egypt named Wadi el-Hol ("Valley of Terror"), just north of the Valley of Queens and across the Nile from the pharaonic capital of Thebes (though at the time of the inscriptions the capital was at Memphis). Carved into the wadi's cliffs are two short alphabetic inscriptions dating from around 1900 to 1800 BC, during the Middle Kingdom, Egypt's literary golden age.

Wadi el-Hol was the site of an Egyptian army encampment along an ancient road. Some army units at the time were composed of Semitic-speaking mercenaries from the lands east of Egypt, relatives or ancestors of the people known to later history as Canaanites, Hebrews, Phoenicians, and Aramaeans. The Middle Kingdom also saw the growth of Semitic-speaking communities living in the Nile delta.

The Egyptians had long had a full set of signs that each stood for a single consonant, but they generally used them only as phonetic complements, resorting to consonant-by-consonant spelling only in rare words or foreign names. Tradition perpetuated a logoconsonantal writing system, but the Semitic mercenaries or delta dwellers who created the Semitic alphabet were not interested in maintaining Egyptian tradition. What interested them greatly was the Egyptian ability to store information, keep accounts, label their possessions, and permanently dedicate objects to the gods.

Some Semitic speakers must have acquired at least some literacy in Egyptian, and they must have grasped the advantage it would be if others of their community could also write. But it was too much to expect them all to learn Egyptian and the complex hieroglyphic writing system that few people knew well, even among native Egyptians. So they created their own bare-bones set of uniconsonantal signs, modeled after the Egyptian ones. This was the "For Dummies" version of writing, stripped of all complexity and redundancy, pared down to something an illiterate soldier could learn in a few sessions. It must have looked funny to the Egyptian scribes: to write any word at all required several signs – how inefficient! The letters did not have to be grouped into boxes, but could just straggle after each other in a line – how ugly! And there was nothing in the spelling of a word that pointed directly to the meaning of the word – no pictographic clue, no determinative – but the word had to be laboriously sounded out before it made any sense – how cumbersome! It was the world's first alphabet, made for people who lacked either the time or the motivation to learn the 500 or so signs that literacy in Egyptian required.

Some of the Egyptian uniconsonantal signs seem to have been designed on the acrophonic principle, by which the first sound in the name of the object depicted became the consonant for which the hieroglyph stood. Though the acrophonic idea may have been Egyptian, and many of the signs used were Egyptian, the names used in creating the alphabet were Semitic. For example, a rippled line, showing waves on water, was *n* in Egyptian, but *m* in this new Semitic alphabet, because the word for "water" in the relevant Semitic language began with *m*-, something like *mēm*. Today, nearly 4,000 years later, we still use a descendant of the ripply line for **M**. Similarly, an ox-head stood for the glottal stop that began the word for "ox," something like *ʔalp*; and a rough enclosure pictured a house, *bēt*. These were the ancestors of **A** and **B**, and the ultimate source of the word *alphabet*.

The letters which resulted from this acrophonic exercise were all consonants; words in the West Semitic languages did not begin with vowels. Like Egyptian, Semitic languages build their words around a core of consonants: writing the consonants recorded the nuclear morpheme of a word, as well as the consonants of any prefixes and suffixes, while the inflectional vowels could be judged by context.

Deducing the story of the early alphabet is very much an exercise in connecting the dots, as the evidence is meager and scattered. From Wadi el-Hol, the next evidence for the alphabet comes from the Sinai, where Semitic speakers were employed in Egyptian mines; and from there the next is in Middle-Bronze-Age Palestine, homeland of the Semitic Canaanites. These early stages of the script, known as proto-Canaanite, are known from only a handful of short inscriptions. Even the total number of letters is not firmly known, though there were probably 27 of them.

Working with the Sinai material, W. F. Albright claimed in 1966 to have deciphered the correct phonemic value of 23 of the letters, though skeptics remain for a number of these values. Only a dozen or so words can be read in the Sinai texts; they are short, and the thread that connects them to later, fully deciphered scripts is weak. Occasional proto-Canaanite inscriptions on stone, metal, and potsherds survive, but anything written on papyrus (probably the vast majority of texts) is long gone, destroyed by the elements.

By about 1400 BC, the pictographic nature of the letters had been largely lost, the letters now formed as simple lines. The transitional stages from proto-Canaanite to this linear Old Canaanite alphabet have not been found, but a roughly contemporary cul-de-sac in the alphabet's history has been. The city of Ugarit, whose ruins are now known as Ras Shamra on the coast of Syria, was a flourishing city-state between 1450 and 1200 BC. Ideally situated to facilitate trade between the Aegean, Anatolia, Mesopotamia, and Egypt, it developed a cosmopolitan civilization. Like most of their colleagues along the Fertile Crescent, Ugaritic scribes wrote Mesopotamian cuneiform on clay tablets. They themselves were speakers of a West Semitic language (closely related to the Canaanite group), and they learned of the simple script their relatives were using. Accustomed to writing in cuneiform, they assigned each of the 27 Canaanite letters a cuneiform sign. At some point they added three more letters to extend the system to write Hurrian, an important regional language of the time which allowed vowel-initial words and had a sibilant (s-like) consonant that didn't appear in Ugaritic.

Written on clay tablets, the Ugaritic texts have withstood the centuries and are the earliest texts of any appreciable length in a West Semitic language (East Semitic, by contrast, is well attested, comprising Akkadian and its Assyrian and Babylonian dialects). They are also the earliest evidence for alphabetical order: a number of tablets bear the signs of the Ugaritic alphabet listed in order – the same order known from later Semitic traditions, and the same order, essentially, as the one we use today.

Alphabetical order was almost as useful an invention as the alphabet itself. We have no certain idea of what inspired the order that we ended up with (other, rival orders existed in the Bronze Age), or whether it ever had any significance. Quite possibly, it was transmitted through a song or rhyme that helped the semi-literate Canaanites remember their letters (just as modern semi-literates, our children, sing the "alphabet song" today). The brevity of the alphabet – so jealously guarded, even for languages with much larger numbers of phonemes – served to keep alphabetical order memorable, while recitation of the fixed list helped discourage additions and changes.

It is remarkable how seldom alphabetical order has been tampered with, despite the fact that the order of the list has no intrinsic meaning. The Greek and Roman alphabets use essentially the same order attested in ancient Ugaritic, as did Phoenician, Old Hebrew, and Aramaic, and most of their descendants. Only a few cultures, such as the Arabs and the Mongols, have dared to reorder the alphabet.

Once firmly ordered, the alphabet could be used to number things. In much of the Near East the letters of the alphabet did double duty as numerals, at least until the introduction of a separate set of numerals from India (the ancestors of what we now call "Arabic" numerals after the people who later introduced them to the Europeans). Today the order of the alphabet serves a vital role, organizing the data of the Information Age. Anything that can be given a name can be put in an ordered, alphabetical list. The potential of alphabetically ordered databases of knowledge – encyclopedias, dictionaries, indexes, telephone books – was well beyond the imagination of the alphabet's inventors, however. Originally a mere mnemonic device, alphabetical order is one of the great serendipitous inventions of history.

The Ugaritic branch of the alphabetic family died out with the fall of Ugarit around 1200. Meanwhile, the Old Canaanite script was used in much of the area archaeologists call (with no political intent) Syria-Palestine, though only hints of its presence have been preserved. A branch following a different alphabetical order migrated southward, mutating significantly along the way, and became Old South Arabian, used for ancient South Semitic languages such as Sabaean, the language of the Queen of Sheba. That script later crossed the Bab el-Mandeb Strait into Africa, where it was used for Classical Ethiopic (Ge'ez or Giiz), the South Semitic written language of the Aksum Empire. At some point, roughly contemporary with the introduction of Christianity into Ethiopia around AD 350, the script was substantially modified to include vowels, written as appendages to consonants in a manner strongly reminiscent of the scripts of India (chapter 10). The new version, now written left to right, became the written vehicle for the distinctive Ethiopian Orthodox Christianity. In modern times the script is also used for the Semitic languages Amharic and Tigrinya in Ethiopia and Eritrea.

Back in Syria-Palestine, by 1050 some important changes had been made (though some would place them later – the dating is difficult due to the scarcity of evidence). The script now ran regularly from right to left, rather than whichever way best fit the inscribed surface. Similarly, the letters faced consistently in the same direction from one text to the next. The number of letters was pared down to 22, not coincidentally the number of consonants in the Canaanite language of those responsible for these changes – the Phoenicians.

The Phoenicians lived along the coast of Syria-Palestine, mostly in the region now known as Lebanon. These times were good for Syria-Palestine. The region had previously found itself on the borders between great empires – the Egyptians to the southwest, the Hittites to the north. But the Hittite Empire fell in 1180 BC, and Egypt's New Kingdom was considerably weakened soon thereafter, both due in part to widespread disturbance caused by the mysterious Sea Peoples (who may also have helped bring about the collapse of Mycenaean civilization). Assyria, at times a threat, was temporarily in a period of decline. In the resulting political vacuum, Phoenician city-states flourished along the coast; the Aramaeans, West Semitic neighbors of the Phoenicians, established a variety of city-states and small kingdoms in modern Syria; and the kingdom of Israel was founded in Palestine by the Hebrews.

Plate 1 Neo-Assyrian cuneiform tablet with observations of the planet Venus. Copied at Nineveh in the seventh century BC; the original observations were made about a thousand years earlier. Image copyright © British Museum/HIP/Art Resource, NY.

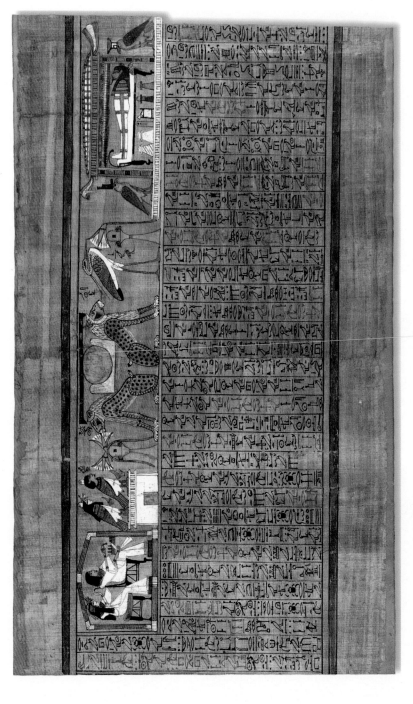

Plate 2 Papyrus with illustrations and cursive hieroglyphs from the Book of the Dead of Any. From Thebes, Egypt, and dating to the nineteenth dynasty, c.1250 BC. Image copyright © British Museum/Art Resource, NY.

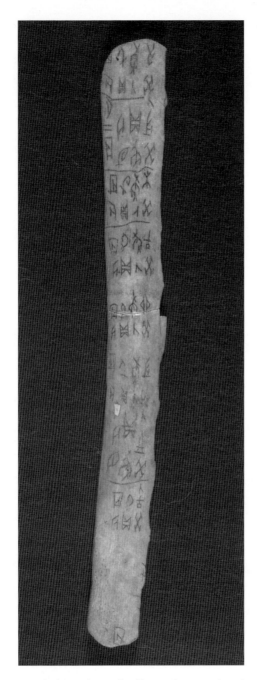

Plate 3 Chinese oracle bone from the Shang dynasty, bearing Chinese characters of the earliest form known. British Museum, London. Image copyright © Art Resource, NY.

Plate 4 Carved sapodilla wood lintel from Temple IV at Tikal, collected in 1877 by the explorer Gustav Bernoulli. Detail showing glyphs. Dated to AD 741. Museum fuer Voelkerkunde, Basel, Switzerland. Photo copyright © Werner Forman/Art Resource, NY.

Plate 5   Linear B written on clay tablets, from the Palace of Knossos, Crete. At top, records of sheep at Phaistos. At bottom, records of oil offered to various deities. These and other Linear B tablets were preserved in the fire that destroyed the palace, around 1350 BC. Image copyright © The Trustees of the British Museum.

Plate 6   Sequoyah with his syllabary. McKenney and Hall: "Se-Quo-Yah," from *History of the Indian Tribes of North America*. c.1837–44. Hand-colored lithograph. Image copyright © Smithsonian American Art Museum, Washington, DC/Art Resource, NY.

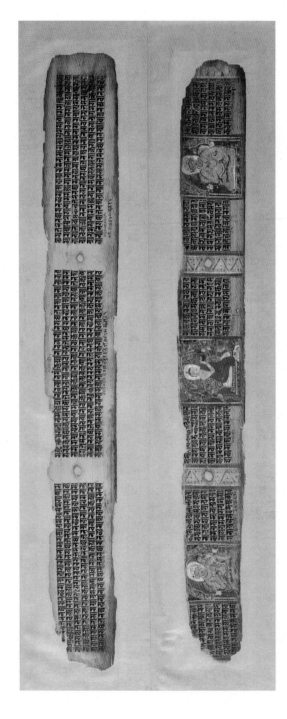

Plate 7 Twelfth-century AD palm-leaf manuscript of a Buddhist Prajnaparamita sutra from West Bengal, India. Image copyright © Freer Gallery of Art and Arthur M. Sackler Gallery.

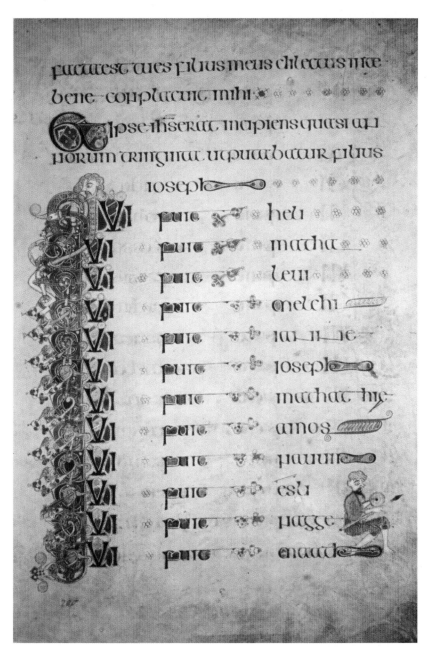

Plate 8 Page from the Book of Kells, showing the genealogy of Christ from the book of Luke. Written in a fine Insular Half Uncial and beautifully illuminated, c. AD 800. Trinity College, Dublin. Image copyright © Art Resource, NY.

Plate 9 Page from the 42-line Gutenberg Bible, produced at Mainz c.1455. The main text is printed with Gothic-style movable type, but the initials and marginalia are hand painted. Page 280, recto, with the prologue to the Book of Job. A picture of Job appears inside the initial V. Staatsbibliothek zu Berlin, Berlin. Image copyright © Bildarchiv Preussischer Kulturbesitz/Art Resource, NY.

These new states required administration. The Phoenicians adapted the linear Old Canaanite alphabet to this purpose and soon passed their easy, 22-letter system on to the Aramaeans and then to the Israelites (see figure 9.1). Neither Aramaic nor Hebrew had 22 consonant phonemes (Aramaic at the time had 26, and Hebrew may have had 25), but neither the Aramaeans nor the Hebrews thought of making any significant changes: the traditionalism of literacy was already beginning to make itself felt. Over the years, however, by a natural process of evolution, Phoenician, Aramaic, and Hebrew became three noticeably distinct national scripts. Each was to play a starring role on the world stage.

The Phoenician script looked westward, along with its seafaring users. In North Africa, the Phoenicians founded the great city of Carthage (in modern-day Tunisia; see appendix, figure A.6) in 825 or 814 BC. The Carthaginian dialect of Phoenician and its version of the Phoenician script, both known as Punic, spread as far as Sicily, Sardinia, Malta, and even into southern Spain. Carthage was eventually destroyed by Rome in 146 BC; but Punic was still spoken in the surrounding rural areas until the fifth century AD. A modified descendant of the Punic script, Tifinagh, is still used by the Tuareg Berbers today.

Closer to their original homeland, the Phoenicians taught writing to the Greeks, who substantially altered the nature of the alphabet by giving vowel phonemes their own letters, and in so doing founded a new family of scripts (chapter 12).

Meanwhile the Old Hebrew, or Palaeo-Hebrew, script stayed closer to home, though it was used for the Canaanite languages Moabite and Edomite (of today's western Jordan) as well as Hebrew. This script gained its claim to fame by being used to write the first parts of the Hebrew Bible. However, it is not the script in which the Hebrew Bible was completed after the Babylonian exile. The Babylonian exile disrupted the Hebrew literary tradition; afterwards the Jews came to use the Aramaic script and a great many Aramaic loanwords in their writing. Some of the Bible is even written in Aramaic rather than Hebrew (e.g. Daniel 2:4–7:28 and Ezra 4:8–6:18 and 7:12–26). The Palaeo-Hebrew script continued to be used for certain purposes: in some of the Dead Sea Scrolls, most of the text is written in the new script, but the tetragrammaton (the four-letter name of God, YHWH) and sometimes the word 'El ("God") are written in Palaeo-Hebrew. Its last use by the Jewish people was on coins struck during the Bar-Kokhba revolt of AD 132–5.

Ugaritic	Phoenician	Aramaic	Hebrew/Moabite	Name	Probable phonetic value	
▬	⚔ Κ	ᚨ	ᚨ	'ālef	[ʔ]	[ʔa] (Ugaritic)
⫫	𐤀	ᚐ	ᚐ	bēt	[b]	
Υ	1 ∧	ᚑ	1	gīmel	[g]	
ꞁ					[x]	
⫯⫯	Δ Λ	ᚑ	ᐊ	dālet	[d]	
⊨	⅃	⅃	ᚱ	hē	[h]	
⊨	Υ Υ	ᚒ	Υ	wāw	[w]	
ꞁ	I	I	ᚎ	zayin	[z]	
⇥	⊟ ⊟	ᚒ	ᚺ	ḥēt	[ħ]	
⇥	⊗ ⊕	⊕	⊗	ṭēt	[tˤ]	
ⱳ	ⴺ ⴺ	ᚱ	ᚎ	yōd	[j]	
⟨⟩	ⴽ ∨	ᚱ	ᛣ	kaf	[k]	
⟨⟩					[ʃ]	
ⱳⱳ	Ꮢ	ᚳ	ᛚ	lāmed	[l]	
⊤	ᛗ	ᚴ	ᚱ	mēm	[m]	
ⱱ					[ð]	
▬	ꞁ	ᚵ	ᚤ	nūn	[n]	
⋈					[ðˤ]	
ᚢ	⅀ ⅀	⅀	⅀	sāmek	[s]	
⟨	Ο	Ο	ο	'ayin	[ʕ]	
⊨	⌐ 1	ᚱ	ᚵ	pē	[p]	
ⱳⱳ	ᚢ	ᚱ	ᚽ	ṣādē	[sˤ]	
⊣	Φ Ϙ	Ϙ	Ϙ	qōf	[q]	
⟝	⟨	ᚨ	ᚵ	rēš	[r]	
ᚤ					[θ]	
⚔					[ɣ]	
	W	W	w	θān/šān/šin	[θ]/[ʃ]	
▬	Χ +	ᚷ	×	tāw	[t]	
⊨					[ʔi]	
⫯⫯⫯					[ʔu]	
⫴					[ç] ?	

Figure 9.1 Ancient alphabets. At left, the Ugaritic cuneiform alphabet, with the original set of 27 consonantal letters plus a three-letter appendix. Next, the Phoenician 22-letter alphabet and its virtually identical daughter scripts, early Aramaic and Old Hebrew (as used also for Moabite). Ugaritic was read from left to right, the others from right to left.

Palaeo-Hebrew continued to be used, however, by the Samaritans, and is still used liturgically by the few hundred members of this nearly extinct community. The Samaritans, who used only the Torah (the first five books of the Bible) rather than the whole Hebrew Bible, claimed to be descended from those people of the northern kingdom of Israel who had not been exiled to Assyria after the fall of Samaria in 722 BC. The Jews, however, considered them to have intermingled with Gentile immigrants to the region and to have the lost the true faith. Acrimony between the Jews and the Samaritans probably encouraged the use of different scripts by the two peoples.

While the Phoenician script looked westward and the Hebrew script wrote the Bible, the Aramaic script looked eastward and proceeded to take over much of the known world. First, however, the Aramaeans introduced a few innovations. The Phoenician script, like Proto-Canaanite before it (and the uniconsonantal signs of Egyptian hieroglyphs before that), had represented only consonants. This was appropriate to the structure of the languages involved and rarely made trouble for readers. *N fct, wrtng wtht vwls cn b dn n Nglsh s wll, s ths sntnc shws.* However, some ambiguities did arise, and the accurate spelling of foreign names was a problem.

The Aramaeans introduced the use of certain letters as *matres lectionis* ("mothers of reading"), beginning in the ninth century BC. A *mater lectionis* was a letter of the alphabet used to spell a long vowel. The letter *hē*, representing the consonant [h], was used as a *mater lectionis* for [aː], [eː], and [oː], while *wāw*, [w], was used for [uː] and *yōd*, [j], for [iː]. The letter *y* has a similar dual function in English, representing a consonant in a word like *yes* and a vowel in a word like *sky*.

At first *matres lectionis* were used only at the end of words, but later inside words as well. Short vowels remained unwritten, but were not particularly regretted. In a time when all writing was done by hand, there was no reason to make the spelling of words more work than it had to be. The use of *matres lectionis* spread from Aramaic to Hebrew and may even have inspired the Greek use of vowel letters. A second useful Aramaic innovation was spaces between words, replacing the earlier dots or slashes.

The Aramaeans become known to history during the eleventh and tenth centuries BC, building small kingdoms and city-states such as Damascus in Syria. Other Aramaeans spread as far east and south

151

as Babylonia, settling in the marshy "Sealand" at its southern end. The warlike Assyrians found themselves surrounded by the upstart Aramaeans. Resolidifying their power, the Assyrians lashed out and subdued tribe after tribe of Aramaeans, starting in the ninth century. They built themselves a larger and larger empire as they went, eventually conquering Damascus in 732 BC.

That should have been the end of the Aramaeans and their script. Nevertheless, there were still Aramaic speakers living along much of the Fertile Crescent from the Persian Gulf to the Mediterranean, going about their business in important trade cities such as Damascus. The Aramaeans had a talent for commerce – and the literacy to keep good accounts – and continued to dominate the trade routes of the Near East despite their political subjugation. Many of their trade practices, including their alphabet and their system of weights and measures, came to be used in the empire of their Assyrian conquerors. By the seventh century BC Aramaic had become the common trade language – the *lingua franca* – of the Near East.

The Assyrians continued to use cuneiform for formal purposes, but Aramaic, with its simple set of only 22 letters, made deepening inroads in more practical areas. The fact that Akkadian and Aramaic were related languages must have helped make Aramaic more attractive. Oddly enough, however, the Aramaic script was not used to write Akkadian; each language was written in its own script, by its own scribes. There were even different words for a scribe who wrote in cuneiform versus one who wrote in Aramaic. Had the Akkadian tradition been willing to consider a change of script, the language might have survived longer.

Some Aramaeans – those living in Babylonia, known as Chaldaeans – assimilated to Babylonian culture and rose to prominence in Babylonian society. When the Babylonians rebelled against their Assyrian overlords, it was a Chaldaean, Nabopolassar (626–605 BC), who ended up on the throne of the Neo-Babylonian Empire. The dynasty he founded included Nebuchadnezzar II (605–562), who captured Jerusalem and was responsible for the Babylonian exile. The Chaldaeans adopted Babylonian cuneiform for official purposes, but their informal language remained Aramaic.

When Cyrus the Great of Persia (559–530 BC) conquered Babylon in 539, Aramaic was once again the clear winner. The Persian Empire soon stretched from Egypt to northern India – the largest empire the world had yet seen – and it needed an administrative language and a script.

Old Persian cuneiform was soon developed for monumental inscriptions, but for administrative purposes the Persians took to Aramaic, despite the lack of any similarity between their Indo-European language and the Semitic Aramaic. They adopted it because it was there, co-opting the bureaucracies of the lands they conquered, many of which were already functioning in Aramaic. It was a long time before anyone thought to use the Aramaic script to write Persian; meanwhile Persian scribes and clerks had to learn Aramaic.

The Aramaic of the Persian period, known as Imperial Aramaic, was a remarkably uniform dialect, written in a uniform script. Local variants of Aramaic were spoken, but the written language was standardized. After Alexander the Great conquered Persia, taking Persepolis in 330 BC, official support for Aramaic was lost in favor of Greek. In the absence of any central authority, Imperial Aramaic evolved over the next few centuries into a number of distinct national scripts which were used both for varieties of Aramaic and for other local languages (see figure 9.2).

One of these scripts was the new Square Hebrew script of Judaea. Cyrus had allowed the Jewish exiles to return to Jerusalem and rebuild the temple, and they had brought the Aramaic language and script with them. Exactly when the Jews began using the Aramaic script for Hebrew is not clear, yet eventually a distinctively Jewish version of the script (known as Square Hebrew, Assyrian Hebrew, or Jewish script) evolved and came to be used for even the most sacred Hebrew texts. Once fully established, the script was remarkably stable: with only a brief adjustment, a reader of modern Hebrew letters can read the two-thousand-year-old Hebrew script of the Dead Sea Scrolls quite easily. Cursive versions of the script have been much less stable, but the square book hand has changed very little.

One change that did occur was the addition of an optional system of vowel notation. Once Hebrew was no longer a spoken language, it became important to preserve the accurate pronunciation of biblical words and to eliminate any potential for ambiguity. An elaborate system of diacritical dots and lines was developed, known as vowel points, which indicated the precise vowel pronunciations used in Hebrew at that time. When added to the consonant *mēm*, מ, for example, the vowel points gave מִ [mi], מֵ [me], מֶ [mɛ], מַ [mɑ], מָ [mɔ], מֹ [mo], and מֻ [mu], with length shown with the addition of the appropriate *mater lectionis*. There were also points for the so-called reduced vowels, extra-short

Aramaic	Syriac (Estrangelo)	Nabataean	Hebrew	Transliteration	Modern Hebrew pronunciation
			א	'	[ʔ] or silent
			ב	b	[b, v]
			ג	g	[g]
			ד	d	[d]
			ה	h	[h]
			ו	w	[v]
			ז	z	[z]
			ח	ḥ	[x]
			ט	ṭ	[t]
			'	y	[j]
			ך כ	k	[k, x]
			ל	l	[l]
			ם מ	m	[m]
			ן נ	n	[n]
			ס	s	[s]
			ע	'	[ʔ] or silent
			ף פ	p	[p, f]
			ץ צ	ṣ	[ts]
			ק	q	[k]
			ר	r	[ʁ]
			ש	š	[s, ʃ]
			ת	t	[t]

Figure 9.2 The Aramaic alphabet and three of its descendants, Estrangelo Syriac, Nabataean, and the Square Hebrew or Jewish script that is used for Hebrew today. As in most Aramaic descendants, the letters have variant forms according to where they occur in a word. The variants are shown only for Hebrew, in which the one on the left is used in word-final position (all these alphabets read from right to left). At right are the standard transliteration and the modern pronunciation of the letters in standard Israeli Hebrew.

pronunciations of vowels that occur in certain unstressed syllables in a word: מֱ [mĕ], מֲ [mă], מֳ [mŏ], and מְ [mə] (sometimes reduced to just [m]). Symbols known as cantillation marks were also added to indicate stress, pauses, and the correct pattern of intonation and voice pitch to be used in the liturgical reading of a phrase.

These marks were included in the Masoretic Text of the Hebrew Bible, the authoritative text assembled and codified between the sixth and tenth centuries AD. With both vowel points and cantillation marks, biblical Hebrew is one of the most painstakingly written languages, recording much more detail than texts written in the Roman alphabet, which do little beyond the occasional piece of punctuation or accent mark to depict stress and intonation. Conscientious inclusion of such detail in a mundane text would serve no useful function and only slow the reader down. It would certainly slow down the writer! Nonbiblical texts, therefore, are not written with cantillation marks, and even the use of vowel pointing is nowadays limited to school books, prayer books, poetry, and occasional places where ambiguity might otherwise arise.

Modern Hebrew is the result of revival efforts in the nineteenth and twentieth centuries. In the last centuries BC, Aramaic gradually ousted Hebrew as the vernacular language of Judaea and Galilee, and Hebrew was reserved for liturgical and literary use until its modern revival. Because of this switch in spoken languages, Aramaic can claim Jesus of Nazareth as its most famous native speaker.

The local Aramaic took on a distinctly Jewish flavor, and was written, like Hebrew, in the Square Hebrew script. This script accompanied the Jews throughout the Diaspora, and has subsequently been used to write distinctively Jewish varieties of Arabic (Judeo-Arabic) and Spanish (Ladino), as well as the Germanic Jewish language, Yiddish, and numerous other Jewish language varieties around the world.

Other varieties of Aramaic persisted in other parts of the former Persian Empire. The city of Palmyra, in Syria, became a prosperous independent state in the centuries after Alexander and went right on writing in Imperial Aramaic, though its inhabitants originally spoke Arabic. Imperial Aramaic evolved smoothly into a specifically Palmyrene variety of the Aramaic language and script. In later centuries, it was to be the first forgotten ancient script to be deciphered, by Abbé Barthélemy in the 1750s.

The local Aramaic of Edessa (now Urfa, in southern Turkey, geographically Syrian) became known as Syriac; it was to become the most important literary dialect of Aramaic. Edessa was the capital of the Arabic kingdom of Osrhoene, founded in 132 BC, and it remained an important city even after it was taken by the Romans in the third century AD. Its literary accomplishments included the Peshitta, an early translation of the Bible into Syriac whose Old Testament predates the codified Masoretic text of the Hebrew Bible and whose New Testament is one of the earliest translations from the original Greek. (Though Jesus and his disciples spoke Aramaic, the New Testament was written in Greek, the *lingua franca* of the eastern Roman Empire.)

Edessa became an important center of Christianity in the lands east of the Roman Empire, and so Syriac became an important literary language, the language of education and religion throughout much of the former Persian Empire. A schism in AD 489 between the Jacobites of the Syrian Orthodox Church (who believed that Christ had a single, divine nature) and the Nestorians of the Church of the East (who believed that Christ had two natures, human and divine, quite independent of each other) brought about a parallel split in the Syriac language and script. The earlier Syriac script, termed Estrangelo, broke into Nestorian (eastern) and Jacobite (western) versions.

After the advent of Islam both forms of Syriac began to be overshadowed by Arabic. The eclipse was not immediate, however, and before Syriac stopped being used as a literary language a number of historically important works were translated from Syriac into Arabic, including works of Greek philosophy and science. These translations helped stimulate the rise of Islamic intellectual culture and preserved much of the Greek tradition that was later lost in the West. Eventually, however, Syriac stopped being spoken and stopped being the language of new literary composition. It is still used as a liturgical language in the Syrian Orthodox Church and by Maronite Catholics.

A very small number of Christians and Jews in the Middle East still use dialects of Aramaic as their mother tongue. Modern Aramaic generally uses Syriac script, except for Mandaic, an Aramaic language used by members of a monotheistic Gnostic religion of southern Iraq and neighboring Iran. Mandaic uses its own version of the Aramaic script, adopted from the Parthian version.

The language that replaced Syriac as the vehicle of culture and religion across the Middle East was Arabic. The origins of the Arabic script are to be found in the kingdom of the Nabataeans, whose capital city of Petra – located south of the Dead Sea in modern Jordan – is famous for its rock-hewn buildings. The Arab Nabataean kingdom arose around 200 BC and adopted Aramaic for its written needs. The Nabataeans spoke Arabic, but like the Palmyrenes and the Edessans they learned to write in Aramaic. Such is the power of written language. However, the Nabataeans continued to speak Arabic, and here and there slipped a few Arabic words into their texts. The oldest surviving example of written Arabic, dating from the first century AD, is written in the Nabataean script.

The Nabataean version of the Aramaic script was to become very cursive, its letters rounded and connected to each other. Eventually a distinctively Arabic script arose from the Nabataean, coming to full maturation with the writing down of the Qur'ān and the need to represent the revealed word of God fully and accurately.

Back in Persia, meanwhile, the overthrow of the empire had ended the homogeneity of written Aramaic, but did little to discourage the use of the Aramaic script. Greek made inroads during the Seleucid period (330 to c.210 BC), but was soon ousted by the Parthians (Indo-European relatives of the Persians) who established their own kingdom in Persia (210 BC to AD 224), later to be succeeded by the Sasanian Persians. The scribes serving the Parthians went right on using the Aramaic language and script, as they had for centuries. The rulers they served, however, did not speak Aramaic. The scribes listened to Parthian, wrote down Aramaic, and read back Parthian. Over time, more and more words of Parthian made their way into the written records. Eventually the texts were more or less completely Parthian, though interspersed with Aramaic words. Those remaining Aramaic words became essentially logograms – word symbols to be read in Parthian. The Aramaic *mlk?* ("king"), for example, would be read as Parthian *ſāh*. That the words were read in Parthian rather than Aramaic is evident from the Parthian inflections added to them.

Officially the language of the following Sasanian period was Middle Persian, written in a script much like Parthian; but other members of the Aramaic family of alphabets flourished as well. The Iranian Sogdian language had its own Aramaic script – or rather, several. The Christian speakers of Sogdian used a descendant of Nestorian Syriac to record their language, and the Manichees, followers of the third-century AD religious teacher Mani, wrote their texts (whether in Persian, Parthian, or Sogdian) in their own Manichaean script derived from Syriac Estrangelo.

A good thing, too. As the Persian script evolved, its letters became connected, and it became what is known as Pahlavi. Many letters were now indistinguishable from each other. By the end of the Sasanian period, the Pahlavi script was nearly illegible. Words in late Pahlavi papyri have to be read as whole entities – almost as logograms – because the individual letters making them up cannot be distinguished. Scholars use spellings in Manichaean texts, as well as earlier, more legible Persian spellings, to break Pahlavi words up into individual letters. Native speakers of the time, applying their top-down reading skills, would not have had anywhere near as much trouble. As is so often the case, the intelligence of readers made up for the deficiencies of the writing system.

The Avesta, the sacred book of the Zoroastrian religion, was first written down in the Sasanian period. These scriptures had been passed down orally for centuries, long after Avestan, the Iranian language they were composed in (a sister language of Old Persian), had become extinct. Since no one spoke Avestan natively anymore, it had to be written more accurately than the living languages of the time. Persian and Parthian were written with *matres lectionis* when vowels were considered necessary, but often vowels were simply left out, *infrble frm cntxt*. In the dead, sacred language of Avestan, however, inferring vowels from context using one's native-speaker knowledge was not going to work. The same problem faced the compilers of the Masoretic text of the Hebrew Bible. So the alphabet was considerably beefed up, and Avestan was given a 51-character fully voweled alphabet to accurately portray its pronunciation. For once, precision trumped tradition.

Having been successfully adapted to the Iranian languages – a linguistic group entirely unrelated to Semitic Aramaic – the Aramaic alphabet was ready to continue eastward, conquering new worlds and new languages. In front of it stretched the wide belt of Inner Asia, from the eastern border of Persia to Mongolia and Manchuria. This was the home of the Altaic language family, comprising, from west to east, the Turkic, Mongolian, and Tungus language groups. The Altaic peoples have historically been nomads. Though they have ruled great empires (those of Genghis and Kublai Khan and of the Ottoman Turks come to mind), they were not themselves progenitors of great civilizations. They did not found great literary traditions, but they did find uses for the technology of writing, especially in periods of empire building (see figure 9.3).

Aramaic original	Uighur letter	Phonetic value	Mongolian letter	Phonetic value	Manchu letter	Phonetic value
		[e]		[a]		[a]
		[a/e]		[e]		[e]
		[w/v]		[i]		[i]
		[ɣ]		[o/u]		[o]
		[o/u]		[ø/y]		[u]
		[ö/ü]				[u] (after [q, ɣ, χ])
		[z]		[n]		[n]
		[ʒ]		[q]		[ŋ]
		[x]		[ɣ]		[q]
		[q]		[b]		[k]
		[j]		[s]		[ɣ]
		[k/g]		[ʃ]		[g]
		[d]		[t/d]		[k] (in loanwords)
		[m]		[d/t]		[g] (in loanwords)
		[n]		[l]		[χ]
		[p]		[m]		[x]
		[tʃ]		[tʃ]		[b]
		[r]		[dʒ]		[p]
		[s]		[j]		[s]
		[ʃ]		[k/g]		[š]
		[t]		[r]		[t] (before [a, o])
		[l]		[w/v]		[d] (before [a, o])
				[h]		[t] (before [e, u])
				[p]		[d] (before [e, u])
				[f]		[l]
						[m]
						[tʃ]
						[dʒ]
						[j]
						[r]
						[f]
						[w/f]

Figure 9.3 Three Altaic descendants of the Aramaic alphabet. Uighur, which follows Aramaic alphabetical order, is shown next to the original Aramaic prototypes. Initial (left) and final (right) forms only are given here, omitting medial forms, except in a few cases where only medial forms exist. Altaic scripts are read from top to bottom.

The ancestral Turkic people – the Türks – were the first Altaic people to write. Originally from Mongolia, they began to expand westward in the sixth century AD, founding an empire that was to reach all the way to the Black Sea. Their oldest surviving inscriptions date to the eighth century and are found along the Orkhon River in their Mongolian homeland. Though inspired by the noncursive version of the Sogdian script, their writing took on an idiosyncratic form, vaguely resembling the runes of Europe rather than the Aramaic scripts of Persia. And while it was written from right to left, like other Aramaic-derived scripts, its rows proceeded from bottom to top. The Türks, clearly, owed little allegiance to Middle Eastern tradition.

In AD 745 control of the Türk Empire passed into the hands of their Turkic kinsmen, the Uighurs, who also learned to write Turkic runes. A century later the Uighurs were themselves displaced from Mongolia by yet another Turkic people, the Kirghiz. They settled in what is now Xinjiang (formerly Chinese Turkestan; see appendix, figure A.4) in northwestern China, where they adopted a sedentary lifestyle and invested in civilization. They cultivated a new script they found in Xinjiang, an adaptation of cursive Sogdian, with which they created significant works of literature.

This Uighur alphabet (also spelled Uyghur, pronounced [wí gər] in English) contained 22 letters (not all of them originally Aramaic, as certain alterations had been made in the transfer from Sogdian). The Uighur language contained 25 consonant and 8 vowel phonemes, so some letters were pressed into double duty. Adding extra letters to the alphabet seems not to have occurred to the Uighurs, just as it did not to the early Hebrews or Aramaeans who used the 22-letter Phoenician alphabet – or to most peoples on the alphabet's eastward march.

At some point, probably under the influence of Chinese, the direction of writing was turned by 90 degrees. Instead of being written in rows from right to left, the page was given a quarter turn counterclockwise, with the result that Uighur was now written from top to bottom in columns that proceeded from left to right across the page (Chinese vertical writing, by contrast, goes from right to left across the page).

With the introduction of Islam in the thirteenth century, the Uighur script was discontinued in favor of the Arabic script, which was itself replaced by Latin-based pīnyīn in the twentieth century (and, across the Chinese border in the Soviet Union, by Cyrillic). First, however, it was passed on to others.

The Mongols were the next Altaic conquerors, overrunning large parts of Asia under Genghis Khan in the early thirteenth century, and even taking China under Genghis' grandson Kublai in 1279. The Mongols mainly left administration to their conquered peoples; but still, an empire needed a script. They borrowed the Uighur vertical script – quite probably by making use of Uighur scribes – and only after the passage of a few centuries added letters to adapt it to their own language. This new Mongolian script was used for translations of Buddhist works which the Mongols, new converts to Buddhism, read enthusiastically, creating a literate culture that still remembers Mongolian script today (though it was replaced in Outer Mongolia by Cyrillic in 1946).

An update of the vertical Mongol script, the so-called clear script, was invented in 1648 to improve the fit of Mongolian writing to the Mongolian language. For the first time in its migration eastward, other than Avestan, an Aramaic alphabet acquired letters for all the short vowels, giving it an unambiguous way of writing all the vowels of the language. Clear script came to be used by Oirat Mongols and is still in use, but the majority of Mongols clung to the classical vertical script. It was more familiar, and it was good enough.

The Mongols were replaced in the arena of empire building by the Manchus, a Tungus people. The Manchus, like the Mongols before them, conquered China, giving it its last imperial dynasty, the Qing (1644–1912). As the Manchu were assembling their empire and preparing to take on China, they realized that they needed writing. Their first solution was to employ literate Mongols as scribes and to do the government's business in Mongolian. Within a few decades, however, the script was adapted to Manchu, first with the addition of some letters, and then with the further addition of diacritical marks. The result included a full set of vowels, and represented Manchu more fully and unambiguously than vertical Mongolian had represented spoken Mongolian. With the Manchu script, the Aramaic alphabet had finally reached easternmost Asia, 3,400 years or so after the first Semitic alphabet was used in Egypt.

Manchu was made an official language of China. Government documents were bilingual in Manchu and Chinese, and Manchu was used as the language of diplomatic correspondence. Many Chinese literary and historical works were translated into Manchu, and Western scholars used these translations to study Chinese. Despite this preferential treatment, spoken Manchu languished as the Manchus became assimilated to the Han Chinese ways and language. Today the language is moribund.

The last Altaic adaptation of the Aramaic script was designed in 1905 for the Buryat dialect of Mongolian. It was a systematic revision of the vertical Mongol and the clear script, designed to fit the phonology of modern Buryat. Type was cast for it, but the alphabet made little headway against the traditional vertical Mongolian.

The alphabet that superseded many of the Aramaic scripts of the Middle East and Inner Asia was Arabic, today the most widely used Semitic alphabet. Since the Arabic script itself was descended from Aramaic, the replacement was a kind of alphabetic fratricide. Early Arabic writing had developed out of Nabataean Aramaic in pre-Islamic days, but the rise of Islam spurred the full development, codification, and spread of a specifically Arabic script.

Even before Muhammad (c. AD 570–632) received the Qur'ān in Arabic, the language had spread from its Arabian homeland into many parts of the Fertile Crescent (though some Arabs, such as the Edessans and Palmyrenes, probably gave up speaking Arabic for Aramaic, keeping only their Arabic names). Spread out as it was, the Arabic language consisted of numerous vernacular dialects. There was also a pan-Arabic formal dialect used in oral poetry. This dialect was the basis for the qur'ānic language, the Qur'ān being the first prose work written in that style. Its formal language and inspired source meant that the style of the Qur'ān became the standard for literary Arabic (known as Classical Arabic) in the succeeding centuries. Classical Arabic was no one's vernacular dialect, though it was more like some people's speech than others'.

Tradition tells us that Muhammad himself was illiterate; his words were memorized or jotted down by his followers. After the death of the prophet and a number of his inner circle, it became clear that Muhammad's revelation was at risk of being lost. The text began to be systematically collected and copied. The third caliph (the caliphs were successors to the prophet in his secular role as leader of the Islamic community) was 'Uthman ibn 'Affan (644–56), who ordered the collation of the authoritative version that is still used today.

As Islam spread along with the Islamic Empire, the Arabic language acquired many new speakers. By the time of 'Uthman, the fledgling empire covered all of Arabia, the Fertile Crescent, and Egypt. By the end of the seventh century it included Morocco (with Spain to follow soon) in the west and Persia in the east. The Sasanian Persian Empire had been absorbed, and the Byzantine Empire had been drastically reduced.

As is frequently the way of new empires, administration was at first transferred wholesale from existing systems. The bureaucracy functioned in Greek in the west and in Pahlavi in the former Persian lands. As the switch to Arabic occurred, in the 690s, knowledge of Arabic became an advantage and the language began to gain speakers.

As the Muslim faith spread within the Islamic Empire, interest in Arabic grew yet further. Arabic held special status, for it was the language in which God had spoken to Muhammad. The Qur'ān, as the revealed Word of God, should not be translated; it could not be the same in another language – it would not be God's word verbatim. Devout Muslims of any language, therefore, had good reason to study Arabic. But unlike native speakers, they needed much more guidance as to how the words should be pronounced. And even native speakers of Arabic might have dialectal disagreements as to the correct pronunciation of words.

To address these concerns, the Arabic script was revamped. The Arabic language had 28 consonants as compared to the 22 consonants available in the Aramaic script. Some letters had been doing double duty for two consonant sounds; now they were divided into distinct letters by the addition of diacritical dots. Thus ث, *θaːʔ* (representing the sound in English *thing*), was distinguished from ت, *taːʔ*.

Additionally, some originally distinct letters of the highly cursive script had come to resemble each other. So ب, *baːʔ*, and ت, *taːʔ*, were also differentiated by the placement of dots. The tendency for letters to resemble each other was especially true in the middle of a word. Most letters in an Arabic word must be joined to the one that follows. At the end of a word, however, they tend to have expressive "tails." Thus the letters developed distinct forms depending on whether they occurred independently or initially, medially, or finally in a word (see figure 9.4). The independent form, usually a combination of the initial form and the final form, is the one shown in simple alphabet charts. Some letters which were distinct in independent form were not distinct in initial or medial form, so diacritics were added to these as well: ي, *jaːʔ*, and ن, *nuːn*, are in initial position ـ and ـ, but for their dots just like initial ت, *taːʔ*, and ب, *baːʔ*. These diacritical dots are now obligatory, forming an integral part of the letter.

Name in IPA	Arabic name	Final	Medial	Initial	Independent
ʔalif	الف	ـا	ـا	ا	ا
baːʔ	باء	ـب	ـبـ	بـ	ب
taːʔ	تاء	ـت	ـتـ	تـ	ت
θaːʔ	ثاء	ـث	ـثـ	ثـ	ث
dʒiːm	جيم	ـج	ـجـ	جـ	ج
ħaːʔ	حاء	ـح	ـحـ	حـ	ح
χaːʔ	خاء	ـخ	ـخـ	خـ	خ
daːl	دال	ـد	ـد	د	د
ðaːl	ذال	ـذ	ـذ	ذ	ذ
raːʔ	راء	ـر	ـر	ر	ر
zaːj	زاي	ـز	ـز	ز	ز
siːn	سين	ـس	ـسـ	سـ	س
ʃiːn	شين	ـش	ـشـ	شـ	ش
sˤaːd	صاد	ـص	ـصـ	صـ	ص
dˤaːd	ضاد	ـض	ـضـ	ضـ	ض
tˤaːʔ	طاء	ـط	ـطـ	طـ	ط
zˤaːʔ	ظاء	ـظ	ـظـ	ظـ	ظ
ʕajn	عين	ـع	ـعـ	عـ	ع
ʁajn	غين	ـغ	ـغـ	غـ	غ
faːʔ	فاء	ـف	ـفـ	فـ	ف
qaːf	قاف	ـق	ـقـ	قـ	ق
kaːf	كاف	ـك	ـكـ	كـ	ك
laːm	لام	ـل	ـلـ	لـ	ل
miːm	ميم	ـم	ـمـ	مـ	م
nuːn	نون	ـن	ـنـ	نـ	ن
haːʔ	هاء	ـه	ـهـ	هـ	ه
waːw	واو	ـو	ـو	و	و
jaːʔ	ياء	ـي	ـيـ	يـ	ي

Figure 9.4 The Arabic alphabet with, from right to left, the independent, initial, medial, and final forms of each letter, plus the letter's name in Arabic and its pronunciation in IPA. As compared to the original Aramaic prototype, Arabic has reordered its letters, putting similarly shaped letters together.

Some letters, in contrast to the norm, must *not* be joined to the following one: the letter *ʔalif*, ا, if joined to a following letter would look just like the connected version of the letter *laːm*, ل. In الكتاب, *al-kitaab*, "the book," for example, the first (rightmost!) letter is an *ʔalif*, which does not connect forward, while the next is a *laːm*. *ʔalif* does join to a preceding letter, however, and the sequence *laːm–ʔalif* is written with a special ligature, لا.

Another part of the writing system that needed to be addressed was the writing of vowels. Arabic has six vowels, three of which are

pronounced short – [i], [u], and [a] – and three long – [iː], [uː], [aː].
Arabic inherited the system of *matres lectionis* from Aramaic and used
it thoroughly, so that all long vowels are written. The *ʔalif*, ١, originally representing a glottal stop, now stands for the long vowel [aː]
except word-initially, while the glottal stop is represented by an extra
symbol that is not considered a true part of the alphabet, the *hamza*, ء.
(This situation arose because the dialect of the Prophet had lost
word-medial and -final glottal stops. When later scribes speaking
other dialects wanted to add them, they felt they should honor the
original spellings and added the *hamza* as merely a diacritical symbol.
Nowadays it may occur on an initial *ʔalif*, as in الف, the name of the
letter, or alone as in باء, the name of the letter *baːʔ*.) Long [uː] is
represented by the letter *waːw*, و, which may stand for either the consonant [w] or the vowel [uː]. Similarly, the *jaːʔ*, ى, stands for either the
consonant [j] (normally transliterated as *y*) or the long vowel [iː].

To show the exact pronunciation of the Qur'ān, and to resolve
all ambiguities of meaning, short vowels had to be represented. The
doubling of consonants also needed to be shown – like the choice of
vowels, consonant doubling is part of the morphological composition
of a word and is traditionally omitted in spelling. So an additional
layer of diacritical marks was added to indicate short vowels, consonant
doubling, the glottal stop (*hamza*), and even the absence of a vowel.
So بَ spells *ba*, بِ is *bi*, and بُ is *bu*, while بّ indicates a *bb* without
intervening vowel, and بْ indicates that no vowel follows the *b*. A
number of other diacritics also exist for accurately showing the proper
pronunciation of words.

The short-vowel marks and other related diacritics are called *vocalization*. Full vocalization is used only for the Qur'ān, for reading textbooks
(for elementary school students and foreigners), and sometimes for
literary classics – parallel to the Hebrew use of vowel pointing. Most
texts just use the "skeleton" of alphabetic letters – the consonants
and long vowels, including the dots which distinguish consonants. A
fully vocalized text exists on three tiers – the central written line, the
obligatory dots above and below the consonants, and the vocalization
shown at the very top and bottom.

To the native speaker and fluent reader, marking of long vowels
only is sufficient. With their top-down processing, fluent readers do
not particularly care to have every phoneme unambiguously spelled
out. In Arabic this is especially true because short vowels can largely

be determined by context. Their placement follows certain specific rules: all words begin with a single consonant, and sequences of more than two consonants do not occur. The identity of the vowels is determined by the morphological form of the word being used. The writing of long vowels helps to reduce potential ambiguity, distinguishing *kitaab*, "book," from *katab*, "wrote", from *kaatab*, "corresponded," all derived from the triconsonantal root *ktb*, which is used for words that involve writing. Since the triconsonantal *ktb* represents the core meaning of the word, a writing system that locates these letters at the core of the spelling and relegates some of the other features to the peripheries matches the structure of the language.

Another reason not to use full vocalization is that modern Arabic, no less than in the time of the Prophet and probably more, is a language rich in spoken dialects. A great deal of dialectal variation exists in the vowels, especially in the short vowels. In fact, if it were not for written Classical Arabic and its somewhat updated version, Modern Standard Arabic, no one would consider Arabic a single language: there are many mutually unintelligible spoken forms. One form, Maltese, is written in the Roman alphabet and is now considered a separate language. Just as Chinese characters unite a diverse group of dialects or languages, so does written Arabic.

In becoming literate, therefore, Arabs must learn a significantly different dialect – almost a new language. To some extent this is true in any written language – one learns to use more formal vocabulary and complex phrasing in writing than in colloquial speech. In Arabic the differences are much greater than in English, to the extent that literate people must become virtually bilingual, a situation known to linguists as *diglossia.* In Arabic, therefore, one could almost say that no one is really literate in their own language, a situation reminiscent of the Nabataeans and Persians who wrote in Aramaic, or the New Kingdom Egyptians who clung to written Middle Egyptian, but in marked contrast to the inventors of the original proto-Canaanite alphabet who developed the script to write their own mother tongue. The benefit derived from diglossia is that it allows the whole Arabic world to share the same literature – and, of course, the same Qur'ān. The omission of short vowels from texts helps make the written language look more familiar to Arabic speakers who have not fully mastered the standard dialect.

With conversion and conquest, Arabic became the language of much of North Africa and the Middle East. Significant holdouts were

Persian and, later, the newcomer Turkish. Yet the religious and cultural significance of Arabic was such that both Turkish and Persian came to be written in Arabic script, as did the other Iranian languages Pashto, Kurdish, and Balochi; the Indo-Aryan languages Urdu, Sindhi, and Kashmiri; many of the Turkic languages of Inner Asia; various languages of North Africa; and Malay. To write these non-Semitic languages a number of new diacritics were added to represent additional consonants: for example, ڤ was made from ف, *faːʔ*, to represent [v], and پ was made from ب, *baːʔ*, to represent [p].

The Arabic script is deeply connected to the Muslim faith. The spread of Islam brought with it a spread of literacy, as did the spread of Buddhism in Central and East Asia and the spread of Christianity in Europe. Islam, like Judaism and Christianity, is a religion "of the Book." In written form, God's word is made available to all: what God has said is as settled and unarguable as a Sumerian tax receipt, though of course the interpretation of what God has said can vary considerably.

Figure 9.5 Islamic zoomorphic calligraphy. From northern India, nineteenth century. Image copyright © Victoria & Albert Museum, London/Art Resource, NY.

In the Hebrew Bible God speaks the world into existence ("Let there be light"). According to one Islamic tradition, by contrast, God made the world by writing it with a pen, and the Qur'ān says that God teaches humans with a pen. As a result, the pen and the craft of writing are highly revered. The art of beautiful writing – calligraphy – plays a central role in Islamic art, the more so as representational arts are frowned upon, especially in a religious setting. Calligraphy is a form of religious expression, particularly in the Sufi tradition of Islam, which emphasizes mysticism and personal experience of God. In beautifully writing one's worship, one draws nearer to God and communes with his transcendent creative spirit.

The maturation of Islamic calligraphy was abetted by the arrival in the Middle East of paper. Paper has a smoother surface than papyrus, allowing for more graceful, smoother lines. After Samarkand fell into Muslim hands in AD 751, the previously well-kept Chinese secret of papermaking spread to the Middle East. Subsequently, the Islamic tradition has produced a magnificent body of calligraphy in a number of styles (figure 9.5). There are plaited letters, mazes, architectural and geometric shapes, and compositions in the shape of a human face, an animal, a fruit or flower, or even a coffee urn, all making creative use of the flowing and curvaceous nature of the Arabic script, the most successful modern form of the Aramaic alphabet.

10

The Empire of Sanskrit

The one word that best describes India is *diversity*. In the cities of the world's largest democracy, cell-phone users and bullock carts share the streets with a dizzying array of buses, cars, scooters, and auto-rickshaws. Historically the region has given birth to four of the world's religions – Hinduism, Buddhism, Sikhism, and Jainism – while the modern nation also boasts a large Muslim population, Christian and Jewish communities that date back to the early centuries AD, one of the world's few Baha'i temples, and the world headquarters of the Theosophical Society. The languages of India belong to five separate, unrelated language families. Yet somehow India today is a single nation, thanks to the fact that in classical times the people of the Indian subcontinent managed to forge elements of a common culture out of myriad local variations. How they did so is closely related to the story of their written words.

According to the People of India ethnographic survey conducted in the late 1980s and early 1990s, Indians use 325 different languages at home. There is no single *lingua franca* with which to sort out this Babel: the survey also found that Indians use 96 different languages when speaking with members of other communities. The survey did not claim to be an exhaustive census, and there is room for endless debate as to whether certain forms of speech are different languages or different dialects of the same language. A definitive tally of India's languages may therefore be impossible, but clearly the total is an impressive number.

Equally impressive is the fact that the survey received 25 different answers to the question of what script people write with, a figure that is the more striking given that many of the 325 mother tongues have no written form. No other nation uses such a profusion of scripts. The modern state of India is three-quarters the size of Europe, but modern Europe uses only three native alphabets (Greek, Roman, and Cyrillic).

India's languages belong to five families. The two most populous families are the Indo-European family (mostly the Indo-Aryan branch), to which many of the northern languages belong, and the Dravidian family, to which the languages of southern India belong. Smaller numbers speak languages of the Austro-Asiatic family (mostly the Munda branch) in central and northeastern India, particularly in tribal communities. Around the edges of India are languages of the Sino-Tibetan family (almost exclusively the Tibeto-Burman branch), located along the Himalayan frontier and in the northeast, and those of the Andaman Islands in the Bay of Bengal, which comprise a family of their own, apparently unrelated to any others on earth.

In sharp contrast to this diversity, all the traditional scripts of India belong to the same family. There are newcomers – the Arabic script (as adapted first for Persian and then for Indian languages), the Roman alphabet, and Ol Chiki (invented for the Munda language, Santali) – but the rest share a single historical source. Despite significant differences in appearance, the native scripts of India generally work on the same principles, encode the same phonemes, and list their letters in the same order. Furthermore, during the first millennium AD they were mostly used to write the same language, Sanskrit.

Although 22 of India's 25 scripts stem from a common source, the first writing in India has left no modern descendants. Between 2600 and 1900 BC, the Indus Valley civilization – one of the world's ancient river valley civilizations and a younger contemporary of the Mesopotamian and Egyptian civilizations – flourished in what is now Pakistan and northwestern India. The Indus Valley culture was apparently literate, as attested by short inscriptions on seals and other durable materials (figure 10.1), particularly from the major cities of Harappa and Mohenjo Daro (see appendix, figure A.7). But these undeciphered inscriptions are so short (averaging only five signs) that some have argued that they are not actually writing. If writing, they are commonly supposed to record an ancient Dravidian language, as the Dravidian languages were spoken in the Indian subcontinent before the arrival of the Indo-European Aryans; but this assumption cannot be proved. Without longer texts or a bilingual inscription, hopes for a decipherment remain slim. After centuries of prosperity,

Figure 10.1 Seal with Indus Valley symbols, from Mohenjo Daro. National Museum of Pakistan, Karachi. Image copyright © Scala/Art Resource, NY.

the Indus Valley civilization withered for unknown reasons, and its unique writing system died with it.

The illiterate Aryans arrived in the subcontinent some four hundred years later. As they mingled with the native population, their language took on distinctively Indian characteristics, absorbing Dravidian words and pronunciations. The Dravidian and Munda languages absorbed Aryan characteristics in return. The Aryans, and many of the Dravidians and Mundas, clung to their individual native tongues, but they allowed each other enough influence that India became what is known as a *linguistic area* – a region in which the various languages share certain characteristics as a result of having borrowed them from each other, rather than having inherited them from a common ancestor. The unification of India had begun.

In time the Aryans developed a distinctively Indian religious tradition, complete with hymns, known as the Vedas, which were composed in the sacred, poetic form of their language, Vedic Sanskrit. The Vedas were transmitted orally, just as the Avesta was in Persia by the Aryans' distant cousins, the Iranians (*Iranian* being another form of the word *Aryan*). As sacred works, the Vedas were carefully preserved, word for word, although the language of everyday use continued to change through the centuries. By the time the Indo-Aryans wrote their language, what they actually spoke was not Sanskrit at all.

The growing gap between the formal language and everyday speech prompted an original Indian invention: grammar. If one was going to use holy language, one had best understand correctly the rules under which it operated; and so the science of linguistic description was born. Sometime around the fourth or fifth century BC the grammarian Pāṇini composed his grammatical summary of Sanskrit, including both its older, Vedic version and the more modern variety in which sacred works were being composed at the time and which became the basis for the classical language. Many other grammatical treatises were composed over the next two millennia, but Pāṇini's *Astādyāyi* ("Eight Chapters") justly remained the paragon of grammars.

It is not clear whether Pāṇini and his contemporaries were literate. The *Astādyāyi* was composed in such a way as to facilitate oral recitation, but whether it originally existed solely in oral form is up for debate. Certainly, the Indian tradition of learning cultivated memory to a degree that is very difficult for us to imagine today. Yet it may have been some of these same early grammarians who designed the distinctively Indian style of scripts. They would have had the linguistic knowledge to do so, but any writing they may have done has not been preserved.

The oldest surviving, clearly datable pieces of writing in India are the edicts of the emperor Aśoka (c.265–238 BC), carved into stone pillars and rock faces. Aśoka, third emperor of the Mauryan dynasty, was a bloody conqueror who subdued most of the Indian subcontinent. Eventually he realized the human cost of his warmongering, renounced bloodshed, and converted to Buddhism. He then ordered his new ethical principles of tolerance, nonviolence, and just rulership inscribed in stone for all to see throughout India. At the frontier between his realm and Seleucid Persia his edicts were written in Greek and Aramaic, but elsewhere they were written in various forms of Prakrit in two different scripts, Brāhmī and Kharoṣṭhī.

Prakrit was a general term used to describe vernacular Indo-Aryan languages as contrasted with the liturgical language, Sanskrit. Pali, the language of Buddhist scriptures, was an early Prakrit. Eventually Pali and certain other Prakrits were themselves fossilized in written texts and became literary languages distinct from the everyday speech of the Indian people. In Aśoka's time, however, using Prakrit was simply using normal language.

The origin of the Brāhmī and Kharoṣṭhī scripts in which Aśoka's edicts were written is a matter of some controversy. Kharoṣṭhī, whose use was restricted to the northwestern portion of the subcontinent and adjacent Inner Asia, eventually became extinct. Brāhmī, on the other hand, spread far and wide, developed numerous regional forms, and is survived today by descendants throughout the subcontinent and Southeast Asia from Punjab to the Philippines.

Kharoṣṭhī was probably the older of the two scripts. It was written from right to left and displays some similarities to Imperial Aramaic. Brāhmī was written from left to right, and is less reminiscent of Aramaic. Yet the similarities between Brāhmī and Kharoṣṭhī are more striking than the similarities between Kharoṣṭhī and Aramaic.

The Indian scripts, starting with Brāhmī and Kharoṣṭhī, are often assumed to be yet another adaptation of the Aramaic script, adding South and Southeast Asia to the portion of the world colonized by the Aramaic alphabet. Others have vigorously denied any link, especially in the case of Brāhmī, claiming an indigenous origin for Indian writing.

The developmental stages – if there were any – of Brāhmī and Kharoṣṭhī are long lost to us, so the controversy may never be fully settled. The most reasonable guess, however, is that writing in India was neither a completely independent discovery nor a slavish borrowing of someone else's technology. Given the presence of the Achaemenid Persian Empire at India's northwest frontier, it is reasonable to assume that Imperial Aramaic played a role in inspiring script development in India. It would be an error, however, to overestimate the similarities of either Brāhmī or Kharoṣṭhī to Aramaic. Brāhmī and Kharoṣṭhī were thoughtfully designed to match the phonemes present in the Indian Prakrits, which were quite different from the Semitic consonants of Aramaic. Rather than making yet another slight modification to the Aramaic alphabet, the Indians discovered an entirely new way to write. They may well have learned from Aramaic-speaking Persians the alphabetic principle of representing each individual consonant with its own symbol, but their approach to representing vowels was novel, quite different from the beefing-up of *matres lectionis* into independent vowel letters that occurred at various points in the Aramaic alphabet's eastward journey. Though probably not an entirely indigenous invention, the scripts of India nevertheless started a new chapter in the history of writing – a case of what anthropologists call *stimulus diffusion*, rather than an outright borrowing or close adaptation.

Kharoṣṭhī, Brāhmī, and the modern descendants of Brāhmī are generally called *alphasyllabaries*, suggesting some combination of an alphabet and a syllabary but leaving unhelpfully vague how such a combination would actually work. The scripts are actually alphabetic in that each phoneme receives its own symbol (with one exception), but the symbols are combined in ways that are foreign to Western alphabets, which (especially since the advent of printing) proceed letter by letter in a single straight line. In native terminology, the Indic writing systems employ units known as *akṣaras*, in which vowel signs are written as appendages to consonant symbols. One vowel is left unwritten, inferred to occur after a consonant if neither the "absence of vowel" sign nor another vowel sign is added.

To take an example from the Devanāgarī script (used for Hindi, Marathi, Nepali, and modern publications in Sanskrit; figure 10.2), क is the letter *k*, read (with the inferred vowel) as *ka*, phonetically [kɐ] or [kə]. If the *k* is followed by any other vowel, a symbol is added to the right, left, top, or bottom of the character, depending on the vowel. So का is *kā* (with a long [aː] vowel), कि is *ki*, की is *kī*, कु is *ku*, कू is *kū*, के is *ke*, को is *ko*, कै is *kai*, and कौ is *kau*. Each of these CV sequences is considered a single *akṣara*, a grouping reminiscent of the syllabic symbols in a syllabary. However, the contribution of each consonant and vowel phoneme is clearly visible, making the system alphabetic despite the fact that the characters do not follow each other linearly as they do in Western alphabets.

So far the system is easy. However, special treatment is needed both for consonants that are not followed by a vowel and for vowels which are not preceded by consonants – in other words, for phonemes that don't fit into CV sequences. Initial vowels were rare in Sanskrit, not because words didn't begin with vowels, but because spaces were not left between words. (The modern languages, by contrast, have adopted word spacing on the European model.) If one word ended in a vowel and the next one began with a vowel, the two vowels were blended into a single one by a set of grammatical rules known as *sandhi*. Thus only vowels that were sentence- or verse-initial did not have a preceding consonant. There were special symbols for these "independent" initial vowels: अ *a*, आ *ā*, इ *i*, ई *ī*, उ *u*, ऊ *ū*, ए e, ऐ *ai*, ओ *o*, and औ *au*.

In principle the independent forms of the vowels could have been used throughout: *kā* would then be written कआ, and *pe* as पए, etc. The resulting linear scripts would be more familiar to those raised with Western-style alphabets, but they would be more cumbersome to write, requiring far more strokes of the pen. With upwards of 45 letters to distinguish, the characters of the Indic scripts are relatively complex; writing vowels as attachments to consonants makes them safely distinct visually and cuts down on the effort of writing them. (The fact that most linear alphabets, by contrast, have fewer than about 30 letters is a historical accident, related more to the number of consonants in Semitic languages than to the number of phonemes a language can have.)

Besides having two versions of the vowels, the other complication of the *akṣara* system occurs with consonants that are not followed by a vowel. Sanskrit abounded in consonant clusters, as Indo-European languages are wont to do. Any sequence of consonants was crammed together into a single *akṣara*. क plus क makes क्क, *kka*, स (*s*) plus क makes स्क, *ska*, and स plus त (*t*) plus व (*v*) makes स्त्व, *stva*. (Prakrit did not have as many consonant clusters, so the complexity of *akṣaras* may have ended up being more than the original designers intended.) Generally the pieces – the individual consonants – of the combination are clearly visible, though usually all but the last lack the vertical bar that stand-alone consonants usually have. However, क्ष (*kṣa*, क + ष) and ज्ञ (*jña*, ज + ञ) are exceptional ligatures that disguise their constituent pieces, and the combination forms of र, *r*, are unusual: क, *k*, plus र, *r*, is क्र, *kra*, while र plus क is र्क, *rka*.

A consonant that occurs without either a following vowel or consonant – because it is mentioned alone, or it occurs at the end of a word or sentence (depending on word-spacing conventions) – traditionally takes a sign known as *halant* or *virāma*, which silences the implied *a* vowel: क is read *ka*, but क् is read as merely *k*.

The modern languages that use Devanāgarī have reduced the use of the inherent vowel. Words that used to end in the default vowel *a* are now pronounced without it, such that राम, *Rāma*, one of the avatars – or incarnations – of the god Vishnu, is now *Rām*. Strictly speaking, this should have caused a proliferation of *virāmas* marking the absence of the vowel, but (sensibly, perhaps) this has not been done. In modern Hindi, therefore, a consonant symbol by itself can stand for either the consonant plus an *a*-vowel or the consonant alone. So "bus" is बस, *bas*, in Hindi, the first consonant being read with the unwritten vowel and the second consonant not. For a speaker of Hindi it is pretty easy to tell where the default vowel is needed on the basis of how words of the language normally sound. Hindi also uses far fewer conjunct consonants than Sanskrit, again on the principle that the presence or absence of the default vowel can be easily judged.

When Brāhmī, Devanāgarī's ancestor, was first used, however, Hindi was still far in the future. Even Sanskrit written literature had yet to be born. Sanskrit was the language of sacred brahminic liturgy, and the records of secular rulers were written in the plainer, everyday Prakrits. Aśoka, a northern king, naturally used the Prakrit language of the northern Indo-Aryans. In the south, however, the people spoke Dravidian languages. For the most part the Dravidian languages remained unwritten until many centuries after Aśoka, with the sole exception of Tamil in the southeast. The oldest known Tamil inscriptions (written in Brāhmī) may date from as early as 254 BC; Tamil was to be the only written Dravidian language for some seven hundred years.

Sanskrit itself remained unwritten (as far as we can tell from preserved inscriptions) for a century of two after the time of Aśoka. Early writing in India served the same kinds of administrative purposes for which writing was usually invented and adopted in cultures around the world. Then something quite remarkable happened. Suddenly writing acquired a higher purpose: India discovered literature. The language for this new artistic use of written language was Sanskrit. The great Indian epics, the *Ramayana* and the *Mahabharata*, were written in Sanskrit. Kings hired poets to compose paeans in their praise – in Sanskrit. These poems were then included as prologues in inscriptions that recorded the acts of the kings. The prosaic details of the king's gift of land to a temple or of tax immunity to a community of Brahmins could be written in Prakrit, but the finely crafted introductory expressions of the king's greatness were in Sanskrit.

With startling speed, the literary use of Sanskrit – in a form now known as Classical Sanskrit – swept the subcontinent. Kings everywhere hired Sanskrit poets and grammarians. To sponsor a work of Sanskrit grammar was a status symbol no self-respecting ruler would want to forgo. No longer confined to brahminic liturgy, Sanskrit was used by all literary people, regardless of their caste, native language, or religion. The Buddhists and Jains, whose sacred texts were originally composed in Prakrits, embraced Sanskrit enthusiastically. Classical Sanskrit was the language of literature, of kingship, of scholarly inquiry, and of education throughout the subcontinent, even in the Dravidian south. Even written Tamil was almost entirely eclipsed by Sanskrit. The Prakrits were largely confined to prosaic, documentary uses and to representing the speech of the common people (no matter what their actual language) in literary works. However, the Prakrits too were increasingly formalized and removed from anyone's actual spoken language. Here was diglossia with a vengeance: anyone who wanted to become literate had to learn a special language.

To write Sanskrit the Brāhmī script was revamped slightly, with added symbols for phonemes that occurred in Sanskrit but not in the Prakrits. Thanks to the careful phonological analysis of the Sanskrit grammarians, the adaptation of Brāhmī to Sanskrit was done scientifically. One of the changes was the addition of syllabic consonants to the repertoire of "vowels." In some languages, such as Sanskrit, a consonant may sometimes take the place of a vowel in a syllable, serving as the syllable's most resonant part. English has some syllabic consonants, such as the *l* of *trouble*, in which the written *e* is usually unpronounced and the *l* provides the resonant sound after the plosive consonant *b*. In Sanskrit the syllabic consonants were considered vowels, as they were doing the work normally done by vowels. So there were separate symbols for *r* when used as a consonant (र in Devanāgarī) and when it was used as a "vowel" (ऋ). As a vowel, the syllabic form usually appeared as an appendage to consonants: कृ was *kr* ([kɹ̩] in IPA). A long version, syllabic *r̄*, also occurred occasionally and received its own symbol, ॠ. Careful attention to the phonology of the formalized language of which they were both students and guardians led the grammarians to realize that the words that shared one particular verb root contained a syllabic *l̥*, which was assigned the symbol ऌ. For the sake of symmetry, it was given a long partner, ॡ, although this letter was never actually used – a classic case of theory driving practice. No syllabic consonants occur in the modern languages, but the symbol for *ṛ* is still retained in many Indian scripts (though pronounced as *ri* or *ru*), and the symbol for *ṝ* remains in some.

From about the first century BC and lasting for about a thousand years, Sanskrit was by far the chief vehicle of written language. The power of Sanskrit was such that it not only conquered the Dravidian peoples of South India but, beginning in about the fourth century AD, it also swept Southeast Asia. From Burma to Java the Southeast Asians took up writing in Sanskrit. Like the Indians, they too praised their kings in Sanskrit verses. They imported Brahmins to teach them about Hinduism, and Buddhist missionaries to teach them about Buddhism. Temples were decorated with scenes from the *Ramayana*, and the Thai capital city was named Ayutthaya, after Ayodhya, the city of Rama in the *Ramayana*. The kings of Thailand still bear the title of Rama, the present King Bhumibol Adulyadej being Rama IX.

One of the remarkable things about the spread of Sanskrit and of Indian learned culture throughout Southeast Asia is that it happened entirely without military or political conquest. The Southeast Asians acknowledged the Chinese emperor as their remote overlord and occasionally sent him tribute. But only the Vietnamese were truly under the control of China. They adopted Chinese writing, Mahayana Buddhism (the form practiced in China), and other aspects of Chinese culture. The rest of the region, freer to choose their cultural models, looked to India, learned Sanskrit and Pali, and chose to adopt Theravada Buddhism (at the time practiced in India and Sri Lanka), Hinduism, or sometimes a combination of both, worshipping Shiva-Buddha.

From the frontier of India in the northwest to Java in the southeast, the language of culture was Sanskrit. It was no one's native tongue. As a vernacular language it had been dead for centuries – if in fact it had ever been one, since it may always have been a formal dialect set apart from colloquial speech. Classical Sanskrit is thus very different from Classical Latin. The original Latin classics were written by people who actually spoke Latin. Although Latin eventually died out as a spoken language and remained in use only as a learned language, medieval scholars who wrote in Latin knew they were writing in the mother tongue of Caesar and Virgil. Classical Sanskrit, by contrast, flourished only after it was "dead." As a purely literary language it belonged to no one people and to no one piece of soil. This ethnic neutrality may have been the secret of its remarkable success. Without it, India might never have been unified, and Southeast Asia might have learned Chinese.

Sanskrit was considered to be eternal, unchanging, and perfect. Although the language of the classics actually did vary somewhat by time and place, the uniformity in the language over thousands of miles and centuries of time is striking. A living, vernacular language would never have been so constant.

Given such remarkable uniformity in the language, what is surprising is that the script with which it was recorded did not remain uniform at all. No one seemed to care if the Brāhmī used in the north diverged from that used in the south, so long as the Sanskrit it recorded was good literary Sanskrit. This lax attitude toward scripts may have been due to the respect that continued to be accorded to the oral tradition and to oral performance of literary texts. If most people experienced written works as dramatic readings, then perhaps the manner in which those works were written was not considered important. The continuing pre-eminence of the spoken word may also account for why there has never been a strong calligraphic tradition in India, despite the fact that the native scripts are inherently quite beautiful. The script was merely a vehicle for the text, and a well-educated person was expected to read many scripts. (By contrast, there are many educated Indians today who speak languages that they cannot read – they may have picked up a language rather easily in conversation, but to read it they would have to master yet another script.)

With no one trying to keep them standardized, the regional forms of Brāhmī diverged from each other quite considerably. At first a simple north/south difference was visible. The northern form of Brāhmī eventually evolved into today's Devanāgarī, Bengali, Gujarati, Gurmukhi (Punjabi), Oriya, Tibetan, and minor scripts such as Meitei-Mayak.

The southern style spread to Southeast Asia and continued to diversify both there and in South India. Additionally, it is possible that Christian missionaries from South India brought the concept of *akṣara* writing to Ethiopia and influenced the fourth-century changes in the script there. In South India and Sri Lanka the Telugu, Kannada, Tamil, Malayalam, and Sinhala scripts are descended from the southern form of Brāhmī. In Southeast Asia Brāhmī-derived scripts are used for Khmer (of the Mon-Khmer branch of the Austro-Asiatic language family), and languages of the Tai family (Thai, Lao, and Shan) and the Tibeto-Burman branch of Sino-Tibetan (Karen and Burmese). Related forms of Indic writing also spread to the Austronesian languages of Java, Bali, Sumatra, Sulawesi, and even parts of the Philippines, where surprised Western missionaries reported universal literacy in the sixteenth century. These insular Southeast Asian scripts, however, have mostly been superseded by the Roman and Arabic alphabets.

In Sulawesi the local language had no consonant clusters and virtually no syllable-final consonants, so conjunct consonants were done away with. When writing spread from there to the Philippines, there was no way to represent final consonants, leaving the resulting scripts closer to syllabaries than Brāhmī ever had been. One surviving insular script is that of the tribal Hanunóo people of Mindoro in the Philippines. The Hanunóo use their script primarily for exchanging love poetry, which they carve into bamboo or other wood with the point of a knife. The script is unusual in being generally written from bottom to top, away from the body – and, of course, for not being associated with administration, bureaucracy, or urban civilization.

A distinctive feature of most Indic alphasyllabaries, whether northern or southern, is the head mark that letters tend to have, derived originally from serifs that resulted from using a reed pen. These serifs are now an integral and distinctive part of the Indic writing systems. In Devanāgarī, Bengali, and Gurmukhi the head marks have become lines running across the top of each letter, which are joined within a word (as in देवनागरी, Devanāgarī). Thus when writing on lined paper in these scripts one suspends the letters *from* the line rather than placing them *on* the line. In Oriya the serifs have become umbrella-like arched lines atop the letters; in Kannada and Telugu a pervasive "checkmark"; in Tamil a tendency for letters to contain a straight line across the top (see figure 10.2).

The traditionally favored writing surfaces in India were birch bark and palm leaves (plate 7). These writing materials were readily available in India in the first millennium, in contrast with Europe and the Middle East, where parchment was rare and costly. In the north a reed pen was used, in the south a metal stylus. Since a metal stylus could easily tear the writing surface, the southern scripts developed more rounded forms, while the northern scripts remain more angular. The Oriya script, located on the border of the northern and southern areas, is closely related to the angular, northern Bengali script; but because it was written with a stylus it developed the more rounded look of a southern script.

Vowels (initial form above, added to k below)

Devanagari	अ क	आ का	इ कि	ई की	उ कु	ऊ कू	ऋ कृ	ॠ कॄ	ऌ कॢ	(ॡ) कॣ
Kannada	ಅ ಕ	ಆ ಕಾ	ಇ ಕಿ	ಈ ಕೀ	ಉ ಕು	ಊ ಕೂ	ಋ ಕೃ	ೠ ಕೄ		
Tamil	அ க	ஆ கா	இ கி	ஈ கீ	உ கு	ஊ கூ				
Roman/IPA	a [e]	ā [aː]	i [ɪ]	ī [iː]	u [ʊ]	ū [uː]	r̥/ri/rʊ][r̥/riː/ruː]		ḷ [ḷ]	

Devanagari	ए के	ऐ कै	ओ को	औ कौ	कँ	कं	कः	क्	
Kannada	ಎ ಕೆ	ಏ ಕೇ	ಐ ಕೈ	ಒ ಕೊ	ಓ ಕೋ	ಔ ಕೌ	ಕಂ	ಕಃ	ಕ್
Tamil	எ கெ	ஏ கே	ஐ கை	ஒ கொ	ஓ கோ	ஔ கெள	Diacritics	க:.	ஃ
Roman/IPA	e [e]	ē [eː]	ai [ai]	o [o]	ō [oː]	au [au]	nasal ṃ	nasal ḥ [h]	no vowel

Consonants (pronounced with following *a*)

Devanagari	क	ख	ग	घ	ङ	च	छ	ज	झ	ञ
Kannada	ಕ	ಖ	ಗ	ಘ	ಙ	ಚ	ಛ	ಜ	ಝ	ಞ
Tamil	க				ங	ச		(ஜ)		ஞ
Roman/IPA	k [k]	kh [kʰ]	g [g]	gh [gʱ]	ṅ [ŋ]	c [ʧ]	ch [ʧʰ]	j [ʤ]	jh [ʤʱ]	ñ [ɲ]

Devanagari	ट	ठ	ड	ढ	ण	त	थ	द	ध	न
Kannada	ಟ	ಠ	ಡ	ಢ	ಣ	ತ	ಥ	ದ	ಧ	ನ
Tamil	ட				ண	த				ந
Roman/IPA	ṭ [t]	ṭh [tʰ]	ḍ [ḍ]	ḍh [ḍʱ]	ṇ [ɳ]	t [t̪]	th [t̪ʰ]	d[d̪]	dh [d̪ʱ]	n [n̪]

Devanagari	प	फ	ब	भ	म	य	र	ल	व	श
Kannada	ಪ	ಫ	ಬ	ಭ	ಮ	ಯ	ರ	ಲ	ವ	ಶ
Tamil	ப				ம	ய	ர	ல	வ	
Roman/IPA	p [p]	ph [pʰ]	b [b]	bh [bʱ]	m [m]	y [j]	r [ɾ]	l [l]	v [ʋ]	ś [ʃ]

Devanagari	ष	स	ह		ळ			
Kannada	ಷ	ಸ	ಹ		ಳ			
Tamil	(ழ)	(ஸ)	(ஹ)	ழ	ள	ற	ன	(Tamil appendix letters in parentheses)
Roman/IPA	ṣ [ṣ]	s [s]	h [ɦ]	zh [ɻ]	ḷ [ḷ]	ṯ [t]/[ɾ]	ṉ [n]	

Figure 10.2 The Devanāgarī, Kannada, and Tamil scripts, all descended from Brāhmī and following the same alphabetical order, though Tamil has reduced the number of letters.

Not only did every region develop its own script, each region also had its own set of Brāhmī-derived numerals, with shapes that evolved freely as they spread throughout South and Southeast Asia. The Brāhmī script is also the ultimate source of the numerals used in most of the world today, though the zero is a late (c. AD 600) addition to the system. In English we call them Arabic numerals, but the Arabs themselves call them Indian. Around AD 800 Arabs from two different regions adopted two different local forms of the Indian numerals; the forms used by the western Arabs were passed on to the Europeans. Some Indian scripts have since given up their local numeral shapes in favor of the European ones, which are now understood everywhere.

The multitude of regional scripts in southern Asia arose mostly in the writing of a single language, Sanskrit – a perfect example of diversity retained in the face of outward conformity. Meanwhile India's many other languages went almost entirely unwritten. Other than the Prakrits, the regional language with the longest recorded history is Tamil, lucky enough to have gotten started on the literary endeavor before Classical Sanskrit really began to dominate. The oldest examples of written Tamil are roughly as old as the Aśokan Prakrit inscriptions. Tamil was given a grammar, the *Tolkāppiyam*, around 100 BC, and a collection of poetry was produced in the following centuries. Yet even Tamil was decisively overshadowed by Sanskrit for several centuries.

The first written Kannada (the language of Bangalore) dates from about AD 450, the first Telugu (the language of Hyderabad) from about 620, and the first Malayalam (the language of the Malabar Coast) from about 830. During the same period, several of the Southeast Asian languages first appear. For centuries after each language was first written, however, the regional languages were used only for prosaic, documentary purposes. Expressive or artistic literary work continued to be done in Sanskrit.

Tamil was the first to shake off the Sanskritic yoke, beginning in the eighth century. Eventually the other major Dravidian languages of South India and the various languages of Southeast Asia followed suit. In the north, the switch to regional vernaculars was several centuries slower in coming. The major regional languages of the north were genetically related to Sanskrit – and even more closely related to Prakrit – so perhaps the need for written vernaculars was less strongly felt. Geography probably also played a role. The movement of peoples and their languages was freer across the broad Gangetic plain of northern

India than it was in other areas with more natural boundaries. The absence of boundaries in a region encourages the development of a *dialect continuum*, in which only slight differences in speech are discernable from one local area to the next. In such a case it would not have been obvious which dialect to reify in writing. Even today it is not always clear where one language in North India ends and another begins; the language known as "Hindi" includes 48 recognized regional variants, not including Urdu, which is much like Hindi but uses the Perso-Arabic script. Many of these other dialects could be considered different languages – and doubtless would be if, like Urdu, they had distinct written traditions.

When the regional languages came to be written down, they were written in whatever local version of the Brāhmī script was used to write Sanskrit. In the south some letters had to be added to represent phonemes used by the Dravidian languages but not Sanskrit. Sanskrit had a great number of consonants; the Dravidian languages had fewer, but nevertheless had some that Sanskrit did not. It was impossible to reuse "extra" letters from Sanskrit, because those letters were still needed for writing Sanskrit, the dominant language. In fact, Sanskrit continued to be written in a multiplicity of local scripts until the introduction of printing in the seventeenth century, since when it has been almost exclusively confined to Devanāgarī. Alphabets all across southern Asia reflect the phonemes of Sanskrit and arrange them in the same order. The order is one carefully worked out by Sanskrit grammarians, who arranged the letters according to how they are pronounced, from the back of the mouth to the front. Extra letters, where needed, generally appear at the end of the list.

The languages of southern Asia soaked up formal Sanskrit vocabulary like so many sponges. When they finally came to be used as literary languages, much of the vocabulary used was actually Sanskrit – a vocabulary refined over the centuries for learned and aesthetic purposes. (Similarly, most learned English vocabulary comes from the classical European languages, Latin and Greek.) The scripts, therefore, went right on writing Sanskrit words, even when embedded in local grammar.

Sanskrit (and the northern Indo-Aryan languages generally) distinguished voiceless plosives from voiced ones (e.g. [p] from [b]), and both of those plain plosives from aspirated ones (e.g. from [pʰ] and [bʰ]). Historically, the Dravidian languages have made no distinction between plain and aspirated plosives and used voiceless and voiced plosives in separate, predictable contexts (so that one can say, for example, that [p] and [b] are alternative pronunciations of a single phoneme, the choice of pronunciation being determined by context). As a result, there are many letters of the alphabet that are actually pronounced alike in colloquial speech. However, people educated in Sanskrit would pronounce Sanskrit words with contrasts of voicing and aspiration duly made. Over time some of the distinctions of Sanskrit consonants have made their way into the local Dravidian languages; certain other distinctions are made only in formal contexts by educated speakers.

The lone rebel in the story is again Tamil. Although the Tamils had a Sanskrit-based alphabet, the Grantha script, when it came to writing their own language they systematically ejected all letters that were not phonemic in Tamil. The result was the shortest Brāhmī-based alphabet in India. Even Sanskrit loanwords were written with the nearest equivalent letters, so that Sanskrit *p*, *b*, *p^h*, and *b^h* are all written ப, *p*. Some Sanskrit sounds were not considered to have close-enough equivalents, so the alphabet was grudgingly given a five-letter appendix of "Grantha letters." The use of any of these letters in a word is a dead giveaway that the word is a loanword, though these days it may be from English, not necessarily Sanskrit.

Across India the basic way the Brāhmī-based scripts work is much the same: consonants and vowels receive separate treatment, sequential consonants are put together in a cluster, vowels other than the default vowel are written as appendages to the consonants except when initial, and the lack of a following vowel is indicated with a *virāma*. Within this general pattern, variations exist. The vowels may each have their own independent letter for when they occur initially, or they may be written initially as diacritics on a "zero consonant" or "vowel support" character. The vowel-killing *virāma* may be written below the character, as in the northern scripts, or it may be written as a mark above it, as in the southern scripts. The conjunction of consonants may be done in different ways. In Kannada and Telugu, for example, the first consonant will be written normal size and the second consonant (sometimes in a simplified shape) written smaller below it. Tamil is the rebel once again, having done away with conjunct characters entirely except for the Grantha letter க்ஷ, which is pronounced *kṣa* and derives from *k* + *ṣ*, but is treated as a single letter, comparable to *x*, [ks], in English. In all other cases, any consonant that is not followed by a vowel receives a dot on top, the Tamil version of the *virāma*.

The adaptation of Sanskrit scripts to the Southeast Asian languages was less straightforward than their adaptation to the Dravidian languages. In the Thai script (see figure 10.3), thanks to the Sanskrit phonemic inventory, there are 44 consonant symbols, but the language as pronounced only has 21 consonant phonemes. Two of the consonants are obsolete – they were used for sounds of Old Thai – but such is the power of a set alphabetic list that they are still considered part of the alphabet. Many of the consonants are pronounced alike: the voiced, voiceless aspirated, and voiced aspirated consonants of Sanskrit are all pronounced in Thai as voiceless aspirates. Furthermore, Thai does not have the retroflex series of consonants so characteristic of languages in India, whether they be Indo-Aryan, Dravidian, Munda, or even Indian English (these sounds are made with the tip of the tongue curled somewhat backward, and are usually transliterated with a dot under them: *ṭ, ḍ, ṇ*). The result is that there are six ways of writing the consonant [tʰ] and three for [kʰ]. These extra consonants have been faithfully preserved in the alphabet and are used in spelling words of Sanskrit and Pali origin. Traditionally the names of the letters consist of the consonant pronounced with the inherent vowel, but as this leaves too many of the letters with the same names, they are also given a further name – a noun which begins with the letter in question. A reverence for original spellings means that there are a number of consonants written (from their original Sanskrit, Pali, or even English forms) that are not pronounced at all, since Thai is very restrictive in what sorts of consonants can be pronounced at the ends of syllables. These consonants are generally (and helpfully!) marked with a diacritic to indicate that they are silent.

Many Southeast Asian languages are tone languages, meaning that each syllable is pronounced with a particular pitch pattern, such as a high pitch, a falling pitch, a low pitch, or a rising pitch. Thai is no exception, with five distinctive tones. Some of the extra consonants are employed to provide information about the tone of the upcoming vowel, with four additional diacritical marks required to represent all tone distinctions. All in all, Thai orthography is quite complex. At least it has (like Tamil) done away with consonant conjuncts.

By contrast, the closely related Lao script (used to write the closely related Lao language) has turned its back on consonants whose only distinctive function is to show a word's Sanskrit etymology. Lao uses only 27 consonant letters to represent its 20 consonant phonemes, with

Consonants

	ก	ข	ค	ฆ	ง	จ	ฉ	ช	ซ	ฌ	ญ	
Initial	[k]	[kʰ]	[kʰ]	[kʰ]	[ŋ]	[ʨ]	[ʨʰ]	[ʨʰ]	[s]	[ʨʰ]	[j]	
Final	[k]	[k]	[k]	[k]	[ŋ]	[t]	[t]	[t]	[t]	[t]	[n]	
Class	M	H	L	L	L	M	H	L	L	L	L	

	ฎ	ฏ	ฐ	ฑ	ฒ	ณ	ด	ต	ถ	ท	ธ	น
Initial	[d]	[t]	[tʰ]	[tʰ]	[tʰ]	[n]	[d]	[t]	[tʰ]	[tʰ]	[tʰ]	[n]
Final	[t]	[t]	[t]	[t]	[t]	[n]	[t]	[t]	[t]	[t]	[t]	[n]
Class	M	M	H	L	L	L	M	M	H	L	L	L

	บ	ป	ผ	ฝ	พ	ฟ	ภ	ม	ย	ร	ล	
Initial	[b]	[p]	[pʰ]	[f]	[pʰ]	[f]	[pʰ]	[m]	[j]	[r]	[l]	
Final	[p]	[p]	[p]	[p]	[p]	[p]	[p]	[m]	[j]	[n]	[n]	
Class	M	M	H	H	L	L	L	L	L	L	L	

	ว	ศ	ษ	ส	ห	ฬ	อ	ฮ	
Initial	[w]	[s]	[s]	[s]	[h]	[l]	zero consonant	[h]	
Final	[w]	[t]	[t]	[t]		[n]			
Class	L	H	H	H	H	L	M	L	

Vowels (shown on "zero consonant," อ)

ออ	อะ	อั	อ้า	อา	อำ	อิ	อี	อึ	อื	อุ	อู
[ɔː]	[a]	[a]	[ua]	[aː]	[am]	[i]	[iː]	[ɨ]	[ɨː]	[u]	[uː]
		(final)	medial								

เอ	เอ้	เอย	เออ	เออะ	เอะ	เอา	เอาะ	เอิ	เอีย	เอียะ	เอือ
[eː]	[e]	[əːj]	[əː]	[ə]	[e]	[aw]	[ɔ]	[əː]	[ia]	[ia]	[ɨa]

แอ	แอ้	แอะ	โอ	โอะ	ใอ	ไอ	Tone marks	`	ˇ	˜	˖
[ɛː]	[ɛ]	[ɛ]	[oː]	[o]	[aj]	[aj]	Tone	varies with class		high	rising

Figure 10.3 The Thai script, descended from the southern form of Brāhmī, and preserving Sanskrit alphabetical order. The Thai language does not distinguish all the consonant phonemes of Sanskrit, so many letters are pronounced alike. Word-finally even fewer consonants are distinguished. On the other hand, Thai has added symbols for its many vowel phonemes. Consonants fall into three classes, which influence the tone on the upcoming vowel. Vowels do not have initial forms; when word-initial they are added to a dummy "zero consonant." Thai does not use spaces between words.

the extras again used as partial indicators of tone. Thai and Lao thus present contrasting choices in the age-old dilemma of literacy: should writing preserve tradition and information about the past (it is, after all, inherently preserving), or should it be easy to learn, modeling the present state of the language as efficiently as possible? Thai still feels the pull of the first-millennium, unified Sanskrit world, while Lao has chosen modernity, simplicity, and regional individuality.

The Sanskritic tradition was firmly on the side of preservation, enabled by the development of the science of grammar. A learned but otherwise dead language has a useful feature: it can be controlled – corralled into following prescriptive norms and largely preserved from change. Over time this becomes yet another argument for using the language: works written in Sanskrit were perceived as perennially accessible, as were works in Latin in medieval Europe. The preserving effect of writing had made it very obvious that while spoken language changes, texts remain the same; the vernaculars were therefore considered unreliable and unstable.

As the study of grammar began to be applied to other languages, first to Tamil in the *Tolkāppiyam* and later to other languages as well, the normative urge of the Sanskrit grammarians was inherited. The grammars were not written to explain how Tamil, say, or Kannada was spoken, but rather to explain how Tamil or Kannada *should* be spoken. Probably it was felt that if the regional languages were to vie with Sanskrit as literary vehicles, they needed officially sanctioned, pure, and relatively changeless forms. To a greater or lesser degree in various languages, this attitude has stuck to the present day.

The result is that both Kannada and Tamil (which were early objects of grammaticization and vernacular literature) are now written in a form that is several centuries older than the spoken language. As a consequence, both languages are marked by strong diglossia. By contrast, while English spelling reflects an older form of the language (with words such as *should*, **knight**, and *laugh*), the archaic spellings are no longer pronounced. Every language with an established literary tradition has a certain amount of diglossia (in English, for example, we rarely write contracted forms such as *hafta*, *gonna*, and *wanna*, though they occur ubiquitously in speech), but in India, as in the Arabic world, the diglossia is much more thoroughgoing. In Kannada, and even more in Tamil, the situation would be analogous to English speakers conversing in twenty-first-century English but writing, reading aloud, and making formal speeches and announcements in Shakespearean English. Unlike English, Kannada and Tamil spell their words as they are pronounced – but only as they are pronounced in the literary form of the language. They are spelled as grammarians feel they *should* be pronounced.

The formal or literary variety is relatively free from dialectal variation, while colloquial styles vary considerably, both by region and by caste. The formal language is no one's spoken style – not even the Brahmins' – but everyone, whatever their class or caste background, will use the literary style in certain formal contexts, provided they have the education to do so. In yet another example of the reifying effect of writing, only the literary variety is considered "real." Highly educated individuals may even believe that they speak the formal variety at home and not notice their instinctive use of their native colloquial. Foreigners are taught only the literary forms and may find themselves corrected if they try to use the colloquial. The literary style is the only form of the language that is traditionally *taught* – the colloquial style is acquired naturally at home. The foreigners may therefore have trouble finding a chance to learn the colloquial language and may continue to find it unintelligible even after they have studied the formal language for years.

Indians have long been used to speaking one language at home and writing another. After the age of Sanskrit, during the Mughal Empire (1526–1857), the court language was Persian, and in modern times English is used as an educated *lingua franca*. However, no single language has absolute sway. As amended in 2004, the Indian constitution recognizes 22 languages: Assamese, Bengali, Bodo, Dogri, Gujarati, Hindi, Kannada, Kashmiri, Konkani, Malayalam, Maithili, Manipuri (Meitei), Marathi, Nepali, Oriya, Punjabi, Santali, Sindhi, Tamil, Telugu, Urdu, and Sanskrit. Except for Sanskrit, these recognized, or "scheduled," languages (so called because they are enumerated in the Eighth Schedule of the Constitution of India) are spoken by at least a million people each. No single community uses Sanskrit as their home language, but it is still widely studied, and the Indian census reports a few thousand people who still claim Sanskrit as their mother tongue (though what this means in practice is not entirely clear). In addition to the scheduled languages, English is tolerated as a de facto national language, alongside Hindi, which officially holds national status.

Languages not on the official list are generally dismissed as "dialects," although this leaves all but one (Santali) of the 20 languages of the Munda group, all but one (Manipuri) of India's 121 Tibeto-Burman languages, and the entire Andamanese language family classified as mere "dialects." Speakers of some of these supposed dialects, such as Tulu (Dravidian) and Bhili (Indo-Aryan), number in the millions. What the so-called dialects lack is neither numbers of speakers nor adequate distinctiveness from other languages, but an established literary tradition.

In the popular mind it is writing that makes a language. Though this is historically backwards, the reifying and standardizing effect of writing is undeniable. In India, where scripts run rampant, one can often recognize what language a text is written in merely by its script. Before 1992 there were only 15 scheduled languages, and they used 10 different scripts. Assamese and Bengali share basically the same script; Hindi, Marathi, and modern publications in Sanskrit share the Devanāgarī script; and Kashmiri, Sindhi, and Urdu are written in the Perso-Arabic script. The rest each had their own.

In fact, the most significant difference between Hindi and Urdu is what script they are written in. Formal and religious styles of Urdu will use more Persian and Arabic loanwords, while the corresponding styles of Hindi will use more Sanskrit loanwords. At a colloquial level, however, Hindi and Urdu sound much the same, to the extent that most linguists consider them a single language. Visually, the two are entirely different. Hindi uses Devanāgarī and Urdu uses the Perso-Arabic alphabet. Their scripts have made of them two different languages.

The recent additions to the list of scheduled languages (Konkani, Manipuri, Nepali, Bodo, Dogri, Maithili, and Santali) have smaller literary traditions and tend to use the more established scripts of other languages – often Devanāgarī, the closest thing India has to a default national script. The exception is Santali, for which Pandit Raghunath Murmu invented the Ol Chiki script in the twentieth century.

The Pandit was reacting to Indians' widespread belief that not only is a real language written down, but any truly self-respecting language has its own script. This attitude has inspired the invention of a number of scripts for so-called "tribal" languages, but Ol Chiki has been the most successful, helping to pave the way for recognition of Santali as a scheduled language.

The People of India project surveyed 4,635 different communities. These traditionally endogamous communities are based on distinctions of caste, tribe, religion, and language. With so many different social and ethnic groups, speaking so many different languages, India seems an unlikely candidate for a nation. The fact that it is one is in no small degree thanks to the unifying work of Sanskrit, whose vocabulary pervades the Indian languages, whose pronunciation has altered the phonemic inventories of unrelated languages, and whose alphabetical order is still followed. In India, it is the script that makes a language; yet it was Sanskrit that made the scripts.

11

King Sejong's One-Man Renaissance

If Sequoyah had been born a royal prince of Korea, he might well have been like Sejong. Born in 1397, Sejong became the fourth king of Korea's Chosŏn dynasty (1392–1910) in 1418 and ruled for 32 years. King Sejong's accomplishments were many and diverse, but today, like Sequoyah, he is best remembered for the script he invented. These visionary men perceived that literacy was vital to the welfare of their peoples, both of which lived in the shadow of a more powerful nation (in Sejong's case, China). With the added benefits of literacy, bilingualism, and a thorough education, Sejong was able to create the most efficient and logical writing system in the world. Those who trumpet the wonders of the Greek alphabet are misguided; it is the Korean alphabet which is the true paragon of scripts.

Sejong was an extraordinary man: a brilliant scholar, an able ruler, and a generous humanitarian. The new Chosŏn (or Yi) dynasty had chosen Neo-Confucianism as its official philosophy, blaming state-sponsored Buddhism for the failings of their predecessors in the Koryŏ dynasty (918–1392, the dynasty from which we get the name *Korea*). Sejong's rare moral vision reflected the best of the Neo-Confucianism under which he had grown up.

The Confucianism Sejong upheld enjoined him to be a wise and benevolent ruler, to cultivate virtue, and to pursue learning as a means to achieve harmony with the cosmos. Few rulers have lived up to these ideals as well as Sejong. He ascended the throne at the age of 21 upon the abdication of his father, King T'aejong, and within two years had launched his very own Korean renaissance.

By 1420 Sejong had revitalized the royal academy (the Academy of Worthies), handpicking its roughly twenty members. With this elite group of men under his personal direction, Sejong presided over Korea's golden age. He directed the scholars to pursue specific projects, but also instituted academic sabbaticals, giving them time off for personal study.

Not content merely to gather knowledge, Sejong turned immediately to its dissemination, and thus to printing. Korea had long ago learned the art of woodblock printing (xylography) from the Chinese and may have heard of Bi Sheng's eleventh-century invention of ceramic movable type (typography). It is also possible that the Koreans had never heard of Bi Sheng, as the Chinese themselves had not taken his invention very seriously. It was Koreans, however, who in 1234 first used metal movable type (a bronze font of Chinese characters), over two centuries before Gutenberg invented his printing press. In 1392 the Publications Office was established, charged with the publishing of books and the casting of type. In practice, the office used only block printing until 1403, when King T'aejong ordered the casting of a new font, declaring the availability of reading material to be essential to good government. This lofty ideal was reportedly greeted with skepticism by some of his officials.

King Sejong, however, followed enthusiastically in his father's footsteps. He ordered a new kind of type cast in 1420 which could be used more efficiently, increasing from about 20 to 100 the number of copies that could be printed from a single form in one day. He had another new font cast in 1434, again with advances in design. In 1436 he experimented with casting type from lead rather than bronze, and brought out a large-print type for the elderly.

Meanwhile, xylography flourished under Sejong as well. Block printing involved considerable expenditure of time and effort in the initial carving of blocks, but once carved a woodblock could last literally for centuries. Movable type was much faster to set up, but the type had to be painstakingly realigned after printing every page, and so printing was slow. Large print orders were therefore usually done with woodblocks, while movable type was used for smaller publications. Given Korea's small population (and its truly tiny literate population), combined with Sejong's concern with disseminating as many publications as possible, movable type was far more practical in Korea than it had ever been in China. In all, 114 works are known to have been printed with movable type and 194 printed with woodblocks during Sejong's reign. By contrast, block printing of books was only just beginning in Europe during this period, and Gutenberg was still experimenting with typography in the late 1440s, thirty years into Sejong's rule.

Like other educated men of his time, Sejong read and wrote in Classical Chinese, the Koreans having been the first people outside of China to adopt Chinese characters. At the latest, Chinese characters entered Korea with the establishment of the Han Prefectures, when China ruled northern Korea from 108 BC to AD 313. The Koreans themselves were using Chinese characters by 414, as evidenced by an inscribed stele erected in honor of King Kwangaet'o (AD 375–413). Chinese characters, however, are designed for the Chinese language, and Korean (aside from a large quantity of Chinese loanwords) is not at all like Chinese. (It is sometimes, though not conclusively, classified with the Altaic languages; it may also be distantly related to Japanese.) So literate Koreans wrote in Chinese. During their long acquaintance with Chinese characters, Koreans invented about 150 characters and added some specifically Korean meanings to Chinese characters. Chinese words entered the Korean language in droves.

Korea accepted China as its "elder brother," with the Chinese emperor – theoretically at least – being the Korean king's overlord. China was considered the source of all culture and learning. The Korean elite therefore thought it natural that becoming literate meant learning the Chinese language: everything worth reading was written in Chinese.

Some attempts were made to write Korean, however. At first, the native style of poetry was written in *hyangchal*, a system of using characters for their pronunciations that was similar to (and may have inspired) the Japanese man'yŏgana. Native Korean poetry declined during the Koryŏ period, however, and with it *hyangchal* went out of use. *Kugyŏl*, analogous to early uses of katakana in Japan, was a system of simple and abbreviated characters that were inserted into Chinese texts to represent Korean grammatical elements and help Korean readers make sense of the Chinese grammar. Korean prose was written in *idu* ("clerk reading"), a system which used some characters for their meanings and others for their sounds. The oldest known *idu* text dates from 754; it remained the dominant method of writing Korean until 1894. Yet *idu* was looked down upon as vulgar by the literati. And indeed, it was a clumsy writing system that cried out to be superseded.

Sejong, while never overtly questioning China's suzerainty, had the audacity to realize that Korea was different from China. He came to the throne at a time when the Chosŏn dynasty was still fresh and hopeful, and the new state-sponsored Neo-Confuncianism was still being defined. Instead of slavishly copying China, Sejong looked for distinctively Korean ways to implement his ideas. Korea needed new rites and ceremonies, and appropriate music for them, so he ordered the compilation of manuals of ritual and protocol, and the composition and arranging of music, in first Chinese style and then native Korean. A unique style of Korean musical notation developed under his reign, the first East Asian system to fully represent rhythm.

To teach Confucian morality, Sejong ordered the compilation of the *Samgang haengsil* ("Illustrated Guide to the Three Relationships"), a book of stories illustrating Confucian virtues. Unlike its earlier models, Sejong's book contained examples drawn from Korean as well as Chinese sources. The king took care to have the book provided with large illustrations, aware that the vast majority of his subjects could not read. He issued statements encouraging the teaching of literacy to all classes of society, including (with a generosity unusual in his time) to women; but with a writing system as complex as *idu* and an educated class intent on keeping the privileges of literacy to themselves, nothing much happened.

Despite his scholarly bent, Sejong was no ivory-tower philosopher. His people needed more than morality and court ritual. Most importantly, the growing population needed food. Sejong set his academy to work on numerous scientific and technological projects directed toward increasing agricultural production. He commissioned a geographical survey of Korea; invented and distributed a rain gauge, instituting a nationwide meteorological network; and implemented irrigation systems. The optimal timing of sowing and harvest required an accurate calendar, he realized, not one calibrated to a Chinese latitude. He would have to derive a Korean calendar from scratch. In the course of his calendrical research Sejong invented (and/or had invented by his academy) an astrolabe, a water clock, and a sundial. His Publications Office printed seven books on agriculture and 32 calendars; it must have weighed on him that his farmers couldn't read them.

King Sejong opened a medical school and even encouraged the education of female physicians so as to improve the health care available to women (who could not with propriety see a male doctor unless very seriously ill). He sponsored a compendious work of herbal medicine in 56 volumes, which again broke with Chinese tradition by emphasizing native Korean herbs, their uses, and where to find them.

For many years, beginning in 1422, Sejong worked on revising the Korean law code. Aware that bad law would make for bad precedents, he personally reviewed each article of the code with his legal scholars. Throughout his reign he showed a passion for justice, working to improve prison conditions, set fairer sentencing standards, implement proper procedures for autopsies, protect slaves from being lynched, punish corrupt officials, set up an appeals process for capital crimes, and limit torture. Nevertheless, one problem continued to vex the king: the litigation process was carried out in Chinese. Were the accused able to adequately defend themselves in a foreign language? Sejong doubted it.

Despite his achievements in agriculture, music, science, printing, and jurisprudence, Sejong was repeatedly stymied by the fact that his subjects couldn't read. How could they learn about advances in technology if they couldn't read? How could they benefit from moral philosophy if they couldn't read? How could they defend themselves properly in a court of law if they couldn't read?

Something must be done about it. Quietly, without telling his academy what he was about, Sejong set out to invent a script that matched the Korean language and could be easily learned by everyday people. The existing script he knew best was Chinese, but he knew that there were other ways to write. His government's school for diplomats offered classes in Japanese, Jurchin, and Mongolian, besides spoken Chinese. Mongolian was taught in both the traditional vertical Mongol script and the newer 'Phags pa script. 'Phags pa was a squarish *aksara*-based script modeled on Tibetan that had been developed at the command of Kublai Khan by the lama 'Phags pa Blo gros rgyal mtshan and completed in 1269. Kublai intended the script to be a universal writing system that could encode all the languages in his empire; in practice it was not used much. Nevertheless official edicts were often issued in 'Phags pa and it was useful for transcribing the correct pronunciation of Chinese characters. When the Mongol Yuan dynasty lost its hold on China in 1368 most people dropped 'Phags pa with relief.

Sejong may well have studied 'Phags pa. He probably realized that some scripts directly represented their languages' pronunciation rather than whole morphemes, thus using far fewer symbols than the logographic Chinese script. Sejong decided that he too would create a phonological script. He studied all the phonological science available at the time. He also learned spoken Chinese, becoming one of the few Koreans who could speak the Mandarin dialect of the time as well as read Classical Chinese.

Chinese phonologists had recognized that syllables contained two parts, an initial (or *onset*) and a final (or *rhyme*). Sejong, perhaps inspired by the representation of consonants in 'Phags pa, realized that a rhyme could have two parts (today known as the *nucleus* and the *coda*), and that the sounds that could end a syllable were the same sorts of sounds as those that could begin a syllable. In other words, the coda and the onset were both filled with consonants. Thus in a word like *kuk*, "country," the [k] sound at the end and the [k] sound at the beginning were "the same thing" and could be represented with the same symbol. Sejong had discovered the phoneme. He went well beyond this discovery and established that phonemes fall into a number of different classes according to traits, or features, which they possess, such as whether they are vowels or consonants, where in the mouth they are pronounced, and whether they are aspirated. Although Sanskrit grammarians had organized the Indian alphabets according to these same sorts of classifications, Sejong took the unusual step of incorporating these phonological features into the design of the individual letters he created.

Known today as han'gŭl, the writing system Sejong invented was a wonder of simplicity and linguistic insight. To make it, he first systematically analyzed the phonology of his language – a job that, like the creation of a Korean calendar, he had to undertake from scratch, as no one had ever yet cared to subject vernacular Korean to linguistic study. First he divided consonants from vowels; that is, he divided the sounds that occur in the onset or coda of a syllable from those that constitute the nucleus of a syllable. Then he divided the consonants into five classes according to where in the mouth they are pronounced (the *place of articulation*, in modern terms), guided by the Chinese philosophical principle of analyzing almost everything into five classes to match the five elemental agents of Water, Wood, Fire, Metal, and Earth. The categories he arrived at were the *labials* (made with the lips, e.g. [m]), the *linguals* (what we now call *alveolars*, made with the tongue tip touching the alveolar ridge behind the top teeth, e.g. [n]), the *dentals* (made with the tongue tip touching or close behind the lower teeth, e.g. [s]; this class is today known as the *sibilants*), the *molars* (what we now call *velars*, made with the back of the tongue against the soft palate inside the back teeth, e.g. [k]), and the *laryngeals* (made in the throat, e.g. [h]; these are also known as *glottals*).

Having thus identified and classified the consonants of Korean, the next task was to assign them each a graphic shape. At this point Sejong had a stroke of absolute genius. He knew that the most basic Chinese characters had originally been pictograms and ideograms, though most characters of the developed script were compounds made up of a semantic radical and a pronunciation clue. The pictograms at the root of the Chinese script were pictures of *things*, as indeed were the pictograms at the root of cuneiform, Egyptian hieroglyphs, and even the Semitic alphabet. Sejong, conscious that he was departing from Chinese practice in designing a script that recorded individual sounds rather than whole morphemes, created a wholly new form of pictogram. He drew *pronunciations*. Choosing one consonant in each of the five categories as basic (the one he considered least harshly articulated), he drew schematics of the formation of the consonant sounds in the mouth (see figure 11.1).

For the basic labial, [m], he drew a pictogram of a mouth, ㅁ, influenced by the Chinese character/pictogram for mouth, 口. For the basic alveolar, [n], he drew the shape of the tongue as seen from the side, with its tip reaching up as it does when it touches the alveolar ridge: ㄴ. For the basic dental, [s], he drew a schematic of a tooth, ㅅ, perhaps influenced by the Chinese character for tooth, 齒, which depicts the incisors inside an open mouth. For the basic velar, [k], he again drew the shape of the tongue, this time with its back raised upward to touch the soft palate: ㄱ. For the basic laryngeal he drew a circle depicting an open throat: ㅇ. What precisely this letter stood for in Sejong's time is unclear, as it now stands for the *absence* of a consonant in the onset of a syllable. What Sejong may have had in mind was the open throat preparatory to the voicing of the upcoming vowel, considering this to be a type of syllable onset in contrast to the closed throat of the glottal stop or the tensed throat that yields the breathy [h].

Armed with five basic shapes for the least harshly articulated consonant of each class, he proceeded to build the remaining consonants around these basic shapes. Plosive consonants were harsher than the nasals, while the affricate [tʃ] was harsher than the fricative [s]. These harsher sounds were given an extra stroke: ㅂ was [p], derived from [m], ㅁ (written so as to require one extra stroke); ㄷ was [t], derived from [n], ㄴ; and ㅈ was [tʃ], derived from [s], ㅅ. The glottal stop, ㆆ,

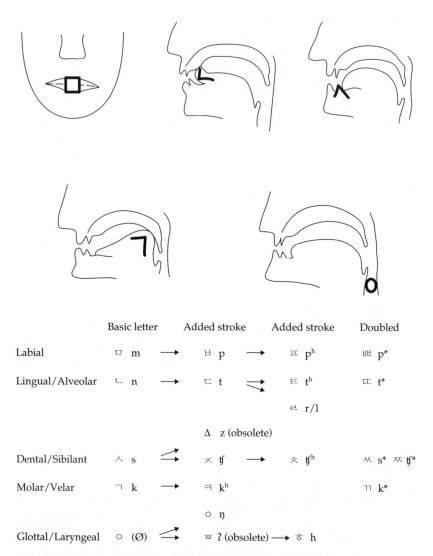

Figure 11.1 The derivation of the han'gŭl letters from their pronunciations. Above, the positions of the lips, tongue, and throat that Sejong used to derive the basic shapes of the consonants. Below, the derivation of further consonants from the basic ones. Note that ○ and ○ are now a single letter.

was similarly derived from the open-throat onset with a line on top of the ㅇ, but the glottal stop and its symbol have since gone out of use in Korean.

Korean has a set of strongly aspirated stops and affricates, and to mark this set of yet harsher sounds the basic symbols were given a further modification, usually a further stroke: ㅍ was [pʰ], ㅌ was [tʰ], ㅊ was [tʃʰ], ㅋ was [kʰ], and ㅎ was [h], the aspirated version of the open throat. Korean also has an unusual set of consonants that are held longer than regular consonants and are similar to doubled consonants in other languages except that they are pronounced with a tense vocal tract. These are sensibly written with double letters: ㅃ, ㄸ, ㅆ, ㅉ, and ㄲ. (Except for ㅆ, these tense phonemes seem not to have existed in Sejong's time, and he used the doubling of a consonant letter to indicate the voiced consonants of Middle Chinese. The Modern Korean tense consonants have arisen since then out of earlier consonant clusters.)

A few consonant phonemes still needed symbols. One of them, pronounced either as [l] or [ɾ], depending on context – [l] when in the coda of a syllable or when doubled, and [ɾ] elsewhere – has an alveolar articulation, so Sejong gave it yet another variation on the basic ㄴ shape: ㄹ. Another exception was the velar nasal, [ŋ]. It is not entirely obvious why Sejong did not consider this the basic sound of the velar series, since the other nasals were considered basic in their classes, but perhaps it was because [ŋ] is unique in not being allowed to begin a Korean morpheme – making it a poor exemplar for the alphabetic principle. Instead he classified this sound with the laryngeals – a reasonable decision (though at odds with modern classification systems) given that in the pronunciation of [ŋ] the mouth is blocked off completely at the very back, leaving the sound to resonate only in the throat and nose. Sejong gave it a symbol based on the open-throat/absence of consonant: ㅇ plus a short vertical line on top, ㆁ. Since Korean morphemes do not begin with [ŋ] and the absence of consonant is not indicated at the ends of syllables, the two symbols have become conflated since Sejong's time: at the beginning of a syllable ㅇ stands for no consonant at all, while at the end it stands for [ŋ].

Having created symbols for consonants, Sejong turned to vowels. Again, he went about it philosophically and systematically. Of the vowels he chose three as basic: the one made with the lowest placement of the tongue [ɒ], the one made with the most forward placement of the tongue, [i], and one of the two made with the tongue drawn up and back, [ɯ] (the unrounded vowel transliterated as *ŭ*). He gave these three vowels symbols representing the mystical triad of heaven, earth, and humankind. The first he represented as a dot, ·, to represent the round heavens (this phoneme is no longer used in Korean). The second he made a vertical stroke, ｜, representing humankind, standing upright. The third became a horizontal line, the flat earth: —. Other vowels were formed as combinations of these. The heavenly dot has evolved into a short line, easier to write with a brush. Thus ㅏ is [a], ㅓ is [ʌ] (transliterated *ŏ*), ㅗ is [o], ㅜ is [u]. Diphthongs starting with a [j] onglide received a second dot (nowadays a line) to make ㅑ [ja], ㅕ [jʌ], ㅛ [jo], and ㅠ [ju]. Other diphthongs were made by combining vowel symbols, though two of these are nowadays pronounced as single vowel phonemes, namely ㅐ (made from ㅏ plus ㅣ and originally [aj] but now [ɛ]) and ㅔ (originally [ʌj] but now [e]). Two other combined vowels, ㅚ and ㅟ, originally [oj] and [uj], are pronounced [we] and [wi] in some modern dialects but as single vowels [ø] and [y] in others.

It was time to put the consonants and vowels together. In Chinese each character is pronounced as a single syllable, and all are written the same size, regardless of complexity. Accordingly, Sejong grouped his newly created letters into <u>syllabic blocks</u>. The initial consonant went at the top left-hand side of the block. Next came the vowel, written to the right of the consonant if it contained a vertical stroke and otherwise below it. Thus 구 is the syllable *ku*, and 가 is *ka*, while a syllable without an initial consonant receives the null sign: 아 is *a*. A final consonant is written at the bottom: 국 is *kuk*, "country," and 말, *mal*, is "language." Syllabic blocks together make up words: 한국말 is *han-kuk-mal*, the Korean language.

If a single consonant occurs between two vowels it is generally assigned to the onset of the second syllable, unless it is [ŋ]; thus the word *ha'nŭl*, "sky," is spelled 하늘, not 한을, but *pang'ul*, "bell," is 방울, with [ŋ] at the end of the first syllable block and the null consonant starting the second. Exceptions in modern orthography (following Sejong's personal practice but revised from most other earlier spelling traditions) arise in order to keep constant the spelling of a morpheme. Thus the verb root 먹 (*mŏk*, "to eat") will be spelled the same, regardless of whether the suffix added to it starts with a vowel or a consonant; the root is clearly visible in both 먹다 and 먹어. The same morphemic convention allows consonant clusters to be *spelled* in syllable codas, even though they are not *pronounced*. The Korean word for "price" is 값, pronounced [kap], with only a single final consonant. The extra ㅅ, *s*, is there because if a vowel-initial suffix is added, there will be room to pronounce it: 값이, with the *-i* suffix marking the word as the subject of the sentence, is pronounced [kapʃi] (*s* being pronounced [ʃ] before [i]). A similar principle drives the spelling in English of a word like *iamb*, with a silent unpronounceable letter that is heard only when a vowel-initial suffix is added, as in *iambic*.

The constant-morpheme principle is also applied to the spelling of single final consonants. The number of consonants that can be pronounced in Korean syllable codas is quite restricted. The phonemes represented by ㅅ, ㅈ, ㅊ, ㅆ, and ㅉ are all pronounced as ㄷ, [t], at the end of a syllable, but they will reappear with their distinctive pronunciations if a vowel-initial morpheme is added. Similarly the tense and aspirated plosives sound like their plain versions in codas but will be spelled according to how they sound when they are followed by a vowel and allowed to show their true colors.

In addition to symbols for all the phonemes of Korean, Sejong (세종) developed a way to record the pitch-accent of the Korean of his time, placing one dot, two dots, or no dots to the left of a syllable to indicate the pitch with which it was to be pronounced. (Pitch-accent is similar to tone except that only one syllable of a word receives a distinctive pitch and the pitch of other syllables is predictable from that one.) Standard modern Korean has lost its system of pitch-accent, and the side dots are no longer used.

While he was about it, Sejong also incorporated extensions of the new script so as to be able to transcribe Chinese. With these modifications, han'gŭl (한글) could be used to teach the proper pronunciation of Chinese.

The system that Sejong ended up with is indeed the paragon of scripts (figure 11.2). It matches the phonology of the Korean language perfectly, and it is elegant and easy to learn. It encodes a large range of linguistic insights. In common with the Indian alphasyllabaries it recognizes the difference between vowels and consonants, a difference that is entirely ignored in linear, Greek-descended alphabets. It encodes individual phonemes, but also provides phonological information on a smaller scale than the phoneme, again in contrast with Western alphabets that recognize only phonemes. Similar phonemes are given predictably similar shapes; this property not only reflects the linguistic

Consonants							
Letter	ㄱ	ㄲ	ㄴ	ㄷ	ㄸ	ㄹ	ㅁ
Name	kiyŏk	ssang-giyŏk	niŭn	tigŭt	ssang-digŭt	riŭl	miŭm
IPA	[k]/[k*]	[k*]	[n]	[t]/[d]	[t*]	[ɾ][l]	[m]
Letter	ㅂ	ㅃ	ㅅ	ㅆ	ㅇ	ㅈ	ㅉ
Name	piŭp	ssang-biŭp	siot	ssang-siot	iŭng	chiŭt	ssang-jiŭt
IPA	[p]/[b]	[p*]	[s]	[s*]	Ø/[ŋ]	[ʧ][ʤ]	[ʧ*]
Letter	ㅊ	ㅋ	ㅌ	ㅍ	ㅎ		
Name	ch'iŭt	k'iŭk	t'iŭt	p'iŭp	hiŭt		
IPA	[ʧʰ]	[kʰ]	[tʰ]	[pʰ]	[h]		
Vowels							
Letter	ㅏ	ㅑ	ㅓ	ㅕ	ㅗ	ㅛ	
Name	a	ya	ŏ	yŏ	o	yo	
IPA	[a]	[ja]	[ʌ]	[jʌ]	[o]	[jo]	
Letter	ㅜ	ㅠ	ㅡ	ㅣ			
Name	u	yu	ŭ	i			
IPA	[u]	[ju]	[ɯ]	[i]			

Figure 11.2 Han'gŭl, the Korean alphabet, listed in the South Korean order. The vowels are here presented separately, but in the alphabetization of actual words all vowel-initial words begin with the dummy consonant ㅇ and will therefore appear after words beginning with ㅆ and before words beginning with ㅈ. The Korean names of the letters are given in Romanization. The name of each consonant contains that consonant twice – as the initial and final letter – which serves to indicate how the letter is pronounced when syllable-initial and when syllable-final. In the phonetic transcriptions given here, the tense consonants of Korean are transcribed with an asterisk. While common among linguists, this usage is not official IPA; these consonants do not yet have a standard IPA transcription.

insight that phonemes are composed of smaller distinctive features, but is a crucial factor in making the han'gŭl alphabet so easy to learn. By contrast, the Roman alphabet abounds with pitfalls for the learner: the graphic similarity between the letters **E** and **F** corresponds to no phonological similarity at all, nor does the similarity between **O** and **Q**, while the similar phonemes written **T** and **D** look entirely dissimilar.

Han'gŭl also recognizes that phonemes are grouped together into syllables and morphemes. Speech as we hear it is naturally divided into syllables; it is also easy to realize that complex words are composed of meaningful parts (morphemes). But the meaningless and often unpronounceable phoneme is a concept that children learning linear alphabets must struggle with. By contrast, han'gŭl is generally taught to children as a pseudosyllabary, being presented first in simple syllables rather than as independent letters. As a result, Korean children can read before they begin their formal education.

The only serious drawback to han'gŭl has been its incompatibility with the typewriter. This Western innovation assumed a linear alphabet, and the non-linear alphabets of Korea and southern Asia – though no harder to read, write, or learn – have sometimes been considered inferior because they are so hard to type (a conclusion no doubt supported by a good measure of ethnocentrism). Fortunately, the word-processing programs of the digital age have largely done away with this objection. The user can type in the letters one after another, and the computer will arrange them into appropriate syllable blocks (similarly, the computer will correctly create Indic *akṣaras*, or choose the word-initial, -medial, or -final version of a letter in Arabic).

Although later historians have tended to assume that Sejong could not have succeeded in designing such a marvelous script without the assistance of his academy, the records of the time are unequivocal in calling the Korean alphabet the king's personal creation, in contrast with other inventions of the period, for which the credit is more evenly divided. He announced his creation in the last month of the lunar year 1443 – somewhere around January 1, 1444, in our solar calendar.

Fierce objections to Sejong's work surfaced almost immediately, led by Ch'oe Mal-li, vice-director of Sejong's own academy. Why was the king endangering good relations with China by so visibly deviating from Chinese practices? Why would the king of a self-respecting country want to imitate barbarians such as the Mongols, the Jurchin, and the Japanese? Only barbarians used scripts other than Chinese characters. Furthermore, by lowering standards of literacy, the new alphabet would lead to rampant cultural illiteracy as people would neglect the study of Classical Chinese and of high culture. Surely the king didn't want that?! The king's hope that a vernacular script would help prevent miscarriages of justice was misplaced, as witness China, where the language matched the writing system but injustice was not unknown. The king was behaving with great imprudence on a matter with potentially profound consequences without having consulted any of his ministers. Was the king further going to endanger his health and the welfare of the nation by continuing to work on his alphabet project on the upcoming retreat he was taking for his health, during which all inessential work was to be handed over to his ministers? And would he meanwhile waste the crown prince's time on it too?

The king may indeed have wished to distance his country from China, and he must have realized that his plan to educate the masses was a threat to the social order treasured by Ch'oe Mal-li and his fellow literati; but he was wise enough not to say so. Instead he issued a sharp rejoinder presenting the new script as a boon to the Korean people – which he as king had every moral right to convey – and emphasizing its application for correcting and standardizing the pronunciation of Chinese characters – a scholarly project for which he was uniquely qualified. The crown prince, he added, would do very well to concern himself with a matter of such great national importance.

Having thus quashed the most vocal criticism, Sejong next put his new script through a rigorous trial run. He set the more alphabet-friendly scholars of his academy to compiling the *Yongbi ŏch'ŏn ka*, or "Songs of Flying Dragons," a work of history and poetry praising Sejong's grandfather and founder of the Chosŏn dynasty, Yi Sŏnggye.

Confident that his new script was working as intended, on October 9, 1446, Sejong finally made public his *Hunmin chŏng'ŭm*, "The Correct Sounds for the Instruction of the People," the name by which he titled both his script and the short promulgation document he wrote explaining it. In the *Hunmin chŏng'ŭm*, each symbol is presented with an example of a Chinese character containing that sound. In its short but moving preface Sejong explains his motivation for introducing a new writing system:

> The speech sounds of our country's language are different from those of the Middle Kingdom and are not communicable with the Chinese characters. Therefore, when my beloved simple people want to say something, many of them are unable to express their feelings. Feeling compassion for this I have newly designed twenty-eight letters, only wishing to have everyone easily learn and use them conveniently every day.

Appended to his brief document was the much longer *Hunmin chŏng'ŭm haerye*, "Explanatory Notes and Examples of Usage of the *Hunmin chŏng'ŭm*," written by scholars of the academy, led by Chŏng

In-ji. The *Hunmin chŏng'ŭm haerye* explained the philosophical and linguistic principles underlying its design, including the rationale for the letter shapes. (This part of the document was unfortunately lost from about 1500 until 1940.) In a laudatory postface Chŏng In-ji wrote "an intelligent man can acquaint himself with them [the letters] before the morning is over, and even the simple man can learn them in the space of ten days," adding, with some justification, that "under our Monarch with his Heaven-endowed wisdom, the codes and measures that have been proclaimed and enacted exceed and excel those of a hundred kings."

Sejong could have issued a proclamation enforcing the exclusive use of han'gŭl, but he did not do so. For someone who had just invented the most rational script in the world he showed prudent restraint in advancing its interests. He sponsored and printed works written in han'gŭl, used it in official documents, and added knowledge of han'gŭl to the subjects tested in the civil service exam. But he stopped far short of imposing the new script on the likes of Ch'oe Mal-li, and the upper classes went right on writing in Chinese.

Sejong died on April 18, 1450. Without him Korea's golden age soon waned, and han'gŭl nearly died of neglect. His successor, Munjong, outlived him by only two years, and his grandson, Tanjong, was soon ousted by Munjong's brother, Sejo. Sejo (1455–68) abolished the Academy of Worthies after usurping the throne, enraged at its members' loyalty to Tanjong. He went on to publish Buddhist texts in han'gŭl for the benefit of the people, but han'gŭl did not enjoy much further support. Among the educated it became known contemptuously as the "vernacular script," "women's script," or even, with undisguised contempt, "morning script," due to its reputation for being learnable in a morning. Anything that was that easy was clearly not worth wasting ink on.

Yet precisely because it was easy to learn, han'gŭl was able to survive this stepchild treatment. Finding refuge among Buddhists, women, and others excluded from power, it put down roots among the people, which enabled it, unlike Korea's printing industry, to survive the sixteenth century. The Imjin War, as the Japanese invasions of 1592–8 were known, devastated the country, killing hundreds of thousands of people, laying waste the crop lands, and dealing the country a great cultural blow that stripped it of many of Sejong's accomplishments. Its fine ceramics industry was destroyed, and the kilns and potters captured by the Japanese were used to jump-start the Japanese porcelain industry, earning the war the nickname of the "pottery war." Korea's type foundries and printing presses were also destroyed, and books, type, and printers were carried off to Japan. Metal type was not recast in Korea until 1668.

Independent of the nation's ruined infrastructure, han'gŭl survived. The seventeenth and eighteenth centuries saw the birth of popular literature written in the vernacular script. It was only in 1894, however, that han'gŭl came into its own as the nationally sanctioned writing system. That year, as part of a series of reforms aimed at modernizing Korea and distancing it from China, King Kojong gave han'gŭl official status. Government edicts were to be written in han'gŭl (with Chinese translation attached if desired) or in a system that mixed Chinese characters and han'gŭl (analogous to the Japanese mixture of kanji and kana). On April 7, 1896, the *Independent* newspaper took the revolutionary step of publishing only in han'gŭl and introduced European-style word spacing.

Meanwhile, the first Protestant missionaries had arrived in Korea, armed with the New Testament in han'gŭl (translated with the help of Koreans living in Manchuria). The use of the people's script in the Bible did much to make Christianity appealing to everyday Koreans, while the existence of the Bible, hymnals, and prayer books in turn promoted the use of han'gŭl.

Resistance to change was strong, however. In 1895 Yu Kil-jun published "Things Seen and Heard While Traveling in the West" in han'gŭl, provoking sharp criticism. As a memoir, it was serious literature and should have used a more serious script.

The Japanese occupation of 1910–45 was unkind to han'gŭl, but this probably sealed its fate as a source of patriotic pride to the Korean people. Han'gŭl received its modern name in 1913 from Chu Si-gyŏng, a Korean linguist, patriot, and editor at the *Independent*, the name being deliberately ambiguous between "Korean script" and "great script." (In North Korea it is nowadays called Chosŏn'gŭl, "Korean script," or simply *uri kŭlcha*, "our characters.") In 1933 the Korean Language Society issued carefully thought-out orthographic principles, codifying the morphophonemic spelling system originally favored by Sejong.

The Japanese government opposed the use of han'gŭl and attempted to officially suppress it in 1938. The Korean language was outlawed in schools; all education was in Japanese. By 1945, the illiteracy rate among Koreans was as high as 78 percent.

The end of World War II brought the end of Japanese domination, and circumstances changed quickly for han'gŭl. North Korea inaugurated an aggressive literacy campaign which virtually eliminated illiteracy by 1949, though further work was needed to regain this level after the devastation of the Korean War. South Korea, while not as single-minded in its efforts, also made rapid progress. Today Korea as a whole boasts one of the world's lowest illiteracy rates (proving, in North Korea, that a high literacy rate is no guarantee of economic success). North Korea abolished the use of Chinese characters in official texts in 1949, but up to 3,000 characters are still taught in secondary school and university for the sake of reading older texts. In South Korea, after much waffling, about 1,800 characters continue to be taught, and in a few contexts, such as space-conscious newspaper headlines, they are still used for words of Chinese origin.

Today Koreans are justly proud of King Sejong and their native script. South Korea observes October 9, the day Sejong promulgated his *Hunmin chŏng'ŭm*, as Han'gŭl Day. Korean linguists point out the inherent logic and systematicity of han'gŭl and champion its potential as an international phonetic alphabet. With modifications along the lines that Sejong pursued in transcribing Chinese, han'gŭl could be adapted to other languages in the world and would do the job more systematically than the present International Phonetic Alphabet, based as it is on the arbitrary shapes of the Roman alphabet. While the chance of this happening may be small, linguists around the world nevertheless laud han'gŭl as the world's easiest, most rational script. Sejong would be pleased.

12

Greek Serendipity

The Greeks of the ninth century BC were barbarians, a situation for which we should all be grateful. Civilization had retreated from the Aegean region with the fall of the Mycenaean city-states around 1200 BC. When the Greeks again began to enjoy some measure of prosperity and to engage in international trade in the ninth century, they did not rush to adopt the ways of the civilized but authoritarian Near Eastern cultures they encountered. Picking and choosing, they accepted only some ideas from the Near East, the most significant being the concept of writing, which they learned from the Phoenicians around 800 or 775 BC. But being dyed-in-the-wool barbarians, the Greeks did not take up writing to learn wisdom from the Phoenicians, to participate in Phoenician culture, or to acquire the cachet of civilization. Feeling no obligation to Phoenician – or other Near Eastern – culture, the Greeks went on to create something quite new, both of their writing system and of their culture. The unique achievements of classical Greece in art, democracy, philosophy, science, and literature were as yet far in the future, but none of them would have been possible without the Greek free-thinking spirit. The Greek alphabet did not create this independent spirit; rather it was one of its early results.

To the powerful Phoenicians, home was a collection of city-states that included Byblos, Tyre, and Sidon and occupied a region roughly equivalent to modern Lebanon. From there their trade networks stretched out across the Mediterranean, reaching westward as far as Spain. The Phoenician alphabet, which they had systematized by about 1050 BC, undoubtedly helped them manage their trading empire, and the script partook of the prestige they acquired along with their mercantile wealth.

Other peoples began to adopt the script. The Hebrews and Aramaeans did, despite the fact that the 22 Phoenician letters were not quite adequate for the consonantal phonemes of their languages. In Asia Minor the Cilicians, speakers of an Indo-European language, began using the Phoenician script around the ninth century. As Phoenician was the prestige language, they wrote in Phoenician, the only Cilician words they wrote being their names. To adequately record their Indo-European language would have required both innovation and independence of thought.

The Greeks, being barbarians and unmoved by prestige, went about learning to write in their own way. Much ink has been spent on debates as to exactly when, where, and how the Greek voweled alphabet was created from the Phoenician consonantal script. These debates will probably never be fully resolved. For my part, I imagine it happened something like this.

Sometime in the first years of the eighth century BC, two men were friends, one Greek and the other Phoenician. The Phoenician may have come to trade on one of the Aegean islands or in one of the Greek cities of Ionia (on the coast of Asia Minor, now in Turkey); or the Greek may have lived in Al-Mina, a city on the coast of Syria that knew much Greek trade and may have been a Greek colony (see appendix, figure A.3). Both men were merchants, and they got to know each other through their work. The Phoenician learned to speak Greek, but the Greek, I suspect, did not learn Phoenician.

One day as the two men were chewing the fat in the Phoenician's workplace, the subject of writing came up. "It's a great help in trade," said the Phoenician. "See, I can tell you without even looking inside that that jar over there contains the finest grade of wine. I can just read the label."

"That's nothing," said the Greek. "I could have told you the same thing. What else would a person put in such a fine jar?"

"Point taken," said the Phoenician. "But how about that crate over there? Would you know, without opening it, that it contains wool?"

"Oh yes," replied the Greek. "I'd know by the smell."

"OK, OK. But writing is useful for much more than that. I can tell you what my profits were ten years ago, for example. Any piece of information I don't want to forget, I just write down."

"And how does that help?" asked the Greek. "How do those silly marks actually help you remember things?"

"Here, I'll show you," said the Phoenician, unwittingly making history as he reached for a piece of wood and a knife to scratch letters

209

into it with. "Here's the first letter. Its name is '*ālef*," he said, pronouncing it with the initial glottal stop – the consonant sound for which the letter stood.

The Greek, not knowing Phoenician, missed the glottal stop entirely. As in English, it made no difference to a Greek word whether it started with a glottal stop or not. It was the [a] which the Greek perceived to be the first sound of the letter's name. As he copied the scratchings, he struggled to pronounce the strange word. The aspirated Greek [pʰ] was as close as he could get to [f], but he had trouble ending a word in a plosive consonant. What he finally managed, and what he remembered later, was something like [alpʰa].

"Very good," said the Phoenician, smiling indulgently at this mispronunciation and not realizing that the very first letter of the alphabet had been misunderstood and that a new kind of writing system – one containing vowel letters – had thereby been born. "Now, here's the next one, *bēt*."

That one wasn't so hard to pronounce, but a little vowel sound did tend to creep in at the end, after the plosive *t*, yielding *bēta*. The next two letters, *gīmel* and *dālet*, also went smoothly (see figure 12.1). The fifth letter, *hē*, seemed straightforward enough at first. It started with [h]. But not much later the eighth letter came along, *ḥēt*. This one started with a voiceless pharyngeal fricative, [ħ]. To a modern speaker of English, this consonant sounds much like someone breathing on eyeglasses preparatory to cleaning them, but to the Greek speaker it probably sounded like a more forceful pronunciation of [h]. He revised his opinion of the fifth letter accordingly. It was the *eighth* letter that started with [h] – *hēta*, as he pronounced it – and he must have been mistaken about hearing [h] in the fifth letter. That one must be simply a vowel sound. He pronounced it *ei* (it was not called *epsilon*, ε ψιλόν or "plain e," until Byzantine times).

Meanwhile, the sixth letter, *wāw*, was easily understood. It began with [w]. The Greek was not to know that this phoneme would soon fall out of use in his language, leaving the letter obsolete (and later to be renamed *digamma* because it looked like a gamma, but with *two* horizontal lines, **F**).

The seventh letter, *zayin*, started with an unfamiliar sound. The sound [z] did not begin words in Greek, but only occurred as a substitute for *s* before a voiced consonant. However, the Phoenician phoneme was not entirely unlike the Greek affricate [dz]. At some point, perhaps not

Phoenician	Name	Archaic Greek	Pronunciation	Later Greek		Name
⨯ Ӄ	'ālef	Α𐌍Α	[a], [aː]	A	α	alpha
𐤄	bēt	𐌁𐌁ΒB	[b]	B	β	bēta
𐌂 𐌠	gīmel	𐌂ΓᴄC	[g]	Γ	γ	gamma
Δ Λ	dālet	▷ΔD	[d]	Δ	δ	delta
𐤄	hē	𐌄ᖴ𐌄E	[ɛ(ː)]	E	ε	ei (e psilon)
Υ Y	wāw	𐤅FFᶠ	[w]		(obsolete)	wau (digamma)
I	zayin	I I	[dz], then [zd]	Z	ζ	zēta
𐤇 𐤇	ḥēt	𐌇𐌇⊟H	[h], then [ɛː]	H	η	hēta/ēta
⊗ ⊕	ṭēt	⊗⊕⊞Ο	[tʰ]	Θ	θ	thēta
𐌆 𐌆	yōd	ꙅꙄꙄꙄ	[i], [iː]	I	ι	iōta
𐌊 V	kaf	𐌊ꓘΚK	[k]	K	κ	kappa
L	lāmed	L𐌋ᐱΛ	[l]	Λ	λ	labda (lambda)
𐤌	mēm	ᴹᴹᴹM	[m]	M	μ	mu
𐤍	nūn	𐌍𐌍ᴎN	[n]	N	ν	nu
𐤎 𐤎	sāmek	𐤎 Ξ X + Xꙅ KM	[ks]	Ξ	ξ	xei (xi)
Ο	'ayin	ΟΟ◊	[ɔ(ː)]	O	o	ou (o mikron)
𐤐 𐤐	pē	𐌓ΓΓΠ	[p]	Π	π	pei (pi)
𐤑	ṣādē	M	[s]		(obsolete)	san
Φ Ϙ	qōf	ϘΦϘ	[k]		(obsolete)	qoppa
𐤓	rēš	𐌓𐌓Ρᴘᴘ	[r], [r̩]	P	ρ	rho
ᗰ	šān/šin	ꙅꙄꙄᶓ	[s]	Σ	σ, ς	sigma
X +	tāw	Τ𐌕	[t]	T	τ	tau
		VΥΥ	[u], [uː], then [y]	Y	υ	hu (u psilon)
		Φ𐤅Φ Γ𐤇 ΓH	[pʰ]	Φ	φ	phei (phi)
		X+ 𐌙VᴪΨ K𐤇 KH	[kʰ]	X	χ	khei (chi)
		VᴪΨ ΓM Γꙅ Φꙅ	[ps]	Ψ	ψ	psei (psi)
		Ω	[ɔː]	Ω	ω	ō (o mega)

Figure 12.1 The derivation of the Greek alphabet from the Phoenician. The early Greek alphabet varied in the direction of writing and in the forms of its letters, as shown. The pronunciation of Modern Greek is rather different from what is shown here.

until he tried writing Greek words on his own, the Greek realized that he could write [dz] with the Phoenician *zayin*. By then it seems he had forgotten the exact name for it, the names being nonsense to him anyway (though not to the Phoenician, for whom they were meaningful words). In his recollection the letter became *dzēta*, rhyming with *bēta* and *hēta*. Our Greek friend was not to know that the [dz] affricate would by classical times be reversed into a sequence of two phonemes, [zd], and that the *dzēta* would then be used for this reversed [zd] as well as for any sequences of *sigma* plus *delta* (s + d, pronounced [zd]) that came along. Nor was he to know that eventually the pronunciation of the letter would be simplified to [z], back to where it started in Phoenician.

The ninth letter, *ṭēt*, started with another sound unknown in Greek, being one of the Semitic "emphatic" consonants, [tˤ] (the superscript indicating pharyngealization, a tightening of the throat). Efforts to pronounce this sound proved useless. The closest thing in Greek was [tʰ], an aspirated consonant, and so the letter became *thēta* (only after the classical period did this letter come to be pronounced as a fricative, [θ]). The aspiration of the Greek consonant and the pharyngealization of the emphatic consonant were not in fact very similar, but both consonants were sounds rather like [t] but with an extra, more forceful aspect to their pronunciation. Whether the Greek arrived at [tʰ] immediately, by means of a mispronunciation, or whether the usefulness of the letter for [tʰ] only occurred to him later, as he found himself needing to write the phoneme, is impossible to say.

The tenth letter, *yōd*, standing for the palatal semivowel [j] in Phoenician, was misunderstood immediately. Greek only used [j] as a reduced version of the vowel [i] in diphthongs. Greek words could not begin with [j], but they could begin with [i]. The Greek would have heard the letter's name as [ioːd] and pronounced it as [ioːda], eventually to become *iōta*. The fledgling Greek alphabet had just acquired another vowel from the consonantal Phoenician alphabet through simple misperception.

Kaf, *lāmed*, *mēm*, and *nūn* were relatively straightforward to the Greek, and he learned them quickly, with some predictable mispronunciation of their names. Then things got quite confusing. The fifteenth, eighteenth, and twenty-first letters all seemed to begin with the same sound, [s]. In reality, they were *sāmek*, plain [s], *ṣādē*, the emphatic [sˤ], and *šān*, probably [ʃ]. For the time being, the Greek learned the three strange names and three arbitrary symbols, hoping it would all make sense when he got to the end of the list and his friend would show him how to actually use the symbols he was memorizing.

The sixteenth letter was every bit as bad. Its name was *'ayin*, which began with a very peculiar sound indeed. It was a voiced pharyngeal fricative, [ʕ], a sound which the Greek might have made as an expression of exasperation, but never as a phoneme in a word. The existence of this sound in Phoenician may well have convinced him that the language was far too hard for him to learn (as its modern counterpart is the bane of second-language learners struggling to pronounce Arabic). He might have tried to skip this one, but his friend was very particular about teaching him the entire list of names and symbols, as though there were something magical about reciting the complete list in the correct order. In trying to pronounce this letter, it was simplest to just leave off the initial throat-clearing sound, which left a back vowel [ɑ] as the next sound, not too different from the [ɔ] which he eventually settled on as its value. The letter came to be called *ou*, and only became known as *omicron* (o μικρόν, or "little o") in the second or third century AD.

The seventeenth letter, *pē*, was easy and was easily translated into *pei* (πει, and eventually *pi*, πι, many centuries later). The nineteenth letter, *qōf*, started with a uvular [q]. Being made further back in the mouth than [k], this sound was not phonemic in Greek, but was not far from the pronunciation of the *k* phoneme when followed by a back vowel. Since the name *qōf* contained a back vowel, the Greek was able to pronounce it to his friend's satisfaction (his friend having by now become used to the Greek's tendency to turn fricatives into plosives and to supplement word-final plosives with extra vowels). Never having heard of a phoneme, the Greek was not troubled by the fact that his *kappa* (κάππα) and *qoppa* (ϙόππα) began with variants of the same phoneme.

The twentieth letter, *rēš*, was not too difficult, though the Greek (ever obedient to the dictates of his native language) insisted on aspirating the *r* at the beginning of a word, turning it voiceless (and inspiring the much later Latin transcription of *rho*). The twenty-second and last letter, *tāw*, was one of the easiest of all.

"Now do it yourself," said the Phoenician. "And then practice over and over until you remember them perfectly. Then, when you really know all your letters, start using them to record words. Listen to yourself say a word, and then write down the letters whose names start with the sounds you hear."

The Greek did as his friend suggested. Perhaps neither of them realized that a significant mutation had occurred in the transfer of the alphabet from one language to the other. In certain cases where the Phoenician had uttered consonant-initial names (in fact, all words in his language began with a consonant), his friend had heard vowel-initial names. Thus when the Greek began to write words, he had symbols for vowel phonemes as well as for (most of) his language's consonants. This was fortunate: Greek, as an Indo-European language, could not be adequately written with only consonants. At the very least, it would have required extensive use of *matres lectionis*. However, using certain symbols that stood uniquely for vowels, and writing down all the vowels in a word, was a better solution for Greek (and later, for many other languages, including English).

My fanciful tale may diverge significantly from the actual events, but some aspects of it are likely to be true. I suspect that the voweled Greek alphabet – a new form of writing at the time – was to some extent an accident caused by misperception. The changes made from the Phoenician to the Greek alphabets were exactly those that a native speaker of Greek would make as mistakes. I also suspect that the Greek alphabet was created by an illiterate, not someone at home with written Phoenician. Creativity is rare in the history of writing, the more so among peoples with well-established literacy. Writing is so conservative in its influences that once one truly knows how to read and write it is virtually impossible to think of doing it any other way (Sejong having been a shining exception). Choe Mal-li was right: generally speaking, only uneducated barbarians have their own scripts. Fortunately, the Greeks at the time fit the description.

One significant addition to the 22 letters had to be made right away. Our anonymous first writer of Greek soon found that he needed a way to write the vowel [u]. Its sound was most like the sixth letter of the list he had learned, *wāw*, but not exactly like it, as it was a vowel not a semivowel. He therefore turned his original *wāw* symbol into two slightly different ones. He put the second one at the end of the alphabet and called it *hu* (ὑ, to be renamed *upsilon*, υ ψιλόν or "plain u," in Byzantine times).

Once the leap had been made from Phoenician to Greek, it was a much easier thing for the new script to spread from one Greek to another along trade routes. Over the eighth and seventh centuries the new alphabet spread throughout Greek lands, from the Ionian settlements in the east to Sicily and the lower boot of Italy in the west. In the absence of established literacy (or anything much to read), variation abounded, both in the shapes and stances of letters and in the direction of writing. Some people, especially in the earliest years, wrote from right to left as the original adapter (under the influence of his Phoenician friend) probably had. Others wrote from left to right or switched the direction of writing at the end of every line, thus writing back and forth *boustrophedon*, "as the ox plows." By about 500 BC, left to right had settled out as the preferred direction.

There was local variation also in the number of letters the alphabet contained as different people tinkered with the technology in an attempt to fit the alphabet more precisely to their language. Although the Greek alphabet was the first in world history to record every vowel as well as every consonant, it was not the case that every Greek phoneme had a unique letter associated with it. In fact, the Greeks *never* achieved the ideal of a one-to-one correspondence between phonemes and letters of the alphabet, neither at the alphabet's creation nor at any other time in its history.

One inadequacy of the original version of the Greek alphabet was that it had no symbols for two of its three aspirated plosives, [pʰ] and [kʰ] (better known to modern readers by their post-classical pronunciations [f] and [x]). On the islands of Crete and Thera this problem was solved by using two letters for one consonant: ΠΗ and ΚΗ. In other areas new letters were invented: φ and Χ in Athens, Corinth, and Ionia, but φ and Ψ in most of the rest of mainland Greece (see appendix, figure A.6).

In certain other cases, a sequence of two phonemes received a single letter. Due to the peculiarities of *s* (which behaves unusually in many languages), sequences of plosive + *s* could occur both at the beginnings and ends of words, making these sequences behave somewhat like single phonemes (most sequences of phonemes, by contrast, occur in reverse order at opposite ends of words, as in English *strap* vs. *parts*). So one of the extra *s*-symbols, Ξ, the one copied from Phoenician *sāmek*, was given the value [ks] in Ionia and Corinth, while in Athens this cluster was spelled ΧΣ, and in the parts of Greece that were using Ψ for [kʰ], it was spelled Χ (hence its later value in the Roman alphabet). Ionia used Ψ for [ps], for which other Greeks used either ΠΣ or φΣ.

Meanwhile, the other two *s*-symbols were giving some trouble. The original adapter had trouble telling them apart, and seems to have confused their names. Out of this confusion, most regions chose one symbol and one name. Thus some local alphabets used the eighteenth letter to stand for [s], writing it **M** (distinguished from M, *mu*) and calling it *san*, like the Phoenician name for the twenty-first letter (*šān*, later *šin*). Other alphabets dropped the eighteenth letter and retained instead the twenty-first letter. This became Σ (with four bars) or Ϟ (with three) and was pronounced *sigma*, more reminiscent of Phoenician *sāmek* (number 15) than *šān* (number 21).

Another issue was the duplication of *kappa* and *qoppa*. The difference between the two was not phonemic, but in Greek (as in English, though rarely noticed by native speakers), a [k] before a back vowel was pronounced a little further back in the mouth than otherwise and was thus a little closer to Phoenician [q]. So K was used before A, E, and I, while Ϙ was used before O and Y. The use of *qoppa* eventually died out except as an abbreviation for "Corinth" on coins and as the numeral 90. The Greeks used two systems of numerals, one based on abbreviations of number names and one based on the order of the alphabet. In the latter system, *alpha* was 1, *bēta* 2, and so forth until *iōta* was 10, *kappa* was 20, and so on. Obviously, a letter could not simply be removed from this system, so *qoppa* remained 90. The F (*wau*, later *digamma*) was also to become obsolete as the Greek dialects lost [w], but its use as the numeral 6 continued.

As with the *sigma*, many letters had variant shapes. The *gamma* used in Athens, Λ, would have been mistaken as a *labda* (later *lambda*) in Ionia or Corinth. The *rho* sometimes had a short tail, approximating later Latin R, but usually appeared as P. The *u* ([u], but fronted to [y] by classical times) could be written with or without a tail, as Y or V.

In Ionia, the local version of Greek had no [h]. The letter other Greeks referred to as *hēta* was therefore pronounced *ēta*. From there it was natural to start using H as a long vowel. E was then used only for the short vowel [ε], while H stood for its long counterpart [ε:]. Faced with the possibility of distinguishing long vowels from short ones, the Ionians made a further innovation. Opening the bottom of O, they made Ω, to be known centuries later (when the distinction in length was no longer made in everyday speech) as ω μέγα, *omega* ("big o"). They could now distinguish in writing between the short [ɔ] vowel and its long [ɔ:] counterpart. However, neither the Ionians nor any other Greeks ever bothered to write the phonemic distinction between long and short [a], [i], or [u], using simply A, I, and Y.

The earliest uses of the alphabet were probably in trade, but the earliest preserved examples of Greek writing are snatches of poetry inscribed on ceramic vessels. Writing and versification served similar purposes: writing was a technology that artificially extended the memory, while hexameter poetry was used in the Greek oral tradition to render information memorable. The epics of Homer were the first lengthy works (that we know of) to be written down, sometime in the first century of the Greek alphabet. As a bard, Homer was a custodian of the Greeks' accumulated wisdom and traditions. He delivered his tales in hexameters, and when they were given over to the artificial memory of letters they were recorded in hexameters.

Most things written in the early centuries of the alphabet are lost to us, having probably been written on leather, papyrus, or wood; but pottery is a great boon to archaeologists. While it breaks easily (requiring more to constantly be made), it never decomposes. Inscriptions scratched or painted onto ceramics are therefore of great help in tracing the early history of the alphabet. Broken potsherds (known as *ostraca*) served as notepads for everyday purposes, as well as for voting ballots in the fifth century BC Athenian unpopularity contest known as *ostracism*, in which the "winner" – generally a politician who was thought to be dangerous to democracy – was exiled from Athens for 10 years.

Despite the relative simplicity of the Greek alphabet, literacy never became the norm in ancient Greece. Learning to read and write requires time and application, even with a largely phonemic alphabet. More importantly, it requires motivation, which is in short supply in a culture where there is as yet little to read, very little to write on, and few jobs for which literacy is a prerequisite. Opportunity is also required, since learning to read requires a teacher. Without widespread motivation and opportunities, literacy rates remain low (as exemplified by Korea, where for all its simplicity han'gŭl, the "morning script," made only modest inroads against illiteracy until the twentieth century). For important merchants and artisans it was a useful job skill; otherwise it was a luxury largely reserved for upper-class men. In all probability, women were almost uniformly illiterate, though with occasional high-born exceptions, of whom the most famous was the poet Sappho (writing roughly 610 to 580 BC).

Sappho's lyric poetry (as opposed to the epic style) is one example of the wider range of uses to which writing began to be put around 600 BC. Another was the Greek vases of the sixth century, which often carry captions and labels, and sometimes the signature of the artist, such as that of the great potter and vase painter Exekias. Having writing on a vase seems to have enhanced its prestige value: some were adorned with letters in meaningless order. Obviously neither the artist nor the buyer of such a vase could read, but the writing was thought to look sophisticated. Meanwhile in Ionia philosophical thought was first committed to written form. More prosaically, writing began to be used for public purposes, in written laws and on coins.

The subsequent classical period (c. 480 to 323 BC) was characterized by a prodigious intellectual output over an astonishingly short period. Led by Athens, Greece in this short century and a half produced such luminaries as historians Herodotus and Thucydides, philosophers Socrates, Plato, and Aristotle, and dramatists such as Aeschylus, Sophocles, Euripides, and Aristophanes, while simultaneously creating works of sculpture and architecture that have never been surpassed.

Classical politics were unusual too, as this was the period of Athenian democracy (begun in 508 BC), in which every free adult male citizen had a voice. The technology of writing served the new political system admirably. Notices were posted for public display, the less important ones painted on wooden boards, but (luckily for posterity) the more important ones chiseled into stone – at least in Athens, which had plentiful quarries nearby. Literacy helped to preserve the new democracy, as citizens who knew how to read could better learn and defend their rights. Not coincidentally, the number of city-dwellers who could read grew significantly during the classical period. Even so, virtually all women, rural people, members of the lower classes, and slaves whose duties were not administrative remained illiterate.

Although Athens was the undisputed intellectual leader of the classical period, the seeds of Greek intellectual achievement were actually sown across the Aegean in Ionia. Here on the coast of Asia Minor the Greeks were in much closer contact with other civilizations. Refugees from the fall of the Neo-Assyrian Empire in 612 BC may have brought Mesopotamian learning to Ionia and contributed to intellectual cross-pollination there. The subsequent Ionian Enlightenment of the sixth century featured the earliest scientific thinkers of the Western tradition, including Pythagoras, still remembered for his theorem about right triangles. Some of these natural philosophers committed their ideas to writing, creating the first Greek prose treatises.

The orthographic result of the Ionian Enlightenment is that the Ionic alphabet acquired a certain prestige in the eyes of other Greeks (who were by now vulnerable to intellectual prestige, being no longer barbarians). Ionian spellings tended to be used by fifth-century Athenian tragedians and writers of serious prose; then in late 403 or early 402 BC Athens officially adopted the Ionic alphabet as part of a series of reforms otherwise aimed at restoring democracy after a period of warfare and instability. The alphabetic reform entailed the adoption of Ω, *omega*, and the reassignment of H from *hēta* to *ēta*, so that two vowel phonemes gained symbols but the [h] ceased to be written at all. Simultaneously the Athenians gained the Ionian Ξ (*xi*) and Ψ (*psi*), though the acquisition was not actually a step forward for the phonemic principle. Loss of subphonemic *qoppa* in favor of *kappa*, however, was. Other changes, such as inverting the *labda*, straightening the *gamma*, and adding a fourth bar to *sigma*, were changes in letter form but not in function.

In private use the new alphabet was not adopted instantaneously, but with time the Ionic alphabet prevailed in Athens and eventually in the entire Greek world. It is not surprising that the Athenians (and other Greeks) welcomed the chance to distinguish long mid vowels from short mid vowels, but it seems perverse to have done so at the price of actually losing a consonant letter. It is true that the Greek [h] was highly restricted in its use, occurring only at the start of morphemes; of all phonemes it was the one that would be least missed if left unwritten. Nevertheless, any Athenian who really wanted an optimally designed alphabet could have found a way to absorb Ionic long vowels without losing *hēta* in the process. But innovation is rare in the history of the written word, and the force of literary prestige is strong.

In the Hellenistic period (reckoned from the death of Alexander the Great in 323 BC to that of the last Hellenistic monarch, Cleopatra VII, in 30 BC), the Greek language spread beyond the borders of the Hellenes, as the Greeks called themselves, to all the lands which had once belonged to the Persians, and which Alexander had conquered. From Sicily to the borders of India, townspeople learned the Greek language and adopted Greek ways, while country people went about their old ways much as ever. Having produced much of the glitter of the classical age, it was Athens' turn to enjoy prestige. The new international form of Greek, called Koine, was based largely on the Attic dialect of Athens (Attica being the area around Athens), though it was written in the Ionic alphabet, by then firmly associated with Athens. Modern Greek is descended from Koine.

One of the new Greek-speaking cities was Alexandria, founded by Alexander in Egypt. In the chaos following Alexander's death, one of his generals, Ptolemy, seized Egypt and got himself crowned pharaoh, founding a dynasty that was to last until Cleopatra's suicide in 30 BC. At Alexandria Ptolemy endowed the Museion, a scholarly academy and library. The library was intended to include all of Greek literature. Texts from all over the Greek world were collected or copied onto papyrus scrolls and placed in the library. The Septuagint, the Greek translation of the Hebrew Bible, was also done at Alexandria. Although the library was eventually destroyed (unfortunately, the Greeks did not keep back-up copies on clay tablets!), we nevertheless owe to the Alexandrian scholars the preservation of texts such as the *Iliad* and the *Odyssey*, which were collected there and served as the basis for further copying.

In the process of accumulating and copying texts, the Alexandrian scholars began to show concern for matters of orthography. They found that at certain points the lack of a written form of [h] made for ambiguity. They noted that the Greeks living in Italy had been more free-thinking than the Athenians. While they had gone along with the adoption of the Ionic alphabet, they continued to write [h] by cutting the *hēta* in half and using ⊢. The Alexandrians adopted the Italian Greeks' half H, but wrote it as a superscript on the following vowel, so that, for example, ὸ was *ho*. Loving symmetry, they made the other half of H stand for the *lack* of an [h] sound before a vowel: ὀ. These diacritics came to be termed "rough breathing" (for [h]) and "smooth breathing" (for lack of [h]). Their use was for many centuries largely reserved for cases where ambiguity could arise without them. These marks later became ʻ and ʼ, so that ὁ was *ho* and ὀ plain *o*.

The Alexandrians were also the first to record the hitherto unwritten pitch-accent of Greek, as unprecedented numbers of non-native learners of Greek prompted a concern for clarity and avoidance of ambiguity. Pitch-accent was marked with an acute accent (e.g. ó) on high-pitched (i.e. accented) vowels, with a circumflex (ô) on long vowels whose first half only was high, or with a grave accent (ò). The grave accent was at first used for low-pitched (i.e. unaccented) vowels, and later for pitch-accents that occurred at the ends of words (in which position the high accent may have been pronounced somewhat lower than usual). As with "breathing," however, pitch-accent was for centuries noted only where its absence might lead to ambiguity.

Only by the ninth century AD (well into the Byzantine period, AD 330–1453) did the use of breathing and accent diacritics become fully regular, with all vowel-initial words marked for "rough" or "smooth" breathing and all words marked for accent. The inclusion of these diacritical marks went a long way toward making up for the fact that Greek did not yet mark word division in any way. Since breathing marks appeared only at the beginnings of words, and words had only one accent apiece, diacritics made individual words easier to find in the continuous text. Word spacing did not become a consistent feature of written Greek until the eighteenth century.

The Byzantine concern for diacritics was prompted by changes in the spoken language. The [h], or "rough breathing," had in fact disappeared from the spoken language centuries before, as had the system of pitch-accent, which was replaced by a stress-accent (similar to stress in English, in which one syllable per word is pronounced more forcefully than others). Pitch-accent and [h] belonged only to an archaic, literary form of the language. No longer preserved in the minds of native speakers, they had to be written down or lost.

Such is the conservatism of written language that the breathing and accent diacritics continued to be used in written Greek until 1976. At that point, the breathings were abandoned and the acute, circumflex, and grave accents all became acute, marking the stressed syllable of a word. Modern Greek is thus unusually helpful in consistently marking for the reader the position of stress.

Another invention of Byzantine times was the small letters, or minuscules. Ancient Greek was written entirely in what we now consider capital letters. All in all, ancient Greek inscriptions are rather difficult for modern readers, used as we are to visual cues such word spacing, punctuation, and capitalization.

The development of minuscule letters was the endpoint in a long line of evolution in the shapes of the letters. Some modifications occurred as the alphabet was borrowed from the Phoenicians, remembered imperfectly, and disseminated around the Greek world. Then, over the course of the classical age, as the Greek alphabet began to be used for public display, the shapes of letters themselves became worthy of care and attention, attaining new balance and symmetry.

By Hellenistic times, inscriptions were often carefully executed works of art. Meanwhile, however, more and more private writing was being done, and the effects of habitually writing with pen and ink on papyrus or parchment began to make themselves felt, even on inscriptions chiseled into stone. Serifs, probably derived from the little splash of ink that tended to be made at the ends of pen strokes, began to be incorporated into stone inscriptions. Meanwhile, some letters developed more rounded shapes: Є, C, and ω were new forms of E, Σ, and Ω.

Eventually a "book hand" distinct from inscriptional styles developed, with pervasive rounding of letter shapes, and eventually, by the ninth century AD, a complete minuscule alphabet which incorporated not only rounded letters but variations in the height of letters and their placement with respect to the line of writing, with descenders plunging below the line and ascenders sticking up above the rest of the text. Given the separate existence of capitals in inscriptions, there were now in effect two separate alphabets. Within a book, capitals were used for titles or marginal comments, but the capitalization of sentences and of proper names within a text did not occur until modern times, after a number of experiments in combining the two letter types.

The Greek alphabet has often been praised for achieving a way of fully recording a language (both vowels and consonants – though not, for centuries, pitch-accent) with a minimum number of symbols. Yet it seems as though a script with a small number of symbols is not after all so desirable: the Greek alphabet and its living descendants, Roman, Cyrillic, and Armenian, are unique in the world for their duplication of letters into capitals and minuscules. (Other short alphabets, such as Hebrew, Arabic, and Syriac, increase their repertoire by using different letter shapes depending on a letter's position in the word.) The Greek total of 24 letters was in the long run not enough; 48 was better, and 49 better still (minuscule *sigma* has two different forms: normally σ, but word-finally ς). Furthermore, a number of additional symbols were used in manuscripts: special abbreviations and ligatures abounded. Ligatures and abbreviations ease the job of the writer (a significant one in the days before printing), while minuscules combined with a consistent capitalization scheme ease the job of the reader. By contrast, having a particularly short list of alphabetical symbols eases only the job of the learner, a concern felt only temporarily by each generation. It was only when Western Europe began to show renewed interest in learning (and then printing) Greek in the fourteenth and fifteenth centuries that the profusion of special symbols abated to meet the needs of non-native speakers and the rigidity of type.

As Western Europeans began to learn Greek for the first time since the fall of Rome a millennium earlier, they were puzzled to find that although there were only five Greek vowel sounds ([a], [e], [i], [o], [u]), there were a great many vowel spellings. The spellings ι, η, υ, ει, οι, and υι were all pronounced [i] (as they still are today – it is only slight hyperbole to say that all Greek vowels are pronounced [i]). The difference in length between o and ω had been lost (both now being [o]), and ε and αι were both pronounced [e]. Had these letters always been read this way? The Greeks themselves thought they had, not realizing how much their language had changed over the centuries, and being used to their language's arcane spellings. However, if the modern Greek pronunciation was the same as that used in classical times, then the ancients were very stupid indeed: they believed that a sheep says "vi vi," the modern pronunciation of βή βή. (Greek consonants have also undergone pronunciation changes; *bēta* is now pronounced [v].) The spelling of Modern Greek vowels is one of the many triumphs of conservatism in the history of writing, having strayed very far from a one-to-one alignment of phonemes and letters in favor of historical spellings.

When the Greeks first developed their alphabet, they were barbarians; but so were all the other inhabitants of Europe. As the first people in post-Bronze-Age Europe to adopt writing and civilization, the Greeks enjoyed the cultural scope to develop both of these as they saw fit. Once they did, they held a monopoly; the other peoples of Europe could only follow their lead.

The first people to copy the Greek alphabet were the Etruscans. The Etruscans lived in what is today still known as *Tuscany* in Italy. They spoke a unique, non-Indo-European language. To their south were the Latins, whose settlements included a small, as yet unremarkable town called Rome. Further south were the newly established Greek colonies.

The Etruscans of the eighth century BC were on the way up, rapidly acquiring power and adopting urban civilization. They extended their influence both northward and southward through Latium, where they encountered the Greeks.

The Etruscans were much taken with Greek culture. They imported fine Greek ceramics, the Greek gods and their associated myths, and, around 700 BC, the early Greek alphabet. They seem to have had a great deal of respect for the alphabet. Indeed, it was a status symbol: they copied it out, exactly as they had learned it, and wrote it on important objects such as grave goods. Nevertheless, the alphabet as they had learned it did not actually fit their language. Etruscan had no voiced plosives, so they found they had no use for the letters *bēta* or *delta*. *Gamma* came to represent a voiceless [k], adding to the confusion caused by *kappa* and *qoppa*. *Kappa* was used before *alpha*, *gamma* before *epsilon* and *iōta*, and *qoppa* before *upsilon* (the *omicron* not being needed in Etruscan, due to a lack of [o]). Eventually *kappa* and *qoppa* were dispensed with (though *kappa* held on in the north). Also lost were *xi* and *chi*. *Hēta* continued to be used for [h] and the *digamma* was used for [w]. *Omega*, the last addition to the Greek alphabet, was not in the original model alphabet that the Etruscans copied; they never missed it. There was no way to write [f] in Greek (φ being pronounced [pʰ] at the time), so the Etruscans first tried *digamma-hēta* (FH), but later invented a new letter for the purpose, written 𐌚 or 8 (see figure 13.1).

Having adopted the alphabet in its early stages when its direction of writing was still feeling Phoenician influence, the Etruscans wrote from right to left, and occasionally boustrophedon. Their first writing, like Greek, had no word division, but in the sixth century BC Etruscan writers began separating words with a dot or colon. They carried word division unusually far, at times putting the dots between individual syllables or other short sequences of letters.

For a time the Etruscans were the dominant culture in non-Greek Italy; according to tradition, the city of Rome itself was ruled by Etruscan kings until the founding of the Roman Republic in 509 BC. Yet over the next centuries Etruria came to be dominated by Rome and eventually the Etruscan language died out. Etruscan works of literature were not preserved and the language is now poorly understood, attested primarily in inscriptions, most of which are short funerary texts. The only remaining relic of the books the Etruscans wrote on long strips of linen fabric is a single religious text containing a ritual calendar. The linen made its way to Egypt, was used to wrap a mummy, and thus survived to be discovered by a Croatian traveler in the nineteenth century. Etruscan inscriptions ceased in the first century BC, as the Etruscan people were absorbed into Roman society and learned Latin. The last record of Etruscan having been spoken is in AD 408, when priests offered to recite Etruscan prayers to help save the city of Rome from besieging Goths. Whether anyone was using the language as a mother tongue anymore is not clear.

Before the Etruscan language died, its alphabet had spread to other people. The most enduring legacy of the Etruscan alphabet was the script of the Latin-speaking Romans, but other early peoples of Italy also borrowed the alphabet to write now-forgotten languages such as Venetic, Faliscan, Oscan, and Umbrian.

In the first centuries AD Greek became the language of Christianity in the eastern part of the Roman Empire (which became the Byzantine Empire with the division of the Roman Empire into western and eastern sections in AD 330). From being an exporter of pagan religion and myths, Greece became a center of Christianity. The Coptic alphabet was one result, created in the first centuries of the Christian era with the addition of a few symbols from the native Egyptian demotic script.

The conversion of the barbarians of Europe inspired the creation of new alphabets based on Greek. In the fourth century AD the Gothic bishop Wulfila designed a Greek-inspired alphabet so as to be able to translate the Bible into his native language (see figure 12.2). Gothic, the sole member of the East Germanic branch of the Germanic languages, eventually became extinct, and Wulfila's alphabet died with it. All that remains is a handful of manuscripts, including parts of Wulfila's translation of the Bible.

The Goths were converted to Christianity, largely through the efforts of Bishop Wulfila. Unfortunately, according to the majority view Wulfila was a heretic: the Christianity which the Goths learned from him was Arian Christianity. Arianism, which taught a more limited version of the divinity of Christ than orthodox Christianity, was popular in the eastern Roman (Byzantine) Empire in Wulfila's time but was soon afterward defeated within the borders of the empire. The continued Arianism of the Goths helped to set them at odds with the Roman Empire and they seemed to have no compunctions about sacking Rome in 410. Orthodox Christians in both halves of the empire took note of this, and it was to be centuries before anyone else in Europe attempted to translate the Bible into a barbarian vernacular, where it might be misunderstood and misinterpreted (though safely off to the east, in Armenia and Georgia, new alphabets based loosely on Greek were created in the fifth century to make Christian texts accessible in the local languages).

Eventually memory of the Goths faded. In 862 the Byzantine emperor received a request from a Slavic prince, Rastislav of Morava (a land encompassing present-day Slovakia, Moravia, and parts of Austria and Hungary). Rastislav and his people had become Christians, he said. Could the emperor send them someone to instruct them in the faith? The emperor turned to the monk (later saint) Cyril, a man known for his facility with languages. Cyril heard the emperor with misgivings. If he tried to teach an illiterate people, how quickly would his words get mutated by the oral tradition, laying the Slavs open to heresy, and himself to accusations thereof? He would go, he said, only if he could set down what he was teaching in an alphabet. Permission was granted.

Since neither the Slavs nor the Byzantines were particularly interested in the Slavs becoming Hellenized, Cyril was free to adapt alphabetic writing as much as he chose so as fit the phonemes of the Slavonic language – a goal the more desirable if the result was to be read by priests, who would not, in the early years of Slavic Christianity, have been native Slavonic speakers. The irony is that the alphabet Cyril designed was probably not the one that we now call Cyrillic. Rather it was a script called *Glagolitic* that he brought to Prince Rastislav in 863. Cyril translated various liturgical works into the Slavonic vernacular. His brother, St. Methodius, accompanied him and continued mission work in Morava after Cyril's death in 869. Methodius was credited by later tradition with having translated the Bible into Slavonic; but if it ever existed, Methodius's Bible has not survived, and the Slavonic Bible that eventually emerged was due to later translation efforts.

After Methodius's death in 884, his disciples were persecuted and scattered, some of them ending up in Bulgaria. Here they helped to inspire a tradition of Bulgarian learning and literacy. As Bulgaria developed, it looked to civilized Byzantium as the source of learning and faith. It was probably here, in the last years of the ninth century, that the Slavonic alphabet was revised so as to look more Greek, yielding the script now known as Cyrillic (figure 12.2).

Cyrillic became the official script of the Slavonic Orthodox Church. Glagolitic was increasingly marginalized, except in Croatia where the population was Roman Catholic. The use of Glagolitic finally petered out in the nineteenth century. Modern Croatian uses the Roman alphabet, while Serbian (linguistically speaking a dialect of the same language, Serbo-Croatian) uses Cyrillic.

Greek	Gothic		Cyrillic (Modern Russian)			
Letter	Letter	Phonetic value	Letter	Phonetic value	Letter	Phonetic value
A	𐌰	[a], [aː]	А a	[a]	Ц ц	[ts]
B	𐌱	[b]	Б б	[b]	Ч ч	[tʃʲ]
			В в	[v]	Ш ш	[ʃ]
Γ	𐌲	[g]	Г г	[g]	Щ щ	[ʃʲtʃʲ]
Δ	𐌳	[d], [ð]	Д д	[d]	Ъ ъ	(absence of palatalization)
E	𐌴	[e], [eː]	Е e	[(j)ɛ]	Ы ы	[i]
	𐌵	[kʷ]	Ж ж	[ʒ]	Ь ь	(palatalization)
Z	𐌶	[z]	З з	[z]	Э э	[ɛ]
H	𐌷	[h]	И и	[i]	Ю ю	[(j)u]
			Й й	[j]	Я я	[(j)a]
Θ	𐍈	[θ]				
I	𐌹	[i], [iː]				
K	𐌺	[k]	К к	[k]		
Λ	𐌻	[l]	Л л	[l]		
M	𐌼	[m]	М м	[m]		
N	𐌽	[n]	Н н	[n]		
Ξ	𐌾	[j]				
O	𐌿	[u], [uː]	О о	[ɔ]		
Π	𐍀	[p]	П п	[p]		
P	𐍂	[r]	Р р	[r]		
Σ	𐍃	[s]	С с	[s]		
T	𐍄	[t]	Т т	[t]		
Y	𐍅	[w], [y]	У у	[u]		
Φ	𐍆	[f]	Ф ф	[f]		
X	𐍇	[kʰ]	Х х	[x]		
Ψ	𐍈	[ʍ]				
Ω	𐍉	[o], [oː]				

Figure 12.2 Two of the descendants of the Greek alphabet, Gothic and Cyrillic. Cyrillic has added letters to the end of the alphabet so as to adapt to the Slavic languages. The Gothic alphabet predates the development of minuscules, so the Gothic letters have only one form each. Cyrillic uses minuscules, but they are less different from the capitals than those of the Greek or Roman alphabet.

St. Cyril was devoted to the cause of vernacularism, pitting himself against the "Trilingualists," who believed that only Hebrew, Greek, and Latin could be used to worship God. Cyril's alphabet and his translations served to bring the Christian faith to the Slavic people in their mother tongue. Ironically, however, the translations of Cyril, Methodius, and their followers had the predictable fossilizing effect. Old Church Slavonic became the language of faith in Orthodox Eastern Europe while the spoken language evolved into the various Slavic languages spoken today. Eventually Slavonic was unintelligible to everyday Slavs.

Today the Cyrillic alphabet is one of the world's major scripts, used for the Slavic languages Russian, Belarusian, Ukrainian, Bulgarian, Macedonian, and Serbian. It has also been adapted to many non-Slavic languages across the former Soviet Union, including Moldovan, Tajik, Turkmen, Tatar, Kazakh, Uzbek, and Kirghiz. The languages of the Northwest Caucasus such as Abkhaz and Kabardian are notable for having around 50 consonants each, with only a couple of vowels. The adaptation of Cyrillic to these languages is therefore quite clumsy, not at all the elegant one-phoneme/one-letter system that Cyril intended. But Cyrillic is now one of the scripts of civilization, and poor alphabetic design is the price many languages have had to pay for a share in civilization.

13

The Age of Latin

According to later tradition, Rome was founded on the morning of April 21, 753 BC, by a bandit warlord, Romulus, whose penchant for waging war against his neighbors was to form part of the national character. After Romulus, six more kings were said to have ruled Rome, of whom the last three were Etruscan. Then in 509 BC the last king, Lucius Tarquinius Superbus, was deposed and the Roman Republic established.

We will probably never know exactly how much of this founding myth is true, but one thing that did happen is that the fledgling city of Rome fell under the influence of expanding Etruria (see appendix, figure A.6). The Romans adopted many aspects of Etruscan religion and culture, plus numerous Etruscan words to go along with them, looking to their more sophisticated neighbors as a source of learning and civilization. More significantly, they also borrowed the Etruscan alphabet, a spin-off of the Greek alphabet created around 700 BC (figure 13.1).

The Romans adapted the technology of writing to their own language, an archaic form of Latin, in the sixth or seventh century BC. The written tradition being young at the time in Etruria, the Romans felt no need to be slavishly faithful to their model. What they arrived at was reasonably well adapted to their language, though it was not a perfect phonemic match. Nor was it exactly the Roman alphabet we know today. Written entirely in capital letters and, at first, occasionally from right to left or boustrophedon, it ran A B C D E F H I K L M N O P Q R S T V. The last letter spelled [u], not [v].

The new Roman alphabet had five vowel letters, A, E, I, O, and V, or as we now write it, U. These letters stood (not coincidentally) for the vowels [a], [e], [i], [o], and [u]. In the spoken language, these

Archaic Greek	Etruscan model alphabet	Inscriptional Etruscan		Roman
ΛꓵΛ	Ꙍ	Ꙍ Ꙍ [a]		A
ꓭꓭꓐB	ꓭ			B
𐤂ΓⲦⲤⲤ	𐤂	) [k]		C
▷ΔD	ᐊ			D
𐌄ꓞꓱꓱE	ꓱ	ꓱ [e]		E
𐌄ꓞFⲤ	𐌅	𐌅 [w]		F
ΙI	Ι	Ιᛚ [ts]		G
⨄ꓥⵔH	目	目 目 Ø [h]		H
⊗⊕⊞Ө	⊗	⊗ O O [tʰ]		
ꙅⵢⵢⵢⵔ	Ι	Ι [i]		I J
ꓘꓘKK	Ⲭ	(Ⲭ) [k]		K
ᒻꓷꓥꓥ	𐌋	𐌋 [l]		L
ꟽꟿꟿM	ꟽ	ꟽ ꟽ [m]		M
ꓩꓭꓩN	ꓩ	ꓩ ꓩ [n]		N
𐌙 Ξ	田			
X +				
OӨ◇	O			O
⅂ΓΓΠ	⅂	⅂ [p]		P
M	M	M [ʃ](?)		
ΦΦϘ	Ϙ	(Ϙ) [k]		Q
ꓷꓷPPꓣꓣ	ꓷ	ꓷ ꓷ [r]		R
ꙅⵢⵢⵢⵉ	ꕷ	ꕷ ꕷ [s]		S
TꓕT	T	T ꓔ [t]		T
VYꓬ	Y	Y V [u]		V U
				W
ⵔΦΦ	X	(X) [s] ?		X
X+	Φ	Φ ⵔ [pʰ]		Y
VꓵΨ	ꓵ	ꓵ V [kʰ]		Z
		Ƨ 8 [f]		

Figure 13.1 The Etruscan and Roman alphabets, as descended from the archaic Greek alphabet. The Etruscans learned the whole alphabet and copied it out (second column), but in inscriptions eliminated some of the letters (third column). The original Roman alphabet is on the left in the right-hand column, with later additions to the right. Sources of the additions are shown with arrows.

vowels could be either long or short, but the alphabet had no way to distinguish them. Although the lack of a length distinction was not usually regretted (length being easily inferred by native speakers), there were occasional efforts to record it, such as by doubling the vowel letter, by using the so-called *I longa* (a taller version of I), or, later, by using a diacritical mark called the apex (shaped ', ⌐, or '). The language also contained the diphthongs [ai], [au], and [oi], which, suitably enough, received digraphs: AE, AU, OE.

As for the consonants, it was a good thing the Romans adopted writing before the Etruscans decided to expel the unnecessary letters B and D (and, for that matter, O) from their alphabet. Although the original Greek letters B and Δ had stood for sounds not present in Etruscan – voiced plosives – the Etruscans' original fascination with the abecedary, or alphabetic list, preserved these letters long enough for the Romans to copy them. As for their pronunciations, the Romans must have learned them either from Etruscans bilingual in Greek or from Greeks living in the colonies of southern Italy.

The Etruscans *had* found a use for Greek Γ, now tilted (and eventually rounded) into C, making it one of their three ways of spelling [k], along with K and Q. In trying to make sense of this profusion, the Romans followed the Etruscans' lead in using Q only before U. The QU letter sequence was used to spell Latin [kʷ], a special two-part consonant pronounced much like *qu-* is in English today, in words like *quick* and *queen*. C was used for most other cases of [k], including in the sequence [ku], and K was relegated to an alphabetic backwater, being rarely used except in a few traditional spellings such as *kalendae*, the first day of a Roman month and the source of our word *calendar*.

This left written Latin in the unsatisfactory position of having no way to distinguish [g] from [k]. The invention of G, by the simple expedient of adding a horizontal line to the end of C, is credited to Spurius Carvilius Ruga, in the third century BC. The letter was placed seventh in the alphabet, in the position of Greek and Etruscan Z, which the Romans were not using. In a fit of conservatism, the abbreviations C. for the first name *Gaius* and Cn. for *Gnaeus* (formerly spelled *Caius* and *Cnaeus*) were retained.

The Etruscans used F, the Greek *digamma*, for bilabial [w] (transliterated *v*). At the time of the Latin adaptation Etruscan was still using FH for [f], a practice the Romans followed at first and then simplified to just F, a letter they were not otherwise using.

Latin did have the bilabial semivowel [w], as well as the palatal semivowel [j], but the Romans considered them variants of the vowels [u] and [i] and used the letters V and I accordingly. Whether to pronounce these letters as vowels or as semivowels was usually pretty obvious: if they occurred before a vowel, they were almost always to be pronounced as semivowels. U was originally a handwritten variant of V, the latter being the norm in formal inscriptions.

Somewhere in the transmission of Greek to Etruscan or from Etruscan to Latin, the letters of the alphabet lost their distinctive Semitic-derived names. Instead of *alpha, beta, gamma*, the Roman alphabet's letters had simple, one-syllable names. The vowels were just called by the long forms of their sounds: [aː], [eː], [iː], [oː], [uː]. Most plosives were called by their sounds plus a long [eː] added to make them pronounceable: B was [beː], C was [keː] (not [seː] until many centuries later), D was [deː], etc. K, following the Etruscan custom of pairing it with A, was [kaː], and H, perhaps to match K, was [haː]. Q was [kuː], also following the letter pairings established by the Etruscans. Other consonants – the nasals, liquids (L and R), and fricatives – could theoretically be pronounced alone without a helping vowel, although such "syllabic" consonants did not occur in any normal Latin words. However, the original pronunciation of the letter names appears to have been syllabic anyway: [f̩], [l̩], [m̩], [n̩], [r̩], [s̩]. The fact that Etruscan, by contrast, did have syllabic consonants strongly suggests that the Latin letter names were derived from Etruscan, but that cannot be proved. Eventually the syllabic pronunciation gave way to one with a short helping [e] in front: [ef], [el], [em], [en], [er], [es]. The later Latin names are basically the ones familiar to speakers of Western European languages. (English, however, replaced long [aː] with [eː], [eː] with [iː], and [iː] with [ai], giving us pronunciations such as A and K; B, D, and E; and I. These changes, which affected all words, not just the letters of the alphabet, were part of the Great Vowel Shift that occurred over the course of the fifteenth century.)

Armed with its alphabet and its military ambitions, Rome grew in power. Having shaken off Etruscan dominance, the Romans subdued most of the other Latin people in the surrounding region of Latium in 338 BC and then, after much bloodshed, the Samnites of the southern Apennines in 290. Rome then began to eye – and conquer – the rich Greek city-states in the south. Finally, war with the other great power in the western Mediterranean, Carthage, was inevitable. The Punic Wars

(*Punic* being the Roman version of *Phoenician*) left Carthage defeated in 201 BC and utterly destroyed and plowed under with salt in 146 BC.

Meanwhile, the Romans had encountered Greek culture. Translations of Greek plays began to be performed, and Roman writers began to copy Greek styles and produce the first Latin literature. Cultured Romans studied Greek, and young scholars traveled to Greece to study philosophy. When mainland Greece was wrested from Macedonian rule in 197 BC, the original Roman intent was to leave the city-states free, as they had been before the coming of Alexander's father, Philip of Macedon. Though this arrangement did not last very long, the Romans retained a respect for the Greeks' cultural achievements. Greek was the language of the eastern Mediterranean – the Hellenistic world – and so it was allowed to remain.

Out of the meeting of Greece and Rome came the civilization that ruled – and shaped – much of the Western world. The Romans loved to fight, but they also loved discipline and order. Thus they made warfare into a science, and the inexorable advance of their legions conquered the known world from Britain to Mesopotamia. The same discipline and order were called upon to rule their empire: they created a strong bureaucracy and legal system to administer it, and built roads, bridges, and aqueducts to sustain it. On the other hand, the Romans looked to Greece for inspiration in literature, philosophy, and the visual arts. Eventually they were also to look to Jerusalem, as they adopted the new Christian religion.

As the Romans absorbed Greek culture, they also absorbed Greek words. This led to an alphabetic problem. The Roman alphabet, though ultimately derived from the Greek, was noticeably different from it. How then were the Romans to spell Greek words in Latin? Greek had aspirated plosives, which they spelled Θ, Φ, and (in the Ionian version of the alphabet) Χ. The Romans had not bothered to include these apparently useless letters in their alphabet. When they found they needed to represent aspirated plosives after all, they fell back on using digraphs, two letters for a single phoneme. These consonants sounded like plosives followed by a heavy breath, so that is how the Romans wrote them: TH, PH, CH.

The Greeks had a couple of letters that stood for a sequence of two consonants, [ps] and [ks]. The Romans, having abundant sequences of [ks], accepted one but not the other, adopting X from a western version of the Greek alphabet in which it stood for [ks] but using PS

233

for the other sequence. The Greeks also used Z, which they now pronounced [z], a foreign sound to the Romans. The Romans therefore readmitted Z to the alphabet, but relegated it to the end, the typical place for new letters. Greek also had a strange vowel sound, Y now being pronounced [y], a rounded front vowel as in French *tu*. Thus Y also joined the alphabet, at the end with Z. Perhaps no one realized that Greek Y and Roman V had originally been the same letter, V having lost its tail along the way. The [y] vowel was never easy for the Romans to pronounce, and even the Greeks eventually began pronouncing it simply as [i]. Since the alphabet could not have two letters named [iː], Y came to be called *y graeca*, Greek I. The name *zeta* was borrowed along with the letter Z and survives in the British name *zed*.

The Roman alphabet thus reached its full classical length of 23 letters. It ran A B C D E F G H I K L M N O P Q R S T V X Y Z. Again, V was a vowel, the shape of the letter we now know as U.

This was the alphabet with which the Roman Empire was ruled. The will of the emperor in Rome (an office instituted under Caesar Augustus in 27 BC) was conveyed to military commanders and governors of the provinces in written letters. Law courts, tax collectors, military clerks, and public officials everywhere depended on writing and its ability to retain information (overcoming time) and to communicate at a distance (overcoming space).

As these uses of writing increased, so did others. As trade flourished and Rome prospered, the finances of the more wealthy citizens became complex enough to demand literacy. With Rome ruling the entire Mediterranean world, people were more mobile than previously, traveling great distances on governmental assignment, on military duty, or for commercial purposes. The use of private letter writing grew accordingly. With the growth of a leisured class, literary endeavors multiplied. Roman authors wrote history, satire, comic plays, epic poetry, odes, and technical manuals.

Nevertheless, Roman society retained a strongly oral character. The majority of the population – almost all of those who were not wealthy, doing business for the wealthy, or employed by the government – were illiterate, particularly in the provinces where neither Latin nor Greek was the language of the native population. Literacy was not assumed: official communication to the public was done through town criers. Even the written word retained a strong oral connection. With no way to mass produce texts, authors gave public readings of their works; this was how they made a name for themselves. The wealthy, though literate, would often have their slaves do the hard work of writing, almost priding themselves on their poor handwriting. Even bookish people, if they wanted to relax, would have their slaves read to them rather than read to themselves. In the days before type, punctuation, and balanced page layout, even reading was work.

The advent of Christianity had a complex effect on literacy in the Roman world. Originally a small and scattered sect, its members maintained unity through letters, with those from its original leaders – the apostles – later forming the Epistles of the Christian New Testament. As an offshoot of Judaism and a religion of the Book, it inherited a great respect for the written word. Literacy was therefore a valuable skill to the early Christians. However, Roman Christians were distressed by the educational curriculum of the time, which featured works with strongly pagan themes. This left them in the ambiguous position of valuing literacy but not education. The net result was that literacy was encouraged among the clergy and members of the growing monastic orders (many of whom would not otherwise have had a chance to learn to read), but not among the laity.

By the time Christianity became widely accepted in the fourth century (Constantine's Edict of Milan in 313 forbade persecution of Christians, and in 391 Theodosius outlawed paganism in favor of Christianity), the Roman Empire was already past its prime. Amidst economic woes and barbarian invasions, even literacy had begun to retreat. In an attempt to shore up the empire, Diocletian had divided it in two in 286 and focused on the eastern, previously Hellenistic half. Constantine reunited the empire temporarily but moved the capital to New Rome, Constantinople (now Istanbul), in 330. Rome was becoming a has-been.

In the Western Empire, the barbarians continued to press. In 410 the Visigoths thoroughly sacked Rome, then moved on to found a kingdom in Gaul. In 406 barbarian tribes had already laid Gaul waste and one of them, the Vandals, went on to conquer Spain, then continued on into North Africa. The Roman legions were brought home from Britain to defend the homeland, and within decades Britain was invaded by Angles, Saxons, and Jutes. Attila the Hun, after inflicting heavy damage on the Eastern Empire, ravaged much of northern Italy in 452. One of his successors, Odoacer, gave the Western Empire its deathblow, proclaiming himself king of Italy in 476. The last Western Emperor, the young Romulus Augustulus, was deposed and pensioned off, too unimportant to assassinate.

So ended the empire of Rome. The empire of Latin, however, kept right on going for another thousand years, and in some arenas – in education and in the Roman Catholic church – for some five hundred years after that. Nor did the Roman alphabet succumb; after some initial retreat it prospered greatly and is used far more widely today than anyone could have imagined in 476. (The Eastern Empire also continued. Considering itself the true Roman Empire, the Eastern, Greek-speaking Byzantine Empire, though shrunken, lasted until the fall of Constantinople in 1453.)

In typical fashion, the barbarians that invaded the empire adopted the language of civilization and learned Latin: they may have conquered the empire, but Latin soon conquered them. Although North Africa (and later much of Spain) was lost to the Arabs – and therefore to Arabic – in the seventh century, much of the rest of the Western Empire went on speaking Latin, whether or not they were now ruled by barbarians. Even today, with the notable exception of Britain, the parts of Western Europe that were inside the Roman Empire generally speak modern forms of colloquial Latin, which we know as the Romance languages.

The Latin the newcomers learned, however, was already slightly different in different regions. As the Romans had conquered each province, they had stationed legions there, sent administrators, and settled colonists. The colonists brought with them the colloquial Latin of the time, which became the new colloquial Latin of the particular province. Since spoken language is forever changing, the colloquial language the colonists brought was different in each province, depending on when the province was settled. From then on, the local Latin evolved somewhat differently than the language back home in Italy. As long as a province remained under Roman rule, it remained in some degree of contact with Italian Latin, and its further evolution was influenced by Italy. Once a province was lost to the Romans, these linguistic updates tapered off, though somewhat maintained in the west by the continued religious importance of Rome.

The Romanian language, for example, began as the Latin of the colonists who first settled in the province of Dacia in AD 107. As Dacia was the last province to be added to the empire, it received a relatively late form of Latin, making Romanian in some ways more like Italian (the Latin that stayed home) than the other Romance languages.

However, Dacia was also the first province to be lost to Rome, in 271. Changes occurring in Italy after this time left Dacian Latin (early Romanian) unaffected, while independent changes were free to occur in Dacian. And thus in other respects Romanian has *less* in common with Italian than other Romance languages.

In the Latin of the Western Empire, contact with the provinces was not lost so quickly or so completely. The local provincial speech contained archaisms, inherited from the Latin of the time of colonization, but also participated in some of the linguistic changes occurring in Italy. Over time, however, with no political or administrative ties to bind the former provinces together, the local forms of Latin grew more and more dissimilar. What had been regional dialects would eventually become separate languages: Italian, French, Rumantsch, Spanish, Portuguese, Provençal, Galician, and Catalan in the west, and Romanian and Dalmatian (now extinct) in the east. Meanwhile the local forms of Latin continued to conquer the former provinces, completely replacing the various indigenous languages, with the exception of Basque in northern Spain.

It was a long time, however, before anyone realized that linguistic fragmentation was underway. As far as anyone was concerned, they were speaking the Latin, or Roman, language. They knew that people from distant parts spoke rather differently, but this did not particularly trouble them, any more than the differences between Australian and American English lead anyone nowadays to conclude that these are two different languages. Like modern Australians and Americans, they shared a written language. That written language had remained relatively stable for centuries, fossilized by being written. From the point of view of early medieval speakers, however, there were numerous silent letters and unpronounced suffixes in that written language – though which ones these were varied from region to region. The grammar of the written language was noticeably different from the spoken language, leading to diglossia among the educated. A good education was rare, however, and many who were called upon to write were increasingly shaky in their grammar and spelling.

In the educational and cultural decline and the linguistic fragmentation of the post-empire centuries, it is no surprise that the alphabet also began to fragment. The early forms of the Roman letters, preserved for us in carved inscriptions, had been exclusively capital letters. From rather crude strokes these had developed over the centuries into artistically balanced forms. Serifs were added, and shading effects were achieved by varying the width of letter strokes. The Roman capitals carved on Trajan's column, erected in the early years of the second century AD in honor of the Emperor Trajan's victories in Dacia, are considered among the finest of their kind. In modern type, the capital letters of serifed fonts are modeled after these ancient exemplars.

Handwriting was something of another matter. Informal writing was done in Old Roman Cursive, while for books the Romans used what we now call Rustic Capitals, somewhat narrower in shape than the inscriptional capitals. In the last centuries of the empire, the Uncial and Half Uncial book hands developed, while the nearly illegible New Roman Cursive was used for less formal purposes. With the Uncial and Half Uncial styles came the first letters with ascenders and descenders extending above and below the main body of the line of text, as in *d* and *p*.

With the fall of the empire, local styles proliferated. Uncial remained popular in Benedictine monasteries until the ninth century. Half Uncial and Christianity were both brought to Ireland by missionary efforts; a Roman Briton, St. Patrick, is credited with the conversion of Ireland, beginning in 432. The Irish, though they had never been part of the Roman Empire, took to Christianity enthusiastically and founded monasteries where churchmen could learn Latin, study, and make books. Although the Irish had their own writing system, Ogham (see figure 13.2), consisting of tally-like marks that could be cut into wood or stone, they learned the Roman alphabet for Latin and eventually used it for Irish as well. The Insular Half Uncial script style they created and cultivated as an art form (and later exported, along with Christianity, to northern England) survives in the famous Book of Kells (plate 8).

In other places, New Roman Cursive mixed with Half Uncials to create the family of letter forms known as minuscules. Different regions developed their own new styles, such as the long-lived Visigothic Minuscule of Spain and Beneventan Minuscule of southern Italy. Monastic centers also created new styles, and the ties between monasteries – and even in some cases the movements of individual people – can be traced by the spread of particular minuscule hands. By the eighth century, Western Europe was beginning to look like India, its multitudinous script styles well on their way to becoming separate alphabets.

The man who took it upon himself to reunite the Roman Empire, language, and alphabet is known to history as Charlemagne, Charles the Great. Charlemagne became king of the Franks in 768. The Franks were a Germanic tribe that under their king Clovis (482–511) had taken over the former Roman province of Gaul (roughly modern France). Clovis converted to Christianity, and his people acquired Latin as the language of civilization, but of course they learned to speak it in its local Gallic form and brought to it their own Frankish accent and a fair number of Frankish words. Unlike the Arian Goths, Clovis converted to orthodox Latin Christianity, establishing a lasting bond between the Frankish kings and the Roman pope. Clovis's dynasty, the Merovingians, was replaced by the Carolingians under Charlemagne's father, Pippin III, in 751.

Charlemagne embodied many medieval ideals in a combination that now seems paradoxical: he was a devout Christian, a capable administrator, a patron of learning, a lover of many women, and a ferocious warrior. His expanded Frankish kingdom covered the lands now known as France, the Low Countries, western Germany, Switzerland, and Austria, while lands now known as eastern Germany, the Czech Republic, Slovakia, Hungary, and Croatia were reduced to tributary status. To a large extent Charlemagne succeeded in reuniting the Western Roman Empire, though (to his frustration) without most of Spain and part of southern Italy. He even extended his realm northward into Germanic lands as far as the border of Denmark. He ruled much of Italy, and had made a gift of part of it to the pope. It was a natural next step, therefore, when Pope Leo III anointed Charlemagne emperor on Christmas Day in the year 800, inaugurating what was to become known as the Holy Roman Empire. (After Charlemagne's death his kingdom was split between his sons, and the heirs to the eastern half, later Germany, took the title of emperor, while the heirs to the western half became the kings of France.)

Part of Charlemagne's conquering vision was to spread and enhance civilization. He gathered to himself some of the greatest minds of his day, instituting what has been termed the Carolingian Renaissance. Scholars came from as far away as Ireland and England, where Latin education had been kept strong; Alcuin of York, a man of great learning, became one of Charlemagne's closest advisors. The assembled scholars noticed something: they each pronounced Latin differently. Furthermore, they could all attest to the abysmally poor Latin grammar displayed by many of their countrymen. Under Charlemagne's direction, they sought to correct and standardize the pronunciation and grammatical usage of Latin.

Thus Charlemagne saved Latin, but in doing so he and his scholars helped found the Romance languages. What had been a slowly growing diglossia between written Latin and the local vernaculars came under conscious scrutiny, and what was perceived as deterioration in written Latin was halted. When read aloud, Latin was no longer to be pronounced as words of the vernacular, but each letter of the original spelling should be pronounced. Thus diglossia became bilingualism as eventually it was recognized that the vernaculars were distinct languages. In time, the Romance languages would themselves have literary forms. In Charlemagne's day, however, vernacular Romance literature was still a long way off, and the long-term consequences of the scholars' work remained unforeseen.

Charlemagne also directed his scholars to create an easily readable, standardized script, to be used throughout his empire. The resulting Carolingian Minuscule was both simple and graceful. Ligatures and abbreviations had run rampant in the earlier minuscules, and very understandably so, as both writing surfaces and the scribes' time and labor were at a premium. In Carolingian Minuscule, however, excessive abbreviations and ligatures were discouraged, though a number survived, such as the ampersand, "&", originally a ligatured version of *et* (Latin "and"). Titles and headings still used capitals or uncials. Capitals, uncials, and minuscules were considered different versions of the alphabet, not the single alphabet with two versions of each letter that we regard capitals and minuscules to be today. However, it was this use of the older script styles alongside the newer ones that helped pave the way for the biform alphabet and the interspersion of capitals and minuscules that characterizes modern text.

Carolingian Minuscule spread through much of Europe and replaced most of the other minuscules. It was even exported to England, where a distinctive local variety developed. In the eleventh and twelfth centuries, however, it began to evolve into the Gothic or Black Letter script styles under an increased demand for books. Gothic hands could be written more quickly and, being very compact, took up less space on the page. Later, the coming of the Renaissance saw the birth of the humanist letter styles in Italy, which deliberately harked back to Carolingian Minuscule. Soon afterward Italian printers were casting type based on the humanist hands of the time. As a result, the letter forms of modern typefaces are strongly reminiscent of Carolingian minuscule.

The modern world is also indebted to the Carolingian Renaissance for its knowledge of many Classical Latin works. Working long hours in royal or monastic scriptoria, medieval men – and some women – copied classical works out of disintegrating papyrus volumes onto strong parchment. Parchment was not a new material, its invention going back to the second century BC, supposedly in Pergamum, in Asia Minor, whence the name *parchment* ultimately derives. Most books of the Roman period, however, were made of papyrus. Official inscriptions were engraved on stone or metal, and temporary, informal writing was done on reusable wax tablets, but books were written on papyrus scrolls imported from Egypt, or occasionally on leather. A single volume was not very long, nor was it inexpensive.

Parchment is a very fine, thinly stretched, untanned leather made from the hides of goats, sheep, cattle, or even sometimes rabbits or squirrels. Vellum is parchment made from cow or calf skin. Parchment is extremely durable and can last for thousands of years. By contrast, papyrus is quite perishable, except in very dry environments such as the Egyptian or Dead Sea deserts. Parchment can be written on on both sides, whereas papyrus and normal leather were used on only one side. The ancient scroll format of books was well served by leather or papyrus, but parchment helped to make possible the codex, or book with pages.

Parchment began to be popular around the fourth century AD, along with the codex. The first known codices date to the first century AD, but at first they were rarities. Some of the earliest people to switch from the scroll to the bound book were Christians, as a codex provided a good format for authoritative texts such as the Gospels or Epistles. The text could be consulted simply by opening it at the desired place rather than unrolling the whole thing from the beginning (a factor that still favors books over scrolling computerized texts today). A codex could accommodate a larger text, allowing the books of the Christian Bible to be bound together into a single volume. Other early texts written in codices also tended to be ones that were frequently consulted for reference rather than read from the beginning in a leisurely fashion. Eventually literary works of all types were using the codex format. In Charlemagne's time books of bound parchment pages were entirely standard.

It has been estimated that a large-format Latin Bible of the early medieval period required over 500 calfskins. Understandably, full texts of the Bible were rare. Wealthy Carolingian nobles and monasteries had a ready supply of hides, but mass production of writing surfaces remained impossible until the introduction of paper. Books, especially religious books, were therefore objects of great value. In inventories of property they were listed under the category of "treasure." The covers of biblical and liturgical volumes were often richly ornamented, sometimes encrusted with jewels in the style of a reliquary. The contents of volume and reliquary were considered equally precious.

The work involved in writing out a manuscript by hand was substantial, and it helped to limit the amount of writing that was done and the amount of reading material that was available. Writing was a job for specialists, somewhat like typing was in the twentieth century before the introduction of the word processor. Even Charlemagne, patron of educational renewal, was never satisfied with his attempts to learn to write as an adult. (This does not necessarily mean that he could not read.) Despite the comparative rarity of reading and writing, Carolingian society was a literate one, depending on access to the written word for a number of purposes. Both reading and writing, however, continued to be mediated through the spoken word, as writers often wrote at dictation, and readers often read aloud.

The Carolingian Renaissance was a revival of learning in Latin. Though Rome was long fallen, Latin still ruled Western civilization, just as Greek ruled the Byzantine Empire, Classical Chinese ruled East Asia, and Sanskrit ruled South Asia. On the fringes of the Latin world, however, lived the inevitable rebels, a people who were not at all sure that Latin was the only valid written language. These people were the English.

When the Romans withdrew from Britain in the early fifth century, most of the population south of the Scottish border spoke British, a Celtic language that was the ancestor of Welsh and of Cornish, a language extinct since about 1800. Writing in the early eighth century, the Venerable Bede, the first English historian, dated the beginning of the Germanic invasions to 449. Three tribes came from the continent – the Angles (whence "English"), the Saxons, and the Jutes – who together are known to history as the Anglo-Saxons. The native Britons resisted fiercely, as later romanticized in the legends of King Arthur, but the British culture and language (though surely not all the British people) were forced westward into Wales and Cornwall or across the Channel to Brittany.

The early Anglo-Saxons were pagan, but the Christian Britons were not particularly interested in trying to convert their enemies. The job was left to Pope Gregory the Great, who sent Augustine (later St. Augustine of Canterbury) as a missionary to southern England in 597, and to the Irish, who sent missionaries to northern England in 634. Christianity spread rapidly among the Anglo-Saxons in the early seventh century, encouraged by the conversion of a number of their tribal kings.

The Anglo-Saxons, like the Irish, produced fine scholars of Latin, among them Bede (c.673–735) and Alcuin of York (c.732–804). However, Latin was only distantly related to English and could never pass for being the written version of their native tongue. Perhaps this is why they dared to create vernacular literature, just as the Tamils did in India.

The Roman alphabet was not the first writing the Anglo-Saxons knew. Their first script, learned back on the continent, was runes (figure 13.2). The runic alphabet, known as the *futhark* after the first six symbols of its sequence ("th" being spelled with a single rune), had originally been inspired by the Roman alphabet or some related script of Etruscan descent in northern Italy. The individual runes were designed to be carved into wood, and so horizontal lines were avoided, being hard to see against the grain of the wood. The earliest known, common Germanic futhark had 24 runes and is first attested in northern Europe around the second century AD. The Angles, Saxons, and Jutes brought the futhark with them to Britain, where with some modifications it became the *futhorc*. The use of runes also spread northward into Scandinavia, where a shorter, 16-rune futhark came to be used. Despite the fact that 16 symbols were barely adequate to represent the Old Norse language, the Scandinavian futhark was nevertheless popular in the Viking Age. Particularly in Sweden, the Vikings erected inscribed rune stones detailing the exploits of deceased relatives, or even, sometimes, of themselves.

The Anglo-Saxons used runes for memorial inscriptions, as labels on objects of value, and as coin legends. Some inscriptions contain verses of poetry. The Anglo-Saxons continued to use runes after their conversion, sometimes using both runes and the Roman alphabet in a single Christian inscription. Although the church had nothing against runes, in the end the script could not compete with the internationally dominant Roman alphabet. The use of runes ceased in the tenth or

Ogham									
[b]	[l]	[w]/[f]	[s]	[n]	[h]	[d]	[t]	[k]	[kʷ]/[k]
[m]	[g]	[gʷ]/[ŋ]	[z]/[st]	[r]	[a]	[o]	[u]	[e]	[i]
[k]/[e]	appendix: inconsistent vocalic values								

Anglo-Saxon runes										
[f]	[u]	[θ]/[ð]	[o]	[r]	[k]/[ʧ]	[g]/[j]	[w]	[h]	[n]	[i]
[j]	[i]/[ç]	[p]	[ks]	[s]	[t]	[b]	[e]	[m]	[l]	[ŋ]
[œ]	[d]	[a]	[æ]	[y]	[ea]	[g]	[k]	[k]		

Figure 13.2 Non-Roman scripts of the British Isles. Above, the Ogham alphabet, used to write Old Irish. An appendix was added to the list of symbols in medieval times, but the values assigned to these vowel letters were not consistent from one manuscript to the next. Below, the Anglo-Saxon runic futhorc, derived from the common Germanic futhark, and named after the first six runes in the alphabetical list. The runic alphabet was the source of some letters used to write Old English in the Roman alphabet: the *thorn*, Þ, and the *wynn*, Ƿ, as well as the name of ᚠ, *ash*, applied to æ. Both of these scripts were probably inspired by the Roman alphabet, but their users felt no obligation to preserve Roman alphabetical order or (especially for Ogham) letter shapes.

eleventh century; if anyone was still using the futhorc at the time of the Norman invasion of 1066, no one did so afterward.

Although runic literacy may never have been high, the Anglo-Saxons knew that their language could be written down. They also knew enough not to regard the 23 letters of the Roman alphabet as immutable (clearly, they were barbarians!). Their language, known today as Old English or Anglo-Saxon, had a different set of phonemes than Latin. (They themselves called their language *Englisc*, pronounced almost exactly as it is today, except that the first vowel was pronounced as spelled, [ɛ] not [ɪ].) They dropped and added letters as needed. Z was not considered necessary, as the [z] sound occurred only as a variant of [s] between voiced sounds. The redundancy of C, K, and Q was reduced to just C.

By the time the English adopted the Roman alphabet, the Latin language no longer had a [w] semivowel. The consonant spelled V or U had hardened, first into a [β] and then to a [v], as in modern French and Italian. The English used U/V only as a vowel. The [v] sound was to them a variant of [f] (as [z] was of [s]), so it was spelled F. *Heaven*, for example, was spelled *heofon*. Old English, like Modern English, also had a [w] sound, and the Latin alphabet of the time provided no way to spell it. The futhorc did, however, so the eighth rune, ƿ, called *wynn*, was incorporated into the alphabet. Old English also had a dental fricative, [θ], with a voiced variant [ð] occurring between voiced sounds. For this they used the third rune, Þ, *thorn*. Probably two different people worked on the problem of how to spell the dental fricative, as the resulting Anglo-Saxon alphabet also included a modification of the letter D for this phoneme. It was called *eth* and written Đ in capital form, ð in minuscule. *Eth* and *thorn* were used interchangeably. Although extinct in English, these letters survive in Modern Icelandic, where *eth* is reserved for the voiced fricative (appropriately symbolized [ð]) and *thorn* is used for the voiceless fricative [θ].

Old English also had a vowel sound unknown to Latin, the low front vowel found in the modern word *hat*. For this they used a ligature of Roman A + E, Æ (æ in minuscule), but called it *ash*, the name of the twenty-sixth rune in the Anglo-Saxon futhorc. Another English vowel, the high front rounded [y], also did not occur in Latin. For this the English appropriated the letter Y, unwittingly returning it to its Classical Greek pronunciation.

To the Anglo-Saxons the [j] semivowel (spelled Y in Modern English) was not a separate phoneme but a variant of [g] that appeared before a front vowel. It was accordingly spelled G, though the Half Uncial G looked something like a modern numeral 5, ᵹ. Carolingian Minuscule brought a more modern-looking G, but the "figure-5" G was retained for Old English. All in all, manuscripts in Anglo-Saxon Minuscule can be difficult to read, containing *wynns*, *thorns*, *eths*, *ashes*, and figure-5 Gs, not to mention abbreviations such as one for "and" that looks like the numeral 7. Punctuation was minimal, and "lines" of poetry were not written as separate lines – that would have been a great waste of parchment.

The first person known to have created Christian poetry in the Anglo-Saxon tradition of alliterative (as opposed to rhyming) poetry was Cædmon, a lay brother in a Yorkshire monastery, sometime between 657 and 680. Anglo-Saxon poetry, like early Germanic poetry generally, was originally oral and devoted to heroic themes. The Anglo-Saxon poets not only added Christian themes to their repertoire, but wrote some of their works down in their adapted version of the Roman alphabet. Thus we still have today not only Cædmon's first hymn, but *Beowulf* as well.

The real stimulus for Anglo-Saxon literature was a decline in the level of Latin learning that followed in the wake of the Viking raids that began in 787 and continued relentlessly for the next century. The Vikings were pagan, and they considered the monasteries of England fine prey, containing much wealth and livestock, and few warriors. The more valuable books in them could be sold or returned for ransom, while the cheaper ones made good kindling.

As the Viking attacks grew from summer-time raids to wars of conquest, Anglo-Saxon England nearly went under. Only under Alfred the Great of Wessex (871–99) was the Viking advance finally halted, though much formerly Anglo-Saxon territory remained in Danish hands.

Alfred was much like Charlemagne. Both were Christian Germanic warrior kings who worked to revive the standard of learning in their lands. Alfred, however, embraced the vernacular. He ordered his ealdermen and reeves to learn to read, and resolved to make important works available in English. Although he encouraged scholarship in Latin, he recognized the futility of expecting everyone to learn Latin in order to become literate.

Like Charlemagne, Alfred gathered around him scholars of international rank. First he had them tutor him in Latin. Then he set out, with their advice, to translate Latin works into Old English. He translated the first 50 Psalms and adapted into English (not as strict translation) the *Pastoral Care* by Pope Gregory the Great, the *Consolation of Philosophy* by Boethius, and St. Augustine's *Soliloquies*. Other works were done under his direction.

This translation was harder than it might at first appear. The Latin language had a well-developed religious and philosophical vocabulary. Old English had a well-developed heroic vocabulary (with many words for swords and shields, to be used according to the demands of the alliterative poetic line), but not a philosophical one. Quite sensibly, languages are well adapted to the contexts in which they are used. If the context changes, speakers will either switch languages or make changes to their native tongue. The clerics learning Latin throughout Christendom were choosing the first alternative, but Alfred chose the second. With his scholastic advisors, he found ways of using native English vocabulary to express theologically and philosophically sophisticated ideas. As a result, English was by far the first vernacular language in Western Europe to have a developed literary form. Even parts of the Bible were translated into English, and a number of its books were adapted into alliterative poetry. (In later centuries translation of the sacred Book was to be condemned as dangerous and illegal.) Latin retained its prestige, however, and continued to be used by the most educated. Some texts were bilingual, with Carolingian Minuscule used for the Latin, and Anglo-Saxon Minuscule for the English translation.

What brought an untimely end to Old English – and its written tradition – was the Norman Conquest of 1066. The Normans, originally Viking "Northmen," had in the previous century taken over what is now Normandy in France and settled down to learn French and rule the native French population. With the invasion of England by William the Conqueror (1066–87), French came to England. Norman noblemen replaced most of the Anglo-Saxon lords, and soon the prestige spoken language of England was French and the only acceptable written language was once more Latin.

Nowadays the surviving words of Old English origin are the simple or even rude ones. Words associated with gentility, courtesy, administration, religion, and education are of French origin or borrowed directly from Latin or Greek. This leaves an inaccurate picture of Anglo-Saxon vocabulary. Old English was not simple, but under the Normans erudite Old English words withered away. What to Alfred would have been *Þrīness* ("threeness") and *welwillendness* are to us the Romance *Trinity* and *benevolence*. English ceased to exist as a literary language and almost ceased to be written at all.

When it finally returned, with tentative stirrings in the late thirteenth century, it was forever marked by French. In part because of its inclusion of French vocabulary, the fourteenth-century Middle English of Chaucer's *Canterbury Tales*, though odd to the modern eye, is recognizable as English, whereas *Beowulf* appears to be in a foreign language.

The Norman Conquest also altered the English alphabet, bringing it under Latin sway. The Normans had adopted the practice of writing [w] as a double U (or, in capitals, a double V). This was the forerunner of the letter W, nemesis of the *wynn*, although it was not recognized as a separate letter until the sixteenth century. The Normans, following the Latin practice of modifying letters with H, introduced TH (formerly Þ or Ð), SH (formerly SC), and CH (formerly just C when next to a front vowel). Under this treatment, the *eth* died out by the fourteenth century. The *thorn* clung to life for some time, although eventually it lost its upper closure and began to look like Y. Even after TH was used in most cases, *thorn* was used as an abbreviation in short words such as "the," eventually yielding misleading pseudo-medieval spellings such as "Ye Olde Tea Shoppe."

French used the Carolingian form of G, while the Anglo-Saxons had used a version descended from the figure-5 Half Uncial version. Since in French the G stood for different sounds than in English (Old French [g] or [ʤ] versus English [g], [j], and sometimes even [x] or [ɣ]), the English G came to be considered a separate letter, 3, called *yogh*, and used for the native English Gs, especially where these were not to be pronounced [g]. The *yogh* eventually lost out to Y. English had lost its rounded [y] vowel in the transition to Middle English, so Y was no longer needed for that. The French, for whom Y sounded the same as I, found Y to be more easily readable than I in the overly compacted Gothic scripts of the later Middle Ages. So Y came to be used as a vowel interchangeably with I, and with the death of *yogh*, as a consonant as well. *Yogh* hung on for a while in Scotland, but printing, with its finite list of reusable characters, was not kind to variant letters. It was replaced with Z.

Meanwhile, the first stirrings of vernacular literature were occurring on the continent. Northern France began experimenting with written French in the eleventh century. The trend spread southward, reaching Spain and Italy in the thirteenth century. At first the vernacular was used only for creative works, while anything formal continued to be written in Latin. Nevertheless, by the end of the Middle Ages Latin had clearly lost its absolute monopoly. It was soon to lose much more ground in the Renaissance and Reformation. The Roman alphabet, however, was to go from strength to strength in its third millennium, being used today for more languages than any script ever has been.

14

The Alphabet Meets
the Machine

One of the most significant events in the history of writing – indeed, in the history of the world – was the completion, in the German city of Mainz around 1450, of Johannes Gutenberg's movable-type printing press. Just as the original technology of writing was central to the development of civilization, so the technology of printing – which mass produced the written word – was central to the development of the modern world. Yet movable type alone could not change the world; the world had to be ready for it. King Sejong could have told us that.

In Europe's case, however, the stage had already been set for the impact of printing during the late Middle Ages. One important aspect of the preparation was the advent of paper. Paper took a thousand years to reach Europe from China; it was first used in Constantinople in 1100 and in Arab-controlled Sicily in 1102. Later in the twelfth century Arabic Spain opened its first paper mill. Somehow the technology fell into Christian hands; legend puts a paper mill in Vidalon, France, in 1157, while more secure records mention paper mills in Fabriano, Italy, in 1276. By the end of the fourteenth century there were several paper-making centers in Christian Europe.

Accustomed to parchment, Europeans wrote with quill pens, rather than Chinese brushes or Islamic reed pens. They therefore needed paper that was strong, scratch resistant, and relatively impervious to ink (to keep the ink from spreading). The solution was to use a gelatine size – a thin layer of glue on the surface of the paper. The result still got mixed reviews: compared with parchment, paper tore easily and was clearly not going to outlast the millennium. Important documents therefore continued to use parchment. But paper was somewhat cheaper, rather lighter, and, most importantly, could be made in greater and greater quantities, at least so long as supplies of the raw materials –

cotton and linen rags – held out. By the end of the fourteenth century the use of paper was finally well established; the printing press appeared promptly not long thereafter. Without paper, a printing press would have been nearly pointless. With paper, printing could create the world's first truly mass communication.

Paper also affected the way printing was done. Neither Bi Sheng nor the Korean printers had ever used an actual press. Their printing was done by rubbing a sheet of paper over the inked type. Asian paper, made to be written on with a brush, was soft and absorbent, making printing easy but restricting it to one side of the paper. When printing was later reinvented in the West, it used a press, by which the paper was forcibly squeezed down onto the inked type. That part of the technology was old, borrowed directly from olive and wine presses. But the reason for the force was European scratch-proof paper: the stuff was so opaque and stubborn that a simple rubbing would not transfer the ink to the paper. And so a press was necessary; the upside was that one could print on both sides of the paper.

The printing press was born, conveniently, into the waning years of the Latin empire. Across Western Europe literate people were reading in Latin. With weak national borders, the press's early products had an international clientele. And that clientele was growing. The number of literate people had been rising since the tenth or eleventh century. Cities and towns had grown, along with the merchant and professional classes. Literacy moved out of the monasteries and upper nobility to meet the needs of urban laypeople. Italy saw the development of commerce and banking, and accordingly led the continent in literacy rates.

With the spread of literacy had come the founding of the first universities, starting with the University of Bologna in the late twelfth century. These universities were centers of an unprecedented demand for books. Lay scribes arose to fill the need, and the crowded Gothic hand developed to help get the books copied quickly and cheaply.

At the same time, the continental vernacular languages were starting to get their first literary attention. Latin was a very old language by this point: the world was changing, but Latin had been fixed by rule and was not changing to keep pace. It was well developed for philosophy and theology, but creativity demanded a living language. Epic, romantic, and chivalrous poetry began to be written in various vernaculars, and folktales were written down. The city of Florence, a wealthy hotbed of literacy (with rates as high as 25–35 percent), produced Dante (1265–1321), Petrarch (1304–74), and Boccaccio (1313–75), literary giants who pioneered in the use of Italian (thus winning for the Tuscan dialect of Florence the honor of setting the standards for written Italian). Vernacular literature could reach a much wider audience than Latin could; even illiterates could enjoy listening to the stories read aloud, as they often were. The printing press was therefore a response to a growing market for books.

Despite their vernacular works, Petrarch and Boccaccio were early Italian humanists, scholars who revered antiquity and looked to classical authors for wisdom. Humanists were more tolerant than their predecessors of Roman paganism, and they sharply criticized the medieval Christian lens through which all classical works had been studied. Humanists were also aware that in the long process of copying and recopying during the Middle Ages many errors had been introduced into ancient works. In the fifteenth century humanists went on a treasure hunt, searching monasteries and libraries for neglected ancient manuscripts. At the same time, they learned Greek and began to read Classical Greek works in the original, tutored by Greek scholars fleeing the tottering Byzantine Empire. These refugee scholars gathered in Florence, where they and the Italian humanists established the Platonic Academy to study Greek philosophy in 1462. The humanists wished to publish complete and corrected versions of ancient works. The new printing technology fit the need admirably: finally, here was a way to reproduce the classics without multiplying errors with every copy.

As he worked on his first press, Johannes Gutenberg (1399–1468) was probably oblivious to the fact that he had been scooped by both Bi Sheng and the Korean government. He did, however, know that others were experimenting with ways to reproduce writing, and (to the frustration of later historians) he kept his work secret. His first products seem to have been a few calendars and a Latin grammar, but it was with his 42-line Bible (so called because there were 42 lines per page) of 1455 that the printed book entered Western history (plate 9).

Gutenberg made about 45 copies of his Bible on vellum (thereby using 7,650 calfskins) and another 135 copies on paper (thereby saving nearly 23,000 skins but requiring an investment of almost 45,000 sheets of paper). The 1,282 pages of each copy were bound into two or three volumes. Before Gutenberg could profit from his work, however, his financial

251

backer, Johann Fust, foreclosed. The next major printed work, and the first to bear a date, was the *Mainz Psalter*, which came out in 1457, purporting to be the work of Johann Fust and his son-in-law, Gutenberg's former assistant Peter Schöffer.

Others in Mainz (and perhaps Gutenberg himself, thought to be the printer of the *Mainz Catholicon* of 1460) soon set up print shops. A three-volume, 36-line Bible was out by 1461. Then in 1462 Mainz was sacked by one of two claimants to the title of archbishop; its printers fled the violence and commercial instability. By the end of the decade Cologne, Basel, Rome, Venice, Paris, Nuremberg, and Utrecht had their own presses. By the end of the following decade, printing had reached England, Spain, and Poland.

The use of type not only revolutionized the scale of book production, but marked a significant conceptual change in the way writing was done. The original process of writing by the *creation* of letters became a process of writing by *selection* from a preformed set of letters. The human hand creates infinite variety. Different people have different handwriting, and even an individual's handwriting will vary from one writing session to the next according to mood, fatigue level, posture, etc. Movable type changes all that. Individual Mycenaean or Carolingian scribes can be still identified by their work; not so the modern writer. Within a single font, the *e* in one word will look just like the *e* in the next, no matter who originally authored the individual words. How many people's words, for example, have been uniformly recorded in Times New Roman type?

Inevitably, there were some who objected to the sterility of the new process. How could the spiritual value of a printed Bible possibly compare to that of one crafted by hand by a praying human soul? Equally inevitably, perhaps, the new technology won the day. The invention of movable type by no means halted to the activity of handwriting, but it did mean that most public texts thereafter were written by selection rather than by creation. At first the privileged domain of print shops, writing by selection has only become more dominant with the invention and widespread use first of typewriters and then of personal computers.

Making a type font for the new selection process was no small undertaking. The first step was to cut a metal *punch* – a raised, reversed image of a letter carved onto the end of a hard metal bar. This punch was then driven into a softer metal to form an indented, unreversed version of the letter called the *matrix* (so called because it was the *mother* of the pieces of type cast from it). The matrix was then placed into a mold, where molten metal was poured over it to create individual pieces of type – again raised and reversed in orientation. Many identical pieces of type could be made from the same matrix to supply the many individual instances of a letter needed to set several pages of type at once (this was one reason not to just print directly from the punches). To set just the previous page of my manuscript, for example, would require 1,605 pieces of type. A full font was about 80,000 pieces. As printing spread, type foundries arose which made enough type to fill the needs of many print shops. Professional type-casters in the early years could make four pieces of type in a minute; by 1900, rotary machines containing the matrices for 100 sorts could make 60,000 pieces of type in an hour (a *sort* being a character in a type font, and "out of sorts" an unpleasant condition for a printer to be in).

The type was housed in the pigeon holes of wooden cases, the less-used capital letters above, in the *upper case*, and the minuscules below, in the *lower case*. The letters were not arranged alphabetically; rather the more used letters were placed within easy reach. Nevertheless, ideas differed as to the ideal arrangement, and it was some time before type cases were standardized within countries (they continued to vary from one country to the next, as the frequency of letter use – and even the set of letters used – varied with the language).

The job of laying out the text belonged to the typesetters or *compositors*, who would assemble individual pieces of type into a *form* held together by a frame or *chase*. They would then *justify* the type by filling up the white spaces so as to keep the type rigidly fixed in the chase. The filled form was placed on the bed of the press and inked. A piece of damp paper was placed on top of it, and the metal plate – the *platen* – of the press lowered to squeeze the paper firmly down onto the ink. Later improvements added a parchment *frisket* that covered the margins of the paper to reduce inadvertent inking, and a *tympan* of felt or flannel placed on top of the paper to add a little "give" that would compensate for slight discrepancies in the height of the type. Forms grew to include several pages of type (printed on a single large sheet), and a counterweight was added to the press to make raising the platen easier. Despite these improvements, the basic technology of printing did not change greatly for several centuries. During the sixteenth and seventeenth centuries experienced pressmen could print a single sheet (containing several pages of text, depending on the size of the resulting book) in 20 seconds.

Fifteenth-century books from the infancy of printing (known as *incunables* or *incunabula* after the Latin word for "cradle") are hefty volumes of impeccable workmanship. When Gutenberg set out to mass produce books, his idea of what books looked like was naturally based on the extant manuscripts of the time. *Those* books were what he wanted to mass produce. And so his Bible looks handwritten. It uses the same Gothic script and the same abbreviations and ligatures that a scribe would use. Rather than the mere 24 letters that Gutenberg's alphabet recognized, he used over 400 different sorts to better imitate scribal practices. Like any copyist of the time, Gutenberg sent his books out to the illuminators to be illustrated by hand. Only when production reached a level where the illuminators and rubricators (those who added the initial capitals in red) could not keep up was this practice abandoned.

Gutenberg's type was of a Gothic style, like the handwriting current in Germany at the time. As printing spread south to Italy, however, printers were exposed to other types of handwriting. In their zeal to resurrect their classical past, the Italian humanists had developed a new style of handwriting based on Carolingian Minuscule, the script of the surviving (parchment) manuscripts of their revered ancient authors. This style of handwriting became the model for roman type styles of the kind we still use today. At first roman type was used only for printing classical works, but its use for Latin, the international language, gave it an international presence.

A cursive and more space-efficient form of the new humanist hand was the inspiration for italic type. Under the direction of the great humanist printer Aldus Manutius, the first italic font was cut in 1,500 to print small-sized editions of the Latin classics. Thus italic and roman were originally cast as separate fonts: a printer would use one or the other for a work. Eventually, however, the more spacious, rounded look of roman type won out, with italic used for special purposes. This conflation of the two type styles led to the development of tilted, or swash, capitals for the italics. Originally, capitals had been a separate script style – their own version of the alphabet. But Gothic manuscripts had over the preceding centuries led to distinctively Gothic-looking capitals; the humanists had reverted to the old Roman capitals as found in classical inscriptions such as Trajan's Column. As long as roman and italic type were used in different books a single set of Roman capitals could serve for both, but once they were put together, italics clearly needed their own set. And so the alphabet came to be thought of as a double list, with each letter having capital and minuscule forms, both of which should be represented in any type style.

Early books imitated handwriting, but printed text brought with it a new authoritative feel. It exuded rigidity and changelessness in a way that handwriting had not. Ever afterward, handwriting has largely imitated type (even to the extent of being called "printing" when not in cursive), but with *a* instead of **a** being a common exception and *g* for **g** even more common. The authoritative aura of print is so strong that the standard shape of the roman letters has changed very little in the last five hundred years.

The German-speaking countries continued to use Gothic type, however, evolving a style known as Fraktur, which was used for German-language publications, while the international roman was used for Latin works. Handwriting imitated Fraktur as well, in a form known as Kurrentschrift. As other countries abandoned the use of Gothic scripts, Fraktur came to be seen as particularly German. Nationalists and internationalists debated the wisdom of retaining this typographical idiosyncrasy; but when the Nazis came to power in the 1930s, Fraktur was embraced as part of the distinctive German heritage. As the Nazis began to conquer peoples who could not easily read Fraktur, however, the regime had a change of heart: Fraktur suddenly became a Jewish invention foisted on the innocent German people, who would hereafter use roman. Today Germany continues to use roman, while Fraktur is perceived as old-fashioned or even suspect, still stigmatized by the Nazis' early support.

Early printed books were simply mechanically produced manuscripts, using the same conventions as books written by hand. Over time, however, the possibilities inherent in the new technology began to assert themselves, and books began to take on a more modern look. Ligatures and abbreviations were reduced, as the need to save scribal effort was gone, replaced by a desire to save trouble cutting extra punches. The open, legible roman type began to be used for all sorts of texts. More white space was included between chapters and between paragraphs. The text was presented in one column per page rather than two. Title pages were added. Page numbers were invented, leading to one of the greatest pre-World Wide Web inventions in information science, the alphabetically ordered index. Books became smaller in size and hence both more portable and more affordable. In sum, books became much easier to read, and more and more people read them. Even the bourgeoisie could have their own small libraries. Reading books for private pleasure rather than aloud became more popular.

The results of printing were many. One of the most significant was to turn the religious reform movement started by Martin Luther into the full-scale propaganda war that was the Protestant Reformation and Catholic Counter-Reformation. At first the religious authorities had been favorably impressed with printing. Monasteries and bishops invested in their own presses; churchmen bought printed liturgical works and editions of the church fathers. And the church hierarchy discovered that presses could produce huge numbers of letters of indulgence, which could be used to raise money for projects such as rebuilding St. Peter's basilica in Rome.

The problem with printing, as the Catholic church soon realized, was that it was very hard to control. If it helped spread good ideas, it could equally spread bad ones. Martin Luther was not the first to attempt to reform the church, but he was the first in the new age of printing. If the Ninety-Five Theses attacking indulgences that he nailed to the door of the Castle church in Wittenberg in 1517 had remained handwritten, it is possible that not much would have happened – at least not at that particular moment. However, Luther translated his theses into German and had them printed and disseminated throughout Germany. The demand for copies helped to convince Luther that the time was ripe for his ideas. The ecclesiastical system really was in need of reform, and Germans were furthermore tired of being dictated to by the Italian papacy. Luther also became convinced of the power of the press. He began to write pamphlets, sermons, and books. Two printers put their presses exclusively at Luther's disposal, and many others published him as well. Luther wrote in German, reaching as wide a lay audience as possible, and emphasizing his split with the Latin church. The German people loved it; over a third of German books sold between 1518 and 1525 were by Luther.

Luther turned his hand to translating the Bible into German. In so doing he did much to set the standards for written High German. Like any vernacular language, German existed in innumerable dialects. Arguably it could have been considered two separate languages: High German, spoken in the southern highlands, and Low German, spoken in the coastal lowlands. But High German won the race to become standardized in print, partly because of Luther. Others before him had written in German, both High and Low, and they had attempted to write in as dialectally neutral a way possible, so as to reach a wider audience. Luther, writing in High German, continued this trend. On the one hand he strove to avoid regionalisms (even those of his own native Lower Saxon dialect), while on the other he used words from a wide variety of dialects, searching for those that would most precisely translate biblical concepts. His use of language decisively shaped the standard German language.

Editions of his Bible sold like hotcakes. By mid-century a million copies had been printed, and an even larger number followed in the second half of the century. Other reformers were quick to seize the power of the press: Geneva became an important printing center publishing the theology of John Calvin – and, frequently, smuggling the product back into Catholic France, where Calvin had come from. Antwerp, Leiden, Basel, and Strasbourg became important Protestant publishing and smuggling centers. Inside France printers and booksellers tended to be Protestant (the Reformation was, after all, very good for the book trade), but as the Catholic Counter-Reformation got underway they had to be very discreet – or pay for it with their lives.

Other printers found business on the Catholic side of the fence. If the Reformers could publish posters and pamphlets denouncing Catholicism, Catholics could return the favor – and printers benefited either way. In a desperate but ultimately futile attempt to control the power and spread of the printed word, the church issued a list of banned books in 1559, the *Index Librorum Prohibitorum*. The index meant work for printers, especially as it needed to be continually updated. In France, a royal edict required all books to be licensed and for a while in 1535 King François I even forbade the printing of any books at all. In 1551 the king forbade the import of any books from Geneva or from Protestant countries. In 1529 the Holy Roman Emperor Charles V (also Charles I of Spain) ordered all copies of Luther's works burned. But banning books only increased the demand for them – and made work for printers.

Printing and bookselling were *business* in a way that manuscript copying never had been. When the furore of the Reformation died down, printers had to look around for cheap projects that would bring in cash. The Bible had been done; devotional works like the *Book of Hours* had been done; the classics had been done. The obvious place to turn next was to books in the vernacular languages. Produced by living authors, these would continue to be in ready supply.

And so it was the economics of the publishing trade that brought the literary languages of modern Europe to maturity. In the process, printers had a significant effect on how these languages came to be written – with what typefaces, with what spellings, and even with what letters.

Vernacular writing had begun some time before, but it had not yet settled into standardized forms. As the Roman alphabet came to be used for its daughter languages, the letters had to do different work than they had done in Latin. Where Latin had originally pronounced **C** as [k], the descendant languages used [s] (as in French *cinq*, "five") or [tʃ] (as in Italian *cinque*) before the front vowels [e] and [i]. Latin [kʷ], however, had become [k], reintroducing that sound before front vowels. To spell it, the letter **K** was retrieved from the dustbin, passed on to the Germanic languages (hence English *king, kid*, and *kitten*), and then replaced in the Romance languages with **QU** under the conservative influence of the humanists (and hence French and Spanish *qui*, "who").

The Spanish language had turned doubled Latin **LL** and **NN** into palatal sounds, [λ] and [ɲ]. The former is still spelled **ll**, but the typography of the latter enshrined one of the many scribal short forms. The double **N** had been written with one **N** above the other, the smaller top **N** degenerating into a wavy line. Thus [ɲ] is spelled **ñ** in Spanish; similarly, the tilde is used over vowels in Portuguese to represent nasalization (originally caused by a following **N**).

Another fossilized short form is the *cedilla*, the symbol at the bottom of **ç**. It was originally a **z** (hence the name, from *zedilla*, "little zed") written below the **c** and was used to represent the affricate [ts] in medieval Spanish. Later the affricate was simplified to [θ] or [s]. As the French language struggled for recognition in the early years of print, Geoffroy Tory proposed improving the writing of French with the cedilla for **cs** that were pronounced [s] where [k] would otherwise be expected, along with vowel accents to distinguish the various additional French vowel qualities, and the apostrophe to show the elision of unpronounced letters. In German, a ligature of the "long s," ſ, and **z** became **ß**, which is used in place of a double **s**.

The French were not alone in adopting vowel accents. The Germanic languages faced challenges adapting the relatively impoverished set of

Latin vowel letters to their richer vowel inventories. German adopted the umlaut, as in **ü**, to depict extra front vowels, while the Scandinavian languages created **å** and **ø** for their non-Latin vowels.

Most shorthand symbols and a number of nonstandard letters (such as the yogh, 3) went by the way, probably because cutting punches for additional symbols was much more work than casting a few more of a smaller set of sorts. Nevertheless, using the Roman alphabet for the various languages of Europe required considerable adaptation. Some languages (such as post-Norman English) chose combinations of letters for distinctive sounds (such as **wh**, **ch**, **sh**, **th**), while others chose to add diacritical marks to create new variants of the Latin letters. Only Icelandic, at the very periphery, dared to retain nonstandard **þ**, and **ð**.

A letter could end up standing for quite different things in different languages. The sequence **ch**, for example, is [tʃ] in English, [k] in Italian, [ʃ] in French, the velar fricative [x] in Dutch, and either [x] or the palatal [ç] in German, depending on context. Overall, the tendency has been not to expand the Latin list of basic letters but to modify letters with diacritics where necessary. In some cases the modified letters are considered new letters, while in others they are merely adorned variants of the original ones. In French, **é**, **è**, and **ê** are all considered variants of **e** and alphabetized as such, but in Swedish, **å**, **ä**, and **ö** are letters of their own and take their place (as additional letters so often do) at the end of the alphabet, after **z**.

One ligature that survived – and altered the list of Latin letters – was the **w**. A doubled **v** (or **u**) had been used for some time: once the Latin consonantal **V** had hardened into a fricative, there was no way to spell the [w] sound that the Romans encountered in Celtic and Germanic names. A double **V** spelling came into being around the first century AD and was later embraced enthusiastically by the Normans (who, with names like *William*, found it very convenient). Overlapping the letters as a **w** was not at first considered necessary to do in print. But in the fifteenth century handwriting was still the norm, and so **w** made its way into print. With the authority of print behind it, it was soon considered a letter of its own. The **w** was not accepted in the Romance languages, however, where even today it is only used in loanwords. The use of World Wide Web URLs (uniform resource locators) prefixed by "www." has brought the **w** to new prominence in these languages.

Another change that eventually affected the list of letters was the distinction of **i/j** and **u/v**. I and V were the formal versions that got inscribed

259

on stone, and **J** and **U** were handwritten forms. When printing first started, **v** and **j** were often used as initial letters, with **u** and **i** later in a word; so the early printers cast type for both. Thus *use* would be printed *vse* and *love* would be *loue*. The use of **v** and **j** for consonants and **u** and **i** for vowels was first suggested in 1465, first used in 1492, and then gradually adopted over the following centuries. For some time, however, **i** and **j**, and **u** and **v**, were still considered the same letter. In Samuel Johnson's dictionary (according to the abridged version of 1756) the letter **V** is defined as having "two powers, expressed in modern English by two characters, *V* consonant and *U* vowel, which ought to be considered as two letters; but as they were long confounded while the two uses were annexed to one form, the old custom still continues to be followed." The entry for *voyager* is followed by *up*. Similarly, the pronoun *I* is followed alphabetically by the verb *jabber*. In Noah Webster's 1806 dictionary, however, the letters were finally separated, with the vowels preceding the consonants.

Ever since then English speakers have considered the Roman alphabet to contain 26 letters, but this idea is a rather parochial one. The ancient Roman alphabet did not have 26; and one look under the "Insert Symbol" command in Microsoft Word, where characters required for various languages are displayed, should be enough to convince anyone that the Roman alphabet in fact exists in much greater variety. There is also great variety in the sounds that the letters represent. There is no longer one Roman alphabet, but many.

The Celtic languages adopted a version of the Roman alphabet, as did a number of Slavic languages; the Baltic languages Lithuanian and Latvian; the Uralic languages Finnish, Estonian, and Hungarian; Maltese Arabic; Basque; and Albanian. The alphabet stretched to cover phonemes it had never encountered before: in Welsh, the lateral fricative [ɬ] received the spelling **ll**, and **w** became a vowel. Polish had two l-like sounds, and spelled one of them (the so-called "dark l," [ɫ]) as **ł**, though with time the pronunciation (but not the spelling) changed to [w]. It also had nasalized vowels, and adopted a subscript hook (rather than the tilde of Portuguese) to make **ą** and **ę**.

Irish had a particular problem: it has way too many consonants for the Roman alphabet, as each consonant comes in both "broad" and "slender" versions (the latter being *palatalized* – almost as though followed by a small palatal glide [j]). Instead of creating new consonant symbols or multiplying consonant digraphs, the Irish chose to indicate the quality of the consonant by the vowel symbols that surround it. Front vowels **i** and **e** were associated with the "slender" consonants, and the back vowels **a**, **o**, and **u** with the "broad" consonants. Thus some vowels letters in Irish are meant to be pronounced as such, while others are there merely to tell the reader something about the nearest consonant. The result, to the foreigner, is a bewildering profusion of vowels in which, for example, the word *buíon* ("host") is merely pronounced [biːn], the **u** and **o** indicating the "broad" quality of the consonants.

The Slavic languages also make use of palatalized consonants, for which they generally use diacritics on the consonants. A particularly Slavic diacritic is the *háček* (which occurs on the third letter of its own name), which evolved from a superscript dot introduced by the fifteenth-century Czech reformer and forerunner of Martin Luther, Jan Hus.

In the twentieth century the Roman alphabet was adopted by Turkish (not without further diacritics) and, by an uncomfortable stretch, Vietnamese. Vietnamese has eleven vowels (requiring the use of diacritics) and six distinct tones (requiring the use of even more diacritics). Another stretch has been the application, beginning in the nineteenth century and still ongoing, of the Roman alphabet to the languages of Africa. Most languages of sub-Saharan Africa have not traditionally been written down, though a few scripts have been invented in West Africa, such as King Njoya's Shü-mom script, the N'ko alphabet, and the Vai, Loma, Kpelle, Mende, and Bambara syllabaries.

Many other African languages have looked to the Roman alphabet. Although it is the script of colonialism, it is a practical choice for sub-Saharan Africa because it looks international, because individuals already educated in the colonial languages (English, French, and Portuguese) already know it (and adults do so hate to learn a new script), and because of the lasting, arguably pernicious influence of the typewriter. Computers are not yet universal, and many in Africa are still dependent on typewriters and their severely limited repertoire of letters.

Adopting the Roman alphabet to African languages is far from straightforward. Most of the languages have more than five vowels, many have tones, and many have a great number of consonants. These consonants may be doubly articulated plosives, which are like [k] and [p] or [g] and [b] pronounced simultaneously; they may be labialized, palatalized, or aspirated; they may be prenasalized (as in the name of President Mbeki, in which the **m** and the **b** represent parts of a single phoneme); or they may be clicks (sounds unlike the phonemes of any other languages, but used by English speakers in non-linguistic utterances to urge on a horse, show disapproval, or mime a kiss). Grudging additions to the typewriter set have been made in some cases, most commonly by adding the vowel symbols ɔ, ɛ, and ə, and the consonant ŋ. ŋ is required because **ng** is needed for prenasalized [ⁿg]. Single phonemes may require up to four letters to write, as in Setswana **tlhw** (technically a "labialized aspirated lateral affricate") and **tshw** (a "labialized postalveolar affricate"), or in Naro **tcg'** (an "alveolar ejective click with fricative release"). Some of the click languages may have over 100 distinct consonant phonemes, though this does depend a little on how you count. (Is the Naro **tcg'** really a single phoneme, or a sequence?) Not even the International Phonetic Alphabet – based as it is on the Roman alphabet – has individual symbols for all these sounds, relying on the conjunction and/or super- and subscripting of symbols. (Setswana **tshw**, for example, is transcribed [tʃʷ].)

The adaptation of the Roman alphabet to the African languages – and even to some of the languages of Europe – makes it less a phonemic alphabet and more a script that records *features*, or aspects of phonemes. In clusters such as Setswana **tlhw**, the individual letters stand for parts of the phoneme. Similarly, with the use of diacritics, such as the Slavic háček, the háček and the letter it is added to also stand for two aspects of a single phoneme. The result is not unlike Sejong's system, in which related phonemes are given related symbols.

Meanwhile, in English the Roman alphabet has picked up traces of both logography and syllabary. The words *heart* and *hart*; *sea* and *see*; *there*, *their*, and *they're*; or *two*, *too*, and *to* are spelled that way not just for historical reasons but because it is useful to have different words look different, even if they are pronounced the same. As in a logogram, the spelling "two" directly tells the reader the meaning of the word, not just its pronunciation. Much ambiguity is thereby avoided.

More recently, the letters of the alphabet have done roaring business as syllabograms. Each letter has a syllabic name – *bee*, *cee*, *dee*, etc. – but the proportion of English syllables covered this way is very small. Nothing daunted, however, the users of text messaging and participants in chat groups, for whom shortness of text is a desideratum, are now typing messages such as **bcnu** ("be seeing you"), **2l8** ("too late"

– here the numerals are also pressed into service as syllabograms), or **ruok** ("are you OK?"). Abbreviations are running rampant again, with messages such as **brb** ("be right back"). The later history of the Roman alphabet, like the history of writing in general, is deeply paradoxical: a never-ending adaptation of a set of symbols that very much prefer to become fixed and fossilized.

The Roman alphabet's initial spread throughout much of Europe was fueled by the power of Rome, followed by the continued power of Latin and of the Catholic church. Later it spread throughout large parts of the world, fueled by European settlement and colonialism, the printing press, and, significantly, the typewriter. As more and more text appeared in the Roman alphabet, more and more languages used it.

All that text had to be printed on something. Paper made printing practical, and printing turned paper into big business. The trade of paper-making exploded in the sixteenth century and again in the eighteenth. Literacy rates were still increasing, and new publications such as newspapers and scientific journals were created. Paper money had also made it from China to the West. But supply could not adequately keep up with demand. Linen rags were not plentiful enough, and desperate measures were undertaken to increase their supply: the English Parliament decreed that the dead should be buried wearing wool, so as to keep the linen in which they were traditionally laid out above-ground. The size of newspaper sheets was also regulated, to save paper. Experiments were undertaken to determine what other kinds of fiber could be used to make paper. Swamp moss, potatoes, cattails, nettles, hops, marshmallows, thistles, and various kinds of bark were all tried. Some of them did result in serviceable paper, but mass production was not economical.

As the modern world unfolded, the demand for the printed word, and the demand for paper, only grew. The mechanization of the Industrial Revolution spurred on the world's voracious appetite for the printed word. In 1798 Nicholas-Louis Robert patented the first paper-making machine, which produced paper in a long unbroken sheet instead of one sheet at a time dipped out of a vat by hand. The invention was slow to take off in Revolutionary France; a version of it was finally manufactured in England beginning in 1807.

Fed with more paper, the printing press responded with its own mechanization. A number of improvements were due to Fredrich König of Germany. First he added a mechanical inking mechanism. Then he added steam power to the mechanism of the press. Finally he wrapped the paper around a cylinder and rolled it over the type. This mechanical single-cylinder press, capable of printing 1,100 sheets per hour, debuted in 1814 with the November 29 issue of *The Times* of London, much to the consternation of its pressmen, who suddenly found themselves unemployed. Suddenly, thick daily newspapers could be printed in the space of a single night – and more paper was needed to produce more print. The next few years saw the introduction of stereotype rotary presses, which wrapped a cast (the stereotype) of the type around a cylinder and rolled the cylinder across the paper (instead of the other way around). Soon the rotary presses could print two sides of the paper at once. With further refinements, mechanical rotary presses could print both sides of 10,000 sheets of paper an hour by 1863.

As early as 1719, the French scientist René Antoine Ferchault de Réaumur had realized that humans were not the first species to make paper. Wasps do it naturally, building their nests in trees. Réaumur rightly concluded that wood fiber could be used to make paper. However, it was some time before wood pulp was successfully used in the paper industry. A machine was needed to grind the wood (patented only in 1840), and the resulting paper was of poor quality. A chemical process to separate the fibrous material from the rest of the wood and produce a paper of more acceptable quality was implemented only in the 1870s. Meanwhile, the desperate search for appropriate fibers had continued, resulting in the commercial production of straw paper and even, in one or two colorful instances, of paper made from the cloth wrappings of Egyptian mummies.

A remaining bottleneck in the printing process was the typesetting. From hesitant beginnings – in which the Gutenberg 42-line Bible probably took two years to typeset – typesetting had grown to a specialized craft. But filling forms with individual pieces of type simply was not fast enough to feed the hungry presses. Machines were needed. On the Linotype or Monotype machines, invented in the late nineteenth century, compositors pressed keys instead of selecting type by hand. The keys controlled the selection of type matrices, and type was cast from the matrices by the line or the complete galley form as it was needed. Not only was the actual typesetting faster, but the type did not need to be broken up and returned to the cases afterwards. Since the 1950s phototypesetting (and, later, digital type) has done away with the need to cast metal type at all.

First, however, metal type had a final important job to do. Stuck onto the ends of metal bars and controlled by levers worked with keys, type entered the realm of the individual with the typewriter. With typewriting the technology of type was applied to the individual copy – type *writing* rather than type *printing*.

The very earliest document written with type is actually the Phaistos Disk, a nondescript little brown clay disk that sits in a small display case in the archaeological museum in Heraklion, Crete (figure 14.1). Dating from somewhere between 1550 and 1200 BC, it is a unique document, written in an undeciphered and (unless more examples come to light) undecipherable script. Its message of 242 characters is impressed into the clay with 46 different punches – one for each of the 46 different characters used. The Cretans of the time were writing Linear A and B, so the mysterious disk may be an import, though from where we do not know. In sharp contrast with the Linear B tablets, where different scribes' handwriting can be identified, if we do ever find another example of the type, we will not know whether it was created by the same "typist" or another.

The first design for an actual typewriting machine was patented in 1714 by the Englishman Henry Mill, but it is not known whether he ever built one. The nineteenth century was full of experiments in mechanical writing, but it was not until 1873 that production began on Christopher Latham Sholes's typewriter at the factory of E. Remington and Sons.

The typewriter placed the pieces of type at the command of a person's fingers, making typing as fast as pressing buttons (though with the early manual typewriters, some force was required to do the pressing). It was a while, however, before the potential speed of the typewriter was realized: touch typing, using all ten fingers, was not invented until about 1880. As the speed of a good typist could just about keep pace with measured dictation – and then, unlike shorthand, did not need to be recopied in order to be legible – typists soon became indispensable to offices and authors.

Mark Twain was supposedly the first author to submit a typed manuscript (*Life on the Mississippi*) to a publisher in 1874. He didn't type it himself, however, but had it copied by a female secretary. Some authors typed their own manuscripts or composed directly onto the typewriter, but typing remained something of a specialized skill, like playing the piano. Also like playing the piano, it was considered an appropriate

Figure 14.1 The Phaistos Disk, the world's oldest typewritten document. The text, in an undeciphered script, was impressed into the clay with punches some time during the Bronze Age. Discovered at Phaistos, Crete, in 1908. Archaeological Museum, Heraklion, Crete. Image copyright © Bridgeman-Girandon/Art Resource, NY.

activity for young ladies, and so many typists were women. (This had, somehow, been foreseen by Remington, who put its new typewriter project in the same division as its sewing machines, not its guns.) Women were paid less than men, and the machines they operated saved a great deal of work. Together, their value to the industrialized world must have been enormous, creating or copying documents cheaply in half the time of handwriting.

Just as early Mesopotamian writing was at the service of state admin-istration, so typing made bureaucracy, administration, and commerce run more smoothly. In the newly global economy that came in the wake of colonialism and saw the growth of new multinational corporations, the result was to advantage those nations whose scripts fit easily onto a typewriter keyboard. Writing longhand benefited neither Chinese characters nor the Roman alphabet; even movable type was relatively unbiased (characters required a much larger font, and a huge case for all the sorts, but at least the typesetter only had to reach for one piece of type per morpheme). But the typewriter was an alphabetic machine.

And it was ugly. The text that came out of typewriters, while even, regular, and legible, was unquestionably ugly. Every letter had to fit into exactly the same amount of space as every other, leading to a very cramped m and w, and a very fat i and l. There was no taking into account the effects of neighboring letters on each other, or of allowing them to overlap in any way (a process known in printing as *kerning*), as in **fi**. And, of course, heaven help you if you wanted to write something that was not on the keyboard. What people could write became constrained to an extent never before imaginable – but in compensation, they could write it very quickly. Even today, the keys available on standard typewriters drive decisions about what writings systems are best for newly written languages.

In short, it was a technology destined to be superseded. The term "word processing" was first used by IBM in 1964 in reference to a typewriter that stored the typed text on magnetic tape and allowed a certain amount of editing. The technology has come a long way since then, from souped-up typewriters to personal computers. Early com-puterized texts combined the flaws of typewriting with poor screen and printer resolution and minimal graphic design. More recent programs, either for word processing, web page design, or presentational aids, have done away with many of these shortcomings.

The move to word processing brought a change from writing that is either physiologically produced (in handwriting) or mechanically produced (in type) to writing that is electronically produced and digitally stored. Although the computer keyboard looks suspiciously like a typewriter keyboard, there are no levers and no pieces of type attached to the computer keys. Instead the stimulus gets converted into an electronic signal that does not look like anything, let alone writing. That signal is converted to an electronic code, which is what the computer works with. The code for the writing – not the writing itself – is what is stored in the computer's memory or conveyed to the printer. It is also conveyed to the screen and reassembled into writing again – but in a very ephemeral form. This digital writing is not fixed in any location: it moves automatically up the screen as new writing appears below it. It can also be erased with convenient but occasionally disastrous ease. Its chief attraction is the ease with which it can be revised. Nowadays we must all be typists. But no matter how poorly we type, the backspace button is there to provide us with orthographic forgiveness. Electronic writing does not have the permanence of a clay tablet or even a sheet of paper. It does not fossilize as readily as traditional writing, and many writers facing the blank screen feel it easier to get started, knowing that they are not committing to the result, but can change it or erase it at any point. Electronic writing is so easy and so fast that one can be fooled into thinking that there is a direct transfer of thought into text – though this may not be either true or a good thing. Writers spend less time planning to write and more time writing, though they often then fritter away the saved time by fiddling with the resulting text.

It will be interesting to see if the new electronic fluidity and impermanence result in a change of attitude toward written language. If writing is no longer permanent, it may lose some of its authority, and "I read it in a book" may no longer be the argument clincher that it has been for so long.

Word processing has also been an equalizing force for the world's scripts, undoing some of the damage done by the typewriter. Within the Roman alphabet proportional spacing can again be taken for granted. The Greek, Cyrillic, Arabic, and Hebrew alphabets as well as mathematical symbols are standard equipment. Chinese, Japanese, Korean, and even Syriac come standard with Windows XP, though typing them straight from the keyboard requires some special installation. Cherokee and Linear B are available on the web. The Unicode project is now in the process of converting all the world's scripts into a single code, giving each unique character a unique computer code. As computer systems adopt the Unicode standards, communication in any script becomes possible. If some of the fossilizing effect of writing does indeed become eroded, orthography projects creating written forms for previously unwritten languages may soon discover that their choices are far wider than the QWERTY keyboard. The expansionist days of the Roman alphabet may be nearly over.

Nevertheless, with all its fonts and font sizes, its cutting and pasting, and its two-column layout options, digital writing still imposes constraints. Many writers, including myself, feel that they can only really perceive and critique their own work when it is printed out. Reading is more difficult on-screen, and proofreading far less effective. The tactile experience of holding the paper and marking on it by hand, and the spatial experience of laying out separate pages side by side for comparison, cannot really be replicated on the screen, no matter how well it tries to simulate three-dimensionality. Thought is mediated by far more than vision alone, and the ability to touch the work and to locate its parts in space is important. The popularity of the computer mouse, I suspect, is not merely due to its ease of operation, but also due to the fact that it mimics natural hand motions such as pointing far more closely than pressing arrow keys does.

The Japanese believe that handwriting is a window to the soul. They are probably right. It is no accident that in the days of typewriters personal letters were still written by hand; a typewritten personal letter would have given offense. There remains a difference between letters that are formed by the motion of the individual body and letters that are selected from a menu – either the menu of the keyboard or the call-up menu that comes of selecting the "Insert Symbol" command. The latest word-processing programs come equipped with dozens of fonts, providing many options in letter style and even color. Programs like PowerPoint provide animation, letting the letters spin, jiggle, or disappear one at a time according to the writer's wish, adding to the written word a temporal element that has been missing since its invention. Nevertheless, as typed text has come to be used for even the most intimate forms of written communication, a certain individuality has been lost.

This is not mere nostalgia speaking. E-mail, instant messaging, chat groups, and text messaging all bring us typed text across great distances at speeds that approach real time. The illusion that one is having a real conversation is easy to succumb to. Yet spoken language, especially in face-to-face contexts, contains many communicative cues that are missing from these contexts. The lift of an eyebrow, the length of a pause, the ironic intonation of a phrase . . . all of these work in the service of communication. Handwriting loses many of them, but may make up for it slightly by variations in letter formation, in expressive squiggles, and inventive use of punctuation. Only the last of these is really available on the Internet, although in some cases one can do one's best with alternative fonts or give way to the urge to qualify remarks with "smileys," :-) or :-(, or a written equivalent, <grin>. However, most people are by now all too familiar with the way an innocently intended e-mail can convey exactly the wrong impression. Typed text is being asked to do jobs previously reserved for speech and handwriting, and the result is not always pretty.

A tome on the history of printed books originally written in 1958 – awed, doubtless, by the recent advances in television, radio, and audio recording – describes the future of the book as "no longer certain." Interestingly, the perceived threats were not the ones that we might think of today—the web, say, or e-books – but rather a previous generation of technology that supplemented the written word but in no way replaced it. With every succeeding advance in technology, rumors of the death of traditional print-and-paper books have similarly been greatly exaggerated. The world still produces nearly a million different new books a year. Printed books have not been replaced; they have merely been outstripped.

Nor has the "paperless office" ever come close to reality; in fact, half the world's paper is used in office documents. In 1940 the United States produced about 13,038,000 metric tonnes of paper. By 2001 it was 81,660,000 tonnes. From 1999 to 2002 the amount of new information stored on paper rose by 36 percent. During that time book publications held steady worldwide (though showing strong growth in the United States), and academic journals decreased paper production (switching to web delivery), but office documents grew by 43 percent. Paper, too, though outstripped, has certainly not been replaced.

The most important apparent threat to the printed book is the World Wide Web, but it is no threat to the written word. Created by Tim Berners-Lee at CERN (the European Organization for Nuclear Research), the first website went up in 1990. By 1994 the web was carrying 400,000 bytes every second (roughly the informational equivalent of an Agatha Christie novel), and by 1999 there were nearly 10 million web servers.

The web is accurately named. What makes it so useful – much more than simply a large, searchable database – is the weblike hypertext links that connect one site to another. In hypertext one document is connected to another in ways other than the traditional, linear one by which one page is always followed by the next. Rather, wherever the author considers one piece of text to be relevant to another, a link can be made, right there. Reading is now transformed into "surfing the web," as users click on one link after another.

Paper books and the web are both dwarfed by the production of more casual text. Researchers at the School of Information Management and Systems at Berkeley estimated in 2003 that in 2002 there were 5 billion instant messages sent a day for a total of 274 Terabytes for the year. A Terabyte is 10^{12} bytes; to print it on paper would take the wood of 50,000 trees. E-mails accounted for a whopping 670,000 Terabytes (though only about 400,000 Terabytes were original, and not all of it was text) per year, with 31 billion e-mails sent daily. By contrast, the print collections of the Library of Congress total only 10 Terabytes. The World Wide Web contains 170 Terabytes (not all of it text) on its "surface," i.e. in fixed web pages, with much more in searchable databases that have been connected to the web.

As the technologies for producing text have expanded, humanity has produced more and more text, and this despite the proliferation of technologies that reproduce the spoken word. Even television news nowadays is frequently accompanied by a line of text at the bottom of the screen, and cell phones, which have greatly expanded the range of the spoken word, are often used for text messaging rather than conversation. Teenagers that a generation ago would have spent hours chatting on the telephone now spend the same amount of time instant messaging their friends in total silence. News headlines such as CNN.com's "Report: Text messaging harms written language" overlook the obvious: there is more written language in the world today than there ever has been.

Written text is not just a cheap substitute for speech, and it never has been. It was invented as an information technology, and while it ended up being an alternative way to express language, it is not recorded speech. Its beauty is that it is actually much *less* than speech.

Much of the informational content of speech is lost in writing. This can certainly lead to e-mail squabbles, but it means that text can be transmitted with much lower bandwidth than speech (i.e. the message takes up far fewer bytes: a printed page is only about 2 kilobytes, but a high-resolution photograph is 2 megabytes and a minute of high-quality recorded sound is 10 megabytes). It also takes less time to process it. Writing may take time and effort, but (silent) reading is very fast. Think of how slow reading aloud is, and then picture accessing all one's information at that speed. (Not surprisingly, those who routinely have to rely on recorded books use special playback controls that increase the speed of the voice without increasing its pitch.) The more the world relies on rapid access to information, the more it will rely on the written word.

So text remains with us. Greater and greater quantities of it are being produced by ordinary people. In a world in which anyone can have a web page and anyone can keep a blog, writing has entered a new phase of democratization. By contrast, the early writing systems of the world were not intended for ordinary people. Nor was the literature of the classical and medieval ages intended for the masses. Even when Sweden mandated universal literacy in the seventeenth century – the first country to do so – reading was the primary goal, not writing.

Until very recently, most written language – and virtually all publicly available written language – was mediated. The author was distinct from the editor, the typesetter, or the publisher. For today's bloggers the word processor does the typesetting, the server does the publishing, and there is (for better or worse) no editor. The result is hand wringing on the part of language purists. They may have a point about stylistic quality, but they have failed to notice that what they are really witnessing is the ultimate triumph of the written word – the point at which the technology becomes second nature to a whole society. We live, therefore, at a turning point in the history of writing. On the one hand, the Information Age has made the Earth flat, leveling the playing field, lowering barriers, enabling collaboration, and encouraging healthy competition. On the other hand, it has opened a digital divide between those individuals and nations that are on-line and those that are not. History has yet to tally the ultimate results. If handwriting ushered in civilization, and print ushered in modernity, it remains to be seen what hypertext will do for us.

Appendix

THE INTERNATIONAL PHONETIC ALPHABET (revised to 2005)

CONSONANTS (PULMONIC)   © 2005 IPA

	Bilabial	Labiodental	Dental	Alveolar	Postalveolar	Retroflex	Palatal	Velar	Uvular	Pharyngeal	Glottal
Plosive	p b			t d		ʈ ɖ	c ɟ	k ɡ	q ɢ		ʔ
Nasal	m	ɱ		n		ɳ	ɲ	ŋ	N		
Trill	B			r					R		
Tap or Flap		ⱱ		ɾ		ɽ					
Fricative	ɸ β	f v	θ ð	s z	ʃ ʒ	ʂ ʐ	ç ʝ	x ɣ	χ ʁ	ħ ʕ	h ɦ
Lateral fricative				ɬ ɮ							
Approximant		ʋ		ɹ		ɻ	j	ɰ			
Lateral approximant				l		ɭ	ʎ	L			

Where symbols appear in pairs, the one to the right represents a voiced consonant. Shaded areas denote articulations judged impossible.

CONSONANTS (NON-PULMONIC)

Clicks	Voiced implosives	Ejectives
ʘ Bilabial	ɓ Bilabial	' Examples:
ǀ Dental	ɗ Dental/alveolar	p' Bilabial
ǃ (Post)alveolar	ʄ Palatal	t' Dental/alveolar
ǂ Palatoalveolar	ɠ Velar	k' Velar
ǁ Alveolar lateral	ʛ Uvular	s' Alveolar fricative

OTHER SYMBOLS

ʍ Voiceless labial-velar fricative
w Voiced labial-velar approximant
ɥ Voiced labial-palatal approximant
ʜ Voiceless epiglottal fricative
ʢ Voiced epiglottal fricative
ʡ Epiglottal plosive

ɕ ʑ Alveolo-palatal fricatives
ɺ Voiced alveolar lateral flap
ɧ Simultaneous ʃ and x

Affricates and double articulations can be represented by two symbols joined by a tie bar if necessary.

k͡p t͡s

VOWELS

Where symbols appear in pairs, the one to the right represents a rounded vowel.

SUPRASEGMENTALS

ˈ Primary stress
ˌ Secondary stress
ˌfoʊnəˈtɪʃən
ː Long eː
ˑ Half-long eˑ
˘ Extra-short ĕ
| Minor (foot) group
‖ Major (intonation) group
. Syllable break ɹi.ækt
‿ Linking (absence of a break)

DIACRITICS Diacritics may be placed above a symbol with a descender, e.g. ŋ̊

̥ Voiceless	n̥ d̥	̤ Breathy voiced	b̤ a̤	̪ Dental	t̪ d̪
̬ Voiced	s̬ t̬	̰ Creaky voiced	b̰ a̰	̺ Apical	t̺ d̺
ʰ Aspirated	tʰ dʰ	̼ Linguolabial	t̼ d̼	̻ Laminal	t̻ d̻
̹ More rounded	ɔ̹	ʷ Labialized	tʷ dʷ	̃ Nasalized	ẽ
̜ Less rounded	ɔ̜	ʲ Palatalized	tʲ dʲ	ⁿ Nasal release	dⁿ
̟ Advanced	u̟	ˠ Velarized	tˠ dˠ	ˡ Lateral release	dˡ
̠ Retracted	e̠	ˤ Pharyngealized	tˤ dˤ	̚ No audible release	d̚
̈ Centralized	ë	̴ Velarized or pharyngealized	ɫ		
̽ Mid-centralized	e̽	̝ Raised	e̝	(ɹ̝ = voiced alveolar fricative)	
̩ Syllabic	n̩	̞ Lowered	e̞	(β̞ = voiced bilabial approximant)	
̯ Non-syllabic	e̯	̘ Advanced Tongue Root	e̘		
˞ Rhoticity	ɚ a˞	̙ Retracted Tongue Root	e̙		

TONES AND WORD ACCENTS

LEVEL				CONTOUR		
e̋	or ˥	Extra high	ě	or ˄	Rising
é	˦	High	ê	˅	Falling
ē	˧	Mid	e᷄	˦	High rising
è	˨	Low	e᷅	˨	Low rising
ȅ	˩	Extra low	e᷈	˪	Rising-falling
↓		Downstep	↗		Global rise
↑		Upstep	↘		Global fall

Figure A.1 The International Phonetic Alphabet.

Consonants				Vowels (Standard American)	
[p]	spot	[f]	fix	[i]	heap
[pʰ]	pot	[v]	vain	[ɪ]	hip
[b]	bob	[θ]	think	[e]	fate (more precisely,
[t]	stop	[ð]	this		[ej])
[tʰ]	top	[s]	seven	[ɛ]	red
[d]	deed	[z]	zoo	[æ]	fad
[tʃ]	church	[ʃ]	sheep	[ɑ]	father (frequently
[dʒ]	judge	[ʒ]	measure		transcribed as [a])
[k]	ski	[l]	leaf	[ə]	cockatoo
[kʰ]	key	[ʍ]	which (for those who	[ɔ]	soft
[g]	give		distinguish *w* and *wh*)	[ɐ]	sun (frequently
[m]	mope	[w]	wagon		transcribed as [ʌ])
[n]	nod	[ɹ]	reed	[o]	boat (more precisely,
[ŋ]	sing	[j]	you		[ow])
		[h]	happy	[ʊ]	book
				[u]	boot
				[ai]	try
				[au]	how
				[oi]	boy

Figure A.2 The International Phonetic Alphabet applied to American English.

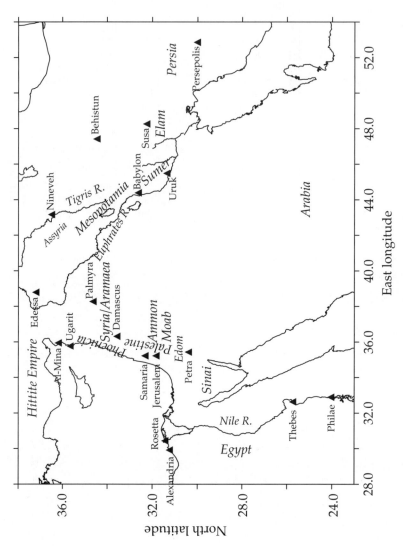

Figure A.3 The ancient Near East.

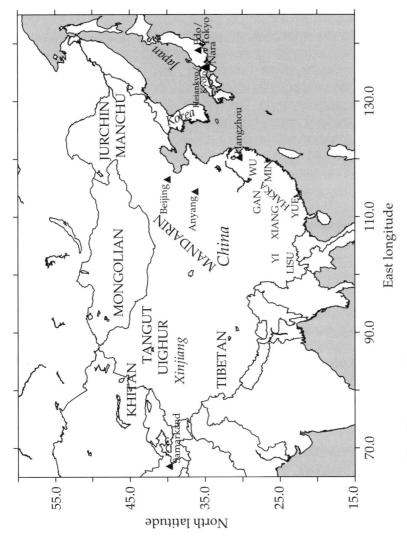

Figure A.4 The Chinese world.

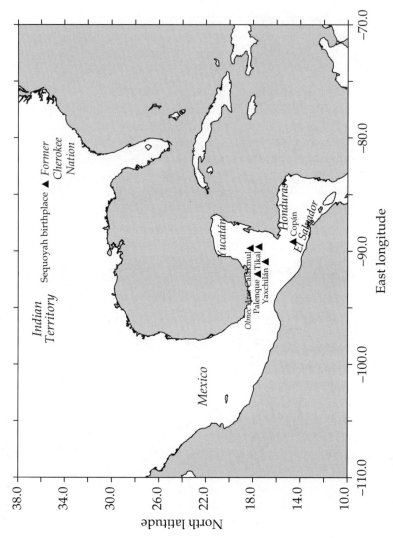

Figure A.5 Mayan Mesoamerica and Cherokee North America.

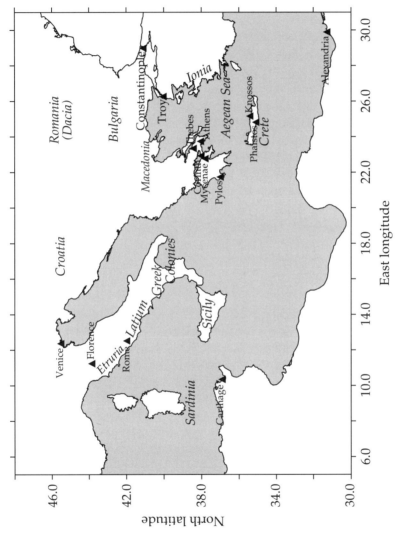

Figure A.6 The Greek and Roman world.

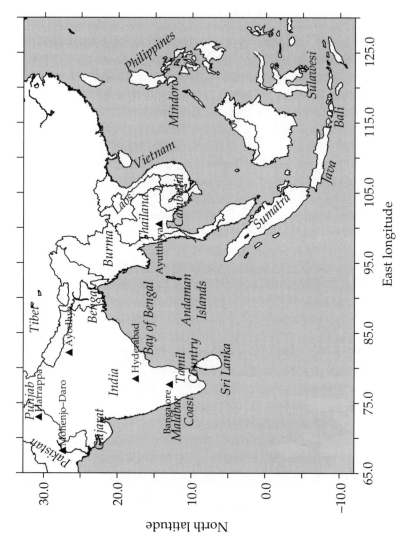

Figure A.7 Southern Asia, the Sanskrit world.

Further Reading

These notes for further reading are both more and less than an academic bibliography. Less, because I have not listed all the many scholarly sources on each subject touched on in this book. More, because I have included synoptic works that are accessible to the general reader. Many such works are textbooks, often the best place to look for synthesis and summary within a given field. I have listed sources separately for each chapter, sometimes with commentary, in order to partially atone for a lack of footnotes or in-text references.

Chapter 1 The First IT Revolution

Those who are serious about the study of writing systems will not want to be without the multi-author volume edited by Daniels and Bright (1996). I acknowledge my substantial debt to that comprehensive work section by section in each chapter's references. Coulmas (1989) and Rogers (2005) are other general works on writing systems that may be consulted for further information on many points that arise in this book. I owe to Harris (1986) the estimate of how many languages have a written literature, to Gordon (2005) the estimate of the world's spoken languages, and to Ladefoged (2005) the estimate of the number of vowels and consonants in the world. It is worth noting that a serious attempt at bypassing language in writing has been made, in the form of Blissymbolics, an ideographically based symbolic system designed to be used in any language. In practice, however, texts using Blissymbolics stick close to the user's language, as pointed out by Rogers (2005).

Coulmas, Florian. 1989. *The Writing Systems of the World*. Oxford: Blackwell.
Daniels, Peter T. and William Bright, eds. 1996. *The World's Writing Systems*. New York: Oxford University Press.
Fagan, Brian M. 1986. *People of the Earth: An Introduction to World Prehistory*, 6th edn. Glenview, IL: Scott, Foresman.

Fromkin, Victoria and Robert Rodman. 1998. *An Introduction to Language*, 6th edn. Fort Worth: Harcourt Brace College Publishers. A good place to start for those interested in language and linguistics.

Gordon, Raymond G., Jr., ed. 2005. *Ethnologue: Languages of the World*, 15th edn. Dallas, TX: SIL International. http://www.ethnologue.com.

Harris, Roy. 1986. *The Origin of Writing*. London: Duckworth. Downplays (too much, I would say) the phonological aspects of writing.

Ladefoged, Peter. 2001. *A Course in Phonetics*, 4th edn. New York: Harcourt Brace. A good place to learn the IPA.

Ladefoged, Peter. 2005. *Vowels and Consonants*, 2nd edn. Malden, MA: Blackwell.

Mafundikwa, Saki. 2004. *Afrikan Alphabets*. West New York, NJ: Mark Batty. Includes the story of King Njoya.

Pinker, Stephen. 1994. *The Language Instinct*. New York: Harper Perennial. An engaging introduction to language and linguistics for the general reader.

Rogers, Henry. 2005. *Writing Systems: A Linguistic Approach*. Blackwell Textbooks in Linguistics. Malden, MA: Blackwell. A systematic introduction.

Röhr, Heinz Markus. 1994. *Writing: Its Evolution and Relation to Speech*. Bochum: Brockmeyer.

The International Phonetic Association. http://www.arts.gla.ac.uk/IPA/index.html. The official IPA website.

Chapter 2 Cuneiform: Forgotten Legacy of a Forgotten People

It is a popularly accepted theory that proto-cuneiform grew out of a system of accounting tokens used throughout preliterate Mesopotamia. These tokens, representing various commodities, were enclosed in clay "envelopes," and representations of the tokens were impressed on the outside. These impressed representations were supposedly the origin of written symbols. However, there has been much scholarly criticism of this theory (see, for example, Glassner 2003), so I do not espouse it here. Whatever its intellectual forerunners, proto-cuneiform writing was an invention substantially different from earlier representational systems.

The cuneiform in figure 2.4 is quoted from Darius (1907).

Caplice, Richard, with Daniel Snell. 1988. *Introduction to Akkadian*, 3rd edn. Studia Pohl: Series Maior: Dissertationes Scientificae de Orientis Antiqui 9. Rome: Biblical Institute Press.

Daniels, Peter T. and William Bright, eds. 1996. *The World's Writing Systems*. New York: Oxford University Press. Sections 2, 3, 8, 9, and 10, by Daniels, Michalowski, Cooper, Gragg, Testen, and Englund.

Darius I, Hystaspes. 1907. *The Sculptures and Inscription of Darius the Great on the Rock of Behistûn in Persia: A New Collation of the Persian, Susian, and Babylonian Texts, with English Translations, etc.* London: British Museum.

Edzard, Dietz Otto. 2003. *Sumerian Grammar.* Handbook of Oriental Studies, Section 1: Near and Middle East 71. Leiden: Brill.

Glassner, Jean-Jacques. 2003. *The Invention of Cuneiform: Writing in Sumer.* Trans. and ed. Zainab Bahrani and Marc Van De Mieroop. Baltimore, MD: Johns Hopkins University Press. Advanced reading on the subject of proto-cuneiform; see especially chapter 7.

Kramer, Samuel Noah. 1966. *In the World of Sumer: An Autobiography.* Detroit: Wayne State University Press. Contains a great deal of information on the Sumerians and their literature, interwoven with the intellectual autobiography of a leading Sumerologist.

Marcus, David. 1978. *A Manual of Akkadian.* Lanham, MD: University Press of America.

Pope, Maurice. 1999. *The Story of Decipherment: From Egyptian Hieroglyphs to Maya Script*, rev. edn. New York: Thames and Hudson. A thorough but dense treatment.

Roux, Georges. 1980. *Ancient Iraq*, 2nd edn. Harmondsworth, UK: Penguin. A good introduction to the history of Mesopotamia.

Thomsen, Marie-Louise. 2001. *The Sumerian Language: An Introduction to its History and Grammatical Structure*, 3rd edn. Mesopotamia: Copenhagen Studies in Assyriology 10. Copenhagen: Akademisk Forlag.

Walker, C. B. F. 1987. *Cuneiform.* Reading the Past 3. Berkeley: University of California Press and the British Museum. A good place to start.

Watt, W. C. 1987. *The Ras Shamra Matrix as a Record of Ancient Phonological Perceptions.* Studies in the Cognitive Sciences 45. Irvine: University of California, Irvine School of Social Sciences. Discusses Ugaritic and the origins of alphabetical order.

Chapter 3 Egyptian Hieroglyphs and the Quest for Eternity

Adkins, Lesley and Roy Adkins. 2000. *The Keys of Egypt: The Obsession to Decipher Egyptian Hieroglyphs.* New York: HarperCollins.

Allen, James P. 2000. *Middle Egyptian: An Introduction to the Language and Culture of Hieroglyphs.* Cambridge: Cambridge University Press. An excellent introduction to the Egyptian language, including hieroglyphs.

Betrò, Maria Carmela. 1996. *Hieroglyphics: The Writings of Ancient Egypt.* English translation. New York: Abbeville Press.

Daniels, Peter T. and William Bright, eds. 1996. *The World's Writing Systems*. New York: Oxford University Press. Sections 4 and 9, by Ritner and Daniels.

Davies, W. V. 1987. *Egyptian Hieroglyphs*. Reading the Past 6. Berkeley: University of California Press and the British Museum.

Fedden, Robin. 1977. *Egypt: Land of the Valley*. London: John Murray. A very readable introduction to Egyptian culture and history, both ancient and modern.

Forman, Werner and Stephen Quirke. 1996. *Hieroglyphs and the Afterlife in Ancient Egypt*. London: British Museum Press.

Pope, Maurice. 1999. *The Story of Decipherment: From Egyption Hieroglyphs to Maya Script*, rev. edn. New York: Thames and Hudson.

Ray, John D. 1986. The Emergence of Writing in Egypt. *World Archaeology* 17, no. 3: 307–16.

Wilson, John A. 1951. *The Culture of Ancient Egypt*. Chicago: University of Chicago Press. A classic text on ancient Egyptian culture.

Chapter 4 Chinese: A Love of Paperwork

Boltz, William G. 1986. Early Chinese Writing. *World Archaeology* 17, no. 3: 420–36.

Creel, Herrlee G. 1937. *The Birth of China: A Study of the Formative Period of Chinese Civilization*. New York: Frederick Ungar. A classic and readable introduction to China of the Shang and Zhou periods.

Daniels, Peter T. and William Bright, eds. 1996. *The World's Writing Systems*. New York: Oxford University Press. Sections 14, 15, 18, and 19, by Boltz, Mair, Kychanov, and Shi.

Fazzioli, Edoardo. 1986. *Chinese Calligraphy: From Pictograph to Ideogram: The History of 214 Essential Chinese/Japanese Characters*. New York: Abbeville Press. An attractive and browsable book.

Hsu Ya-hwei. 2002. *Ancient Chinese Writing: Oracle Bone Inscriptions from the Ruins of Yin*. Trans. Mark Caltonhill and Jeffrey Moser. Taipei: National Palace Museum.

Hunter, Dard. 1943. *Papermaking: The History and Technique of an Ancient Craft*. New York: Alfred Knopf. A fascinating volume dedicated entirely to the history of paper; it even includes samples.

Keightley, David N, ed. 1983. *The Origins of Chinese Civilization*. Studies on China 1. Berkeley: University of California Press. Includes technical treatment of various aspects of ancient China.

Mair, Victor H. and Yongquan Liu, eds. 1991. *Characters and Computers*. Amsterdam: IOS Press.

Ramsey, S. Robert. 1987. *The Languages of China*. Princeton, NJ: Princeton University Press. A clear description of modern Chinese, its history, script, and dialects, and its relation to other languages within China.

Roberts, J. A. G. 1996. *A History of China*. Phoenix Mill, Stroud, Gloucestershire: Alan Sutton. A good overview of general Chinese history.

Taylor, Insup and M. Martin Taylor. 1995. *Writing and Literacy in Chinese, Korean and Japanese*. Studies in Written Language and Literacy 3. Amsterdam: John Benjamins. Discusses the Chinese writing system and issues surrounding literacy in a logographic script.

Chapter 5 Maya Glyphs: Calendars of Kings

Due to the recent nature of the decipherment, works on Maya writing from before about 1985 are out of date. For the same reason, works that truly explain how the writing system functioned, as opposed to works publishing only recent conjectures and advances, are still rare. For those who would actually like to learn to read Maya glyphs, an excellent place to start is Montgomery (2002) or Coe and Van Stone (2005). I owe to Justeson (1986) the idea that the conjunction of numerals and calendar or commodity symbols inspired the first writing both in Mesoamerica and in Mesopotamia. In addition to the works cited below, see Pope (1999), cited in chapters 2 and 3, for the decipherment of Palmyrene, Phoenician and Sassanian.

Coe, Michael. 1987. *The Maya*, 4th edn. New York: Thames and Hudson.

Coe, Michael. 1992. *Breaking the Maya Code*. New York: Thames and Hudson.

Coe, Michael and Justin Kerr. 1997. *The Art of the Maya Scribe*. New York: Thames and Hudson.

Coe, Michael and Mark Van Stone. 2005. *Reading the Maya Glyphs*, 2nd edn. London: Thames and Hudson.

Daniels, Peter T. and William Bright, eds. 1996. *The World's Writing Systems*. New York: Oxford University Press. Section 12, by Macri.

Houston, Stephen. 1989. *Maya Glyphs*. Reading the Past. London: British Museum.

Houston, Stephen, Oswaldo Chinchilla Mazariegos, and David Stuart, eds. 2001. *The Decipherment of Ancient Maya Writing*. Norman, OK: University of Oklahoma Press. A collection of primary sources in the history of the Maya decipherment.

Justeson, John S. 1986. The Origin of Writing Systems: Preclassic Mesoamerica. *World Archaeology* 17, no. 3: 437–58.

Marcus, Joyce. 1992. *Mesoamerican Writing Systems: Propaganda, Myth, and History in Four Ancient Civilizations*. Princeton, NJ: Princeton University Press.

Montgomery, John. 2002. *How to Read Maya Hieroglyphs*. New York: Hippocrene Books.

Pohl, Mary E. D., Kevin O. Pope, and Christopher von Nagy. 2002. Olmec Origins of Mesoamerican Writing. *Science* 298: 1984–7.

Saturno, William A., David Stuart, and Boris Beltrán. 2006. Early Maya Writing at San Bartolo, Guatemala. *Sciencexpress*. www.sciencexpress.org. January 4; 10.1126/science.1121745. Recent discoveries in the field.

Schele, Linda and David Freidel. 1990. *A Forest of Kings: The Untold Story of the Ancient Maya*. New York: William Morrow.

Wichmann, Søren, ed. 2004. *The Linguistics of Maya Writing*. Salt Lake City, UT: University of Utah Press. Discusses ongoing issues in decipherment and linguistic analysis of Maya texts.

Chapter 6 Linear B: The Clerks of Agamemnon

The archaeology of the Aegean Bronze Age is a subject of perennial interest, and there are many good works on the topic. On the other hand, the Minoans have been also the subject of much speculation, some of it outright fanciful, since their rediscovery by Sir Arthur Evans. The following are some sound works that I consulted in the course of writing this chapter and that I have enjoyed reading. For those who may be wondering why there is no description of the eruption of Thera in this chapter, it is because the present-day consensus is that, immense as the eruption certainly was, it occurred well before the downfall of the Minoans and did not lead to the occupation of Crete by the Mycenaeans.

John Chadwick, who collaborated with Michael Ventris in the final stages of his decipherment, has been the foremost popularizer of Linear B (1967, 1976, 1987). A more personal view of the decipherment can be found in Robinson (2002), a biography of Michael Ventris, who died in 1956 at age 34, not long after his decipherment.

Many questions surround the life and identity of the poet Homer. By tradition he was blind, but the evidence for this is slight to nonexistent. So little is known about him, in fact, that some have even questioned whether such a person existed – whether a single person could have composed both the *Iliad* and the *Odyssey*. But it could well have been a single person: poetic geniuses could not have been so very common. If there was a Homer, and if he was blind, then someone else must have written down his words. If he was not blind, it would probably have been easier for him to do it himself. My own presentation of him in the final portion of this chapter is admittedly speculative, but (I hope) within the bounds of plausibility. The role played in his compositions by the oral tradition on the one hand, and by literacy on the other, has received much scholarly attention in the past century. Outstanding modern verse translations of the *Iliad* and the *Odyssey* can be found in Fagles (1990 and 1996, from which I took the quotation regarding Greeks on Crete). These are accompanied by introductions by Bernard Knox that competently summarize modern speculation and research on Homer. Ong (1982) illuminates the substantial differences between oral and literate cultures, with frequent reference to epic poetry generally and to Homer specifically, though certain references to the pre-eminence of the Greek alphabet should be taken with a grain of salt.

Chadwick, John. 1967. *The Decipherment of Linear B*, 2nd edn. Cambridge: Cambridge University Press.

Chadwick, John. 1976. *The Mycenaean World*. Cambridge: Cambridge University Press.

Chadwick, John. 1987. *Linear B and Related Scripts*. Reading the Past. London: British Museum.

Daniels, Peter T. and William Bright, eds. 1996. *The World's Writing Systems*. New York: Oxford University Press. Section 7, by Bennett.

Fagles, Robert, trans. 1990. *The Iliad*. With introduction and notes by Bernard Knox. New York: Penguin.

Fagles, Robert, trans. 1996. *The Odyssey*. With introduction and notes by Bernard Knox. New York: Penguin.

Fitton, J. Lesley. 2002. *Minoans*. People of the Past. London: British Museum Press. Summarizes what is actually known about the culture and eschews overinterpretation.

Higgins, Reynold. 1981. *Minoan and Mycenaean Art*, rev. edn. London: Thames and Hudson. A beautifully illustrated work that gives a good sense of the cultural achievements of the period.

Hooker, J. T. 1980. *Linear B: An Introduction*. Bristol: Bristol Classical Press. Best for those already somewhat familiar with Greek.

Horwitz, Sylvia L. 1981. *The Find of a Lifetime: Sir Arthur Evans and the Discovery of Knossos*. New York: Viking.

Ong, Walter. 1982. *Orality and Literacy: The Technologizing of the Word*. London: Methuen.

Robinson, Andrew. 2002. *The Man Who Deciphered Linear B: The Story of Michael Ventris*. London: Thames and Hudson.

Vermeule, Emily. 1972. *Greece in the Bronze Age*. Chicago: Chicago University Press. Though somewhat dated by now, still a good introduction to the archaeology of Bronze-Age Greece, including the Mycenaean period.

Chapter 7 Japanese: Three Scripts are Better than One

Daniels, Peter T. and William Bright, eds. 1996. *The World's Writing Systems*. New York: Oxford University Press. Section 16, by Smith.

Gottlieb, Nanette. 2000. *Word-Processing Technology in Japan: Kanji and the Keyboard*. Richmond, Surrey: Curzon.

Habein, Yaeko Sato. 1984. *The History of the Japanese Written Language*. Tokyo: University of Tokyo Press.

Hadamitzky, Wolfgang and Mark Spahn. 1981. *Kanji and Kana: A Handbook and Dictionary of the Japanese Writing System*. Rutland, VT: Tuttle. A compact yet comprehensive volume that presents hiragana, katakana, and the full list of common kanji, together with rules for their use. For anyone who wants to learn the Japanese writing system. Less dedicated script lovers will also find it enjoyable browsing.

Murasaki Shikibu. 1960. *The Tale of Genji*. Trans. Arthur Waley. New York: Random House.

Perez, Louis G. 1998. *The History of Japan*. Westport, CT: Greenwood. A readable introduction for the nonspecialist.

Shibatani, Masayoshi. 1990. *The Languages of Japan*. Cambridge: Cambridge University Press.

Taylor, Insup and M. Martin Taylor. 1995. *Writing and Literacy in Chinese, Korean and Japanese*. Studies in Written Language and Literacy 3. Amsterdam: John Benjamins.

Chapter 8 Cherokee: Sequoyah Reverse-Engineers

The life and deeds of Sequoyah were poorly documented during his lifetime. What remain are a few descriptions of reminiscences (or translations thereof) on the part of Sequoyah and those who knew him. Foreman (1938) contains a collection of several of these, many of them conflicting somewhat in detail but agreeing on the basic story. Lowery and Payne (1977) contains some as well. The account I present here relies on the common elements of these descriptions and my best guesses in cases of conflict.

Holmes and Smith (1976) is an introduction to the Cherokee language, using Sequoyah's syllabary. It also contains photographs of Sequoyah's handwriting and signature. Walker and Sarbaugh (1993) discuss the early history of the syllabary, adducing evidence that Sequoyah himself was responsible for certain modifications that gave the characters their modern forms, and not Samuel Worcester as has sometimes been claimed (as, for example, in Holmes and Smith).

Bender, Margaret. 2002. *Signs of Cherokee Culture: Sequoyah's Syllabary in Eastern Cherokee Life*. Chapel Hill, NC: University of North Carolina Press.

Daniels, Peter T. and William Bright, eds. 1996. *The World's Writing Systems*. New York: Oxford University Press. Section 53, by Scancarelli.

Ehle, John. 1988. *Trail of Tears: The Rise and Fall of the Cherokee Nation*. New York: Anchor. An engrossing history of the Cherokee Nation during Sequoyah's lifetime.

Foreman, Grant. 1938. *Sequoyah*. Norman, OK: University of Oklahoma Press.

Holmes, Ruth Bradley and Betty Sharp Smith. 1976. *Beginning Cherokee*. Norman, OK: University of Oklahoma Press.

Hutchins, John. 1977. The Trial of Reverend Samuel A. Worcester. *Journal of Cherokee Studies* 2, no. 4: 356–74.

Lowery, George, with introduction and transcription by John Howard Payne. 1977. Notable Persons in Cherokee History: Sequoyah or George Gist. *Journal of Cherokee Studies* 2, no. 4: 385–93.

Walker, Willard and James Sarbaugh. 1993. The Early History of the Cherokee Syllabary. *Ethnohistory* 40, no. 1: 70–94.

Chapter 9 The Semitic Alphabet: Egypt to Manchuria in 3,400 Years

Naveh (1982) is a classic reference on the early alphabet, but see Sass (2005) for arguments that the Phoenician alphabet is younger than the 1050 BC date generally accepted, and Hamilton (2006) on the origins of the alphabet. For the Altaic languages, see also Ramsey (1987), listed under chapter 4. For Ugaritic, see also Watt (1987) under chapter 2.

Bender, M. L., J. D. Bowen, R. L. Cooper, and C. A. Ferguson, eds. 1976. *Language in Ethiopia*. Ford Foundation Language Surveys. London: Oxford University Press.

Beyer, Klaus. 1986. *The Aramaic Language: Its Distribution and Subdivisions*. Trans. John F. Healey. Göttingen: Vandenhoeck und Ruprecht.

Brustad, Kristen, Mahmoud Al-Batal, and Abbas Al-Tonsi. 1995. *Alif Baa: Introduction to Arabic Letters and Sounds*. Washington, DC: Georgetown University Press.

Daniels, Peter T. and William Bright, eds. 1996. *The World's Writing Systems*. New York: Oxford University Press. Sections 5, 46, 47, 48, 49, 50, 51, 61, 62, and 68, by O'Connor, Swiggers, Goerwitz, Daniels, Hoberman, Skjærvø, Kara, Bauer, Haile, Hary, Aronson, and Kaye.

Dunstan, William E. 1998. *The Ancient Near East*. Fort Worth, TX: Harcourt Brace.

Gaur, Albertine. 1994. *A History of Calligraphy*. London: British Library.

Hamilton, Gordon J. 2002. W. F. Albright and Early Alphabetic Epigraphy. *Near Eastern Archaeology* 65, no. 1: 35–42.

Hamilton, Gordon J. 2006. *The Origins of the West Semitic Alphabet in Egyptian Scripts*. Monograph Series 40 Washington, DC: Catholic Biblical Quarterly.

Healey, John F. 1990. *The Early Alphabet*. Reading the Past. London: British Museum.

Hourani, Albert. 1991. *A History of the Arab Peoples*. Cambridge, MA: Harvard University Press.

Kaltner, John and Steven L. McKenzie, eds. 2002. *Beyond Babel: A Handbook for Biblical Hebrew and Related Languages*. Resources for Biblical Study 42. Atlanta: Society of Biblical Literature.

Khan, Gabriel Mandel. 2001. *Arabic Script: Styles, Variants, and Calligraphic Adaptations*. Trans. Rosanna M. Giammanco Frongia. New York: Abbeville Press.

Lipiński, Edward. 2000. *The Aramaeans: Their Ancient History, Culture, Religion*. Orientalia Lovaniensia analecta 100. Leuven: Uitgeverij Peeters. A dense tome only for the truly dedicated.

Millard, A. R. 1986. The Infancy of the Alphabet. *World Archaeology* 17, no. 3: 390–8.

Naveh, Joseph. 1982. *Early History of the Alphabet: An Introducton to West Semitic Epigraphy and Palaeography*. Jerusalem: Magnes Press, Hebrew University.

Sass, Benjamin. 2005. *The Alphabet at the Turn of the Millennium: The West Semitic Alphabet ca. 1150–850 BCE: The Antiquity of the Arabian, Greek and Phrygian Alphabets*. Journal of the Institute of Archaeology of Tel Aviv University Occasional Publications, 4. Tel Aviv: Emery and Claire Yass Publications in Archaeology.

Thackston, Wheeler M. 1999. *Introduction to Syriac: An Elementary Grammar with Readings from Syriac Literature*. Bethesda, MD: Ibex.

Wilford, John Noble. 1999. Finds in Egypt Date Alphabet in Earlier Era. *New York Times*, November 14.

Yardeni, Ada. 1997. *The Book of Hebrew Script: History, Palaeography, Script Styles, Calligraphy and Design*. Jerusalem: Carta.

Chapter 10 The Empire of Sanskrit

The ethnographic survey cited in the text is published as Singh and Manoharan (1993). See Farmer *et al.* (2004) for an argument (not fully convincing in my view) that the Indus Valley symbols could not have been a writing system.

Abbi, Anvita. 2001. *A Manual of Linguistic Field Work and Structures of Indian Languages*. Munich: Lincom Europa.

Bright, William. 1990. *Language Variation in South Asia*. New York: Oxford University Press.

Coulson, Michael. 1976. *Sanskrit: An Introduction to the Classical Language*. Teach Yourself Books. Sevenoaks: Hodder and Stoughton.

Daniels, Peter T. and William Bright, eds. 1996. *The World's Writing Systems*. New York: Oxford University Press. Sections 11, 30–45, 56, 65, 69, by Parpola, Salomon, Bright, Mistry, Gill, Bagchi, Mahapatra, Gair, Mohanan, Steever, van der Kuip, Court, Wheatley, Diller, Schiller, Kuipers, McDermott, Zide, Masica, and Pettersson.

Farmer, Steve, Richard Sproat, and Michael Witzel. 2004. The Collapse of the Indus-Script Thesis: The Myth of a Literate Harappan Civilization. *Electronic Journal of Vedic Studies* 11, no. 2: 19–57.

Government of India, Ministry of Home Affairs. Sequence of Events with Reference to Official Language of the Union. http://rajbhasha.nic.in/eventseng.htm.

Hart, Kausalya. 1992. *Tamil for Beginners*. Berkeley: Centers for South and Southeast Asia Studies, University of California at Berkeley.

Pollock, Sheldon. 2006. *The Language of the Gods in the World of Men: Sanskrit, Culture, and Power in Premodern India*. Berkeley: University of California Press.

SarDesai, D. R. 1994. *Southeast Asia: Past and Present*, 3rd edn. Boulder, CO: Westview Press.

Singh, K. S. and S. Manoharan. 1993. *Languages and Scripts*. People of India, National Series IX. Delhi: Oxford University Press.

Smyth, David. 2002. *Thai: An Essential Grammar*. London: Routledge.

Snell, Rupert and Simon Weightman. 1989. *Hindi: A Complete Course for Beginners*. Teach Yourself Books. Chicago: NTC Publishing Group.

Steever, Sanford, ed. 1998. *The Dravidian Languages*. London: Routledge. Includes a chapter on Dravidian scripts.

Walsh, Judith. 2006. *A Brief History of India*. New York: Facts on File.

Chapter 11 King Sejong's One-Man Renaissance

The quotations from Sejong's preface to the *Hunmin chŏng'ŭm* and Chŏng In-ji's postface to the *Hunmin chŏng'ŭm haeryae* are from Kim-Cho (2001), though I have omitted bracketed material interpolated for the sake of the reader by Kim-Cho but which I consider unnecessary.

Ahn, Sang-Cheol. 1998. *An Introduction to Korean Phonology*. Seoul: Hanshin Publishing.

Daniels, Peter T. and William Bright, eds. 1996. *The World's Writing Systems*. New York: Oxford University Press. Section 17, by King.

Kim, Djun Kil. 2005. *The History of Korea*. Greenwood Histories of Modern Nations. Westport, CT: Greenwood Press.

Kim Jeongsu. 2005. *The History and Future of Hangeul: Korea's Indigenous Script*. Trans. Ross King. Folkestone, Kent: Global Oriental.

Kim-Cho, Sek Yen. 2001. *The Korean Alphabet of 1446: Expositions, OPA, the Visible Speech Sounds, Annotated Translation, Future Applicability*. Amherst, NY: Humanity Books. Includes both a translation and a copy of the *Hunmin chŏng'ŭm* and *Hunmin chŏng'ŭm haeryae*.

Kim-Renaud, Young-Key, ed. 1997. *King Sejong the Great: The Light of Fifteenth Century Korea*, rev. edn. Washington, DC: International Circle of Korean Linguistics. Readable and well illustrated.

Kim-Renaud, Young-Key, ed. 1997. *The Korean Alphabet: Its History and Structure*. Honolulu: University of Hawai'i Press.

Ministry of Culture and Information, Republic of Korea. 1970. *A History of Korean Alphabet and Movable Types*. Seoul: Ministry of Culture and Information. Contains copies of the *Hunmin chŏng'ŭm*, *Hunmin chŏng'ŭm haeryae*, and early printed material.

Sohn, Ho-Min. 1999. *The Korean Language*. Cambridge Language Surveys. Cambridge: Cambridge University Press.

Taylor, Insup and M. Martin Taylor. 1995. *Writing and Literacy in Chinese, Korean and Japanese*. Studies in Written Language and Literacy 3. Amsterdam: John Benjamins.

Chapter 12 Greek Serendipity

The Greek alphabet is the perennial subject of scholarly debate, particularly with respect to its origins and its historical significance. Near Eastern scholars tend to date its creation earlier (around 1100 BC), before the stance of the letters and the direction of the script were standardized in the parent Phoenician script. Greek archaeologists, however, point to the absence of any surviving writing from that time and advocate a date closer to 800 BC. The version I have presented here, in which the Greek alphabet was created in the context of illiteracy (and was therefore subject to much variety as learners struggled with the new technology), takes into account both the varying stances and directions and the more modern date that fits the Greek archaeological record. But see Sass (2005, listed under chapter 9) for a reconciliation that places the standardization of the Phoenician alphabet much later as well. How the semivowels and laryngeal consonants of the Phoenician alphabet were reinterpreted as vowels is also open to debate: I have presented what I as a phonologist think is the most likely process (i.e. the misunderstanding of a foreigner, for which see also Brixhe in the Baurain et al. volume) which also fits with the explanation of the varying directions and stances. However, semivowels and laryngeals are easily elided or used for vowels in many languages, as witness the Aramaic invention and subsequent widespread use of *matres lectionis*. For those wanting to know more about the various theories, see Baurain et al. (1991) and Havelock (1982) below, as well as Sass (2005), Healey (1990), and Naveh (1982) listed under chapter 9.

Allen, W. Sidney. 1987. *Vox Graeca: A Guide to the Pronunciation of Classical Greek*, 3rd edn. Cambridge: Cambridge University Press. Highly recommended for anyone wanting to learn about Greek pronunciation in depth.

Baurain, C., C. Bonnet, and V. Krings, eds. 1991. *Phoinikeia Grammata: Lire et écrire en Méditerranée*. Namur: Société des Études Classiques. Contains articles presenting a range of scholarly opinion on the origins of the Greek alphabet. Very technical and in a variety of languages, but the article by Claude Brixhe is especially recommended.

Bonfante, Larissa. 1990. *Etruscan*. Reading the Past. London: British Museum.

Cook, B. F. 1987. *Greek Inscriptions*. Reading the Past 5. Berkeley: University of California Press.

Cooper, Henry R. 2003. *Slavic Scriptures: The Formation of the Church Slavonic Version of the Holy Bible*. Madison, NJ: Farleigh Dickinson University Press.

Daniels, Peter T. and William Bright, eds. 1996. *The World's Writing Systems*. New York: Oxford University Press. Sections 21, 22, 23, 27, 28, 29, 60, 64, 67, by Swiggers, Threatte, Jenniges, Ritner, Ebbinghaus, Bonfante, Cubberley, Sanjian, Holisky, Comrie, Feldman, and Barac-Cikoja.

Easterling, Pat and Carol Handley, eds. 2001. *Greek Scripts: An Illustrated Introduction*. London: Society for the Promotion of Hellenic Studies. Accessible and well illustrated.

Harris, William V. 1989. *Ancient Literacy*. Cambridge, MA: Harvard University Press.

Havelock, Eric A. 1982. *The Literate Revolution in Greece and Its Cultural Consequences*. Princeton, NJ: Princeton University Press. Overstates the uniqueness of the Greek alphabet and is strangely dismissive of Near Eastern scripts, literacy, and literature, but is valuable on the transition from orality to literacy in Greece.

Jones, Peter. 1998. *Learn Ancient Greek: A Lively Introduction to Reading the Language*. New York: Barnes and Noble. A good place to start learning Greek, if you don't mind the "lively" tone.

Morris, Ian and Barry B. Powell. 2006. *The Greeks: History, Culture, and Society*. Upper Saddle River, NJ: Pearson. Despite talking down to its intended audience (undergraduates), this book presents a thoughtful synthesis combined with extensive quotation from primary sources.

Chapter 13 The Age of Latin

Besides the works listed below, see also Gaur (1994), listed under chapter 9, and Harris (1989), under chapter 12.

Abels, Richard. 1998. *Alfred the Great: War, Kingship and Culture in Anglo-Saxon England*. London: Longman.

Allen, W. Sidney. 1978. *Vox Latina: A Guide to the Pronunciation of Classical Latin*, 2nd edn. Cambridge: Cambridge University Press. A thorough and excellent work.

Baugh, Albert C. and Thomas Cable. 1963. *A History of the English Language*, 3rd edn. Englewood Cliffs, NJ: Prentice Hall. A classic.

Becher, Matthias. *Charlemagne*. Trans. David S. Bachrach. New Haven, CT: Yale University Press.

Bede. 1968. *A History of the English Church and People*. Trans. Leo Shirley-Price and R. E. Latham. London: Penguin.

Bonfante, Giuliano. 1999. *The Origin of the Romance Languages: Stages in the Development of Latin*. Ed. Larissa Bonfante. Bibliothek der klassichen Altertumswissenschaftern: Reihe 2; N. F., Bd. 100. Heidelberg: Universitätsverlag C. Winter.

Cassidy, Frederic G. and Richard N. Ringler, eds. 1971. *Bright's Old English Grammar and Reader*. New York: Holt, Rinehart and Winston. A classic textbook.

Daniels, Peter T. and William Bright, eds. 1996. *The World's Writing Systems*. New York: Oxford University Press. Sections 23, 24, 25, and 26, by Bonfante, Knight, Elliott, and McManus.

Gordon, Arthur E. 1973. *The Letter Names of the Latin Alphabet*. Berkeley: University of California Press.

Humez, Alexander and Nicholas Humez. 1985. *A B C Et Cetera: The Life and Times of the Roman Alphabet*. Boston: Godine. Surprisingly, most of this book is not about the Roman alphabet, but it does contain information about the later additions to the alphabet, as well as social history of the Roman period written in an accessible style.

Janson, Tore. 2004. *A Natural History of Latin*. Trans. Merethe Damsgård Sørensen and Nigel Vincent. Oxford: Oxford University Press.

McKitterick, Rosamond. 1989. *The Carolingians and the Written Word*. Cambridge: Cambridge University Press.

Mitchell, Bruce. 1995. *An Invitation to Old English and Anglo-Saxon England*. Oxford: Blackwell. Both thorough and accessible.

Page, R. I. 1987. *Runes*. Reading the Past. London: British Museum.

Payne, Robert. 2001. *Ancient Rome*. New York: ibooks.

Peters, Edward. 1996. *Europe and the Middle Ages*, 3rd edn. Upper Saddle River, NJ: Prentice Hall.

Sacks, David. 2003. *Letter Perfect: The Marvelous History of our Alphabet from A to Z*. New York: Broadway Books. Written for a general audience.

Chapter 14 The Alphabet Meets the Machine

Estimates vary on the number of Bibles Gutenberg printed and how many calfskins went into making a vellum copy. I have taken my numbers from the British Library website cited below. In addition to the works listed below, see also Mafundikwa (2004) listed under chapter 1, Hunter (1943) listed under chapter 4, and Allen (1978), Janson (2004), Peters (1996), and Sacks (2003) listed under chapter 13. The book that speculated on the "no longer certain" future of the printed book is Febvre and Martin (1976, originally published in French in 1958). The numbers I quote on the amount of information and paper in 2002 come from Lyman and Varian (2003).

British Library. Treasures in Full: Gutenberg Bible. http://www.bl.uk/treasures/gutenberg/homepage.html.

Crystal, David. *Language and the Internet*, 2nd edn. Cambridge: Cambridge University Press. A timely and readable work.

Daniels, Peter T. and William Bright, eds. 1996. *The World's Writing Systems*. New York: Oxford University Press. Sections 23, 24, 59, 63, 74, by Bonfante, Knight, Tuttle, Senner, Daniels, McManus, Hamp, Comrie, Bendor-Samuel, Đinh-Hoà, Augst, and Daniels.

Febvre, Lucien and Henri-Jean Martin. 1976. *The Coming of the Book: The Impact of Printing 1450–1800*. Trans. David Gerard. London: Verso. A classic.

Friedman, Thomas L. 2006. *The World is Flat: A Brief History of the Twenty-First Century*, updated and expanded edn. New York: Farrar, Straus and Giroux.

Gillies, James and Robert Cailliau. 2000. *How the Web was Born: The Story of the World Wide Web*. Oxford: Oxford University Press.

Godart, Louis. 1995. *The Phaistos Disc: The Enigma of an Aegean Script*. Itanos Publications.

Graff, Harvey J. *The Legacies of Literacy: Continuities and Contradictions in Western Culture and Society*. Bloomington: Indiana University Press.

Haas, Christina. 1996. *Writing Technology: Studies on the Materiality of Literacy*. Mahwah, NJ: Lawrence Erlbaum. Describes experiments done to determine how word processing affects writing.

Further Reading

Heim, Michael. 1999. *Electric Language: A Philosophical Study of Word Processing,* 2nd edn. New Haven, CT: Yale University Press.

Howard, Nicole. 2005. *The Book: The Life Story of a Technology.* Westport, CT: Greenwood Press. Greenwood Technographies.

Johnson, Samuel. 1994. *A Dictionary of the English Language: In Which the Words are Deduced from their Originals Explained in their Different Meanings, and Authorized by the Names of the Writers in whose Works They are Found.* New York: Barnes and Noble.

Lawson, Alexander. 1990. *Anatomy of a Typeface.* Boston: Godine.

Lyman, Peter and Hal R. Varian. 2003. How Much Information. http://www.sims.berkeley.edu/how-much-info-2003.

Prah, Kwesi Kwaa, ed. 2002. *Writing African: The Harmonisation of Orthographic Conventions in African Languages.* CASAS 25. Cape Town: Centre for Advanced Studies of African Society.

Report: Text Messaging Harms Written Language. http://www.cnn.com/2007/TECH/04/26/Ireland.text.message.reut/index.html.

Sonn, William. 2006. *Paradigms Lost: The Life and Deaths of the Printed Word.* Lanham, MD: Scarecrow Press.

Southall, Richard. 1984. First Principles of Typographic Design for Document Production. *TUGboat* 5.2. http://www.tug.org/TUGboat.

Werschler-Henry, Darren. 2005. *The Iron Whim: A Fragmented History of Typewriting.* Toronto: McClelland and Stewart. Aptly named, a whimsically selective cultural history.

What is Unicode? http://www.unicode.org/standard/WhatIsUnicode.html.

Winks, Robin W. and Lee Palmer Wandel. 2003. *Europe in a Wider World: 1350–1650.* New York: Oxford University Press.

Index